C0-ALU-954

Asia: Reference Works

G. Raymond Nunn is also the compiler of *Japanese Periodicals and Newspapers in Western Languages: An International Union List* and *Southeast Asian Periodicals: An International Union List*, which are both published by Mansell.

Asia : Reference Works

A SELECT ANNOTATED GUIDE

By G. Raymond Nunn

Mansell
London 1980

ISBN 0 7201 0921 3

Mansell Publishing,
a member of Bemrose U.K. Limited,
3 Bloomsbury Place, London WC1A 2QA

First published 1980

British Library Cataloguing in Publication Data

Nunn, Godfrey Raymond
Asia, reference works.
1. Asia—Bibliography
I. Title
016.95 Z3001

ISBN 0-7201-0921-3

Printed photolitho in Great Britain by Ebenezer Baylis & Son Ltd.,
The Trinity Press, Worcester and London

CONTENTS

PREFACE

Asia, a selected and annotated guide to reference works was published by The M.I.T. Press in 1971, and it was planned to issue revised editions from time to time. Since 1971 a world-wide search has been conducted in libraries in Asia, Europe and the United States to identify additional and new reference works. This search was completed in the beginning of 1979, and it was found that the volume of new material was so substantial that what was required was not a new edition, but a new work. Of the 1,567 books and periodicals cited in this guide, less than 500 have been retained unchanged from the original publication.

In the original publication it was stated that the writing of the guide was prompted by the gaps which exist in the reference bibliography for Asia. Since 1971 other country reference bibliographies have been published, but these are too frequently oriented to publications issued in their own countries, and usually stress works in their own Asian language. For countries other than China, India and Japan, there has been little accounting of their reference materials, and most are still without a country guide.

The problem of selection has been a difficult one. It was comparatively easy to reject a large number of reference works which have been superseded by other more current or more comprehensive works. Over 100 of the titles in the original publication have been superseded and are not included in this guide.

The second step in selection was the establishment of a number of categories. These were encyclopedias and handbooks, yearbooks, dictionaries, biographical dictionaries, directories, atlases, gazetteers, chronological tables, statistics and bibliography. A search was made to secure at least one or two works for each of these categories. For many countries this was not possible. On the other hand, other categories were well represented, and selection had to take place. For example, in the case of dictionaries, it was decided to radically restrict the number of works cited. If possible, at least two were to be represented, stressing use for the English-speaking reader. Not only contemporary interests were to be served, but the user should find reference works which refer to earlier periods, where these are available.

Well over half the entries belong to the bibliography category. A number of sub-categories were established, such as general bibliography, descriptive of a country as a whole, trade bibliography, national library catalogues, official publications, indexes to periodicals and newspapers, and subject bibliography. In the case of some countries all related bibliographies could be cited—there were so few. In others, there were a substantial number, and the most comprehensive and representative were selected. Emphasis was also laid on those more useful to the Western reader, but this did not necessarily restrict selection to those published in the West, or in Western languages. However, reference books in Western languages are much more represented than in similar guides published in China, Japan and Korea, and related to these three countries.

All items have been personally examined by the author. This has been done to ensure the greatest possible accuracy of description, and also to avoid a number of bibliographical ghosts which do exist in the literature.

No diacritical marks have been used, principally to simplify composition procedures. To avoid possible misunderstandings, titles of works and names of organizations in Asian languages have been translated into English. When a translated title has been supplied in the work cited, this is indicated by the absence of parentheses. There is an index which lists Chinese-, Japanese- and Korean-language titles in characters and syllabaries where appropriate. With these aids it should be possible to render the transliterated and romanized titles back into the original script.

I wish to acknowledge the generous assistance of Dr. Masato Matsui, Mrs. Lan-hiang Char, Mrs. Lynette Wageman and Mr. Sam S. Hahn and Mrs. Chau Mun Lau, area specialists in the Asia Collection of the University of Hawaii Library, Mr. Frank J. Shulman of the University of Maryland Library, Mr. Key Paik Yang of the Asia Division of the Library of Congress, and Dr. Eugene Wu of the Chinese-Japanese Library of the Harvard-Yenching Institute. They have all brought titles of new reference works to my attention. Mrs. Aiko Crandall wrote the characters for the Chinese, Japanese and Korean index.

Every effort has been made to avoid errors in this multilingual guide containing reference works in six European and sixteen Asian languages, many of which are known imperfectly to the author. For this reason mistakes in judgement and language may appear, in spite of assistance from language consultants. For these and other errors, the indulgence of the reader is requested. The responsibility for these, and for the final selection and arrangement rests with the author.

Asian Studies Program,
University of Hawaii at Manoa, Honolulu.
August 1979.

A. ASIA

The term Asia is used in a geographical sense to include the whole continent from the Suez Canal to the Bering Straits, and from the Urals to Indonesia. This guide deals only with that part of Asia within the arc from Pakistan to Japan and excludes Soviet Asia.

ENCYCLOPEDIAS AND HANDBOOKS

A 1 Malalasekara, G. P. *Encyclopedia of Buddhism*. Ceylon, Government of Ceylon, 1961–
Projected to be completed in 1971 in 15,000 pages but actually proceeding at a much slower rate of publication. Buddhism in all countries is included, in both Mahayana and Theravada forms. Written by a team of international authorities, including Japanese and Chinese scholars. Fourth fascicule of volume 3 published in 1977 noted.

A 2 University of London. School of Oriental and African Studies. *Handbook of Oriental history*. London, Royal Historical Society, 1963. 265 p.
Written by members of the School's Department of History and intended as an aid to a number of problems in the study of Asia, such as personal and place names, transliteration and pronunciation, glossaries of terms and chronological systems. There are five sections: Near and Middle East, India and Pakistan, Southeast Asia and the Archipelago, China, and Japan. The pre-Islamic Near East is not covered. A reprint of the 1951 edition.

A 3 Ling, T. O. *Dictionary of Buddhism*. New York, Charles Scribner's, 1972. 244 p.
Over 200 entries extracted from Professor S. G. F. Brandon *Dictionary of comparative religion* (1970) provide a useful but elementary introduction to Buddhism

A 4 *Dictionary of Oriental literatures*. New York, Basic Books, 1973. 3 v.
The first volume deals with East Asia, the second with South and Southeast Asia, and the third with West Asia and North Africa. Major writers and styles are discussed, and there are altogether some 2,000 brief signed articles by principal international authorities.

A 5 Frederic, Louis. *Encyclopedia of Asian civilizations*. Villecresnes, Louis Frederic, 1977–
100,000 entries have been compiled from 3,000 sources, and will be published in a projected ten volumes. Volumes 1–3 seen. The area covered will be East, South, Southeast and Central Asia.

Articles are short, and emphasis is on personal and place names and terms.

YEARBOOK

A 6 *Asia yearbook*. Hong Kong, Far Eastern Economic Review, 1960–
A systematic annual review by country of Asian politics, foreign relations, economy, trade, agriculture, industry and transport. Includes the whole Asian area and New Zealand and Australia. Has substantial regional economics section. 1978 issue seen. Continues *Far Eastern economic review yearbook*, 1960–74.

DIRECTORIES

A 7 *Asia who's who*. Hong Kong, Pan Asia Newspaper Alliance, 1957–60. 3 v.
Issues noted for 1957, 1958 and 1960. The 1960 issue contains some 3,500 biographies, about 500 more than that for 1957. All countries of Asia, from Afghanistan to Japan, and including Outer Mongolia, are covered, and the emphasis is on politicians and government officials. The information supplied is brief, but this reference work remains an important source for countries where there is no collective biography.

A 8 Conference of Asian Affairs. *American institutions and organizations interested in Asia*, second edition. New York, Taplinger, 1961. 581 p.
Important but dated directory lists some 1,000 programs related to Asia, including Afghanistan, but excluding Soviet Asia and the Near East. The programs are at American universities, religious and educational organizations, foundations, museums and libraries. Valuable since it can lead to sources of information not otherwise available through bibliographies. Well indexed. A revision of the 1957 edition.

A 9 United Nations Educational, Scientific and Cultural Organization. *Research facilities in science and technology in Asia, a preliminary survey*. Paris, UNESCO, 1968. 701 p.
Lists some 960 institutes, giving addresses, fields of activity, budget, library resources. Arranged by country.

A 10 *The Far East and Australasia, a survey and directory of Asia and the Pacific*, 1969–. London, Europa Publications, 1968–
The only directory giving current information on all Asian countries, covering historical introduction, government, diplomatic representation, political parties, religion, press, finance, trade, education, educational institutions and bibliography. Some 1,500 biographies in the who's who section. 1977–8 last edition seen.

A 11 *The Asia press and media directory*. Hong Kong, Press Foundation of Asia, 1974–
Newspapers, selected periodicals, news agencies, radio and television stations are arranged by country, with brief directory-type information. 1976–7 issue seen.

A 12 East-West Center. East-West Communication Institute. *Sources of information on population/family planning, a handbook Asia*. Honolulu, 1975. 263 p.
A directory of 64 national, regional and international organizations, with a detailed subject index. Information under each entry includes publication and library holdings.

A 13 United Nations Asian Development Institute. *Directory of development documentation and information facilities in Asia and the Pacific*. Bangkok, 1976.
Some 350 facilities are arranged by country, with directory-type information for each, including purpose and size of library collections. Index to names of facilities and subject index. Loose-leaf format.

ATLAS

A 14 Penkala, Maria. *A correlated history of the Far East, China/Korea, Japan*. Rutland, Tuttle, 1966. 76 p.
18 large black and white maps with excellent detail illustrate the history of Asia from prehistoric times to the present, with a gap from the Ming dynasty to the thirties. Accompanied by a comparative chronology of Japanese, Chinese and Korean history. 1975 issue seen.

BIBLIOGRAPHY

A 15 Kyoto Daigaku. Jimbun Kagaku Kenkyujo (Kyoto University. Research Institute of Humanistic Studies). . . . *Toyogaku bunken mokuroku* Annual bibliography of Oriental studies, 1934–. Kyoto, Kyoto Jimbun Gakkai, Showa 10– (1935–).
This major bibliography includes books, periodicals and periodical articles in Japanese, Chinese, Korean and Western languages, with an area coverage for the whole of Asia, including the Middle East and Russian Asia. The bibliography is organized into two sections; the first for materials in Chinese, Japanese and Korean, and the second for materials in Western languages, with the first being generally twice the volume of that in the second. Each section is further subdivided into books and periodical articles, and then arranged by broad subjects. Indexes to Japanese authors by the Japanese syllabary, to Chinese and Korean authors by characters, to Russian authors by the Cyrillic alphabet, and an

alphabetical index to Western authors. All areas of knowledge are covered, but that of history is emphasized. This important listing suffers from a lack of cumulation and of an area and country approach, which make it less useful. 1974 issue published 1976. Title varies: from 1936 to 1962 *Toyoshigaku kenkyu bunken mokuroku*.

A 16 Tohogakkai, Tokyo (Institute of Eastern Culture). *Books and articles on Oriental subjects published in Japanese during 1954–*. Tokyo, 1955–. Annual.

The 1964 issue indexes 213 periodicals and 6 festschriften, and contains entries for approximately 1,000 articles. A separate section lists 157 books, most of which are abstracted. The emphasis is on East Asia, excluding Japan, but materials on South and Southeast Asia are included. Arrangement is by country, then by subject, with books in a separate section. Author index from 1958 issue. 1973 issue seen.

A 17 *Bibliography of Asian studies*, 1956–. Ann Arbor, Asssociation for Asian Studies, 1957–. Annual.

Continues the *Far Eastern bibliography*, 1941–55, itself a continuation of the *Bulletin of Far Eastern bibliography*, 1936–40. With the name change for the 1956 issue, the scope of this bibliography was considerably enlarged to include South Asia, and its size was expanded to cite annually some 13,000 Western-language books and periodical articles, published in Asia and the West, and arranged by country and then by an extensive array of subject divisions. Author index. Unevenness in the bibliography reflects the varying qualities of the materials available, and the work of a number of separate voluntary contributors. The single most important bibliographical contribution to the field of Asian studies. Cumulated by Association for Asian Studies *Cumulative bibliography of Asian studies, 1941–1965* (Boston, G. K. Hall, 1969–70. 8 v.) and *Cumulative bibliography of Asian Studies, 1966–1970* (Boston, G. K. Hall, 1972. 6 v). Ceased to be part of the *Journal of Asian studies* with *Bibliography of Asian studies, 1969*.

A 18 Hewitt, Arthur R. *Union list of Commonwealth newspapers in London, Oxford and Cambridge*. London, Institute of Commonwealth Studies, 1960. 101 p.

A union list of 2,426 newspapers mostly in English, which have been preserved, in many cases only in the United Kingdom. There are, for example, 155 newspapers listed for India. The British Museum collection at Colindale in North London has the strongest representation. The newspapers are arranged first by country, and then by place and title. There is a title index. Holdings and locations are given.

A 19 Nunn, G. Raymond. 'Asia'. American Universities Field Staff. *A select bibliography, Asia, Africa, Eastern Europe, Latin America*. New York, 1960. pp. 1–191.

The Asia section was based on the University of Michigan Undergraduate Library collection on Asia, and was reviewed by two teams of specialists, one at the University of Michigan, and the other with the American Universities Field Staff. The 2,748 books cited are almost entirely in English and have been graded. 'A' and 'B' entries, amounting to 30% of the total have been annotated. The arrangement is by country, with separate author and title indexes. The Asia section includes the Middle East, but excludes Soviet Asia, and the selection is a recommended one for the college library. *Cumulative supplement, 1961–1971* published 1973.

A 20 Kumar, Girja and V. Machwe. *Documentation on Asia*. Delhi, Vikas Publishing House, 1960–
An English-language bibliography, with an initial volume of 4,044 entries, and arranged by geographical area, with subdivisions for countries. Many entries are from Asian sources, and this work is useful as a supplement to the annual *Bibliography of Asian studies* (A 17). Author and subject indexes. Volume 5, covering 1964 and published 1976, last seen.

A 21 Kyriak, Theodore E. *Catalog cards in book form to United States Joint Publications Research Service translations*, 1957–68. Annapolis, Research and Microfilm Publications, 1962–9.
Worldwide in scope, including the Soviet Union, Eastern Europe, Southeast Asia, North Korea, as well as mainland China. For each area the JPRS reports are listed numerically, referring to a reproduction of a card outlining contents. Beyond this rudimentary regional approach there is no subject approach, and this listing is a slight improvement on that in the *Monthy Catalog of United States Government Publications*, which lists the reports by number. Continued by CCM Information Corporation *Catalog cards in book form to United States Joint Publications Research Service translations*, from 1969. Itself continued by *Transdex, bibliography and index to the United States Joint Publications Research Service (JPRS) translations*, v. 9–12, 1970–4. 1978 issues seen.

A 22 University of London. School of Oriental and African Studies. Library. *Library catalogue of the School of Oriental and African Studies, University of London*. Boston, G. K. Hall, 1963. 26 v.
554,000 catalogue cards representing some 200,000 titles, have been reproduced in this catalogue. A substantial proportion is concerned with Asia, although the Middle East, Africa and the Pacific Islands are also covered by the Library. The general series section is divided into an author catalogue, a title index, and subject catalogues subdivided by major geographical regions. The five-volume Chinese catalogue is similarly arranged. There is a single-volume Japanese catalogue, and a catalogue of manuscripts and microfilms. A key to one of the principal library collections of Asia. . . . *First supplement* (1968) in 16 volumes

lists 60,000 titles. . . . *Second supplement* (1973) in 16 volumes. . . . *Third supplement* (1979) in 19 volumes.

A 23 Yunesuko Higashi Ajia Bunka Kenkyu Senta, Tokyo (Centre for East Asian Cultural Studies). *A survey of Japanese bibliographies concerning Asian studies.* Tokyo, 1963. 300 p.
Some 1,200 bibliographies almost entirely in Japanese are arranged under 34 headings. No annotations. Alphabetical index to titles.

A 24 Yunesuko Higashi Ajia Bunka Kenkyu Senta, Tokyo (Centre for East Asian Cultural Studes). *Bibliography of bibliographies of East Asian studies in Japan.* Tokyo, 1964. 190 p. (Bibliography no. 3).
Compiled as a supplement to *A survey of Japanese bibliographies concerning Asian studies* (A 23), but actually there is duplication. 854 bibliographies in book and article form on East Asia and Southeast Asia, excluding Japan, are arranged by area. Nearly all entries are in Japanese. Title index.

A 25 Pearson, James D. *Oriental and Asian bibliography, an introduction with some reference to Africa.* Hamden, Shoestring Press, 1966. 261 p.
The first part consists of an account of the history of Oriental studies, and the second the literature of this field, including over 330 entries for reference books in Oriental and Western languages, which are annotated through the accompanying text. The third part is concerned with library collections and problems.

A 26 State University of New York. Foreign Area Materials Center. *Reprints and microforms in Asian studies.* Ann Arbor, Association for Asian Studies, 1968. 145 p. (*Newsletter of the Association for Asian Studies*, volume xiii, supplement no. 1).
Nearly one-half lists reprints of books and journals in Western languages, separating books from journals, and arranging the former by major area. There are some 700 entries. The second part lists some 1,000 microforms, again dividing these into books and into newspapers and periodicals. Both sections are subdivided regionally. The Near and Middle East is not included. There is no index. This most useful listing is by no means complete for microforms, principally since its sources for compilation are limited.

A 27 Nunn, G. Raymond. *Asia, a core collection.* Ann Arbor, Xerox University Microfilms, 1973. 101 p.
A selection of 1,000 books in English on Asia, with each entry annotated. The first 10% of the selection has been graded I, the second 20% II. Selection has been based on quality, not on in-print status of books and arrangements have been made to reproduce out-of-print books. The selection is compiled for the undergraduate college collection. Arranged by country, subarranged by discipline. Author and title index.

A 28 U.S. Library of Congress. *Newspapers in microform, foreign*

countries. 1948–72. Washington, 1973. 269 p.
Approximately one-sixth of the newspapers listed are published in Asia, and this provides a most valuable guide to locations of these materials in the United States and Canada. 1948 is date of compilation, not contents. Supersedes for Asia, George A. Schwegman *Newspapers on microfilm* (1967).

A 29 Besterman, Theodore. *A world bibliography of Oriental bibliography*, revised and brought up to date by J. D. Pearson. Totowa, New Jersey, Rowman and Littlefield, 1975. 727 columns.
11,033 bibliographies which have appeared in book form are listed, and include the 6,562 bibliographies noted in the fourth edition of the author's *A world bibliography of bibliographies*. Entries are arranged by region and country, with an author and title index.

Theses and Dissertations

A 30 Bloomfield, B. C. *Theses on Asia accepted by universities in the United Kingdom and Ireland, 1877–1964*. London, Frank Cass, 1967. 127 p.
2,571 masters' and doctoral dissertations relating to Asia are arranged by geographical areas and subdivided by major subjects. Oceania, Islam and the Near and Middle East are included. There is a brief statement on the availability of theses for photocopying and inter-library lending. Unfortunately most of this material is still not accessible outside the universities where the dissertations were published. Sources are ASLIB *Index to theses accepted for higher degrees* and university calendars. Regularly updated in *Bulletin of the Association of British Orientalists*.

A 31 Stucki, Curtis W. *American doctoral dissertations on Asia . . .* Ithaca, Southeast Asia Program, Department of Asian Studies, Cornell University, 1968. 304 p. (Cornell University, Department of Asian Studies, Southeast Asia Program, data paper no. 71).
Doctoral dissertations in the standard bibliographies are usually listed under major disciplinary categories, and this makes the area approach for locating dissertations difficult. The important feature of this listing is its arrangement by region, and subdivision by country and then by subject. Dissertations are arranged chronologically under subject. Approximately 3,200 doctoral dissertations on Asia, published from 1933 to 1966 are listed. Author index. Revision of the 1959 and 1963 editions.

A 32 Bishop, Enid. *Australian theses on Asia*. Canberra, Faculty of Asian Studies, Australian National University, 1972. 35 p. (Occasional paper 12).
Lists theses accepted by Australian universities for higher degrees to the end of 1970. Author index.

A 33 Shulman, Frank J. *Doctoral dissertations on Asia, an annotated*

biographical journal of current international research. Ann Arbor, Xerox University Microfilms for Association for Asian Studies, 1957–
Continues the listing of dissertations which appeared in the *Association for Asian Studies Newsletter*, 1969–71, and in the *Asian Studies Professional Review*, 1971–4. Arranged by country, with further subdivision for Japan, China and India. Includes American, Canadian, French, and British dissertations. Author index. Volume 2 nos. 1 and 2, for 1976–7 last issue seen.

Subject Bibliography

RELIGION AND THOUGHT

A 34 Streit, Robert and Johannes Dindinger. *Biblioteca missionum.* Aachen, Internationales Institut fur Missionswissenschaftliche Forschung, 1916–.
Bibliography of books and periodical articles on the Catholic mission movement, with an emphasis on Asia. Each volume is arranged chronologically, with author, person, place, country and peoples, and language indexes. The following volumes are on Asia, and the number of entries is noted in parentheses:

4. *Asiatische Missionsliteratur, 1245–1599.* 1928. 626 p. (2,052).
5. *Asiatische Missionsliteratur, 1600–1699.* 1929. 1,114 p. (2,811).
6. *Missionsliteratur Indiens, der Philippinen, Japans und Indochinas, 1700–1799.* 1931. 616 p. (2,005).
7. *Chinesische Missionsliteratur, 1700–1799.* 1931. 544 p. (4,035).
8. *Missionsliteratur Indiens und Indonesiens, 1800–1909.* 1934. 1,028 p. (3,201).
9. *Missionsliteratur der Philippinen, 1800–1909.* 1937. 996 p. (2,408).
10. *Missionsliteratur Japans und Koreas, 1800–1909.* 1938. 565 p. (1,475).
11. *Missionsliteratur Indochinas, 1800–1909.* 1939. 817 p. (2,062).
12. *Chinesische Missionsliteratur, 1800–1884.* 1958. 745 p. (1,217).
13. *Chinesische Missionsliteratur, 1885–1909.* 1959. 807 p. (752).
14. *Chinesische Missionsliteratur, 1910–1950.* 1959–61. 3 v. (3,496).
27. *Missionsliteratur Indiens, 1910–1946.* 1970. (2,260).
28. *Missionsliteratur Sudasiens (Indien, Pakistan, Burma, Ceylon), 1947–1968.* 1971. 579 p. (3,994). No. 3,994 is a list of 701 Catholic periodicals published in South Asia.
29. *Missionsliteratur Sudostasiens, 1910–1970.* 1973. 678 p. (2,847).

30. *Missionsliteratur Japans und Koreas, 1910–1970*. 1975. 481 p. (1,914).

A 35 Gard, Richard A. *Buddhist political thought, a bibliography*. Baltimore, 1952. 73 p.
Syllabus and bibliography of course on Buddhist political thought taught at the School of Advanced International Studies. Some 500 books and articles, but mostly books, are arranged by topic, following the outline of the syllabus.

A 36 Hanayama, Shinsho. *Bibliography on Buddhism*. Tokyo, Hokuseido Press, 1961. 869 p.
Some 15,073 books and periodical articles in English, French, German and Italian on Buddhism are arranged in alphabetical order by author. The entries are not annotated, and include materials published to 1928. Materials published after 1928 will be found in *Bibliographie bouddhique*, 1928– (Paris, P. Geuthner, 1930–), the first volume of which covers January 1928 to May 1934, the second from May 1934 to May 1950, and the third from May 1950 to May 1958. The arrangement of materials in the *Bibliographie bouddhique* is by subject, with an index in the last number of each volume. The *Bibliography on Buddhism* is supplementary to *Bussho kaisetsu daijiten* (R 148).

A 37 Bechert, Heinz. *Buddhismus, Staat und Gesellschaft in den Landern des Theravada Buddhismus, Band III* (Buddhism, state and society in the countries of Theravada Buddhism, v. 3). Wiesbaden, Otto Harrosowitz, 1973. 662 p.
1,947 books and articles in Western languages are arranged by author, with some annotation. Entries 1948–93 are in Sinhalese. Subject index.

A 38 Satyaprakash. *Buddhism, a select bibliography*. Gurgaon, Indian Documentation Service, 1976. 172 p. (Subject bibliography series no. 1).
2,565 articles from 88 Indian periodicals published from 1962–76, and 450 books published during the same period and before in an alphabetical author-subject arrangement.

SOCIAL SCIENCES

A 39 United Nations. Economic and Social Commission for Asia and the Pacific. Library. *Asian bibliography*, 1952–. Bangkok, 1952–. Semi-annual.
Lists selected acquisitions of the Library of the Economic Commission for Asia and the Far East in Bangkok. Its Asian-language content is limited, and its emphasis is on the social sciences. Materials are collected from 33 Asian countries, and from Australia and New Zealand. Arranged by the Universal Decimal Classification with a country and subject index. January–June 1978 issue noted.

A 40 University of Texas. Population Research Center. *International population census bibliography, Asia*. Austin, Bureau of Business

Research, Graduate School of Business, 1966. 1 v. (various paging) (Census bibliography no. 5).
Arranged on a country-by-country basis, and covering the whole of Asia, including the Middle East, but not Soviet Asia. Attempts to be a comprehensive guide to population statistics, and includes other sources in addition to those found in the census reports.

A 41 Fong, Monica. *A bibliography of population censuses of Asia and the Pacific in the libraries at the University of Hawaii*, as of October 1970. East-West Center, East-West Center Population Institute, 1971. 68 p.
Valuable since it gives locations for one of the largest collections of Asian statistics and population data in the United States.

A 42 Nunn, G. Raymond. *Asian libraries and librarianship, an annotated bibliography of selected books and periodicals, and a draft syllabus*. Metuchen, Scarecrow Press, 1973. 137 p.
353 books and periodicals are arranged by country, then by subject, and cover publishing, libraries, national libraries, university libraries, special libraries, public libraries, school libraries, cataloguing and classification. Each entry annotated. The draft syllabus is suggested for course on Asian libraries and librarianship. Author and title index. Characters given in an appendix for titles in Chinese, Japanese and Korean.

A 43 Lent, John A. *Asian mass communications, a comprehensive bibliography*. Philadelphia, Temple University, 1974. 708 p.
Over 11,000 books, reports and articles are arranged by country, and then by major topics, such as advertising, and public relations, film, government information, news agencies, printed media, radio and television. No annotation and no index.

NATURAL SCIENCES

A 44 Merrill, Elmer D. and Egbert Hamilton Walker. *A bibliography of Eastern Asiatic botany*. Jamaica Plain, Mass., Arnold Arboretum of Harvard University. 1938. 719 p.
Brought to the end of the 1950s by Egbert Hamilton Walker *A bibliography of Eastern Asiatic botany, supplement* (Washington, American Institute of Biological Sciences, 1960). Eastern Asia includes China, Japan, Korea, Eastern and Southern Siberia, the Philippines, Thailand, Burma, Indochina and India. The period covered is from 1800, and there are no language limitations. Books and periodical articles are cited, and the arrangement is by author, with subject, geographical and classified indexes.

ART AND MUSIC

A 45 Waterman, Richard A. *Bibliography of Asiatic Musics*. (n.p.)
3,488 books and periodical articles in Western languages and Russian are cited in 14 instalments, each of which is limited to a region. Over half concerned with the music of the Near East. The

instalments originally appeared in *Music Library Association notes*, second series, v. 5–8, December 1947 to March 1951.

A 46 Gerboth, Walter. *Music of East and Southeast Asia, a selected bibliography of books, pamphlets, articles and recordings.* Albany, University of the State of New York, the State Education Department, 1963. 23 p.
228 books and periodical articles and 75 recordings are arranged by country. Almost entirely in English, and all items located in libraries in New York City. No annotations.

A 47 Bijutsu Kenkyujo (Institute of Art Research). *Nihon Toyo kobijitsu bunken mokuroku* (Bibliography on early Oriental and Japanese art). Tokyo, Chuo Koron, Showa 44 (1969). 698 p.
In the first two volumes published in 1941, over 28,000 articles selected from some 250 periodicals are arranged under 28 subjects, too broad a classification for rapid use. There is an author index. The third volume has some 7,500 articles distributed under 56 headings. Some 36,000 articles selected from over 250 periodicals, arranged by subject. Author index. New single-volume edition of *Toyo Kobijutsu bunken mokuroku*.

HISTORY AND GEOGRAPHY

A 48 Le Gear, Clara Egli. *A list of geographic atlases in the Library of Congress*. Washington, U.S. Government Printing Office, 1963. 681 p.
This is the second supplement to Phillips' compilation of atlases at the Library of Congress, and is arranged by area. A valuable feature is the section on Asia (9,475–10,084). Titles are translated and contents described in English. The index lists authors, editors and areas in one sequence.

A 49 Toyoshi Kenkyu Rombun Mokuroku Henshu Iinkai (Committee for the Compilation of a Catalogue of Articles on Oriental History Appearing in Japan). *Nihon ni okeru Toyoshi rombun mokuroku* Japanese studies on Asian history, a catalogue of articles. Tokyo, Showa 39–42 (1964–7). 4 v.
In the first three volumes 62,456 articles are compiled from some 550 periodicals and collected works on Asian history, excluding Japan. The bibliography is arranged by name of periodical or collected work, then by volume and issue, or by its place in the collected works. The fourth volume is an alphabetical author index. No subject index is provided, which is a major disadvantage. Publications surveyed dated from 1880 to 1962.

B. BANGLADESH

Bangladesh, the former East Pakistan, was formed as an independent country in 1971. Much of the reference material now found under Pakistan and India will also refer to Bangladesh.

HANDBOOK

B 1 American University, Washington, D.C. Foreign Area Studies. *Area handbook for Bangladesh*. Washington, D.C., U.S. Government Printing Office, 1975. 346 p.
A country summary is followed by sections on social, political and economic affairs, and national security. Bibliography. Research completed April 1975.

YEARBOOKS

B 2 *East Pakistan yearbook*, 1958–. Chittagong, The Tempest, 1958–
A series of economic, political, social and literary articles on the former East Pakistan are included in each issue. No index, and little biographical and directory-type information. Volume 1–3 for 1958–60 noted.

B 3 *East Pakistan annual*, 1961–. Chittagong, 1961–
In the 1963/4 issue a series of general articles of mainly economic interest is followed by a substantial classified trade directory. Indexed. No directory or index in the fourth volume for 1966/7.

DIRECTORIES

B 4 East Pakistan. *East Pakistan civil list*. 1947?–
List of East Pakistan civil servants, with major arrangement by department, and an index arranged alphabetically under the last part of the name. No. 9 for 1963–4 and No. 10 for 1965–6 noted.

B 5 Indian International Trade Centre. *Business guide to Bangladesh*. Bombay, 1972. 292 p.
A directory of firms arranged by areas of economic activity. Index to advertisers, but no index to firms in directory.

B 6 *Bangladesh directory and year book, 1976*. Calcutta, Associated Book Promoters, 1976. 1 v. (various paging).
Principally a directory of exporters in Bangladesh, arranged by type of trade, with almost no yearbook information.

GAZETTEER

B 7 U.S. Board on Geographic Names. *Bangladesh* . . . Washington, U.S. Government Printing Office, 1976. 526 p.
33,700 entries for place and feature names in Bangladesh, with their classification, longitude and latitude.

STATISTICS

B 8 East Pakistan. Bureau of Statistics. *Statistical digest of East Pakistan*, 1963–. Dacca, 1964–. Annual.
A survey of statistical information for food, agriculture, industry, trade, education, health, communication and finance. 1969 issue last seen.

B 9 Society and Commerce Publications. Economic Research Bureau. *Statistical abstract of Bangladesh*. Calcutta, Society and Commerce Publications, 1972–
A lengthy introduction surveys the economy of Bangladesh, its population, trade, education and health, and is followed by appendices of statistical tables. Fuller earlier information on Bangladesh will be found in *Twenty-five years of Pakistan in statistics, 1947–1972* (E 21).

B 10 Bangladesh. Bureau of Statistics. *Statistical yearbook of Bangladesh*, 1975–. Dacca, 1976–
An earlier nine volumes were published under the title *Statistical digest*, which is now discontinued. Over 300 tables cover meteorology, agriculture, manufacturing, trade, finance, education, prices and wages, health, labour, transport, consumption and national income. Statistics cover period 1964–5 to 1973–4.

B 11 Bangladesh. Bureau of Statistics. *Statistical pocketbook of Bangladesh*, 1978–. Dacca, 1977–
Covers general features, area and population, meteorology, agriculture, industry, trade, finance, education, prices, labour, energy, transport and consumption.

BIBLIOGRAPHY

B 12 'Catalogue of books and periodicals registered in the Province of East Pakistan during the quarter ending . . . .' *Dacca Gazette*, appendix.
The issue for the quarter ending 31 March 1967 contains 336 entries, nearly all in English or Bengali, arranged by subject, and with full bibliographical information. In addition 74 periodicals were also listed, including some official publications.

B 13 Haq, Shamsul. *Bamla sahitya, granthapanji, 1947–1969* Bengala

literature, a bibliography, 1947–1969. Dacca, Pakistan Jatiya Granthakendra, 1970. 470 p.
A bibliography, listing some 2,200 authors and their works in Bengali, and restricted to Bangladesh. Author index and title index.

B 14 U.S. Library of Congress. American Libraries Book Procurement Center, New Delhi. *Accessions list, Bangladesh*, 1972– New Delhi, 1972–.
Volumes 1 and 2 cover publications for 1972 and 1973 respectively, and represent a very much reduced output compared with that for the former East Pakistan. Each issue is divided into books, serials and a subject index. 1977 volume seen.

B 15 Shamsuddoulah, A.B.M. *Introducing Bangladesh through books, a select bibliography, with introduction and annotations, 1855–1976*. Dacca, Great Eastern Books, 1976. 45 p.
255 books in English, arranged under 17 major subjects. Most entries are not annotated. No index.

B 16 Satyaprakash. *Bangladesh, a select bibliography*. Gurgaon, Indian Documentation Service, 1976. 218 p. (International bibliography series no. 3).
Some 2,500 articles on Bangladesh published in 91 Indian periodicals from 1962–76 and 135 books in an alphabetical author-subject arrangement.

B 17 Serajul Haque. *Bangladesh demography: a select bibliography*. Dacca, Bangladesh Institute of Development Studies, 1976. 59 p. (BIDS Library bibliography series no. 11).
518 entries for research reports, working papers, seminar papers, discussion papers, periodical articles, reprint articles, documents and 'work in progress' type material, and covering the period 1947–75. Arranged by 18 major subjects. Author index.

B 18 Talukder, Alauddin. *Bangladesh economy: a select bibliography*. Dacca, Bangladesh Institute of Development Studies, 1976. 211 p.
2,132 references to books and periodical articles published from 1947 to 1974. Arranged under 23 major subjects, with further subdivision. Author index.

C. INDIA
(Including South and Southern Asia)

Britain became the paramount power in India after the Maratha War of 1817–19, and independence did not come to the subcontinent until 1947, when it was divided into two parts, with the largely Muslim areas of the former Indian Empire becoming the new state of Pakistan.

REFERENCE WORKS

C 1 Sharma, Hari Dev. *Indian reference sources, an annotated guide to Indian reference books*. Varanasi, Indian Bibliographic Center, 1972. 313 p.
Lists some 2,200 titles, arranged under four main divisions, generalia, social sciences, and pure and applied sciences. Each division is further subdivided. Items are in all major Indian languages, with about one-half in English. Emphasis is placed on books which are currently available. Annotations are descriptive and frequently critical. Combined author, title and subject index.

C 2 Gidwani, N. N. and K. Navalani. *A guide to reference materials on India*. Jaipur, Saraswati Publications, 1974. 2 v.
Some 20,000 books and periodicals published up to the beginning of 1972 are arranged by major form and subject divisions, with detailed subarrangement, constituting a comprehensive guide to reference works on India, with some minor annotation. The section on dictionaries, subarranged by language, contains over 2,800 works. Author, subject index, also contains some titles.

ENCYCLOPEDIAS AND HANDBOOKS

C 3 Balfour, Edward. *The cyclopaedia of India and of Eastern and Southern Asia*. Graz, Akademische Druck- u. Verlaganstalt, 1967–8. 3 v.
A reprint of the third edition published in 1885, and containing 35,000 articles, in most cases short, on the flora and fauna, geography, history, biography, customs, religion and literature of South and Southeast Asia, but with a concentration on South Asia. Articles often have short bibliographical notes. Much of the information is now dated, but there remains a substantial proportion not readily accessible through other reference sources.

C 4 *Imperial gazetteer of India*, revised edition. Oxford, Clarendon Press, 1907–31. 26 v.
Work commenced on this gazetteer in 1871, and the first four

volumes are in a different binding and have title *The Indian Empire*. Volumes 5–25 were published in 1908, and are in the form of an alphabetical gazetteer. Volume 25 is an index to volumes 5–24. Volume 26 is an atlas of 66 maps and plans, and was published in 1931. Although much information is now dated, this is still a principal historical source for India. The *Imperial gazetteer of India, provincial series*, (Calcutta, Superintendent of Government Printing, 1908–9. 25 v.) rearranges the same information by province. Reprinted by Today and Tomorrow's Printers and Publishers, New Delhi, 1972.

C 5 *Hindi vishwakosa* (Hindi Encyclopedia). Varanasi (i.e. Benares), Nagari Pracharini Sabha, 1966?–
An excellent and well illustrated encyclopedia in Hindi, which should not be confused with an encyclopedia with the same name published in Calcutta in 1914–31. 12 volumes noted, with volume 12 published in 1970.

C 6 Bhattacharya, Sachchidananda. *A dictionary of Indian history*. New York, George Braziller, 1967, 888 p.
A new dictionary with 2,785 entries for persons, places, institutions important in Indian history from earliest times until the present.

C 7 Walker, George Benjamin. *The Hindu world, an encylopedic survey of Hinduism*. New York, Praeger, 1968. 2 v.
665 articles averaging one to two pages in length cover Hinduism. Each article has a bibliography. Detailed index, referring the reader to the main article, where topics are not covered in specific articles.

C 8 American University, Washington, D.C. Foreign Area Studies. *Area handbook for India*. Washington, U.S. Government Printing Office, 1975. 648 p.
A revision of the 1969 edition, and with April 1974 as the date for completion of research. A brief summary is followed by sections on social, political and economic affairs, and two chapters on national security. Bibliography.

C 9 Sharma, Jagdish Saran, *Encylopedia Indica*. New Delhi, S. Chand and Co., 1975. 715 p.
Some 8,000 short articles, mostly biographical and geographical, but other subjects are included also, and related to India, which is covered to 1975.

YEARBOOKS

C 10 Mitra, H. N. *Indian annual register*, 1919–47. Calcutta, Annual Register Office, 1919–47.
Each volume commences with a chronicle of events followed by summary accounts of proceedings in central and provincial assemblies. Later issues give fuller accounts of Congress activities

and important national affairs. The *Register* appeared annually from 1919–23, and 1930–47, and quarterly with the title *Indian quarterly register*, from 1924–9. Available on microfiche published by the International Documentation Center, Zug.

C 11 *Times of India directory and yearbook, including who's who*, 1953/4–. Bombay, Times of India, 1953–.
In continuation of the *Indian yearbook and who's who*, 1914–47, and the *India and Pakistan yearbook and who's who*, 1948–53, gives short statements on a wide variety of subjects concerned with India, such as meteorology, defence, agriculture, railroads, foreign investment, currency, banking and industry. In addition it has information on the States and cities, with a classified list of trades and professions. There is a short biographical dictionary with some 1,000 biographies, but biographical section much smaller in later issues. Indexed. 1978 last issue noted.

C 12 *India, a reference annual*, 1953–. Delhi, Ministry of Information and Broadcasting, 1953–.
Compiled from official sources, and covers political, constitutional, educational, cultural, scientific, financial and other aspects of India. There are a great number of statistics, and bibliography is well represented. Succeeding issues duplicate each other considerably. 1976 issue last noted.

DICTIONARIES

C 13 Monier-Williams, Monier. *A dictionary, English and Sanskrit*. Varanasi, Chowkambra Sanskrit Series Office, 1961. 859 p. (Chowkambra Sanskrit series, studies v. 13).
The best one-volume dictionary of the Sanskrit language, with over 25,000 words. The most used and the most usable. Entries are clearly stated. Based on Bohtlingk *Sanskrit-Worterbuch*. Another useful dictionary is Arthur Anthony Macdonnell *A practical Sanskrit dictionary* (London, Oxford University Press, 1924. 382 p.) with some 8,000 Sanskrit words, with usage and English equivalents.

C 14 Bohtlingk, Otto von. *Sanskrit-Worterbuch in kurzerer Fassung*. Graz, Akademische Druck- u. Verlaganstalt, 1959. 7 v. (in 3).
A reprint of the abridgement of Bohtlingk *Sanskrit-Worterbuch* 1855–77. 7 v.), the definitive dictionary of Sanskrit. The abridgement contains some 120,000 entries and their equivalents in German, and was originally published in St. Petersburg in 1879–89.

C 15 Platts, John Thompson. *A dictionary of Urdu, classical Hindi and English*. New York, Oxford University Press, 1930. 1,259 p.
Old, but it has been frequently reprinted, and is essential for use with classical and courtly Urdu. It has a tendency to be formal, but is a necessary tool when working with written documents. A reprint of the 1884 edition.

C 16 *Bhargava's standard illustrated dictionary of the Hindi language* (Hindi-English edition), sixth revised and enlarged edition. Banaras, Shree Ganga Pustakalaya, 195–? 1,280 p.
Lists of some 35,000 Hindi works and with its companion volume *Bhargava's standard illustrated dictionary of the English language* (Anglo-Hindi edition), ninth edition (Banaras, Shree Ganga Pustakalaya, 1951. 1 v.) with over 30,000 words, is sketchy, simplistic and not reliable since usage is not stated. However it is the only dictionary of its type widely available. For students who cannot read the Devanagari script in which Hindi is normally written, there is *The student's practical dictionary romanized, Hindustani-English, and English-Hindustani* (Allahabad, Ram Narain Lal, 1952. 363, 563 p.), 1974 revised edition seen.

BIOGRAPHICAL DICTIONARIES

C 17 Beale, Thomas William. *An Oriental biographical dictionary.* New York, Kraus Reprint Corporation, 1965. 431 p.
Contains approximately 5,000 names of historical figures and also some mythical, religious and social terms. The use of word the Oriental in the title is misleading, since the dictionary concerns itself almost exclusively with Muslim and Arabic names gathered from the Muslim histories. The Arabic equivalent is frequently used following the transliterated form of the name. Useful for the Muslim period of Indian history. A reprint of the 1894 edition.

C 18 Buckland, Charles E. *Dictionary of Indian biography.* London, Swan Sonnenschein, 1906. 494 p.
Includes some 2,600 biographies, mostly of persons of British descent, for the period of Indian history from about 1750 to the time of publication. A short bibliography and list of works consulted is included. Reprinted by Haskell House, New York, 1968 and by Greenwood Press, Westport.

C 19 Hayavadana Rao, Conjeevaram. *The Indian biographical dictionary, 1915.* Madras, Pillar, 1915. 472 p.
Some 2,000 European and Indian living persons are arranged alphabetically with appendices including the warrant of precedence for India, salutes in India, Indian Clubs and Indian titles.

C 20 *Who's who in India, Burma and Ceylon,* 1930–9. Bombay, Modern Press and Publications, 1930–9.
The 1937 edition contains some 1,800 biographies divided into three sections, of which the most important are the second, listing Indian princes, chiefs and nobles, and the third, a general section in three parts, each arranged alphabetically. Index to names.

C 21 Kabadi, Waman P. *Indian who's who.* Bombay, 1935. 600 p.
Contains some 1,200 biographies of men and women residing in India, and of Indian or British descent. The length of the

description depends on the importance of the person. Works are listed for authors.

C 22 India (Republic). Ministry of Home Affairs. *The Civil list of Indian Administrative Service.* Delhi, Manager of Publications, 1956–
A listing of senior officials, giving their birth date, present position, pay, and arranged by the province on whose administrative cadre they happen to be. Issues noted for 1961–7, and the 1967 issue lists some 4,500 officials. Index to names. Continues the *India Office list*, 1876–1947 published on microfiche by the International Documentation Center, Zug. There are also departmental and State Civil Lists.

C 23 Chitrava, Siddheswarshastri Vishnu. *Bharatavarshiya pracina caritrakosa* (Dictionary of ancient Indian biography). Puna (i.e. Poona), Bharatiya Caritra Kosa Mandala, 1964. 1,204 p.
The most authoritative and comprehensive biographical dictionary for early India, with some 18,000 names of persons cited in early Hindu, Buddhist and Jain literature. Bibliography of sources. In Hindi.

C 24 Sahitya Akademi, New Delhi. *Who's who of Indian writers.* Honolulu, East-West Center Press, 1964. 410 p.
Some 6,000 living Indian writers arranged alphabetically. The family name is usually placed first, and personal names have been used in place of the family name only when the latter is not in general use. Date and place of birth, titles, pseudonyms and at the most six titles of the author's publications are listed.

C 25 *India who's who*, 1969–. New Delhi, INFA Publications, 1969–
1971 issue noted as third year of publication, and lists some 2,500 personalities, arranged under eight main headings and subarranged. Appendixes for classified listing of organizations, ministers and officials. Alphabetical index. 1977/8 issue seen.

C 26 Sharma, Jagdish Saran. *The national biographical dictionary of India.* New Delhi, Sterling Publishers, 1972. 302 p.
Contains entries for some 1,300 biographies, including modern and earlier persons from Indian history, with brief identifying notes and birth and death dates, if known. Valuable subject index. Non-Indians usually disregarded.

C 27 Sen, Siba Pada. *Dictionary of national biography.* Calcutta, Institute of Historical Studies, 1972–4. 4 v.
Includes some 1,800 selected Indians and foreigners in India from 1800 to 1947. Biographies are full and sources are stated.

DIRECTORIES

C 28 *Thacker's Indian directory and the world trade*, 1865–. Calcutta, Thacker's Directory, 1865–.

Divided into an official directory, subdivided by States, and a commercial directory, also subdivided by States, and major urban centers. Separate sections for newspapers, hotels, transport, mining, plantations, foreign trade, and a classified list of firms.

C 29 *Trado Indian directory* . . . New Delhi, Trade Builders, 1942–.

A directory of commercial firms, educational, medical and scientific organizations. Divided into 21 sections, the first two being for national organizations, and followed by a section each for the 19 regions of India. Each section indexed separately, and there is no index for the whole volume. The information given consists mostly of addresses. Official organizations not included. 1970 issue last examined.

C 30 Indian Association of Special Libraries and Information Centres. *Directory of special and research libraries in India.* Calcutta, 1962. 282 p.

Possibly less than half of the 400 special libraries in India are represented, and detailed information for 173 arranged by name, includes size of collections and staff. Another 700 libraries, not all special, are listed by State. Place and subject indexes.

C 31 Khosla, Raj K. *Men of library science and libraries in India.* New Delhi, Premier Publications, 1967. 1 v. (various paging).

Some 650 biographies of librarians are followed by a listing of some 1,400 libraries arranged by name, with a short note on each, sometimes including size of collection. A third part lists some 3,000 academic libraries, some 360 special libraries, and some 1,100 state and public libraries. No index.

C 32 Indian National Scientific Documentation Centre. *The directory of scientific research institutions in India, 1969.* New Delhi, 1969. 1,120 p.

Information on budgets, staffing, history, library collections and publications of 913 institutions based on 768 replies out of 1,374 questionnaires sent out, and 145 institutions with descriptions from other sources. Unanswered questionnaires were mostly those sent to state agricultural institutions and university science departments. Arranged by kind of institution, with listings by subject, location and date of establishment. Personal name index, periodical index, subject index. Covers some 90% of major research and development in India.

C 33 Holmes, W. Robert. *Research facilities in Delhi*, second edition. Delhi, 1969. 1 v.

Lists 173 institutions which can give assistance to researchers, with addresses, notes on purpose of the institution, publications, and size of library. A subject index to institutions provided.

C 34 Holmes, W. Robert. *Research facilities in Bangalore, Mysore and Ahmedabad.* Delhi, 1969. 1 v.

71 institutions are arranged by city, and subarranged alphabetically noting addresses, purpose, size of library and publications.

C 35 Aggarwala, Dharma Vira. *All India educational directory.* Chandigarh, All India Directories Publishers, 1972. 1,262 p.
A thorough survey of higher education in India, including a directory of universities and colleges, of research institutes and professional societies, arranged by subject, libraries, archives. Only ten pages devoted to non-higher education. Who's who in education arranged by subject with 2,500 biographies.

C 36 Guha, Partha Subir. *Directory of economic research centres in India.* Calcutta, Information Research Academy, 1972. 426 p.
Provides directory-type information on some 250 centres, giving addresses, staff, objects, history, library and publications. Research completed from 1966 to 1971 is also noted. Indexes for institutions, periodical publications, and subject index to research projects and personal names index appended.

C 37 Surender Kumar. *Directory of Libraries in Delhi.* Jullunder, Sterling Publishers, 1973. 63 p.
332 libraries, excluding those in high schools, are listed with addresses, budget, number of volumes and a subject index under 11 major headings.

C 38 *Directory of Indian publishers*, edited by Dinkar Trivedi. New Delhi, Federation of Publishers and Booksellers Associations of India, 1973. 591 p.
In four sections. The first section, arranged by language, lists some 10,250 commercial publishers and excludes booksellers who are not publishers; the second notes some 1,000 public and corporate publishers, arranged by type of institution; the third lists related activities; and the fourth is a geographical index to publishers.

C 39 Singh, Mohinder. *Learned societies and institutions in India, activities and publications*, revised and enlarged edition. Delhi, Metropolitan Book Co., 1975. 459 p.
395 learned societies and institutions in India, are arranged alphabetically by name of the organization, with a short descriptive statement and lists of research monographs, periodical and series publications for each entry. Index to institutional journals, author index and subject classification of institutions. Revision of 1969 edition.

C 40 *Universities handbook, India, 1975.* New Delhi, Association of Indian Universities, 1975. 1,035 p.
Directory and description of 79 universities, 17 agricultural universities, nine institutes and ten other major institutions. Index to degrees and subjects. Revision of 1973 edition, and continuation of Inter-University Board of Indian and Ceylon *Universities' handbook, India and Ceylon*, issued in 1964, 1969 and 1971. 1977 edition seen.

ATLASES

C 41 India (Republic). National Atlas Organization. *National atlas of India (preliminary edition).* Calcutta, 1957. 26 maps.
A collection of specialized maps, emphasizing social and economic conditions, with a text in Hindi and English. The maps are coloured, and at a scale of 192 miles to the inch.

C 42 India (Republic). Survey of India. *School atlas*, 1964. Dehra Dun, 1964. 77 maps.
Atlas of general, physical, climatological and economic features of India, and showing the latest administrative divisions at the time of publication.

C 43 India (Republic). National Atlas Organization. *Tourist atlas of India*. Calcutta, 1974.
Ten general maps of India, illustrating physical features, climate, archaeology, political divisions, are followed by 15 regional maps, at a scale of 1:1,000,000. No index.

C 44 Schwartzberg, Joseph E. *A historical atlas of South Asia.* Chicago, University of Chicago Press, 1978. 382 p. (Association for Asian Studies reference series no. 2)
152 pages of plates, almost all in colour, contain nearly 700 maps. Covers South Asian history from prehistoric times to the present day. For the more modern maps there is an emphasis on comparing the base years of 1931 and 1961. Countries covered include not only India, but Pakistan, Bangladesh, Afghanistan, and Sri Lanka. Related historical maps for Southeast Asia also included. Extensive discussion of the maps and their sources. A bibliography of over 3,500 entries is, in itself, a significant contribution. 15,000 entry index.

GEOGRAPHICAL DICTIONARIES AND GAZETTERS

C 45 Sharma, Jagdish Saran. *The national geographic dictionary of India*. New Delhi, Sterling Publishers, 1972. 223 p.
Lists some 2,000 places, important in Indian history, or in the Independence movement, with locations according to the latest political re-organization, and with some descriptions.

C 46 U.S. Office of Geography. *India, preliminary NIS gazetteer.* Washington, Central Intelligence Agency, 1952. 2 v.
Issued as part of the National Intelligence Survey program. The first volume covers Bhutan, French India, Jammu and Kashmir, Nepal, Portuguese India and India A–J. The second volume covers India K–Z. Gives 30,650 place and feature names, with their classification and longitude and latitude.

CHRONOLOGY

C 47 Rickmers, Christian Mabel (Duff). *The chronology of India, from the earliest times to the beginning of the sixteenth century.* Westminster, A. Constable and Co., 1899. 409 p.
A useful, but somewhat dated chronology, listing historical events from the birth of Buddha to the death of Babar in 1530. Sources are cited for almost all entries. The chronology is supported by a full index and a number of chronological and dynastic lists.

C 48 Burgess, James. *The chronology of modern India, for four hundred years, from the close of the fifteenth century, A.D. 1494–1894.* Delhi, S. Chand and Co., 1970. 817 p.
Over four-fifths of the chronology on the period from 1895. 35-page index.

C 49 Sharma, Jagdish Saran. *India since the advent of the British, a descriptive chronology from 1600 to Oct. 2, 1969.* Delhi, S. Chand and Co., 1970. 817 p.
Arranged according to the reign or administration of the head of the state at the time, and emphasizes political events. Index often more full than text, giving ranks to names and adding districts to place names.

C 50 Vidya, Sagar. *India in world affairs, chronology of events, 1947–72.* New Delhi, Swastik Prakashan, 1973. 248 p.
Lists the most important events connected with India in the first 25 years of independence, with an index. Author worked in the Library of the Ministry of External Affairs, Delhi.

CHRONOLOGICAL TABLES

C 51 Sewell, Robert and Sankara Balkrishna Dikshit. *The Indian calendar, with tables for the conversion of Hindu and Muhammedan dates in A.D. dates and vice versa . . .* London, Swan Sonnenschein, 1896. 106, cxxxvi, 169 p.
The main text consists of conversion tables for Hindu and Muslim dates, with an explanatory preface. Originally written to help detect forged documents with spurious dating, but now valuable for the historian handling historical materials.

C 52 Andhra Pradesh. Bureau of Economics and Statistics. *Diglott calendar.* Hyderabad, 1961–7. 2 v.
The first volume covers the period A.D. 1879–1930 and the second from A.D. 1931 to 2000. The first volume is restricted to the Muslim and Gregorian calendars, and the second includes the Saka and Vikrama calendars also, in both cases giving equivalents for years, months and days.

CENSUS

C 53 India (Republic). Census Commissioner. *Census of India, 1951.* Delhi, Manager of Publications, 1952–. 447 v. (projected).
Although censuses were taken by the British administration in different parts of India before 1872, the main national series commenced in that year, and the second census was taken in 1881, and decennially from that year to the present. A full listing of the census volumes may be found in *International population census bibliography, Asia* (A 40). The census was generally divided into a number of provincial volumes, usually subdivided into at least two parts, an administrative part and a part for tables. The number of parts in the 1951 census represented a major advance in the size of the census reporting.

C 54 India (Republic). Office of the Registrar-General. *Census of India, 1961*. New Delhi, Manager of Publications, 1962–.
The 1961 census publication program was projected to have 1,476 volumes. The general section was to be in ten parts in 29 volumes. In addition there are 26 States and Union territories, and all of these will have at least two parts, a general report, and a general population table. Others may have as many as 22 parts, and each part may be published in a number of volumes. The most numerous group will be the village surveys, planned to cover 580 villages. For a more complete description refer to India (Republic), Office of the Registrar-General, *Census of India, guide to the 1961 census publication program* (1965. 230 p.).

C 55 India (Republic). Office of the Registrar-General. *Census of India, 1971*. Delhi, Manager of Publications, 1972–.
A major publication appearing in 29 series. The first is for India as a whole, and each of the second and following series cover States and other political divisions of India.

STATISTICAL YEARBOOKS

C 56 India. Department of Commercial Intelligence and Statistics. *Statistical abstract for British India*, 1st–18th issue, 1911–40. New Delhi, Manager of Publications, 1923–43.
Each issue covers the preceding ten years, and includes some 270 tables under approximately 40 headings, as emigration, vital statistics, area and population, pilgrims, railroads, lunatic asylums, etc. There are four appendices, for customs tariffs, rates of excise duty on liquor, opium and other drugs, currency, and rates of income tax. Indexed. Continues *Statistical abstract relating to British India*, Volumes 1 (1840–65) – 36 (1891/2–1900/1), London, 1867–1902. Published on microfiche by Inter Documentation Company, Zug.

C 57 India (Republic). Central Statistical Organization. *Statistical abstract, India*, 1949–. Delhi, Manager of Publications, Government of India, 1950–.
The period of coverage is from five to ten years, and the tables under some 39 headings include economic and social development, including area and population, national income, agriculture, livestock, forests, printing presses, publication and education. Brief explanatory notes precede sections of the abstract, which is in itself a useful guide to the Indian central statistical services. Title varies: *Statistical abstract of the Indian Union*. 1975 last issue noted.

BIBLIOGRAPHY

Bibliography of Bibliographies

C 58 Kalia, D. R. and M. K. Jain. *A bibliography of bibliographies on India*. Delhi Concept Publishing Co., 1975. 204 p.
1,243 bibliographies, mostly in English, and appearing in book form, are arranged by an alphabetical subject order. No annotations. Index to authors and subjects.

General Bibliography

C 59 Calcutta. Imperial Library. *Catalogue*. Calcutta, Superintendent of Government Printing, 1904–18. 2 v. (in 4).
Lists books in Western languages in the Imperial Library, now the National Library of India. The first part, in 2 volumes, is an author-catalogue of printed books in European languages and was published in 1904. It also contains a list of newspapers. The second part is a subject index to the author catalogue, and is also in 2 volumes. Supplements 1–2 were published from 1906 to 1939, and include materials received to 1937. Each supplement is in two parts, the first is an author catalogue, and the second a subject index.

C 60 Calcutta. National Library. *Author catalogue of printed books in European languages*. Calcutta, Manager, Government of India Press, 1941–64. 10 v.
A later and more inclusive listing than the Imperial Library *Catalogue* (C 59) but lacks the subject index which makes it less valuable. Some 40,000 books are listed, and these are mostly in English, and only one-third were published in India. Official publications not included. *Supplement, 1951–1961*, published in 1964, reported.

C 61 U.S. Library of Congress. Orientalia Division. *Southern Asia accessions list, 1952–60*. Washington, 1952–60.

Issued as a quarterly through volume 5 published in 1956, with title *Southern Asia, publications in Western languages, a quarterly accessions list*, then issued monthly to December 1960. Lists books and periodical articles in Western and in selected Southern Asian languages, books from 1945, Western-language articles from January 1951, and from April 1953 for Southern Asian-language articles. Materials cited have been acquired by the Library of Congress and some 80 co-operating libraries, and library locations are stated. The list helps to fill the gap in coverage for Southern Asia at a time when national bibliography and the *Far Eastern bibliography* did not undertake this responsibility. Divided into a Western-language section subarranged by country, and minor Southern Asian-language section arranged by country and subdivided by language. There are no annotations and no published index. Reprinted by Arno, New York, 1971 (6 v.).

C 62 Calcutta. National Library. *A bibliography of Indology.* Calcutta, Government of India Press, 1960–.

A series of volumes listing 'basic books on all aspects of Indian culture'. Most books are in the National Library. Volumes published include:

1. *Indian anthropology.* 1960. 2,067 entries. Subject arrangement with author index.

2. *Indian botany, part I, A–J.* 1961. 5,346 entries. *Part II, K–Z.* 1965. 5,764 entries. Author arrangement and no index.

3. *Bengali language and literature, part I, early period.* 1964. 1,769 entries. Subject arrangement. Indexed. *Part II* (1965) reported.

C 63 *An up-to-date encyclopedia of all Indological publications published in India, and other countries related to ancient India, classified and arranged subjectwise in alphabetical order.* Delhi, Mehar Chand Lachman Das, 1962. 385 p.

A trade catalogue listing more than 12,962 titles. The first section includes books in English and Indian languages published in India; the second, books published outside India and the third, books published in Indian languages on Ayurveda, a traditional system of Indian medicine. The first section is arranged under the following subjects: Vedas, philosophy, language and linguistics, history and arts, and the sciences. No index.

C 64 Patterson, Maureen L. P. and R. B. Inden. *South Asia, an introductory bibliography.* Chicago, University of Chicago Press, Syllabus Division, 1962. 412 p.

4,369 entries, mostly in English, for books and periodical articles, arranged under eight major headings: general; history; social structure, political and economic structure; political, economic and social change; religion and philosophy; literature, science and the arts. Over 80% of the books are in the library of the University of Chicago. No annotations. Author and title index.

C 65 Diehl, Katherine Smith. *Early Indian imprints*. New York, Scarecrow Press, 1964. 533 p.
1,038 annotated titles based on the William Carey Historical Library of Serampore College near Calcutta, and includes all materials dated to 1850, and all titles published at Serampore to 1873. Divided into three major sections: books in Indian languages; books, other than bibles, in chronological order; and bibles arranged by language.

C 66 Great Britain. India Office Library. *Catalogue of European printed books*. Boston, G. K. Hall, 1964. 10 v.
Lists some 90,000 volumes in Western languages in the India Office Library, but excludes translations, which are placed with the original languages. Materials acquired to 1936 were catalogued in a sheaf catalogue (a loose-leaf catalogue of slips on which were pasted entries from printed catalogues and supplementary lists). This comprises volume 1–2, volume 3–6 reproduce the new author catalogue on cards for accessions from 1936, and including about one-fifth of the books in the sheaf catalogue. Volume 7–9 are a subject index to volume 3–6. Volume 10 notes the periodicals held by the Library. Since the India Office Library was a depository library for a substantial period between 1867 and 1947, and has collected after Independence, this catalogue is one of the principal reference tools for the study of Indian history.

C 67 Mahar, J. Michael. *India, a critical bibliography*. Tucson, University of Arizona Press, 1964. 119 p.
A select bibliography of 2,023 entries, mostly in English, and almost entirely books, emphasizing those published after 1940. Arranged by subject, with almost one-half on history, and a quarter on religion and philosophy. Entries are annotated, but these are sometimes much less than critical. Some errors suggest books not all examined by compiler. Author index.

C 68 Ajia Keizai Kenkyujo, Tokyo (Institute of the Developing Economies). *Union catalogue of documentary materials on Southeast Asia*. Tokyo, 1964, 5 v.
Lists Western-language books, mostly in English, on South and Southeast Asia in 31 Japanese institutions. Textbooks, juveniles, novels and Buddhist materials are excluded. There are sections for Asia as a whole, Southeast Asia, i.e. South Asia, and for individual countries. These are further subdivided into uniform subject divisions. Half of the approximately 20,000 titles are on India. Volume 5 is an author index. A convenient listing, making no claim to be comprehensive, brings together a great number of important books in a small and handy compass.

C 69 Indian Council for Cultural Relations. *Aspects of Indian culture, selected bibliographies*. New Delhi, Bhatkal Books International, 1966.
Bibliographies consists of introductory, selected and annotated

materials arranged in subject groups. The following volumes have been published:

1. *The arts*. 1966.
2. *History and culture*. 1970.
3. *Indian literature*. 1972.

C 70 Harvard University Library. *Southern Asia*. Cambridge, Harvard University Library, distributed by Harvard University Press, 1968. 543 p. (Widener Library shelflist 19).
Some 10,242 titles are arranged in a classified order, primarily by country and region, with a strong emphasis on South Asia. There is an index by both author and title, and listing of items by date of publication.

C 71 Jacob, Louis. *South Asia, a bibliography for undergraduate libraries*. Williamsport, Brodart, 1970. 103 p.
1,610 entries for books include India, Pakistan, Ceylon, Nepal and Afghanistan with coverage for the humanities and social sciences. Entries are graded and have references to annotations elsewhere and reviews. Author index.

C 72 U.S. Department of the Army. *South Asia and the strategic Indian Ocean, a bibliographic survey of the literature*. Washington. Government Printing Office, 1973. 359 p.
Consists of entries on contemporary topics for the region, very fully annotated, and arranged by countries. Excellent coloured maps are included.

C 73 Sharma, Jagdish Saran. *Sources of Indian Civilization, a bibliography of works by world orientalists, other than India*. Delhi, Vikas Publishing House, 1974. 360 p.
2,573 books, mostly in English, are arranged by subject, and subarranged by author. No author index.

C 74 Kaul, H. K. *Early writings on India, a union catalogue of books on India in English language published up to 1900, and available in Delhi libraries*. New Delhi, Arnold-Heinemann, 1975. 324 p.
3,277 books arranged in a detailed subject order, giving library locations in Delhi. Author and title index.

Current Bibliography

C 75 Calcutta. National Library. *Indian national bibliography*, 1957–. Calcutta, 1958–.
Originally issued quarterly, with annual cumulations for 1958–63 now issued monthly. Includes works in English and the major Indian languages, recorded in transliteration, and central and local official publications. It depends on the deposit of books provided under the Delivery of Books and Newspapers (Public Libraries) Act of 1954, but it has been estimated that 30% of these publications are not deposited, and many have to be purchased by the National Library. Maps, music scores, periodicals and

newspapers (except for the first issue under a new title) and ephemeral materials are excluded. Arranged in two parts, the first for general publications, and the second for official materials. General and official publications in one sequence after January 1973. Dewey Decimal Classification is used. Author and subject index. 1975 annual issue seen.

C 76 *Impex reference catalogue of Indian books, the list of all important books (in English) in print . . .* New Delhi, Indian Book Export and Import Co., 1960. 236, 468 p.

Some 10,000 books published in India and still in print are arranged by 48 subjects, and subarranged by author. Title, publisher, and price are given, but most entries lack pagination. A second section arranges the books by authors. The list lacks professional bibliographical standards with its different forms of titles and author names. *Impex supplement 1960–62* was published in 1962, and has 4,000 titles, over half of which are central and local official publications. Important since it helps to cover the period before the publication of the *Indian national bibliography* (C 75).

C 77 U.S. Library of Congress. American Libraries Book Procurement Center, New Delhi. *Accessions list, India*, 1962–. New Delhi, 1962–.

A monthly record of the publications acquired by the Center, including both commercial and official publications, newspapers and periodicals. Arranged by language, and within each language section, by author. Cumulative author index is issued annually, and also an annual list of serials. The list records deliveries to some 22 selected libraries in the United States, but unfortunately not all these libraries have the materials under sound bibliographical control and accessible for inter-library loan, a condition of deposit. Since the entry in the *Accessions list* may not always agree with that finally decided upon at the Library of Congress, it may be difficult to locate the book. Also, where the number of copies are short, they are distributed on a priority list, and not all libraries may receive a copy. Finally many libraries are following individual discard policies. In India, the Center attempts some selection, particularly in the field of fiction which is strongly scaled down. In spite of all these limitations, the list is more current and sometimes more complete than the *Indian national bibliography* (C 75). June 1977 issue seen.

C 78 *Indian books.* Varanasi, Indian Bibliographic Centre, 1970–.

The first issue lists some 3,000 books in English, and covers 1969 publications. The main arrangement is by author, and a fuller arrangement is provided by subject. The title index also gives substantial information. 1974 edition, with no title arrangement, published in 1975.

C 79 *Indian books, an annual bibliography.* Delhi, Researchco Reprints, 1972–.

The 1974–5 edition published in 1975, lists books in English printed or reprinted in India including official publications. Some 5,000 titles are arranged in separate sequences by author, and by subject. A directory of publishers is appended.

C 80 Sher Singh. *Indian books in print, 1972, a bibliography of Indian books published up to December 1971.* Delhi, Indian Bureau of Bibliographers, 1972–3. 3 v.
The first volume is a listing by authors, the second by title, and the third by subject. First edition published in 1969 listed 20,000 titles published from 1955 to 1967.

Publications in South Asian Languages

BENGALI

C 81 Long, James. *A descriptive catalogue of Bengali works, containing a classified list of fourteen hundred Bengali books and pamphlets which have been issued from the press during the last sixty years with occasional notices of the subjects, the price, and where printed.* Calcutta, Sanders, Cones and Co., 1855. 108 p.
488 entries for books in Bengali, with annotations and titles in English. Contains in addition much useful information on the early history of printing in Bengal.

C 82 Blumhardt, James Fuller. *Catalogue of Bengali printed books in the Library of the British Museum.* London, British Museum, 1886. 150 p.
Some 1,310 books are listed by author and title, and include three types of publication: books in the Bengali language, books translated into other languages, and polyglot publications in which Bengali books appear either in the original or in translation. There is a general index of titles, including variant forms of the author's name found on the title page. There are two series of catalogues of South Asian language materials issued in London during the late 19th and early twentieth century. The materials catalogued were frequently the same, and the compilers of the catalogues the same individuals. However, the series issued by the British Museum is better organized, more inclusive, and easier for the general reader to understand, than that issued by the Indian Office Library. For these reasons it has been preferred for entry here.

C 83 Blumhardt, James Fuller. *Supplementary catalogue of Bengali books in the Library of the British Museum acquired during the years 1886–1910.* London, British Museum, 1910. 470 cols.
2,500 books listed by author and title according to the British Museum cataloguing rules. General index of titles, and a subject index providing a subject approach to the original catalogue and to this supplement.

C 84 Blumhardt, James Fuller. *Second supplementary catalogue of Bengali books in the Library of the British Museum acquired during the years 1911–1934*. London, British Museum, 1939. 678 cols.

Lists some 5,000 books with a similar arrangement to the above catalogue.

C 85 Calcutta. National Library. *Author catalogue of printed books in Bengali language.* Calcutta, Manager, Government of India Press, 1941–63. 4 v.

Some 15,000 books and periodicals in Bengali, acquired up to the end of 1937, are arranged by author. Titles are transliterated and translated. For a more up-to-date, but selective listing, *The national bibliography of Indian literature* (C 199), lists some 5,700 entries in Bengali.

C 86 Mukherji, Jagomohon. *Bengali literature in English, a bibliography*. Calcutta, M. C. Sarkar, 1970. 108 p.

A list of some 200 books and articles, with a supplement covering publications through 1969, translated from Bengali into English. Index to English and Bengali titles and to personal names.

HINDI

C 87 Blumhardt, James Fuller. *Catalogues of the Hindi, Panjabi, Sindhi, and Pushtu books in the Library of the British Museum.* London, British Museum, 1893. 284, 64, 24, 54 cols.

An author catalogue in four parts. The first contains some 1,800 titles in Hindi, the second some 400 in Panjabi, the third some 150 books in Pushtu, and the fourth some 160 in Sindhi. Each part has its own title and subject index.

C 88 Blumhardt, James Fuller. *A supplementary catalogue of Hindi books in the Library of the British Museum acquired during the years 1893–1912*. London, British Museum, 1913. 470 cols.

Some 3,000 books arranged by author, or by title for anonymous works. Title and subject index.

C 89 Barnett, Lionel David and others. *A second supplementary catalogue of printed books in Hindi, Bihari and Pahri in the Library of the British Museum*. London, British Museum, 1957. 1,678 cols.

Over 6,000 titles are arranged by author, with subject and title indexes. Books on the *Adi granth* have been excluded since this is regarded as part of Panjabi literature.

C 90 Singh, Mangalnath. *Hindi mem uccatara sahitya* (The best of Hindi books). Varanasi (i.e. Benares), Rajnagari Pracharini Sabha, Vikrama 2014 (1957). 732 p.

Some 13,000 titles are arranged into 39 subject divisions. For each book, author, title, publication date and price given. Authors are listed by first name under each division. No index.

C 91 Tandon, Prem Narayan. *Hindi sevi samsara* (A dictionary of Hindi writers). Lakhanav (i.e. Lucknow), Hindi Sevi Samsara Karyalaya, 1963–5. 2 v.

Lists some 418 bookstores and libraries, 401 publishing houses,

1,806 newspapers and periodicals and 1,077 living writers and their works. Volume 1 covers the situation to 1947, and volume 2 from 1947 to 1963.

C 92 Mahajan, Yash Pal and Krishna Mahajan. *Brahad Hindi grantha suchi* (A Hindi bibliography). Delhi, Bharatiya Granth Niketana, 1965. 584 p.
Some 24,000 books are arranged by author under family name. The name of the publisher, publishing date, subject and price are given. *Parisishta* (Supplement, 1966) (1967. 141 p.) contains an additional 5,000 titles.

C 93 Pitambar, Narain. *Hindi sahitya sarini* (Bibliography of Hindi books). Hoshiarpur, Viveshvaranand Institute, 1971–4. 2 v. (Vishveshvaranand Indological series 50, 65).
Some 40,000 Hindi books, published to 1964, and arranged in a detailed subject order. Author and title indexes. The most comprehensive of the Hindi bibliographies.

HINDUSTANI

C 94 Blumhardt, James Fuller. *Catalogue of Hindustani printed books in the Library of the British Museum.* London, British Museum, 1889. 458 cols.
Lists some 2,500 works in Hindustani, and written almost entirely in Perso-Arabic script.

C 95 Blumhardt, James Fuller. *Supplementary catalogue of Hindustani books in the Library of the British Museum acquired during the years 1889–1908.* London, British Museum, 1909. 678 cols.
An author catalogue of some 7,500 books with a title index and a classified subject index.

KANNADA

C 96 Barnett, Lionel David. *Catalogue of the Kannada, Badaga and Kurg books in the Library of the British Museum.* London, British Museum, 1910. 278 cols.
1,600 entries are arranged by author, with a title and subject index. Only nine books are in Badaga and Kurg. 3,000 titles in Kannada are listed in *The national bibliography of Indian literature* (C 199).

MALAYALAM

C 97 Gaur, Albertine. *Catalogue of Malayalam books in the British Museum, with an appendix listing the books in Brahui, Gondi, Kui, Malto, Oraon (Kurukh), Toda and Tulu.* London, British Museum, 1971. 587 p.
Some 6,000 entries in Malayalam for books in the British Library held up to 1966. Arrangement is by author, with a title index and subject index.

C 98 Govi, K. M. *Malayala granthasuchi.* A retrospective bibliography of Malayalam books published to the end of 1970. Trichur, Kerala Sahitya Akademi, 1973–4. 2 v.
26,013 titles are arranged by subject, with full bibliographical descriptions and some annotations, and published from 1772 to 1970. Author index and title index. Author is an assistant editor of the *Indian national bibliography* (C 75).

MARATHI

C 99 Blumhardt, James Fuller. *Catalogue of the Marathi and Gujarati printed books in the Library of the British Museum.* London, British Museum, 1892. 232, 196 cols.
In two sections, the first listing some 1,200 Marathi books and the second some 1,000 Gujarati books. Both sections are arranged in author order. Subject and title indexes.

C 100 Blumhardt, James Fuller. *A supplementary catalogue of Marathi and Gujarati books in the British Museum.* London, British Museum, 1915. 256, 336 cols.
In two sections, the first containing some 2,000 books in Marathi, and the second some 2,300 in Gujarati. Separate subject and title indexes to both sections. 4,500 books in Gujarati are included in *The national bibliography of Indian literature, 1901–1953.*

C 101 Date, Shankar Ganesh. *Marathi grantha suchi, 1800–1937* (Bibliography of Marathi publications, 1800–1937). Puna (i.e. Poona), 1943. 1,072, 376 p.
A classified catalogue arranged by the Dewey Decimal Classification, with some Colon Classification modifications, of 18,768 books in Marathi or on Marathi language, literature and grammar. Manuscripts, periodicals, textbooks, guidebooks, almanacs, reports, liturgical materials and maps are excluded. There is a chronological list of books published from 1805 to 1855. Author and title index. Date's unaided lifetime contribution to Marathi bibliography, with all entries personally inspected by him.

C 102 Date, Shankar Ganesh. *Marathi grantha suchi, 1938–1950* (Bibliography of Marathi publications, 1938–1950). Puna, 1951. 658 p.
A classified catalogue similar to the above bibliography, of 7,839 books, with author and title index. Completed with some assistance from the Sahitya Akademi and the Bombay State Education Department.

C 103 Date, Shankar Ganesh. *Marathi niyatakalikanci suci, 1800–1950.* Mumbai (i.e. Bombay), Marathi Granth Sangrahalaya, 1969–. v. 1–.
An attempt at a comprehensive listing of Marathi publications. The first volume covers periodicals, excluding weekly and daily publications. Volume 2, parts 1 and 2 seen.

PANJABI

C 104 Barnet, Lionel David. *Panjabi printed books in the British Museum, a supplementary catalogue.* London, British Museum, 1961. 121 p.
1,300 books arranged in author order, with a subject and title index. Books in Panjabi are in both the Devanagri and the Gurmukhi script. Supplements James Fuller Blumhardt *Catalogues of the Hindi, Panjabi, Sindhi and Pushto books in the Library of the British Museum* (C 87).

C 105 Ramdev, Jogindar Singh. *Panjabi likhari kosha* (Dictionary of Panjabi authors). Jallandara (i.e. Jullundur), Niu Buk Kampani, 1964. 336 p.
1,700 authors are listed, with a short account of their lives and list of their published works. Based on a questionnaire. 80% of the authors sent materials for this compilation, and the other 20% include some older writers and many no longer living. The first book of its kind.

SANSKRIT, PALI AND PRAKRIT

C 106 Haas, Ernst. *Catalogue of Sanskrit and Pali books in the British Museum.* London, Trubner and Co., 1876. 188 p.
An author catalogue of some 3,400 works, with a title index. The entries are usually, but not always published in India.

C 107 Bendall, Cecil. *Catalogue of Sanskrit, Pali and Prakrit books in the British Museum acquired during the years 1876–92.* London, British Museum, 1893. 624 cols.
Approximately 5,000 books, mostly current. Shows an increase in the number of Jain texts, mostly in Prakrit, over the previous catalogue of Ernst Haas. Index of titles and a select subject index.

C 108 Barnett, Lionel David. *Supplementary catalogue of Sanskrit, Pali, and Prakrit books in the Library of the British Museum acquired during the years 1892–1906.* London, British Museum, 1908. 1,096 cols. An author catalogue of some 8,900 books with a separate title and select subject index. Includes some Burmese titles.

C 109 Barnett, Lionel David. *Supplementary catalogue of the Sanskrit, Pali, and Prakrit books in the Library of the British Museum acquired during the years 1906–1928.* London, British Museum, 1928. 1,694 cols.
Author catalogue for some 13,500 books, with separate general index of titles and a select subject index. Contains a few titles in Burmese.

C 110 Emeneau, Murray Barnson. *Union list of printed Indic texts and translations in American libraries.* New Haven, American Oriental Society, 1935. 540 p. (American Oriental series 7).
An excellent guide to resources in the United States and aid for the bibliographer and cataloguer. Since it was published there has been a very great expansion of South Asian literature in American

libraries, and it is estimated that there are at least twice the number of the 4,491 titles listed in American libraries, with many new locations. Almost all the works were written before 1800, and are in Sanskrit, Pali, Prakrit and Apabhramsa. An appendix lists the serial publication of texts. Holdings of the University of California not included.

TAMIL

C 111 Murdoch, John. *Classified catalogue of Tamil printed books, with introductory notices.* Madras, Tamil Development and Research Council, Government of Tamilnad, 1968. 287 p.
1,755 titles are listed, but some are missionary publications in English. The entries are arranged in subject order, with sections including religion, jurisprudence, philosophy, literature, history, periodicals and newspapers. Index of titles, but not of authors. The extensive introduction surveys Tamil literature and language. Reprint of 1865 edition.

C 112 Barnett, Lionel David and G. U. Pope. *Catalogue of the Tamil books in the Library of the British Museum.* London, British Museum, 1909. 590 cols.
An author catalogue of over 3,600 books, mostly in Tamil, but some in English or French, with a general index of titles and a select subject index. Includes a short note on Tamil literature.

C 113 Barnett, Lionel David. *Supplementary catalogue of the Tamil books in the Library of the British Museum.* London, British Museum, 1931. 696 cols.
Some 3,900 books are in author order, with a general index to titles and a select subject index.

C 114 Madras (State). Tamil Development and Research Council. *Tamil nul vivara attavanai* Madras State Tamil bibliography, 1867–1910. Madras, 1961–5. 2 v. (in 7 parts).
The first volume in three parts, lists 3,718 books published from 1867 to 1900, arranged by the Dewey Decimal Classification, with an author-title index. The second volume lists 4,860 books, also arranged by Dewey, and with author-title index.

C 115 Nayagam, Xavier S. Thani. *A reference guide to Tamil studies, books.* Kuala Lumpur, University of Malaya Press, 1966. 122 p.
Lists 1,322 books arranged in a classified order. The first section notes translations and summaries of Tamil literature. Author index. No annotations.

C 116 Pattapiraman, K. *Tamilp pattirikaikal.* A guide to Tamil dailies and periodicals. Madras, Arunodayam, 1968. 108 p.
Lists 500 periodicals and dailies, giving date of first issue, and directory-type information. No index.

TELUGU

C 117 Barnett, Lionel David. *A catalogue of the Telugu books in the*

Library of the British Museum. London, British Museum, 1912. 444 cols.
Over 6,000 entries are arranged by author, with a general index to titles and a select subject index.

Official Publications

C 118 Campbell, Francis Bunbury Fitzgerald. *Index-catalogue of Indian official publications in the Library, British Museum.* London, Library Supply Co., 1900. 193, 314, 72 p.
A subject catalogue of approximately 7,500 publications issued mostly subsequent to 1857. Entries are arranged primarily by geographical area and subdivided by subject.

C 119 India. Office of the Superintendent of Government Printing, Calcutta. *General catalogue of government publications, corrected up to 31st December, 1912, part I.* Calcutta, 1913, 329 p.
Includes all publications, except acts, regulations and publications not for sale, and is noted as no. 21 in the series. The first part deals with India as a whole, and is divided into twelve major divisions. The second part is divided into nine provinces. Subject index. A revised edition, corrected up to 30 June 1921, in 506 p. was published in 1921.

C 120 India (Republic). Publication Branch. *Catalogue of Government of India civil publications.* Delhi, Manager of Publications, 1926–.
Publications are listed by subject, and cover acts and laws, agriculture, arts and sciences, administration, finance, medical, trade, commerce and industries. When in Indian languages, the title is given in English only. Kept up to date with annual supplements. Revised issues for 1948 and 1953 noted. No index. The 1959 catalogue is the basis for a new series of supplements which were issued for 1960/1964, 1965, 1966 and 1967. *Indian national bibliography* (C 75) also lists official publications.

C 121 India (Republic). Lok Sabha. Secretariat. *List of publications (periodical or ad hoc) issued by various ministries of the Government of India,* third edition. New Delhi, Lok Sabha Secretariat, 1958. 282 p.
Some 3,000 publications are arranged by issuing agency, with information on periodicity, price and source of availability, and whether in print. Valuable as a supplement to the *Catalogue of Government of India civil publications* (C 120). No subject index.

C 122 Singh, Mohinder. *Government publications of India, a survey of their nature, bibliographical control and distribution system.* Delhi, Metropolitan Book Co., 1967, 270 p.
With the government being the largest publisher in India, and issuing so much of value, it is important that the controls and distribution system for this material be understood. This work

discusses the organization of the government, and follows this with a detailed statement by 31 divisions, covering publications, distribution and controls. Over 1,500 titles are cited.

C 123 Datta, Rajeshwari. *Union catalogue of the Central Government of India publications held by libraries in London, Oxford and Cambridge*. London, Mansell, 1970. 471 cols.
Arranges some 4,700 books and periodicals in an alphabetical author sequence. The materials noted are in English only and relate broadly to the social sciences. Locations stated for 12 major collections.

Periodicals and Newspapers

C 124 Calcutta. National Library. *Catalogue of periodicals, newspapers and gazettes.* Calcutta, Government of India Press, 1956. 285 p.
1,697 periodicals, gazettes and newspapers in Western languages only and published from the late 18th century, are arranged in Dewey Decimal Classification order, with a full bibliographical citation including holdings. Title and subject index. Over three-quarters of the titles published outside India.

C 125 *Indian press yearbook*, 1949–. Madras, Indian Press Publications, 1949–.
A journalists' yearbook of which only one-third is concerned with a select list of newspapers and periodicals arranged by state. For each entry, editorial staff and circulation stated. No index. The third issue for 1954 latest noted.

C 126 India (Republic). National Information Service. *NIFOR guide to Indian periodicals, 1955–1956.* Poona [preface, 1955]. 385 p.
Lists both newspapers and periodicals, with 2,127 titles. There is also listed another 1,526 concerning which the compiler had little information. Index to titles and subjects.

C 127 India (Republic). Office of the Registrar of Newspapers. *Press in India, part II*, 1956–. New Delhi, Ministry of Information and Broadcasting, 1957–. Annual.
Includes all serials, with frequency ranging from daily to annual. Arranged by state, then by language of publication, together with information on date of establishment, address, publisher and circulation. Title index. The most comprehensive listing of periodicals in India. Title to 1964: *Annual report*. 1973 issue seen.

C 128 Gidwani, N. N. *Indian periodicals, an annotated guide*. Jaipur, 1969. 191 p.
Lists over 5,000 periodicals currently published. In the first part these are arranged by subjects, and the second part is an index to the first. Excludes ephemera, juveniles, too cheap materials, catalogues of publications, annual reports, debates, telephone directories. Selective annotations, which are provided only when considered helpful.

C 129 Gandhi, H. N. D. *Indian periodicals in print, 1973*. Delhi, Vidya Mandal, 1973. 2 v.
16,483 periodicals are listed alphabetically, with language, date of first publication, frequency, address and price noted. Volume 2 arranges these titles under 35 headings, with a further subdivision into 152 groupings, and then by language. In addition there is a sponsoring institution index, a subject index, a list of cessations, and statistics on Indian periodical publication.

INDEXES

C 130 *Guide to Indian periodical literature*, v. 1, no. 1–, 1964–. Gurgaon, 1964–.
Started somewhat unsatisfactorily, but now being issued quarterly, and covering some 150 Indian periodicals. Each issue has some 7,000 entries, and the standard of bibliographical work is high. April–June 1978 issue seen.

C 131 *Index India*. Jaipur, Rajasthan University Library, 1967–74. In 1969 there were 51,049 entries for some 1,100 periodicals and newspapers, over half of which were non-Indian. Entries were arranged by subject, and separate subject and author indexes were provided.

C 132 *Indian press index*, v. 1–, April 1968–. Delhi, Delhi Library Association, 1968–.
Indexes 25 English-language newspapers. In 1969, 40,559 entries were arranged in subject order. Monthly issues. Author index and geographic index. April–May 1977 last issue noted.

Theses and Dissertations

C 133 Kozicki, Richard J. and Peter Ananda. *South and Southeast Asia, doctoral dissertations and masters' theses completed at the University of California at Berkeley, 1906–1973*, revised edition. Berkeley, University of California, Center for South and Southeast Asia Studies, 1974. 49 p. (Occasional paper no. 11).
168 doctoral dissertations and 211 masters' theses are arranged by country. Revision of the 1969 edition.

C 134 Shulman, Frank J. *Doctoral dissertations on South Asia, 1966–1970, an annotated bibliography covering North America, Europe and Australia*. Ann Arbor, Center for South and Southeast Asia Studies, University of Michigan, 1971. 228 p. (Michigan papers on South and Southeast Asia 4).
1,303 dissertations are arranged by country, then by detailed subjects. Over half the entries have a short annotation, which is intended to be descriptive and not critical. Contributions for 1970 are incomplete, except for United States, and 107 dissertations are noted for the United States for 1971. Valuable notes on distribution and subject range of entries and availability. Author,

institution and subject indexes. 650 dissertations are listed in Margaret H. Case *South Asian history, 1750–1950* (C 222).

C 135 Inter-University Board of India and Ceylon. *A bibliography of doctoral dissertations accepted by Indian universities, 1857–1970*. New Delhi, 1972–5. 24 v.
Arranged by major disciplines, and with an author index to each volume. Location of dissertation stated. The most comprehensive list.

C 136 *Indian dissertation abstracts*, v. 1–. Bombay, Popular Prakashan, 1973–.
A publication of the Indian Council of Social Science Research and of the Inter-University Board of India. The first issue seen contains 36 abstracts, including dissertations in the fields of history, and social sciences.

C 137 Gopal, Krishnan. *Theses on Indian sub-continent, 1877–1971* . . . Delhi, Hindustan Publishing Corporation (India), 1977. 462 p.
3,769 dissertations, published in Australia, Canada, Great Britain and the United States, related to South Asia and in the social sciences and humanities, are arranged by country, and subarranged in a detailed subject classification. A small number are annotated. Author index and subject index. Fills a major gap in the coverage for dissertations on Asia.

Russian Language

C 138 Birman, D. A. and others. *Bibliografiia Indii*. Moskva, Nauka, 1976. 682 p.
11,277 entries for books, articles, reviews, translations arranged by eleven major subjects, with further subdivision. Some annotation. Author and title index. Second edition.

Films

C 139 Mosher, William and Edward Schulick. *Annotated South Asia film catalogue*. New Delhi, Educational Resources Centre, 197–. 146 p.
An annotated list of some 400 films, with list of film sources.

Subject Bibliography

RELIGION AND THOUGHT

C 140 Guerinot, Armand Albert. *Essai de bibliographie Jaina*. Paris, 1906. 568 p. (Annales du Musee Guimet, Bibliotheque d'etudes 22).
852 books and periodical articles in Western and Indian languages arranged in a classified order, and annotated. Indexes for authors, titles, subjects, places and periodicals surveyed.

C 141 Renou, Louis. *Bibliographie vedique*. Paris, Adrien-Maisonneuve, 1931. 339 p.
6,500 books and articles in Western languages, Hindi and Sanskrit are arranged in 16 subject groups, and then chronologically. Subjects covered include the Vedas, Hindu civilization, the Vedic language, Sanskrit philology, and Indian religion. 68 periodicals are cited, and one-third of the entries are briefly annotated. Index to titles and authors.

C 142 Jain, Chhote Lal. *Jaina bibliography*. Calcutta, Bharati Jaina Parisat, 1945. 377 p. (Jaina bibliography series no. 1).
509 books and periodical articles in Western languages arranged in seven sections, and chronologically within each section. Annotated. Excludes material listed in Armand Albert Guerinot *Essai de bibliographie Jaina* (C 140).

C 143 Dandekar, R. N. *Vedic bibliography*. Bombay, Karnatak Publishing House, 1946. 398 p.
Some 3,500 books and articles in Western and Indian languages are arranged by subject. Some 450 periodicals are cited. The subjects covered include the Indus Valley civilization, the Vedas, Vedic and Indic languages, and Indian religion. There are annotations in English for about one-sixth of the entries, but no translation of titles. The standard Indian works tend to be in more modern editions than those cited by Louis Renou *Bibliographie vedique* (C 141). Index to titles and subjects.

C 144 Dandekar, R. N. *Vedic bibliography, volume 2*. Poona, University of Poona, 1961. 760 p.
Supplements the previous bibliography with 6,500 books and periodical articles in Western and Indian languages, and arranged into 20 chapters and 93 subsections. One-third of the entries are annotated. Title and author index. Volume 3, published 1973, has over 7,000 entries.

C 145 Smith, Harry Daniel. *Profile of a library in transition*. Syracuse (Syracuse University), for the program of South Asia Studies, 1966. 205 p.
The principal part of the text is a bibliography of the history of religion in South Asia based on the holdings of the Syracuse University Library in 1966. Some 3,000 books are arranged in subject order, with library call numbers. No index and no annotation.

C 146 *Encyclopedia of Indian philosophies, volume 1, bibliography*. Delhi, Motilal Banarsidass, 1970. 811 p.
Does not list the major works, but commentaries and expositions of these. Approximately 9,222 entries emphasize Bengali publications. The bibliography is divided into three sections, the first of datable Sanskrit texts by date, the second of non-datable Sanskrit texts by title, and the third of other literature, arranged by literature, then by title. Index of names, index of titles, and an index by topic.

SOCIAL SCIENCES

C 147 Gilbert, William Harlen. *Caste in India, a bibliography, part 1.* Washington, D.C., 1948. 174 p.
A major introductory statement explains how the bibliography was compiled, and this is followed by a detailed list of contents in which 5,345 entries for materials published to March 1943 were projected. However part 1 contains only 1,970 entries nearly all in English. No annotations and no index. No further parts reported.

C 148 Mandelbaum, David G. *Materials for a bibliography of the ethnology of India.* Berkeley, Department of Anthropology, University of California, 1949. 220 p.
2,250 unannotated entries in Western languages are arranged by cultural area and subject. Only a few of the entries were personally inspected by the compiler, and those that are considered important have an asterisk before them. Compiled in 1940–1. Author and subject index.

C 149 U.N.E.S.C.O. Research Centre for the Social Implications of Industrialization in Southern Asia. *Southern Asia social science bibliography.* Calcutta, 1952–65. 14 nos.
Books, articles and reports in English and published in India, Pakistan and Ceylon, are divided into five major subject classes, and further subdivided. Some selected items are annotated. Author and subject index.

C 150 Bacon, Elizabeth E., Morris E. Opler and Edward E. LeClair Jr. *Selected and annotated bibliography of the sociology of India.* New Haven, Human Relations Area Files, 1957. 116 p.
559 annotated entries are arranged by subject, and by author within each subject. Table of contents the only key to this bibliography since there is no index.

C 151 Furer-Haimendorf, Elizabeth von. *An anthropological bibliography of South Asia, together with a directory of recent anthropological field work.* Paris, Mouton, 1958–70. 3 v. New series, volume 1, 1965–9, published 1976.
Based upon and continues David G. Mandelbaum *Materials for a bibliography of the ethnology of India* (C 148). The first volume covers the period 1940–54, with 5,316 books and periodical articles in Western languages, and the second for 1955–9, has 2,761 entries. The main part of both volumes is divided into 19 regional sections and one general section. Author index at the end of each volume. The field research directory entered by researcher is a valuable guide for future research publication. The third volume covers publications from 1960 to 1964, with 3,524 entries.

C 152 Alexandrowicz, Charles Henry. *A bibliography of Indian law.* New York, Oxford University Press, 1958. 69 p.
The first part is a short introduction to Indian law arranged in much the same order as the second part or bibliography, which lists some 700 books and periodicals. Annotation for a limited number of important legal works cited.

C 153 India (Republic). Directorate of Economics and Statistics. *Agricultural economics in India, a bibliography*, second edition. Delhi, Government of India Press, 1960. 342 p.
A substantial revision of the 1953 edition, contains 3,400 annotated entries arranged by subject, and covering agriculture in general, planning, utilization, technology, administration, labour, land problems, legislation, taxation and statistics. No index.

C 154 *Indian agricultural economics, a bibliography, supplement*. 1964 164 p.
Contains an additional 1,600 books and official reports, arranged by subject. No index.

C 155 Damle, Y. B. *Caste, a review of the literature on caste*. Cambridge, Massachusetts Institute of Technology, Center for International Studies, 1961. 125 p.
In three parts. The first is a review of research in the field, and divides publications into 28 categories. The second lists 281 books and articles published between 1950–9 in subject order, and the third contains 116 abstracts of important books on caste arranged by author. No table of contents and no index. No cross references between sections.

C 156 Cohn, Bernard S. *Development and impact of British administration in India, a bibliographical essay*. New Delhi, Indian Institute of Public Administration, 1961. 88 p.
Lists some 400 books, mostly in English, in an essay, where they receive the equivalent of an annotation. Bibliography is arranged by author.

C 157 Gupta, G. P. *Economic investigations in India, a bibliography of researches in commerce and economics, approved by Indian universities*. Agra, Ramprasad and Sons, 1961–6. 3 v.
Since only 5% of university theses are published, much valuable material is not made accessible. This bibliography attempts to redress this situation. The first part lists dissertations under 18 universities, by date of degree. The second rearranges these materials by topic. Thesis topics which have been approved are listed in the same way. The 1962 supplement includes another six universities. 1966 supplement also.

C 158 Pai Panandiker, V. A. *A bibliography on public administration in India, the Central and State governments*. New Delhi, Indian Institute of Public Administration, 1963. 58 p.
Arranges some 500 books, reports and articles in English by topic. Author index.

C 159 Indian Law Institute. *Index to Indian legal periodicals*, 1963–. New Delhi, 1963–. Semi-annual.
32 periodicals are indexed under subject and author, with the author entries referring to the subject. The scope is not restricted to Indian law, and only a small proportion of the total Indian law literature is covered.

C 160 National Council of Education Research and Training. New Delhi. *Educational investigations in Indian universities, 1939–1961*. New Delhi, 1966. 286 p.
85 doctoral dissertations and 2,856 masters' theses in the field of education, are arranged by institution granting the degrees. Name and subject indexes. Continued by *Educational investigations in Indian universities, 1962–1966* (1968) with a similar arrangement and listing an additional 65 doctoral dissertations and 2,159 masters' theses.

C 161 Brembeck, Cole S. and Edward W. Weidner. *Education and development in India and Pakistan, a select and annotated bibliography*. East Lansing, Michigan State University College of Education and International Programs, 1963? 221 p. (Michigan State University Education in Asia series 1).
Divided into two sections, one for India and the other for Pakistan. Each of these subdivided into a number of subjects. 241 books and periodical articles, all in English, are given critical and descriptive annotations. No index.

C 162 Mukerjee, A. K. *Bibliography of periodicals*. Delhi, Central Institute of Education, 1964. 118 p.
491 periodicals, including those not published in India, located in the National Council on Education Research and Training, and in bound volumes in its different libraries. Arranged by the Dewey Decimal Classification, with an alphabetical title index.

C 163 Jaipur, India (Rajasthan). University of Rajasthan. Library. *A select bibliography on Indian government and politics*. Jaipur, Rajasthan University Library, 1965. 196 p.
A select bibliography of 1,601 books and articles in English, and located in the University of Rajasthan Library. Entries are arranged by subject. No annotations. Lists the 42 periodicals surveyed since 1950. Author index.

C 164 Kirkland, Edwin Capers. *A bibliography of South Asian folklore*. Bloomington, Indiana University Research Center in Anthropology, Folklore and Linguistics, 1966. 292 p. (Indiana University Folklore Institute, Folklore series 21).
6,852 books and periodical articles cover the whole South Asian region and Tibet, in Western and Asian languages, and are arranged by author. Entries are annotated, with information on the area, linguistic, tribal and ethnic group to which it belongs. This information is brought together in the index. Indian classical literature is included within the term folklore.

C 165 De Benko, Eugene and V. N. Krishnan. *Research sources for South Asian studies in economic development, a select bibliography of serial publications*. East Lansing, Asian Studies Center, Michigan State University, 1966. 97 p.
918 entries for official, academic, commercial and private industrial periodicals, with items starred held by Michigan State University, comprising one-fifth of the total. The two principal

parts, one on economic development, and the other on related social science fields, are arranged by country, and then by author. No annotation. Subject index.

C 166 Pareek, Udai. *Behavioural science research in India, a directory, 1925–65*. Delhi, Behavioural Science Centre, 1966–71. 2 v.
The first volume contains 16,729 entries, mostly periodical articles, arranged in a detailed subject order, with 22 main divisions, and over 175 subdivisions. Volume 2 covers 1966 through 1968. Continued by *Indian behavioural science abstracts*, 1970–. This is a bibliography, not a directory. Author index.

C 167 *Index to Indian economic journals*. Calcutta, Information Research Academy, 1966–. Quarterly.
January 1972 issue indexes 110 serials, mostly periodicals. Subject and author indexes. December 1972 issue last seen.

C 168 *Education in India, keyword in context index and bibliography*. Ann Arbor, Comparative Education Program, School of Education, University of Michigan, 1966. 220 p. (University of Michigan Comparative Education series).
The main body of this bibliography is formed by the keyword in context index (Kwik) and is based on books, periodical articles and Indian unpublished dissertations, mostly in English. Author index, but no statement of sources surveyed.

C 169 Sethi, Narendra K. *A bibliography of Indian management*. Bombay, Popular Prakashan, 1967. 116 p.
Over 500 articles in English are arranged under eight major headings, with an emphasis on economic management. Author index.

C 170 Sen Gupta, Sanker. *A bibliography of Indian folklore and related subjects*. Calcutta, Indian Publications, 1967. 196 p. (Indian folklore series no. 11).
Approximately 5,000 books and articles are arranged by topic. Author index. Does not refer to Edwin Capers Kirkland *A bibliography of South Asian folklore* (C 164).

C 171 Greaves, Monica A. *Education in British India, 1698–1947, a bibliographical guide to the sources of information in London*. London, University of London Institute of Education, 1967. 182 p. (Education Libraries Bulletin supplement 13).
1,379 books and periodical articles mostly in English, are arranged by author, with a subject index. In addition there is a short section on manuscripts and records. The most complete bibliography of its type.

C 172 Menge, Paul E. *Government administration in South Asia, a bibliography*. Washington, American Society for Public Administration, Comparative Administrative Group, 1968. 100 p. (Papers in comparative public administration, special series no. 9).
Over 1,025 books and articles in English published almost entirely from 1947 to 1967 are arranged by country, with subject divisions

for India and Pakistan. The materials listed are available in the United States. Bibliographies and periodicals only are annotated. No index.

C 173 Jadhav, C. G. *Bibliography of social studies in India*. Delhi, Manager of Publications, 1968. 955 p. (Census of India, 1961, volume 1, part I (III-B)).
Covers systematically the period from 1955 to 1961, but includes materials dated after 1961, since materials published before 1955 may be found in *A bibliography of Indology, volume 1, Indian anthropology* (C 62); Elizabeth von Furer-Haimendorf *An anthropological bibliography of South Asia* (C 151); and David G. Mandelbaum *Materials for a bibliography of the ethnology of India* (C 148). Some 11,000 entries for books, articles, reports, including those from the Census of India, are arranged by State and Union territories, and subarranged by 11 major subject divisions. Materials on Pakistan are included where they relate to India. Author index.

C 174 Indian Institute of Public Administration. *A bibliography on public enterprises in India*. New Delhi, 1968. 135 p.
A revision of the 1961 edition. 1,148 books, articles and reports are arranged by subject. No index or annotation. Includes materials published to June 1966.

C 175 India (Republic). Department of Labour and Employment. Library. *Bibliography on industrial relations in India, 1951–1968*. New Delhi, 1969? 264 p. (Bibliographical series 23).
2,696 entries, nearly all articles, arranged by subject. Subject index provided, but no author index.

C 176 Shukla, Modan Mohan, Jagmal Singh Chauhan and Knod Kumar Maheshwari. *Banks and banking in India, with special reference to bank nationalization*. Delhi, New Star Publishers, 1970. 283 p.
Some 1,800 articles in English published in the 1960s are presented in detailed subject arrangement. Author index and subject index.

C 177 Pareek, Udai. *Foreign behavioural research on India*. Delhi, Acharan Sahkar, 1970. 159 p.
Some 1,600 books, articles, theses and dissertations in English are arranged in a detailed subject order. Directory of 165 researchers appended. Author index.

C 178 Roy, Sachin. *Anthropologists in India, short biography, bibliography and current projects*. New Delhi, Indian Anthropological Association, 1970. 218 p.
Contains 180 biographies, and a bibliography arranged by author, with a short introduction to the history and present development of anthropology in India.

C 179 Goil, N. K. *Asia social science bibliography, 1966–*. Delhi, Vikas Publishing House, 1970–.
May be viewed as a continuation of *Southern Asia social science bibliography* (C 149). The 1967 volume was published in 1974,

and contains selected entries for 600 books and 1,685 periodical articles, in English, arranged by major social science divisions, and subarranged by country and locality. Annotated. Author, subject and geographical indexes. 1968 and 1969 volumes are projected. Over half of this bibliography on India, and there are no entries on the People's Republic of China.

C 180 Bose, Ashish. *Urbanization in India, an inventory of source materials*. New Delhi, Academic Books, 1970. 370 p.
Surveys the 1951 and 1961 Census of India, the 120 National Sample Surveys, and the 16 city surveys of the Research Programs Committee of the Planning Commission. The inventory has a demographic bias, and contains no materials in Indian languages, no local materials from municipalities, and omits some important works. 1,529 citations. Index.

C 181 Rath, Vimal. *Index of Indian economic journals, 1916–1965*. Poona, Gokhale Institute of Politics and Economics, Orient Longman, 1971. 302 p. (Gokhale Institute studies no. 57).
Indexes 32 periodicals including official periodicals, in a subject arrangement. Author index.

C 182 Prasher, Ram Gopal. *Indian library literature, an annotated bibliography*. New Delhi, Today and Tomorrow's, 1971. 504 p.
Contains over 3,500 entries, including books, periodical articles and dissertations, published from 1955. Arranged in the Dewey Decimal Classification, with subject and author indexes. Some entries annotated.

C 183 Delhi. Institute of Applied Manpower Research. Documentation Centre. *Employment, unemployment and underemployment in India, an annotated bibliography*. New Delhi, 1972. 200 p.
Lists 798 books and articles, most of which are annotated and cover the period 1947–71, but some earlier work is also included. Classified author index, journal index and area indexes.

C 184 India (Republic). Office of the Registrar General. *Bibliography of census publications in India*. Delhi, Manager of Publications, 1972. 520 p. (Census centenary publication no. 5).
Attempts to make a comprehensive listing of all census publications through the 1961 Census, and includes countries formerly covered by the Indian census. Some 2,820 publications arranged by State and Union territories. Author index.

C 185 Rana, M. S. *Writings on Indian constitution, 1861–1972*. Delhi, Indian Bureau of Bibliography, 1973. 496 p.
7,419 newspaper and periodical articles, books and reports are arranged in a highly detailed division. In addition there are 236 theses and dissertations and 2,500 cases arranged by article of the Constitution. The bibliography attempts to be inclusive. Author index.

C 186 Sharma, Jagdish Saran. *Indian socialism, a descriptive bibliography*. Delhi, Vikas Publishing House, 1975. 349 p.
Some 6,000 books, periodicals and articles are arranged by a

detailed subject order. Author index.

C 187 Chekki, Danesh A. *The social system and culture of modern India, a research bibliography*. New York, Garland Publishing, 1975. 843 p.

5,475 books and articles related to sociology and social and cultural anthropology, almost entirely in English, are arranged in detailed classification. The entries were published between 1947 and 1974. No index.

C 188 Bose, Ashish. *Bibliography on urbanization in India, 1947–1976*. New Delhi, Tata McGraw-Hill, 1976. 179 p.

2,711 books, articles and reports in English, arranged under 55 headings, and covering demography, geography, history, politics, administration and sociology. Author index.

C 189 Ghosh, Arun and Ranjit Ghosh. *Indian political movement, 1919–1971: a systematic bibliography*. Calcutta, India Book Exchange, 1976. 499 p.

6,564 entries for books, articles and reports. Arranged by political parties in six time periods: 1919–33; 1934–9; 1940–7; 1948–55; 1956–64; and 1965–71. Appendix (entries 6120–564) contains a selected list of related books, pamphlets and articles. Author index and subject index.

C 190 Mehrotra, R. K. *Mass communication in India, an annotated bibliography*. Singapore, Asian Mass Communication Research and Information Centre, 1976. 216 p. (Asian Mass Communication bibliography series 2).

836 entries for periodicals, books, periodical articles and reports in English, arranged under 21 major subjects. Published materials included from 1945 to 1973, and unpublished material from 1960 to 1973. Well annotated. Index.

C 191 Institute of Development Studies. Village Studies Program. *Village studies, data analysis and bibliography*. London, Mansell, 1976–8. 2 v.

An annotated bibliography of approximately 1,000 village studies, arranged by region, then by author. The information on each village is coded. The first volume (1976) is concerned with India. The second volume (1978), reported but not seen, deals with other developing countries. Author, institution and topics indexes.

NATURAL AND APPLIED SCIENCES

C 192 Ranganathan, Shiyali Ramamrita. *Union catalogue of learned periodicals in South Asia, volume 1, physical and biological sciences*. Delhi, Indian Library Association, 1953. 390 p. (Indian Library Association, English series 7).

Locations and holdings are given for some 6,000 periodicals arranged in subject order, with an alphabetical and subject index. Burma, Indonesia, Malaya and Ceylon were asked to cooperate, but most of the library locations are for India. Pakistan is not covered. The list is dated, and in 1965 it was estimated that there were over 10,000 different periodical titles in India alone.

C 193 Guha, Roy K. K. *Bibliography of soil science and fertilizers with reference to India.* Delhi, Manager of Publications, 1954. 131 p. (Indian Council of Agricultural Research, Bulletin no. 74).
2,156 periodical articles in Western languages are arranged by subject. Author index. Contains a brief history of soil science in India.

C 194 U.N.E.S.C.O. Science Cooperation Offices for South and South East Asia. *Bibliography of scientific publications of South and South East Asia*, 1955–64. New Delhi, Indian National Science Documentation Centre, National Physical Laboratory, 1955–64. Monthly.
Continues U.N.E.S.C.O. South Asia Science Cooperation Office *Bibliography of scientific publications of South Asia (India, Burma, Ceylon)*, 1949–54 (Delhi, 1949–54), which appeared semi-annually in 12 numbers. A bibliography of unannotated English language articles selected from some 400 periodicals, published mostly in India, but with some representation from the Philippines. The items are arranged by subject, and there are annual cumulated subject and author indexes. In 1964 10,253 entries covered a broad range of the sciences, including education, geography and town planning. Partly replaced by the Indian National Scientific Documentation Centre *Indian science abstracts*, January 1965–.

C 195 *Index to Indian medical periodicals*, 1959–. New Delhi, Central Medical Library, 1959–. Semi-annual.
75–100 periodicals are surveyed. The index is divided into two parts; the first arranges the articles by subject, and the second indexes by author. Some 1,200 articles, almost entirely in English, are indexed each year. Volume 28, 1972 last issue seen.

C 196 Delhi. National Science Library. *Catalogue of serials in the National Science Library*. New Delhi, Union Catalogue Division, National Science Library, Indian National Science Documentation Centre, 1965. 407 p.
3,447 periodical titles, of which 2,250 are current, and one-quarter published in India. The periodicals are arranged alphabetically, with holdings. Classified index, index of issuing organizations, and an index by language.

C 197 Wilson, Patrick. *Science in South Asia, past and present, a preliminary bibliography* . . . New York, Foreign Area Materials Center, University of the State of New York, 1966. 100 p. (Foreign Area Materials Center occasional publication no. 3).
Over 1,100 printed books and periodical articles in Western languages arranged by subject. The materials are concerned with the history of science and technology in South Asia, and the post-World War II state of scientific research and education. Scientific works, as opposed to books about science, have been

excluded. Nearly all entries personally examined by the compiler. Author index.

C 198 National Institute of Community Development. *Agriculture and food production in India, a bibliography*. Hyderabad, 1971. 151 p.

2,378 books, reports and articles in English are arranged under 14 subjects, with some subdivision, and survey agricultural input, administrative support, crops, labour, education, prices and other problems related to food production.

LANGUAGE, LITERATURE, DRAMA AND PAINTING

C 199 *The national bibliography of Indian literature*, 1901–1953. New Delhi, Sahitya Akademi, 1962–74. 4 v.

Not restricted strictly to literature, but includes books in other subject fields when these have value as literature. Although selected, it supplements the British Museum series of catalogues of books in South Asian languages. The only English books listed are those published in India, or by Indian writers. The first volume includes works in Assamese (1,500), Bengali (5,700), English (7,200), and Gujarati (4,500). The second, works in Hindi (7,500), Kannada (3,000), Kashmiri (120), and Malayalam (3,900). The third, works in Marathi (4,500), Oriya (3,000), Punjabi (3,000), and Sanskrit (4,800). The fourth volume has Sindhi (1,000), Tamil (6,000), Telugu (5,700), and Urdu (6,000). The approximate number of titles in each language is stated in brackets after the language above. Each volume has own index. The size of subject groups in this bibliography makes searching difficult. Index suffers from inadequate editing.

C 200 Mehta, Chandravadan Chimanlal. *Bibliography of stageable plays in Indian languages, volume 1*. New Delhi. Published under the joint auspices of the M.S. University of Baroda and Bharatiya Natya Sangha, 1963. 292 p.

5,000 plays in the 14 main languages of India, published between 1901 and 1960. The entries are divided by language, and subarranged by author. For each play the number of acts or scenes, the number of characters and the theme is given.

C 201 Calcutta. National Library. *Bibliography of dictionaries and encyclopedias in Indian languages*. Calcutta, 1964. 165 p.

Lists 2,088 dictionaries and 102 encyclopedias. Arranged by language with an index to authors and titles.

C 202 Pattanayak, D. P. *Indian languages bibliography*. New Delhi, Educational Resources Centre, 1967. 84 p.

Over 1,600 selected books and periodical articles arranged under 14 major South Asian languages. The books cited are mostly grammars and dictionaries. No annotations and no index. Revised edition 1973.

C 203 Roadarmel, Gordon C. *A bibliography of English source materials for the study of modern Hindi literature*. Berkeley,

Center for South and Southeast Asian Studies, University of California, 1969. 96 p.
1,453 entries for books and periodical articles on Hindi poetry, short stories, plays, novels, and essays in translation, books and articles on Hindi literature, and reviews and commentaries on it. Author index.

C 204 Summer Institute of Linguistics (Nepal). *A bibliographical index of the lesser known languages and dialects of India and Nepal.* Kathmandu, 1970. 312 p.
2,218 books and articles are arranged by author, and are proceeded by a language index to the entries.

C 205 Mahajan, Yash Pal. *Hindi sahitya, alocana grantha suci* Hindi literature, books on Hindi literary criticism and linguistics. Dilli (i.e. Delhi), Bharatiya Granth Niketan, 1971. 336 p.
Lists some 7,500 books in a classified arrangement. Not annotated. Index.

C 206 Navalani, K. *Dictionaries in Indian languages, a bibliography.* Jaipur, Saraswati Publications, 1972. 370 p.
Approximately 3,000 language dictionaries are arranged by language, with some annotation. The most extensive listing of Indian language dictionaries now available. No index.

C 207 Central Institute of English and Foreign Languages. *A bibliography of Indian English.* Hyderabad, 1972. 2 v. in 1.
In two parts, the first concerned with Indian literature in English, lists 1,847 critical works, works of drama, fiction, poetry, arranged by type of literature, and published since 1827. Index to authors. The second minor part notes some 200 works on Indian English.

C 208 Gupta, Brijen Kishore. *India in English fiction, 1800–1970, an annotated bibliography.* Metuchen, Scarecrow Press, 1973. 296 p.
2,272 books are arranged by author, with some entries annotated. The books listed are novels, tales, and collections of short stories on India, written originally in English or translated into English. Title index and theme index.

C 209 Van Zile, Judy. *Dance in India, an annotated guide to source materials.* Providence, Asian Music Publications, Music Department, Brown University, 1973. 129 p.
839 entries for books, articles, films and phonorecords are listed in a detailed subject order, with annotation. Periodical and author indexes.

C 210 Karkala, John A. and Leena Karkala. *Bibliography of Indo-English literature, a checklist of works by Indian authors in English, 1800–1966.* Bombay, Sadanand Publishers, 1974. 167 p.
A short introduction takes note of bibliographical problems. The bibliography lists some 1,700 works, arranged by type of literature. No annotation. Author index.

C 211 Agesthialingom, S. *A bibliography of Dravidian linguistics.* Annamalainager, Annamalai University, 1973. 362 p.

(Annamalainagar University, Department of Linguistics, Publication no. 30).
4,121 books and periodical articles, arranged by author, but with no breakdown by language, no index and no annotation. Included in the entries are 211 dictionaries and 203 book reviews.

C 212 Hingorani, Ratan Pribhdas. *Painting in South Asia: a bibliography*. Delhi, Bharatiya Publishing House, 1976. 253 p.
1,500 entries for books and articles published up to 1972 and by 19 major sections with further subdivision. Author index, anonymous works index, subject index, manuscript titles index, dated paintings index, artists index, index of patrons, sites index and collections index. Includes articles found in the Kern Institute, Leiden *Annual bibliography of Indian Archaeology* (C 214).

HISTORY AND GEOGRAPHY

C 213 *Cambridge history of India*. Cambridge, Cambridge University Press, 1922–37. v. 1, 3–6.
The bibliographies for each chapter of the history are placed in a section at the end of each volume. Collectively they form one of the finest bibliographies for South Asian history, with some 3,500 entries for primary and secondary sources in South Asian and Western languages. Reprinted by S. Chand, Delhi, 1958–64. A more up-to-date bibliography may be found at the end of each volume of R. C. Majumdar *The history and culture of the Indian people* (1957–65); this helps to complete the gap in the coverage of the *Cambridge history of India*, of which volume 2 was not published.

C 214 Kern Institute, Leiden. *Annual bibliography of Indian archaeology*, 1926–. Leyden, E. Brill, 1926–.
Coverage includes both South Asia and the regions of Southeast Asia under Indian cultural influence. Entries for both historical studies and art in addition to archaeology. The 1954–7 issue contains monographs and periodical articles selected from 160 Indian and non-Indian Western-language periodicals, with annotations. Author index. 1964–6 volume published 1972.

C 215 Fernandes, Braz A. *Annual bibliography of Indian history and Indology*, 1938–42. Bombay, Bombay Historical Society, 1938–49. 5 v.
An annotated and classified list of books and articles from some 80 periodicals, with a separate index to authors and subjects, and continuing the 'Bibliography of Indian history for the years 1927–30', *Journal of the Bombay Historical Society*, nos. 1–4, 1928–32, which selected articles from some 50 periodicals.

C 216 Moraes, George Mark. *Bibliography of Indological studies, 1942–3*. Bombay, Examiner Press, 1945–52. 2 v.
The 1942 issue contains 1,974 entries for books and articles in English from 104 periodicals, published mostly in India.

Arranged by subject, with a subject and author index. Most entries are annotated.

C 217 Singhal, C. R. *Bibliography of Indian coins*. Bombay, Numismatic Society of India, 1950–2. 2 v. and first supplement 1952–60.

The first volume lists non-Muhammedan series, and the second Muhammedan series. Lists papers and periodical articles, with abstracts, and is arranged by kind of coin. Index of authors and index of rulers and dynasties.

C 218 Sharma, Jagdish Saran. *Mahatma Gandhi, a descriptive bibliography*. Delhi, S. Chand, 1955. 565 p. (National bibliographies no. 1).

3,671 annotated books and periodical articles in Western and Indian languages (but almost entirely in English) by and about Gandhi, covering the period from 1891 to 1955. Divided into three parts, the first discusses sources of the literature on Gandhi; the second lists biographies of Gandhi in a chronological order, with an alphabetical subject bibliography of books and periodical articles by and about Gandhi; and the third lists books which influenced Gandhi, books for which he wrote forewords, and periodicals he edited. A supplement covers additional writings from April 1954 to April 1955. Second edition published 1968 has 90-page supplement for material from 1955.

C 219 Sharma, Jagdish Saran. *Jawaharlal Nehru, a descriptive bibliography*. Delhi, S. Chand, 1955. 421 p. (National bibliographies no. 2).

3,710 annotated entries for books and periodical articles by and about Nehru in Western languages, covering the period from 1889 to 1955. Divided into three parts in much the same way as the author's bibliography on Gandhi. The first part lists sources, and biographies arranged chronologically; the second is a subject bibliography of books and articles by and about Nehru; and the third lists books which influenced him and for which he wrote forwards.

C 220 Wilson, Patrick. *Government and politics of India and Pakistan, 1885–1955, a bibliography of works in Western languages*. Berkeley, South Asia Studies, University of California, 1956. 365 p. (Modern India Project bibliographical study no. 2).

5,294 books, mostly published in India, arranged by broad subjects, with chronological arrangement within each subject. History, political affairs, biographies, constitutional history, and international relations are covered. Locations of books in the United States noted. Author index. Available in xerox copies from General Library, University of California, Berkeley.

C 221 Sharma, Jagdish Saran. *Indian National Congress, a descriptive bibliography of India's struggle for freedom*. Delhi, S. Chand, 1959. 816 p.

The subject covered is broader than the title indicates, being concerned with the cultural, economic, and political development of India, in addition to the major theme of the struggle for freedom. 9,135 books, articles, addresses, reports and resolutions from 1885 to 1958 are included. The materials are in Western languages, and are annotated. Arranged into three parts, the first gives sources and a subject bibliography, the second has a chronology, and the third lists material for the post-Independence period. Index.

C 222 Case, Margaret H. *South Asian history, 1750–1950, a guide to periodicals, dissertations and newspapers.* Princeton, Princeton University Press, 1968. 561 p.
5,400 articles, over half of which are annotated, and selected from 351 periodicals and 650 dissertations, are arranged under some 150 headings. The articles are arranged in the first part, and the dissertations in the second. The third part lists some 341 English-language and 251 Indian-language newspapers by place of publication and notes holdings in American, British, Canadian and Indian libraries. Author and subject indexes.

C 223 Scholberg, Henry. *The district gazetteers of British India, a bibliography.* Zug, Inter Documentation Company, 1970. 131 p. (Biblioteca Asiatica 3).
The most comprehensive listing of district gazetteers for India, including Burma. Historical account of the gazetteers is followed by a series list, arranged by province, for 1,344 gazetteers. Index by place and author.

C 224 Kaul, Hari Krishen. *Sri Aurobindo, a descriptive bibliography.* New Delhi, Munshiram Manoharlal, 1972. 222 p.
Some 2,000 books, and articles arranged in twelve major sections. Name and title index.

C 225 Scholberg, Henry and Emmanuel Divien. *Bibliographie des Français dans l'Inde.* Pondicherry, All India Press, 1973. 216 p.
1,168 books in French and English, covering the period from the 17th through the 20th century, are arranged in a detailed subject classification. Locations of the books in libraries stated. Author, subject and anonymous works title index.

C 226 Sukhwal, B. L. *South Asia, a systematic geographic bibliography.* Metuchen, Scarecrow Press, 1974. 827 p.
10,346 books and articles are arranged by country, then by a detailed subject order, and then divided into books. journals, articles and dissertations. Tibet is included in South Asia. The emphasis is on geography, but the bibliography is useful for the study of related fields. No annotations. Author index.

C 227 Moodgal, Hari Mohan K. *Indira Gandhi, a select bibliography.* New Delhi, Gitanjali Prakasha, 1976. 275 p.
3,274 books, reports and newspapers and periodical articles in a detailed subject arrangement. Useful for the Indian political scene since 1966. Index.

C 228 Kalia, D. R. and M. K. Jain. *Eminent Indians, a bibliography of*

biographies. New Delhi, Marwah Publications, 1977. 200 p.
1,544 entries are arranged in two parts. The first section contains biographies, including autobiographies and is arranged by the name of the biographee; the second section contains collective biographies, arranged by author. Index to biographees.

C 229 Satyaprakash. *Gandhiana, 1962–1976*. Gurgaon, Indian Documentation Service, 1977. 184 p. (Subject bibliography series no. 2).
2,652 articles from 100 Indian English-language journals and the *Times of India* in an alphabetical author-subject arrangement.

C 230 *Annotated bibliography on the economic history of India, 1500 A.D. to 1947 A.D.* Pune, Gokhale Institute of Politics and Economics, 1977–.
A major bibliography to be completed in four volumes, with the first two volumes indexing Indian and British official publications. Arrangement provides for an extremely detailed subject classification. Subject index and regional index for the first two volumes. Author index for volume 2.

REGIONAL BIBLIOGRAPHY

C 231 Singh, Ganda. *A bibliography of the Panjab*. Patiala, Punjabi University, 1966. 245 p.
A bibliography of some 4,000 periodicals, manuscripts, books and articles arranged by language, and then by author. No annotation. No index.

C 232 Schappert, Linda G. *Sikkim, 1800–1968, an annotated bibliography*. Honolulu, East-West Center Library, East-West Center, 1968. 69 p. (Occasional papers of the East-West Center Library no. 10).
342 books, periodical articles and reports are arranged under 16 headings and annotated. Library locations are given in the Boston area. Combined author, title and subject index. Sikkim is a protectorate of the Republic of India.

C 233 Barrier, Norman Gerald. *The Punjab in nineteenth-century tracts, an introduction to the Pamphlet Collection in the British Museum and India Office*. East Lansing, Asian Studies Center, Michigan State University, 1969. 76 p. (Research series on the Punjab 1).
An historical survey of this research source is followed by a select and annotated list of 286 tracts in Indian languages and in English, representing some 5% of the total volume of this source. Two appendices give samples of the tracts.

C 234 Barrier, Norman Gerald. *Punjab history in printed British documents, a bibliographic guide to Parliamentary papers, and select non-serial publications, 1843–1947*. Columbia, University of Missouri Press, 1969. 108 p.
Printed sources are important since much of the official and

private manuscript resources has been destroyed. An annotated review of 488 sources. Index.

C 235 Barrier, Norman Gerald. *The Sikhs and their literature, a guide to tracts, books and periodicals, 1849–1919.* Delhi, Manohar Book Service, 1970. 153 p.

Covers the period when the Sikhs were under British rule, a long introduction is followed by an author list of books and tracts in English and Panjabi, anonymous publications, institutional publications and an annotated list of 59 periodicals.

C 236 Kharbas, Datta Shankarrao. *Maharashtra and the Marathas, their history and culture, a bibliographic guide to Western-language materials.* Rochester, South Asia Center, University of Rochester, 1973. 326 p.

5,535 books, periodical articles (but excluding articles from newspapers, weekly and biweekly journals), and doctoral dissertations are arranged by author. Government publications are included on a selective basis. Two useful short sections on bibliography and reference works on India and on Maharashtra and the Marathas precede the main list. Items in the University of Rochester Library are marked. No index. Expanded edition with 5,809 entries published by G. K. Hall, Boston, 1975.

C 237 Satyaprakash. *Andhra Pradesh: a select bibliography, 1962–1975.* Gurgaon, Indian Documentation Service, 1975. 175 p. (Indian states bibliography series no. 1).

2,687 entries for periodical and newspaper articles, book reviews, editorials and signed articles published in selected 116 Indian English-language journals and the *Times of India* from 1962–75. About 200 books are included. Entries in an alphabetical author-subject arrangement. Mostly in English.

C 238 Satyaprakash. *Assam: a select bibliography, 1962–1975.* Gurgaon, Indian Documentation Service, 1976. 100 p. (Indian states bibliography series no. 2).

1,500 articles published in 76 Indian English-language journals and some 170 books mostly in English. Entries are in an alphabetical author-subject arrangement.

C 239 Satyaprakash. *Bihar, a select bibliography, 1962–1975.* Gurgaon, Indian Documentation Service, 1976. 155 p. (Indian states bibliography series, no. 3).

2,536 articles, published in 113 Indian English-language periodicals and the *Times of India*, from 1962–75 and 98 books mostly in English, in an alphabetical author-subject arrangement.

C 240 Satyaprakash. *Gujarat: a select bibliography.* Gurgaon, Indian Documentation Service, 1976. 168 p. (Indian states bibliography series no. 4.)

2,451 articles from 119 journals and the *Times of India*, published from 1962 to mid-1976, and 500 books. Entries in an alphabetical author subject arrangement.

C 241 Warikoo, Kulbushan. *Jammu, Kashmir and Ladakh, a classified*

and comprehensive bibliography. New Delhi, Sterling Publishers, 1976. 555 p.
7,686 articles, books and reports, mostly in English, arranged under 23 headings. Subject index and author index.

D. NEPAL

Nepal became a British Protectorate in 1816, and did not become completely independent until 1923.

HANDBOOKS

D 1 Hedrick, Basil C. and Anne K. Hedrick. *Historical and cultural dictionary of Nepal.* Metuchen, Scarecrow Press, 1972. 198 p. (Historical and cultural dictionaries of Asia series no. 2).
A collection of historical, religious, political, place and local gossip data on Nepal arranged in dictionary form. A select bibliography almost entirely in English of some 240 books and articles is appended.

D 2 American University, Washington, D.C. Foreign Area Studies. *Area handbook for Nepal, Bhutan and Sikkim.* Washington, U.S. Government Printing Office, 1973. 431 p.
A survey of social, political and economic affairs in Nepal, followed by an account of national security. Separate chapters for Bhutan and Sikkim. Separate indexes and bibliography for each country, with a general bibliography. Research completed November 1972. Replaces 1964 edition.

DICTIONARIES

D 3 Turner, Ralph Lilley. *A comparative and etymological dictionary of the Nepali language.* London, Routledge and Kegan Paul, 1931. 932 p.
26,000 entries in Nepali with their equivalents in English. Some examples of usage.

D 4 Pradhan, Paras Mani. *New standard dictionary, English-Nepali,* revised new edition. Kalimpong, Bhagyalaxmi Prakashan, 1970. 830 p.
32,000 English words with their equivalents in Nepali. No examples of usage. Includes an appendix on technical terminology.

BIOGRAPHICAL DICTIONARY AND DIRECTORIES

D 5 *Who is who—Nepal, 1972–74.* Kathmandu, Kathmandu School of Journalism, 1974. 391 p.

Contains some 400 biographies, and section on officials arranged by organization.

D 6 *Nepal, trade and information directory*, 1972/3–. Kathmandu, Eastern Trading and Investment Co. Annual.
Yearbook-type information in first major undertaking of its kind for Nepal. Combines background information on history with economic data and a commercial directory.

CENSUS AND STATISTICS

D 7 Nepal. Department of Statistics. *Census of population, Nepal*, 1952/4 Kathmandu, 1958. 81 p.
The eastern portion of Nepal was enumerated in 1952 and the western in 1954. This publication abstracts the more important results of the census.

D 8 Nepal. Department of Statistics. *Preliminary report of the national population census, 1961, provisional figures*. Kathmandu, 1962. 10 p.
In distinction to the 1952/4 census, the whole population was enumerated at one time. Tables show male and female population by region and district, urban and rural population by region, urban population and housing by towns, and absent population by districts.

D 9 Nepal. Central Bureau of Statistics. *Population Census 1971*. Kathmandu, 1975–
In five volumes as follows:
1. *General characteristic tables.*
2. *Social characteristics* (in two parts).
3. *Economic characteristics* (in two parts).
4. *Female fertility characteristics tables.*
5. *Selected localities tables.* Reported.

D 10 Nepal. Central Bureau of Statistics. *Statistical pocket book, Nepal, 1974*. Kathmandu, Central Bureau of Statistics, National Planning Commission, 1974. 134 p.
114 tables arranged under 18 major subjects, with statistical information generally for the late 1960s, and in some cases up to 1972.

BIBLIOGRAPHY

D 11 U.S. Library of Congress. American Libraries Book Procurement Center, New Delhi. *Accessions list, Nepal*, 1966–. Delhi, 1966–. Quarterly.
Some 450 books and periodicals are recorded for 1967. There is an author index in the last issue for each year. This list will now become the principal bibliographical source for Nepal. 1977 issue seen.

D 12 *Bibliographie du Nepal.* Paris, Centre National de la Recherche Scientifique, 1969–
The following volumes have appeared:
1. *Sciences humaines, references en langues europeennes.* 1969. 4,515 entries. *Supplement 1967–1973* (1973) lists 3,991 entries.
3. *Sciences naturelles.* Tome 1, 'Cartes du Nepal' (1973), 371 entries. Tome 2, 'Botanique' (1972), 1,006 entries.
Volume 1 and supplement are arranged by subject, with author index, and both books and articles are covered. No annotation. The first volume provides a basis for the *Bibliography of Nepal* (D 17).

D 13 Bernier, Ronald M. *A bibliography of Nepalese art.* Kathmandu, Voice of Nepal (distributed by Educational Enterprises), 1970. 46 p.
Some 600 books and periodical articles are arranged in alphabetical order by author. Special attention is paid to architecture.

D 14 Centre for Economic Development and Administration. *Nepal documentation.* Kathmandu, Centre for Economic Development and Administration, Tribhuvan University Campus, 1972–3. 4 v. (CEDA occasional bibliography nos. 1–4).
Each volume in two sections, the first in English and the second in Nepali, and includes books, periodicals and reports. The first volume contains 607 entries.

D 15 Gyawali, Bharat M. and Garland L. Stanford. *Information resources on Nepal.* Kathmandu, Documentation Centre, Centre for Economic Development and Administration, 1973. 84 p.
In two principal parts, the first being a selected list of some 240 titles, mostly books on Nepal, and the second listing and discussing library resources in Nepal and the U.S. and U.K. There are lists of foreign agencies in Nepal and Nepalese official bodies.

D 16 Birman, D. A. and M. N. Kafitina. *Bibliografiia Nepala, 1917–1967.* Moskva, Nauka, 1973, 22 p.
254 entries for books, articles, and dissertations, arranged by major subject fields. Author and title index. Some annotations.

D 17 *Bibliography of Nepal* (Nepalako granthasuci), compiled and edited by Khadga Man Malla. Kathmandu, Royal Nepal Academy, 1975. 529 p.
8,327 entries for books and articles in European languages published to 1972. Materials are classified under 15 major subjects. Includes brief annotations in Nepali. Index of anonymous works. Author index. Supersedes a number of other bibliographies on Nepal. The most comprehensive bibliography on Nepal, containing much material such as official and minor publications not available outside the country. However the amassing of this number of entries under a relatively small number of subjects make the bibliography rather difficult to handle.

E. PAKISTAN

Pakistan was formed in 1947 from the predominantly Muslim areas of East Bengal and the western part of the Indian subcontinent. These two widely separated areas are known as East Pakistan and West Pakistan. In the one Bengali is the leading language, and in the other Urdu. East Pakistan became Bangladesh, an independent country in 1971.

REFERENCE WORKS

E 1 Siddiqui, Akhtar H. *A guide to reference books published in Pakistan*. Karachi, Pakistan Reference Publications, 1966. 41 p.
473 English-language reference works published from August 1947 to December 1965 are arranged in an alphabetical subject order. The list has been made as comprehensive as possible. Author index.

HANDBOOK

E 2 American University, Washington, D.C. Foreign Area Studies. *Area Handbook for Pakistan*. Washington, U.S. Government Printing Office, 1975. 455 p.
A country summary is followed by accounts of social, political and economic affairs, and national security. Bibliography. Research completed September 1974. Revision of 1971 edition.

YEARBOOKS

E 3 *Pakistan*, 1947/8–. Karachi, Pakistan Publications, 1948–.
Each issue is divided into two parts. The first deals with Pakistan as a whole, and is divided into broad subject headings, further subdivided into minor topics. The second has the same arrangement, but is concerned with the provinces, states and frontier regions of Pakistan. The table of contents serves as an index. 1963/4 last issue noted. Title from 1947/53 *1st to 6th year*.

E 4 *West Pakistan year book*, 1957–. Lahore, Directorate of Publications, Research and Films, Information Department, West Pakistan, 1957–.
An official review of political, economic and social activity in West Pakistan, with statistics. No index and no biographical or directory-type information. Issues for 1957 through 1968 noted.

E 5 *Pakistan yearbook*, 1969–. Karachi, National Publishing House, 1968–.

A continuation of *Twenty years of Pakistan, 1947–1967* (1968) emphasizing current development, but also a useful general survey of Pakistan, with background and contemporary problems, arranged under 39 subject headings. Statistical tables and bibliography included. Indexed. 1978 issue seen. Published by East and West Publishing Company, Karachi from 1973.

DIRECTORIES

E 6 *Ansari's trade and industrial directory of Pakistan*, 1950/1–. Karachi, Ansari Publishing House, 1950–.
The first part consists of short and valuable summaries of ten important aspects of Pakistan's economic development, together with a classification of industry, a classification of importers and exporters, and a classification of merchants and agents, separated into East and West Pakistan. The second part is an alphabetical list of merchants and manufacturers, again with a separate listing for East and West Pakistan. Information taken from the most recent government publications. Title varies: *Ansari's trade directory of Pakistan and who's who*. 1950/1, and *Ansari's industrial directory of Pakistan*, 1957–.

E 7 U.N.E.S.C.O. South Asia Science Cooperation Office. *Scientific institutions and scientists in Pakistan.* New Delhi, 1958. 501 p.
Divided into three parts: scientific organizations arranged by subject; scientific associations, societies and technical periodicals of which 46 are listed; and a list of some 2,000 scientists arranged by the Universal Decimal Classification, with their date of birth, position, research interest and publications. Only the natural and applied sciences are included.

E 8 Pakistan Bibliographical Working Group. *A guide to Pakistan libraries, learned and scientific societies and education institutions, biographies of librarians*, revised edition. Karachi 1960. 166 p.
The first section lists libraries, giving addresses, size of collections, and their nature, annual additions and other information; the second lists educational institutions, noting their departments; the third lists eight museums and art galleries; the fourth lists learned societies and institutions arranged geographically; and the final section contains 65 biographies of librarians in Pakistan. Indexed. Revision of the 1956 edition.

E 9 Mian, Tasnin Q. *Principal research institutions in Pakistan.* Lahore, Social Science Research Centre, University of the Panjab, 1964. 2 v.
52 institutions, excluding universities, arranged in broad subject groups, stating the history, objectives, research staff, library for each. Analysis of the data.

E 10 *Barque's Pakistan trade directory and who's who*, 1963/4–. Lahore, Barque and Company, 1965–?
Noted as the first edition, and in continuation of the first edition of *Barque's All-India trade directory and who's who*, and also containing the biographical material in A.M. Barque *Who's who in Pakistan*, 1962/3 (1963), there are four sections: industries, classified; firms arranged under an alphabetical listing of places; a classified trades, professions and commerce section; a listing of importers and exporters by commodity; and the who's who section. 1975/6 volume seen.

E 11 *Libraries of Pakistan, a comprehensive list*. Karachi, Library Promotion Bureau, 1970. 54 p.
Lists some 1,500 libraries, arranged alphabetically by city.

BIOGRAPHICAL DICTIONARIES

E 12 Khan, Tahawar Ali. *Biographical encyclopedia of Pakistan*, 1955/6–. Lahore, Biographical Research Institute, Pakistan, 1956–.
The fourth edition (1971–2) contains some 2,500 biographies, arranged under 21 major professional headings, with portraits for most entries.

E 13 *Azam's who's who of Pakistan, 1962–63*. Lahore, Azam Publications, 196–. 176 p.
Some 300 living persons are arranged alphabetically by surname. More informal than the *Biographical encyclopedia of Pakistan* (E 12) and useful as a supplement to that work.

E 14 Pakistan. Establishment Division. *Civil list of Class I officers serving under Government of Pakistan*, January 1961–. Karachi, Manager of Publications, 1961–.
List officers arranged by department, giving their date of birth, present appointment and emoluments. No index to names. 1964 issue published in 1965 last noted. A *Pakistan civil list*, no. 1– (Lahore, Civil and Military Gazette, 1950–) also listed higher civil servants. Civil lists and similar directories exist for the governments of East and West Pakistan.

E 15 Pakistan Association of Scientists and Scientific Professions. *Scientists and technologists of Pakistan, a directory*. Karachi, 1966. 367 p.
Lists over 3,000 persons, and is based on returned questionnaires to which there was a 40% response. Arranged by subject fields, with a name index.

GAZETTEER

E 16 U.S. Office of Geography. *Pakistan* . . . Washington, U.S.

Government Printing Office, 1962. 883 p.
Contains 63,300 entries for places and feature names in Pakistan, together with their classification and longitude and latitude.

CENSUS AND STATISTICS

E 17 Pakistan. Commercial Intelligence and Statistics Department. *Statistical digest of Pakistan*, 1950–. Karachi, 1950–.
A cyclostyled issue of the digest was reported for 1947, but the 1950 issue is noted as the first. Population, production, economy, finance, trade, communications, education, prices and foreign trade are surveyed. The 1950 issue has information for 1947 and 1948.

E 18 Pakistan. Central Statistical Office. *Pakistan statistical yearbook*, 1952–. Karachi, Manager of Publications, 1954–.
Issues have not appeared annually, since the 1963 issue is noted as the sixth, and was published in 1964. Divided into 15 major sections, such as area and population, climate, labour, etc. Each section has introductory information, followed by charts and statistical tables. 1965/6 issue with title *Pakistan statistical annual*. 1975 issue seen.

E 19 Pakistan. Office of the Census Commissioner. *Census of Pakistan*, 1951. Karachi, Manager of Publications, Government of Pakistan, 1954–6. 9 v.
The first volume covers the whole of Pakistan, volumes 2–6 regional reports and tables, volume 7 economic conditions of West Pakistan, and volume 8 economic conditions for East Pakistan. Volume 9 is an administrative report issued for official and research scholar use only. Information for the period prior to 1947 will be contained in the census and statistical series noted under India.

E 20 Pakistan. Office of the Census Commissioner. *Census of Pakistan*, 1961. Karachi, Manager of Publications, Government of Pakistan, 1962–4. 10 v. (in 13).
A census of all persons resident in Pakistan for the areas in which they are normally resident. Age, sex, religion, nationality, place of birth, mother tongue, literacy, education, land holding, economic activity, and fertility of women were surveyed. For the first time an attempt was made to survey the number of educated persons in each of the technical and professional fields. The 1961 series includes the Housing Census taken in 1960. Volume 6 is in two parts. Volume 7, in three parts, is for official use only. In addition to the 13 parts of the census, there are 46 district census reports, and six census bulletins. *District Census reports*, v. 1–20 seen of *Population Census of 1972*.

E 21 *Pakistan.* Central Statistical Office. *Twenty-five years of*

Pakistan in statistics, 1947–1972. Karachi, Printing Corporation of Pakistan Press, 1972. 551 p.
Updates 20 years of Pakistan in statistics, and includes information on Bangladesh, the former East Pakistan. A valuable review covering population, labour, agriculture, industry, transport, finance and trade, and social and cultural affairs.

BIBLIOGRAPHY

For pre-1947 materials on the regions now in Pakistan, bibliographies in the section for India should be consulted. For the period after 1971 refer to Bangladesh for the former East Pakistan.

E 22 Usmani, M. Adil. *Status of bibliography in Pakistan.* Karachi, Library Promotion Bureau, 1968. 106 p. (Library Promotion Bureau publication no. 4).
421 bibliographies relating in whole or in part to Pakistan, with subject and form divisions. Author and title index. Preceded by a major essay on bibliography in Pakistan.

E 23 Ghani, A. R. *Pakistan, a select bibliography.* Lahore, Pakistan Association for the Advancement of Science, 1951. 339 p.
9,000 books and periodical articles in English on the history, description, natural resources and economy of Pakistan, arranged in a detailed subject order, but with no index. Among the subjects omitted are art, architecture, language, education literature and folklore. Compiled to a considerable extent from other bibliographies.

E 24 U.S. Library of Congress. American Libraries Book Procurement Center, Karachi. *Accessions list, Pakistan,* 1962–. Karachi, 1962–.
Records Public Law 480 selections and deliveries to libraries in the United States, but is the only current and substantial bibliographical listing for Pakistan. Commercial, official and serial publications are included, in both English and the languages of Pakistan. Books are arranged by language and there is a monthly and annual cumulated author index. 1978 issue seen.

E 25 Pakistan Bibliographical Working Group. *The Pakistan national bibliography, 1947–1961.* Karachi, 1973–.
Entries are arranged by subject classes similar to the *Indian national bibliography* (C 75). To be completed in seven fascicules. First two fascicules noted.

E 26 Pakistan. National Bibliographical Unit. *The Pakistan national bibliography, annual volume,* 1962–. Karachi, Manager, Government of Pakistan Press, 1966–.
Divided into two parts, the first containing publications not issued by the government, and the second official materials, each part is arranged according to the Dewey Decimal Classification.

Index lists authors, titles, and subjects in one sequence. 1962, 1963–4, 1968, 1969, 1972 volumes seen.

E 27 National Book Centre of Pakistan. *Books from Pakistan published during the decade of reforms, 1958–1968*. Karachi, 1968. 159 p.
Succeeds and supersedes *English-language publications from Pakistan, a guide list*, and contains over 2,000 entries for books in English, arranged by subject. List of publishers appended. No index. Continued by *Books from Pakistan*, 1969–; 1974 issue last seen.

E 28 Birman, D. A. and M. N. Kafitina. *Bibliografiia Pakistana, 1947–1967*. Moskva, Nauka, 1973, 53 p.
804 entries for books, articles and dissertations, arranged by subject fields. Author and title index.

E 29 Satyaprakash. *Pakistan: a bibliography, 1962–1974*. Gurgaon, Indian Documentation Service, 1975. 338 p.
Some 6,500 articles from 109 Indian journals and the *Times of India* and published from 1962–74. Entries are arranged in an alphabetical author-subject arrangement.

Official Publications

E 30 Moreland, George B. and Akhtar H. Siddiqui. *Publications of the Government of Pakistan, 1947–1957*. Karachi, University of Karachi, 1958. 187 p.
1,578 entries in English concerned with Pakistan, including Government of India Acts which apply to Pakistan. The bibliography is arranged under issuing ministry, and is inclusive of the *Catalogue of the Government of Pakistan publications*, 1956 edition. There is a subject index.

E 31 Pakistan. Manager of Publications. *Catalogue of the Government of Pakistan publications*. Karachi, 1962. 168 p. 1966 issue last noted.
Lists 1,000 entries in English, arranged by issuing ministry. Includes Acts, including Government of India Acts issued prior to 1947. Materials listed are for sale.

E 32 Pakistan. Administrative Staff College, Lahore. *Alphabetico-classed catalogue of government reports, pamphlets, and miscellaneous publications, corrected up to 30th June, 1963*. Lahore, 1963. 122 p.
Approximately 1,200 entries in English, arranged under some 100 general subject sections. There is no alphabetical approach to issuing bodies and titles are abbreviated. A key to the National Administration Library in Lahore, and should be used together with other bibliographies for Pakistan official publications.

E 33 Datta, Rajeshwari. *Union catalogue of the Government of*

Pakistan publications held by libraries in London, Oxford and Cambridge. London, Mansell, 1967. 116 cols.
Some 1,050 entries for books and periodicals were arranged in author order, with locations in 11 major libraries.

E 34 Downey, J. A. *Pakistan Central Government and quasi-governmental organizations, a preliminary directory and list of IDS library holdings*, 1947–71. Brighton, Institute of Development Studies at the University of Sussex Library, 1973? 1 v. (Institute of Development Studies Library, Occasional guides no. 5).
Government and quasi-government organizations are listed in alphabetical order, and for each its history, functions and publications are noted. An index to organizations.

E 35 Siddiqui, Akhtar H. *A guide to Pakistan government publications, 1958–1970*. Karachi, National Book Centre of Pakistan, 1973. 276 p.
3,331 publications, arranged by ministry and subordinate bureaus. No annotations. A continuation of George B. Moreland *Publications of the Government of Pakistan, 1947–1957* (E 30). Items 3265–331 list periodicals arranged by ministries and bureaus. Important since the *Catalogue of the Government of Pakistan publications* was last issued in 1966 (E 31). Subject index with small author and periodical indexes.

Periodicals and Newspapers

E 36 Moid, A. and Akhtar H. Siddiqui. *A guide to periodical publications and newspapers of Pakistan*. Karachi, Pakistan Bibliographical Working Group, Karachi University, [preface, 1953]. 60 p. (Publication no. 2).
300 periodicals, with language of publication stated, are arranged under 50 subjects. Also listed are 50 daily newspapers of which 35 are in Urdu; 10 biweekly and 144 weekly newspapers.

E 37 *Pakistan press index, a monthly index to newspapers of Pakistan*. Karachi. Documentation and Information Bureau, 1966–.
A continuation of *Dawn index, June 1965–February 1966* and providing a detailed subject index for *Dawn* and *Pakistan Times*. Last issue noted: v. 4, no. 4/5, April/May 1969.

E 38 National Book Centre of Pakistan. *English-language periodicals from Pakistan, a guidelist*. Karachi, 1967. 55p.
Some 400 periodicals are arranged under 64 subject headings. Annuals are included. No annotations. Title index.

E 39 Cheema, Pervaiz Iqbal. *A select bibliography of periodical literature on India and Pakistan, volume 1, Pakistan*. Islamabad, National Commission on Historical and Cultural Research, 1976. 187 p.
Some 2,200 articles selected from 575 periodicals, mostly from the United States and the United Kingdom, and published from 1947

to 1970, have been arranged in a detailed subject classification. No index.

Theses and Dissertations

E 40 University of the Punjab, Lahore. *Bibliography of theses, dissertations and research reports, University of the Punjab.* Lahore, West Pakistan Bureau of Education, 1961. 212 p.
2,086 theses arranged by subject for the period 1947 to 1959.

Subject Bibliography

SOCIAL SCIENCES

E 41 Keddie, Nikki R. and Elizabeth K. Bauer. *Annotated bibliography for Pakistan sociology, economics and politics.* Berkeley, University of California, Human Relations Area Files South Asia Project, 1956. 64 p.
Over 400 books, periodicals, and periodical articles arranged in subject order, with annotations. No index.

E 42 Eberhard, Wolfram. *Studies on Pakistan's social and economic conditions, a bibliographical note.* Berkeley, University of California, Institute of International Studies, Center for South Asia Studies, 1958. 47 p.
Some 450 studies or urban and rural social conditions in Pakistan, mostly unpublished masters' and doctoral dissertations available at the University of the Punjab at Lahore and at the Agricultural College at Lyallpur. Arranged by author, with subject references in the same alphabetical sequence.

E 43 Elahi, Fazal and Akhtar H. Siddiqui. *Union catalogue of periodicals in social sciences held by the libraries in Pakistan.* Karachi, Pakistan Bibliographical Working Group, 1961. 92 p. (Publication no. 5).
Lists over 1,000 periodicals of which one-quarter are U.S., and one-fifth each are Pakistani, Indian and British. Locations and holdings are stated for 55 libraries.

E 44 Siddiqui, Akhtar H. *The economy of Pakistan, a select bibliography, 1947–1962.* Karachi, Institute of Development Economics, 1963. 162 p.
4,248 books, reports and articles selected from some 190 periodicals are arranged in a detailed subject order with separate author and subject indexes. Materials are in English. The most comprehensive bibliography on the economy of Pakistan. The same author's *The economy of Pakistan, a select bibliography, 1963–1965* (E 47) provides a supplement.

E 45 Bhatti, Allah Ditta. *A bibliography of Pakistan demography.* Karachi, Pakistan Institute of Development Economics, 1965. 59 p.
301 books, reports, periodical articles and papers in progress, with a subject index. No annotation. No author index.

E 46 Braibanti, Ralph. *Research on the bureaucracy of Pakistan, a critique of sources, conditions and issues, with appended documents*. Durham, N. C., Duke University Press, 1966. 569 p. (Duke University Commonwealth Studies Center publication no. 26).
A study of the general conditions under which research may be conducted, together with a major number of references to reports with valuable critical comments.

E 47 Siddiqui, Akhtar H. *The economy of Pakistan, a select bibliography, 1963–1965*. Karachi, Pakistan Institute of Development Economics, 1967. 42 p.
Over 1,100 books, official publications, and periodical articles arranged by subject. No annotations. Author index.

E 48 West Pakistan. Bureau of Education. *Bibliography on education in Pakistan*. Lahore, 1970. 112 p.
Contains some 1,400 books, articles, reports and theses in English arranged under some 200 headings. A list of periodicals surveyed is appended.

E 49 Fuyyaz, Muhammad and Qaiyum Lodhi. *Thesis index, 1957–1967*, a tenth anniversary publication of the Department of Sociology, Lahore, University of the Punjab. Lahore, 1968. 61 p.
Some 300 masters' theses arranged by year, with a subject index.

E 50 Jones, Garth N. and Shaukat Ali. *Pakistan government and administration, a comprehensive bibliography*. Lahore, Pakistan Public Administration Research Centre, 1970–2. 3 v.
A major bibliography covering some 7,800 books, reports and articles published between 1947 and 1968. Each of the three volumes has a similar subject arrangement, and its own author index. Volume 2 was published by the Pakistan Academy for Rural Development, Peshawar, and volume 3 by the Department of Political Science, Colorado State University.

E 51 Bhatti, K. M. *Bibliography on rural development in Pakistan*. Peshawar, Pakistan Academy for Rural Development, 1973. 127 p.
871 books, articles and reports in English arranged by five major subject divisions. No annotations. Index.

E 52 Khurshid, Zahiruddin. *Ten years' work in librarianship in Pakistan, 1963–1972*. Karachi, Department of Library Science, University of Karachi, 1974. 214 p.
Supplements Anis Khurshid and Syed Irshad Ali *Fifteen years' work in librarianship in Pakistan, 1947–1962*, and is organized in an author-subject arrangement. Most of the entries are in English, but some are in Bengali, Urdu and Sindhi.

E 53 *Pakistan and Bangladesh: bibliographic essays in social science*. edited by W. Eric Gustafson. Islamabad, University of Islamabad Press, 1976. viii, 364 p.
A collection of bibliographical essays with some 2,000 entries on Muslim separatism; political science 1947–72; social

anthropology; sociology; economics; foreign policy; and bibliographies.

LITERATURE

E 54 Waheed, K. A. *A bibliography of Iqbal.* Karachi, Iqbal Academy, 1965. 224 p.
A comprehensive bibliography of books and articles by or related to Iqbal in Urdu and English.

HISTORY AND GEOGRAPHY

E 55 Rahman, Mustaqur. *Bibliography of Pakistan geography, 1947–1967.* Karachi, University of Karachi, 1968. 89 p.
Approximately 900 books and periodical articles, mostly in English, are arranged under 25 subject headings. No annotation and no index. Revised edition covering 1947–73 (1974. 117 p.) reported.

E 56 Aziz, Khursheed Kamal. *The historical background of Pakistan, 1857–1947, an annotated digest of source material.* Karachi, Pakistan Institute of International Affairs, 1970. 626 p.
Contains 9,244 entries, including 2,872 books arranged by broad subjects, then alphabetically by author. 5,304 periodical articles are arranged by year of publication, then alphabetically by author. Another 1,066 entries are in a supplement. Entries are mostly in English, although some are in French. There are none in Urdu. All have been seen by the author personally. Annotated. Separate author and subject index. A list of periodicals consulted is appended.

E 57 Muhammad Anwar. *Qaid E Azam Jinnah, a selected bibliography.* Karachi, National Publishing House, 1970. 110 p.
Contains a chronology of Jinnah's life, a general bibliography of 1,625 books and articles in an author/subject arrangement, and index of authors.

F. SRI LANKA

Sri Lanka (Ceylon) was occupied by British troops in 1796, and did not gain its independence until 1948.

ENCYCLOPEDIA AND HANDBOOK

F 1 American University, Washington, D.C. Foreign Area Studies. *Area handbook for Ceylon*. Washington, U.S. Government Printing Office, 1971. 525 p.
A country summary is followed by surveys of social, political and economic affairs and national security, 28-page bibliography and glossary. Research completed August 1970.

F 2 *Simhala visvakosaya* Sinhalese encyclopedia. Kolamba, Samskrtika Departmentuva, Rajaye Mudranalaya, 1963–
A general encyclopedia, with approximately one-fifth of its contents concerned with Ceylon. Articles are not signed and do not have bibliographies, but there is a list of the authorities responsible for the compilation of the encyclopedia. Volume 2, published in 1965, noted.

YEARBOOK

F 3 Ceylon. Department of Census and Statistics. *Ceylon yearbook*, 1948–. Colombo, 1948–
Official yearbook of the social, economic and general conditions of Ceylon. It does not claim to be exhaustive, but attempts to give the salient information. Ceylon's history, geography, constitution, government and programs of the government in economic and social fields are covered. The issue for 1948 surveys the period from 1939 to 1946. 1971 isue noted.

DICTIONARIES

F 4 Carter, Charles. *A Sinhalese-English dictionary*. Colombo, M. D. Gunasena, 1965. 806 p.
A reprint of the 1924 edition, containing some 56,000 Sinhala words in Sinhala script, with their equivalents in English.

F 5 Carter, Charles. *An English-Sinhalese dictionary*, revised edition. Colombo, M.D. Gunasena, 1965. 535 p.
A reprint of the 1936 revision of the 1891 edition. The 1936 edition added a considerable number of new scientific terms and

removed many antiquated expressions, replacing them with modern forms. Some 30,000 English words are given in their Sinhala equivalents in Sinhala script.

DIRECTORIES

F 6 *Ferguson's Ceylon directory*, 1858–. Colombo, Ceylon Observer Press, 1858–. Annual.
Covers recent legislation, statistics, government developments, lists trades in a classified arrangement and discusses the institutions, agriculture, trade, finance and history of Ceylon. Contains maps and a detailed alphabetical index. 1975/6 last issue seen.

F 7 Ceylon. *Ceylon civil list*. Colombo, Government Press.
A listing of senior civil servants, arranged by departments, with an index to names. Each entry has date of birth, degrees, salary, and appointments held. This series commenced in the 19th century. Last issue 1959. Continued by *Lanka Sivil Layistuva*, 1960–. Last noted issue published 1965 for 1963.

ATLAS

F 8 Kalyanavamsa, Kudavalle Dhirananda. *Lankave aitihasika bhumi situvam* (Historical atlas of Ceylon). Kolomba, M.D. Gunasena, 1967.
84 maps of India and Ceylon with descriptive matter. Directory of place names. In Sinhalese.

GAZETTEER

F 9 U.S. Office of Geography. *Ceylon*. Washington, U.S. Government Printing Office, 1960. 359 p. (Gazetteers no. 49)
29,600 entries for place and feature names in Ceylon, including variant forms cross-indexed to the standard names approved by the U.S. Board on Geographic Names. Each name has its longitude and latitude and indication of its associated administrative unit stated.

CENSUS AND STATISTICS

F 10 Ceylon. Department of Census and Statistics. *Census of Ceylon*, 1946. Colombo, Government Press, 1950–2. 4 v. (in 7)
There have been decennial censuses of Ceylon from 1871 to 1931. There was no census in 1941. The 1946 census has its first volume in two parts. The first is a general report and the second a

statistical digest. The second volume classifies the population; the third the female population; and the fourth by race, religion and literacy.

F 11 Ceylon. Department of Census and Statistics. *Statistical abstract of Ceylon*, 1949–. Colombo, Government Publications Bureau, 1949–

Statistics collected from government and business sources survey climate, population, social conditions, education, economy, trade and communication, finance and prices. Nearly all the tables cover a number of years. The Department's *Quarterly bulletin of statistics* ceased publication from the first quarter of 1961. 1969 last issue seen.

F 12 Ceylon. Department of Census and Statistics. *Census of Ceylon*, 1953. Colombo, Ceylon Government Press, 1957–62. 4 v. (in 10)

The first volume discusses the census procedures and has a number of tables concerned with population, race and religion. Volume 2 is in three parts, and surveys population and growth. Volume 3 is concerned with race, religion and literacy in two parts. Volume 4 is also in two parts, with one part in three sections, and surveys gainfully employed population and income.

BIBLIOGRAPHY

F 13 Wikremasinghe, Martino de Zilva. *Catalogue of the Sinhalese printed books in the Library of the British Museum*. London, British Museum, 1908. 308 cols.

An author catalogue of some 2,400 books acquired by purchase or under the Colonial Copyright Acts, and including examples of early Sinhalese printing from the 18th century. Titles are transliterated and translated. There is a title index.

F 14 Gard, Richard A. *A bibliography for the study of Buddhism in Ceylon in Western languages*. Berkeley, 195–. 49 p.

Some 300 books and articles arranged by subject, with some annotation or contents notes.

F 15 Ceylon. Office of the Registrar of Books and newspapers. *Catalogue of books. . .* ,1960–4? Colombo, Government Press, 1960–4? Quarterly.

Continues part 5 of the *Ceylon Government gazette* which was first issued in 1885. This list suspended publication during World War II and resumed publication in 1951. Retrospective lists covered the period from 1942 to 1951. Each quarterly issue contained some 1,000 entries, arranged in a classified order, and included government publications. The last issue noted was for January–March 1964.

F 16 *Ceylon national bibliography*, v. 1–, 1963–. Nugegoda, National Bibliography Branch, Department of the Government Archivist, 1964–.

Based on books deposited with the Registrar of Books and Newspapers, and excluding newspapers and periodicals, except for first issues, maps, ephemeral materials, etc. All parts have a classified section arranged by the Dewey system, but modified for Ceylon. Alphabetical index by authors and titles. Number 2 of a preliminary *Ceylon national bibliography*, published in 1962, noted. April 1972 issue received in 1977. Renamed *Sri Lanka national bibliography*. 1976 issues seen.

F 17 U.S. Library of Congress. American Libraries Book Procurement Center, New Delhi. *Accessions list, Sri Lanka*, 1967–. New Delhi, 1967–. Quarterly.

1967 issues include some 500 books and periodicals in English and Sinhala. December 1978 last issue seen.

F 18 National Museum Library, Colombo. *Ceylon periodical index*. Colombo, 1969–

v. 1, 1969 and v. 4, 1972 only seen of this index.

F 19 Goonetileke, H. A. I. *A bibliography on Ceylon*. Zug, Inter Documentation Company, 1970–. 3 v.

Volumes 1 and 2 list 9,948 books, articles, official publications, and unpublished theses are arranged by subject, with coverage through 1967. Some entries are annotated. Author index. Volume index. Volume 3 contains additional materials to June 1973.

F 20 Macdonald, Teresa. *Union catalogue of the Government of Ceylon publications held by libraries in London, Oxford and Cambridge*. London, Mansell, 1970. 75 cols.

Some 1,400 entries, with library locations for Government of Ceylon publications, on modern studies, emphasizing social sciences.

F 21 *Ceylon press directory, 1971*. Colombo, Central Press Agency, 1971. 38 p.

Lists 63 newspapers and 86 periodicals including annuals, with directory-type information, including personnel and information on subject coverage. Serials in English, Tamili and Sinhalese are included.

F 22 Birman, D. A. and M. N. Kafitina. *Bibliografiia Tseilona, 1917–67*. Moskva, Nauka, 1973. 37 p.

521 entries for books, articles and dissertions, arranged by subject fields. Author and title index.

G. SOUTHEAST ASIA

This region, which until recently has often been placed within the Far East, includes the Asian mainland countries of Burma, Thailand, Democratic Kampuchea, Laos and Vietnam, the island nations of Indonesia and the Philippines, and the peninsular and island kingdom of Malaysia, from which Singapore is now independent.

REFERENCE WORKS

G 1 Johnson, Donald Clay. *A guide to reference materials on Southeast Asia*. New Haven, Yale University Press, 1970. 176 p. (Yale Southeast Asia studies 6).
Lists over 2,200 reference works written in the Roman alphabet and located in the Yale and Cornell University libraries. Arrangement is by form and subject and not by country. Index.

DIRECTORIES

G 2 Tilman, Robert O. *International biographical directory of Southeast Asian specialists, 1969*. Ann Arbor, Interuniversity Southeast Asia Committee, Association for Asian Studies, 1969. 337 p.
Based on 1,150 completed questionnaires, but including none from the Soviet Union and the People's Republic of China. Actually only 950 specialists listed, since some of the replies were from specialists in other areas. Gives personal history, career history, education, country and discipline of specialization, languages, publications, research and address. Indexes by nationality and language.

G 3 *Directory of selected scholars and researchers in Southeast Asia*. Singapore, Regional Institute of Higher Education and Development, 1974. 1,214 p.
5,045 persons listed, with over 1,000 each from Indonesia, Thailand and the Philippines. No representation for Burma. The initial selection was based on academic qualifications, established recognition, and if relevant, university ranking. Only 50% of those selected replied to the questionnaire. Each entry gives information on personal history, education, career, publications, current research and language skills. Indexes for age, nationality, qualifications, discipline, rank and sex.

ATLASES

G 4 *Atlas of South East Asia*. New York, St. Martin's Press, 1964. 92 p.
130 coloured maps, including eight coloured historical maps as endpapers. Each country has been given separate treatment with a group of maps, ranging in number from 10 to 16. Indochina is treated as a unit. A typical section contains maps for physical features, climate, vegetation, and land use, agricultural products, population, including ethnic and linguistic groups, communications and minerals as well as large scale maps of the major cities. 24 pages of historical introduction by Professor D. G. E. Hall. Index to place-names.

G 5 United Nations. *Atlas of physical, economic and social resources of the Lower Mekong Basin,* prepared under the direction of the United States Agency for International Development . . . the Engineers Agency for Resources Inventories and the Tennessee Valley Authority for the Committee for Coordination of Investigation of the Lower Mekong Basin, United Nations Economic Commission for Asia and the Far East. Washington, 1968. 256 p.
Maps, descriptions and statistical data are arranged under 38 subject headings. The information in the maps includes the Republic of Vietnam, Cambodia, Laos, and Thailand, less its southernmost provinces, and covers development, transportation, communication, power, tourism, industry, urban areas, health, education, ethnic groups, population, land use, agriculture, minerals, geology and climate. An outstanding atlas and a major contribution to the reference literature of Asia.

BIBLIOGRAPHY

G 6 Monash University. Library. *Gravel and golddust, the Southeast Asia pamphlet collection at Monash University Library*. Clayton, 1975, i.e. 1976. 112, 112 p.
Some 2,500 pamphlets are arranged in two parts, the first listing by author or title, and the second by subject. A valuable listing of ephemeral material.

G 7 Cornell University Libraries. *Southeast Asia catalog*. Boston, G. K. Hall, 1976. 7 v.
Volumes 1–3 list Western monographs by country, and volumes 4–6 monographs in Southeast Asian languages by country. Volume 6 has a Chinese- and Japanese-language section; in addition it lists Asian serials, and serials for Burma and Cambodia. Volume 7 lists serials for Indonesia to Vietnam, and newspapers and maps. A major bibliography surveying the largest

collection of publications on Southeast Asia in the world. Can be kept up to date by Cornell University Libraries *Southeast Asia Accession List.*

Western Languages

G 8 Cordier, Henri. *Bibliotheca indosinica, dictionnaire bibliographique des ouvrages relatifs a la peninsule indochinoise.* Paris, Imprimerie Nationale, E. Leroux, 1912–32. 5 v. (Publications de l'Ecole Francaise d'Extreme-Orient, 17–20, 15 bis).
The great bibliographical work for mainland Southeast Asia, covering books and periodical articles in Western languages, with an emphasis on French materials published to 1913. There are approximately 60,000 entries, which include 17,600 books and in addition articles from 160 periodicals. The first volume covers Laos, Siam, Assam and Burma; the second, Malaya; the third and fourth, French Indochina and Cambodia. There is a detailed table of contents. Four volumes were published from 1912 to 1915, and the author and subject index was published in 1932. Primary arrangement by country, then by subject divisions, including languages, customs, history, geography, government, religion, literature, etc. Some annotations. Continued for Indochina by Paul Boudet and Remy Bourgeois *Bibliographie de l'Indochine francaise* (O 29). Reprinted by Burt Franklin, New York, 1968.

G 9 Embree, John Fee and Lillian Ota Dotson. *Bibliography of the peoples and cultures of mainland Southeast Asia.* New Haven, Yale University Press, 1950. 821 p.
12,000 books and periodical articles published to 1949, with an emphasis on modern materials. Organized by culture and by political area, and includes Assam, Chittagong, Burma, Thailand, Laos, Cambodia, Vietnam, and the tribes of South China. Each section is further divided into races, social organization and law, religion and folklore, language and writings. Political history, economics and welfare are not included. Only a few short annotations, and no translation of titles. 34 other bibliographies were consulted to compile this bibliography. No author index. Reprinted by Russell and Russell, New York, 1972.

G 10 U.S. Library of Congress. Division of Orientalia. *Southeast Asia, an annotated bibliography of selected reference sources in Western languages,* compiled by Cecil Hobbs. Washington, Library of Congress, 1952. 163 p.
345 annotated entries for books, arranged by country, then by subject. Author, title and selected subject index. Continued by the Division's *Southeast Asia, an annotated bibliography of selected reference sources in Western languages,* compiled by Cecil Hobbs (Washington, Library of Congress, 1964. 180 p.) with 535 entries, mostly published between 1952 and 1962, and with similar

arrangement, extensive annotation and indexing. Reprinted by G. K. Hall, Boston, 1968. Continuation reprinted by Greenwood Press, Westport.

G 11 Sternstein, Larry and Carl Springer. *An annotated bibliography of material concerning Southeast Asia from Petermanns Geographische Mitteilungen, 1855–1966.* Bangkok, Siam Society, 1967. 389 p.

Some 2,700 reviews of books, 250 maps and illustrative material, 147 articles and 664 notes all in Western languages. Included also are a list of 350 periodicals cited, and keys to the entries by area.

G 12 Tregonning, Kennedy G. *Southeast Asia, a critical bibliography.* Tucson, University of Arizona Press, 1969. 103 p.

2,058 annotated entries for books, periodicals and periodical articles, almost entirely in English and published since 1945. Arrangement is by country, subarranged by subject, with introductory paragraphs for the more important. In each subject section entries are arranged with the most authoritative, the most general and the most easily obtainable first.

G 13 United Nations. *Selected bibliography, lower Mekong basin.* Washington, Department of the Army, Engineer Agency for Resources Inventories, 1969. 2 v.

3,000 books, periodical articles and reports are arranged by country, and subdivided by subject under agriculture, climate, education, electricity, fisheries, forestry and vegetation, geology, health, industry, minerals, population, soils, telecommunications, transportation, urban areas, and water resources. Not annotated, but selected on basis of value, currency and availability, all items cited being located in a library. Looseleaf format.

G 14 Johnson, Donald Clay. *Southeast Asia, a bibliography for undergraduate libraries.* Williamsport, Brodart, 1970. 59 p.

Lists 750 books and periodicals, arranged by country, and subarranged by subject. There are no annotations, but references to other annotated bibliographies and to reviews are noted. Availability was a major criterion of selection, emphasizing books published in the 1960s.

G 15 U.S. Department of the Army. Army Library. *Insular Southeast Asia, a bibliographic survey.* Washington, U.S. Government Printing Office, 1971. 419 p. (DA PAM550–12).

Only one-third consists of a bibliography of books and articles in English, fully annotated, and with a subject arrangement contemporarily oriented. Coverage is for Malaya, Singapore, Indonesia, the Philippines and Australia and New Zealand. The remainder consists of data and maps emphasizing the current situation.

G 16 U.S. Department of the Army. Army Library. *Peninsular Southeast Asia, a bibliographic survey of literature, 1972.* Washington, U.S. Government Printing Office, 1972. 424 p. (DA PAM550–14).

Less than half consists of entries for books and articles in English oriented towards the contemporary political situation. Each entry is abstracted. The remainder consists of appendices with maps and other data. Coverage is for Burma, Cambodia, Laos and Thailand.

G 17 U.S. Library of Congress. Division of Orientalia. South Asia Section. *Southeast Asia subject catalog*, edited by Cecil Hobbs. Boston, G. K. Hall, 1972. 6 v.

Over 66,000 entries for books, periodical articles and theses, mostly in Western languages, are divided by country, then by subject. The 350 periodicals and newspapers indexed are listed in the appendix. Includes entries published to 1969.

G 18 Bixler, Paul Howard. *Southeast Asia, bibliographic direction in a complex area*. Middletown, Choice, 1973. 98 p. (Choice bibliographical essay series no. 2).

With an introduction, and introductions to each section, and with sections on Southeast Asia, Burma, Thailand, Indochina, Indonesia, Malaysia, Singapore and Brunei, the Philippines and Overseas Chinese. Each section has a selected bibliography. Author and title index.

G 19 U.S. Library of Congress. American Libraries Book Procurement Center, Djakarta. *Accessions list, Southeast Asia*. Djakarta, 1975?–.

Continuation of *Accessions list, Indonesia* from 1964–70 and *Accessions list, Indonesia, Malaysia, Singapore and Brunei* 1970–5?. Materials selected are arranged by country. Issued monthly or bimonthly, with an annual author index. Cumulated list of Malaysia, Singapore and Brunei serials, and cumulated list of Indonesian serials included. June 1978 issue seen.

G 20 University of Malaya. Library. *Bibliography on literature, drama and dance in Southeast Asia.* Kuala Lumpur, 1976. 137 p.

Based mainly on the holdings of the University of Malaya Library, includes some 4,000 books and articles on customs, folklore, dance, music, and literature, mainly of the post-World War II period. An appendix of graduation exercises submitted to the Department of Malay Studies, University of Malaya, 1957–74, on these topics is included. Emphasis is on Malaysia and Indonesia.

G 20a Partaningrat, Winarti. *Master list of Southeast Asian microforms.* Singapore, Singapore University Press, 1978. 682 p.

12,504 entries for microforms of books, reports, manuscripts, newspapers and periodicals are arranged by country and then alphabetically. Location stated for positive and negative copies. A key to a great amount of unusual and difficult to secure research materials.

Chinese Language

G 21 Oey, Giok P. *Survey of Chinese-language materials on Southeast Asia in the Hoover Institute and Library*. Ithaca, Department of Far Eastern Studies, Southeast Asia Program, Cornell University, 1953. 73 p. (Cornell Southeast Asia Program data research no. 8).
287 books in Chinese are arranged by subject, with the largest section on Overseas Chinese. Annotations vary from 50 to 150 words in length. One of the most useful sections is a list of Overseas Chinese newspapers, giving considerable information concerning each paper. No index.

G 22 Shu, Austin C. W. and William W. L. Wan. *Twentieth-century Chinese works on Southeast Asia, a bibliography*. Honolulu, Research Translations, East-West Center, 1968. 201 p. (Annotated bibliography series no. 3).
758 entries with romanization in the Wade-Giles system, translation of titles, and characters, with extensive annotations in English. Materials are arranged by country, and 80% have library locations. Based to some extent on Hsu Yun-chiao, 'Preliminary bibliography of the Southeast Asian studies', *Bulletin of the Institute of Southeast Asia, Nanyang University, Singapore* Nan yang yen chiu, v. 1, no. 1, 1959, pp. 1–160, and Li Yih-yuan, 'Studies on Overseas Chinese in East Asia, a catalogue of books and articles in Chinese and Japanese', *Bulletin of the Institute of Ethnology, Academia Sinica*, v. 18, Autumn 1964, pp. 46–235, but has the advantage of having annotation in English, and employing Wade-Giles romanization. Author and broad subject index.

G 23 Nanyang University, Singapore. Institute of Southeast Asia. *Index to Chinese periodical literature on Southeast Asia, 1905–1966* Nan yang yen chiu Chung wen ch'i kan tz'u liao so yin. Singapore, 1968. 363 p.
Indexes nearly 10,000 articles from over 500 periodicals in Chinese published from 1905 to 1966. Entries are arranged first by country, and further subdivided by country. No index or annotations.

Japanese Language

G 24 Irikura, James K. *Southeast Asia, selected annotated bibliography of Japanese publications*. New Haven, Southeast Asia Studies, Yale University, in association with Human Relations Area Files, 1956. 544 p. (Behaviour science bibliographies).
965 books covering reference materials, geography, history, political affairs, foreign relations, trade, health, education and minorities from the late nineteenth century to 1955. Titles are

translated into English, and descriptive annotations are provided. Arranged by geographical areas, then broken down into broad subject groups. Locations in the Library of Congress, and Yale, Harvard and Columbia universities. Author index.

G 25 Ichikawa, Kenjiro. *Southeast Asia viewed from Japan, a bibliography of Japanese works on Southeast Asian societies, 1940–1963*. Ithaca, Department of Asian Studies, Southeast Asia Program, Cornell University, 1965. 112 p. (Cornell University, Department of Asian Studies, Southeast Asia Program, data paper no. 56).
2,594 entries are divided into five sections: reference works and bibliographies; Southeast Asia as a whole; mainland Southeast Asia, excluding Malaya; island Southeast Asia, including Malaya; and publications based on field research in South China, the Himalayan region and East India when subjects studied are related to Southeast Asia. Appendices include a list of serial publications, and indexes to authors and editors. The emphasis of the bibliography is on social science materials.

Russian Language

G 26 McVey, Ruth Thomas. *Bibliography of Soviet publications on Southeast Asia as listed in the Library of Congress Monthly Index of Russian acquisitions.* Ithaca, Department of Far Eastern Studies, Southeast Asia Program, Cornell University, 1959. 109 p. (Cornell University, Department of Far Eastern Studies, Southeast Asia Program, data paper no. 34).
Approximately 2,000 books and periodicals referring to Southeast Asia and published from 1945 for books, and from 1947 for periodical articles. Entries are divided into 13 sections, and arranged by author in each section. No index.

G 27 *Bibliografiia Iugo-Vostochnoi Azii, dorevoliutsionnaia i sovetskaia na russkom iazyke, original naia i perevednaia.* Moskva, Izdaltelstvo Vostochnoi Literaturi, 1960. 256 p.
3,752 books and periodical articles, but mostly articles, divided by country, and then by a detailed subject arrangement. Author title index. Also available on microfilm from Inter Documentation Company, Zug.

G 28 Berton, Peter and Alvin Z. Rubinstein. *Soviet works on Southeast Asia, a bibliography of non-periodical literature, 1946–1965*. Los Angeles, University of Southern California Press, 1967. 201 p. (School of Political and International Relations, University of Southern California, Far Eastern and Russian research series no. 3).
Over 400 books are arranged by country, and then by broad subject divisions. No annotations. Author index. Contains an extensive introduction to Soviet Southeast Asian studies and translations into Russian from Southeast Asian languages.

Periodicals

G 29 Johnson, Donald Clay. *Index to Southeast Asian journals, 1960–1974, a guide to articles, book reviews and composite works.* Boston, G. K. Hall, 1977. 811 p.
10,636 articles, some appearing more than once, from 44 journals related to Southeast Asia, and 115 composite works in an alphabetical subject arrangement. Publications indexed issued from 1960 to 1974. Some 2,400 books are listed with reviews from the journals cited. Author index to articles, and title index to reviews.

G 30 Nunn, G. Raymond. *Southeast Asian periodicals, an international union list.* London, Mansell, 1977. 456 p.
Some 26,000 different periodicals published in Southeast Asia from the beginning of the 19th century to 1975 have been arranged by country, and then alphabetically by title. Available imprint information, and note of continuations have been given where possible. Holdings information has been given for libraries in Southeast Asia, Western Europe, and the United States. Official publications and annuals have been included, and newspapers excluded.

G 30a Moon, Brenda. *Periodicals for South East Asian Studies, a union catalogue of holdings in British and selected European libraries.* London, Mansell, 1979. 610 p.
Approximately 14,000 periodicals are arranged in one alphabetical sequence. The catalogue includes periodicals related to South East Asia but published outside the region. Complements G. Raymond Nunn *Southeast Asian periodicals, an international union list* in that it records British and a number of European library holdings far more fully.

Theses and Dissertations

G 31 The, Lian and Paul W. Van de Veur. *Treasures and trivia, doctoral dissertations on South East Asia, accepted by universities in the United States.* Athens, Ohio University, Center for International Studies, 1968. 141 p.
958 doctoral dissertations are arranged by country and sub-arranged by major subject. Author index, no annotations. Entries asterisked are to be found in *Dissertation abstracts, international.*

G 32 SarDesai, D. R. and Bhanu D. SarDesai. *Theses and dissertations on Southeast Asia.* Zug, Inter Documentation Company, 1970. 176 p. (Biblioteca Asiatica 6).
Some 2,800 theses and dissertations are arranged first by subject field, then by country, with an author index. Doctoral dissertations are included from the United States, Soviet Union, British Isles, Malaysia, Singapore, Australia, New Zealand,

Philippines, Netherlands and Japan, and to a lesser extent from France and Germany. Over 40% of the entries are for master's theses, but represent a less systematic coverage. Bibliographical sources used not stated.

Maps

G 33 South-East Asia Library Group. *Draft survey of map resources.* Hull, 1971. 35 p.
An international directory of map resources, indicating the location of some of the major collections, but disappointing in its description of holdings.

Subject Bibliography

SOCIAL SCIENCES

G 34 Breese, Gerald. *Urban Southeast Asia, a selected bibliography of accessible research, reports and related materials on urbanism and urbanization.* New York, Asia Society, Southeast Asia Development Advisory Group, 1973. 165 p.
Some 3,000 books, reports and periodical articles cover the problem of urbanization and urbanism in Southeast Asia, arranged by country, and then by major divisions and alphabetically. Hong Kong is included, and Burma excluded. The entries are not annotated.

G 35 Halpern, Joel M. *Mekong Basin development, Laos and Thailand selected bibliographies.* Bruxelles, Centre d'Etude du SudEst Asiatique et de l'Extreme Orient, 1974. 234 p.
Arranged under such major headings as 'Education in the Kingdom of Laos', 'Laos and Mekong Basin development' with some 1,100 entries, and 'Thailand and Mekong Basin development' with some 700 entries. The latter two divisions are further subdivided. No annotations and no index.

LITERATURE

G 36 Nemenzo, Catalina A. *Southeast Asian languages and literature in English, an annotated bibliography.* Quezon City, University of the Philippines, 1967. 984 p.
7,458 books and articles are arranged by country, then by subjects. Entries are annotated. Indexes by author, organization and subject. Published in *Philippine Social Sciences and Humanities Review*, vol. XXIV, nos. 1–4.

G 37 Jenner, Philip N. *Southeast Asian literatures in translation, a preliminary bibliography.* Honolulu, University Press of Hawaii, 1973. 198 p. (Asian Studies at Hawaii no. 9).
3,690 entries, mostly in English and French, for books and articles, are arranged by country, and subarranged by type of literature. Very little annotation. No index.

G 38 Bernardo, Gabriel A. *A critical and annotated bibliography of Philippine, Indonesian and other Malayan folklore*. Cagayan de Oro City, 1972. 150 p. (Xavier University, Folklore Museum and Archives publication no. 5).
A revision of Professor Bernardo's master's thesis (1923) which was based on collections in three major public libraries in Manila. 417 entries for books and articles. Annotated. Author and title index.

HISTORY

G 39 Hay, Stephen N. and Margaret M. Case. *Southeast Asian history, a bibliographic guide*. New York, Praeger, 1962. 138 p.
632 books, periodical articles and theses, mostly in English, and with no materials in Southeast Asian languages, are arranged by country, with further subdivision into bibliographies, books, articles and dissertations. Selection has been limited to materials most useful for the beginning student or teacher in Southeast Asian history. Separate author and subject indexes. Ceylon is included.

G 40 Anderson, Gerald H. *Christianity in Southeast Asia, a bibliographical guide, an annotated bibliography of selected references in Western languages*. New York, Missionary Research Library, 1966. 69 p.
1,200 books, periodicals and periodical articles, not limited to Christianity, but including background history for Southeast Asia. New Guinea, Taiwan and Ceylon are also included. Nearly all entries have short annotations. Author index.

G 41 Morrison, Gayle. *A guide to books on Southeast Asian history (1961–1966)* Santa Barbara, ABC-Clio Press, 1969. 105 p.
556 annotated entries for books, almost entirely in English, are arranged by country, and then by author. The annotations are full and keyed to reviews. Supplements Stephen N. Hay *Southeast Asian history, a bibliographic guide* (G 39) and includes a few books published before 1961, and not found in this bibliography. Subject and author index.

G 42 Nevadomsky, Joseph-John and Alice Li. *The Chinese in Southeast Asia, a selected and annotated bibliography of publications in Western languages, 1960–1970*. Berkeley, Center for South and Southeast Asia Studies, University of California, 1970. 119 p. (Center for South and Southeast Asian Studies, University of California, Occasional paper no. 6).
662 entries for books and periodical articles, divided by country and further divided if necessary. Almost all entries are annotated. Author index. 1973 revision reported.

H. BURMA

Lower Burma was acquired by Britain in 1852, following the Second Anglo-Burmese War, and much of the information concerning Burma from 1852 to 1937, when Burma became independent of India, can be found in Indian official publications. Burma became a sovereign state in 1948.

ENCYCLOPEDIA, HANDBOOKS AND YEARBOOK

H 1 *Myanma svezon kyan* (Burmese encyclopedia). Yangon (i.e. Rangoon), Bathapyan Sabei Athin, 1954–76. 15 v.
A well-produced encyclopedia in an attractive format, but initially giving little space to Burmese matters. The proportion of space on Burma has increased as publication has proceeded. No bibliographical notes with articles.

H 2 *Burma yearbook and directory*, 1957/8–. Rangoon, Student Press, 1957–.
Surveys government structure; lists officials, the diplomatic corps and the press; has materials on Rangoon, and the States, communication, foreign aid, education, health and the economy; and has a short classified trades directory, now primarily of historical interest.

H 3 American University, Washington, D.C. Foreign Area Studies. *Area handbook for Burma*. Washington, U.S. Government Printing Office, 1971. 341 p.
A country summary is followed by a survey of social, political and economic affairs, and of national security. Bibliography and glossary. Research completed April 1971.

H 4 Maring, Ester G. and Joel M. Maring. *Historical and cultural dictionary of Burma*. Metuchen, Scarecrow Press, 1973. 290 p. (Historical and cultural dictionaries of Asia series no. 4)
Has some 1,600 entries on Burmese history and culture, covering from earliest times to the early 1970s.

DICTIONARIES

H 5 Judson, Adoniram. *The Judson Burmese-English dictionary . . .* Rangoon, Baptist Board of Publications, 1953. 1,123 p.
Some 22,000 Burmese words are given with their English equivalents A reprint of the 1921 edition.

H 6 Judson, Adoniram. *English and Burmese dictionary . . .* Rangoon, Baptist Board of Publications, 1956. 928 p.
A reprint of the 1922 edition, unchanged except for page size, and containing some 27,000 words, with their equivalents in Burmese. Technical terms have been omitted and much of the work on the

development of Burmese vocabulary in recent times is not represented. A new dictionary, J. A. S. Stewart and C. W. Dunn *Burmese-English dictionary* (London, Luzac, 1940–), which is based on 420,000 slips with words in their context, drawing from Burmese literature from the 15th century, and including colloquial and technical vocabulary, is in progress. The first five parts, representing a small fraction of the material, have been published.

H 7 Ba Han, Maung. *The University English-Burmese dictionary.* Rangoon, Hanthawaddy Press, 1951–65. 2,292 p.
Extremely thorough dictionary, including up-to-date and colloquial vocabulary. Examples of usage in English, with Burmese equivalents. The first dictionary to be compiled after Adoniram Judson *English and Burmese dictionary* (H 6).

BIOGRAPHICAL DICTIONARIES

H 8 *Who's who in Burma*, 1961. Rangoon, People's Literature Committee and House, 1961. 220 p.
Not intended to be comprehensive and containing some 500 biographies only. Since the Burmese do not have family names, the last part of the given name of a biographee has been listed alphabetically. Occupation, date of birth, and brief information including a list of publications and address are given. Many persons listed are now out of office, and those now in office are often not listed. Of less value today than in 1961.

H 9 Maung Thu-ta. *Sa hso daw mya at htok pat ti* (Biographies of authors). Yangon, Zwe, 1971. 642 p.
171 non-living authors are arranged in chronological order, from 13th to 20th century, with accounts of their lives and works.

H 10 Kin Thet Htar. *Who's who in medicine in Burma.* Rangoon, Department of Medical Research, Ministry of Health, 1973. 203 p. (Burma Medical Research Council, Special report series no. 9)
541 medical specialists are listed, with their education, career, membership of professional societies, publications, current research and address. In addition there is a directory of health institutions, medical associations and laboratories.

DIRECTORY

H 11 *Burma trade directory*, 1952–. Rangoon, Burma Commerce, 1952–.
Arranged alphabetically by subject, with firms under each subject by nationality, 23 trades are listed. Appendices have information on Burmese trade and customs, and list commission agents, importers and exporters. There is also a classified list of trades and of individual industrialists. Burmese industry is now

nationalized and much of the information will be of historical value only. Issue for 1963/4 last noted.

GAZETTEER

H 12 U.S. Board on Geographic Names. *Burma* . . . Washington, Army Map Service, 1966. 725 p. (Gazetteer no. 96)
52,600 entries for place and feature names in Burma. Each name is classified, and its longitude and latitude given.

CENSUS AND STATISTICS

H 13 Burma (Union). Census Division. *First stage census, 1953.* Rangoon, Government Printing and Stationery, 1957–8. 4 v.
The published work in four volumes includes the data collected for the first stage in 1953, where 248 cities in Burma and four in the Kachin area were surveyed, and for the second stage in 1954, when 2,143 villages in Burma and 1,016 in the Kachin area were covered. The first volume is for population and housing, the second for industry, the third for the Chin special division, and the fourth for agriculture. Since the census does not follow the pattern of previous ones, comparisons are difficult. The fourth volume and a second stage census, 1954, in four volumes are reported in *International population census bibliography, Asia* (A 40), but not seen. Previous census information will be found in the one or more Burma volumes of the decennial *Census of India*, from 1881 to 1931. The records of the 1941 census were destroyed during the Japanese occupation.

H 14 Burma (Union). Central Statistical and Economics Department. *Quarterly bulletin of statistics*, 1951–. Rangoon, Superintendent, Central Press, Burma, 1951–.
Issued quarterly, but often irregular, in Burmese and English text, and arranged under 15 headings, including population, labour, agriculture and forestry, industry, foreign trade, transportation, prices, indices, banking and taxation. Issues for 1963 last noted.

H 15 Burma (Union). Central Statistics and Economics Department. *Statistical yearbook*. Rangoon, 19––.
The 1963 issue (362 p.) covers statistics, in some cases going back to the early 1950s, for population, health, education, labour, agriculture, forestry, industry, foreign trade, transportation, prices, and public finance. In 1967 a *Statistical pocket book* (104 p.) was issued by the Department.

BIBLIOGRAPHY

H 16 Barnett, Lionel David. *Catalogue of Burmese books in the British Museum*. London, British Museum, 1913. 346 cols.

1,800 books published from the early 19th century are listed with an index of titles and an index of subjects including arts and sciences, grammar, lexicography and orthography, law, poetry and religion.

H 17 Burma (Union). Government Book Depot. *Catalogue of publications in stock at the Book Depot, Rangoon*, 1963, corrected up to 30 September 1963. Rangoon, Central Press, 1964. 91 p.
A similar catalogue has been issued under various titles since 1919. This issue lists some 2,500 publications, which are mostly acts, ordinances and statutes. Substantial publications account for a very small proportion of the total number of entries.

H 18 Bernot, Denise. *Bibliographie birmane, annees 1950–1960*. Paris, Editions du Centre National de la Recherche Scientifique, 1968. 230 p.
Some 1,700 books and periodical articles are arranged by subject, and then by author. The author arrangement has the full citation together with brief annotations. There is an ethno-linguistic index. This bibliography is valuable since it contains some 230 items in Burmese.

H 19 Whitbread, Kenneth. *Catalogue of Burmese printed books in the India Office Library*. London, Her Majesty's Stationery Office, 1969. 231 p.
Lists some 2,800 titles arranged by title and representing the largest collection of Burmese books, and books translated from Burmese outside Burma. Author and subject index.

H 20 Nunn, G. Raymond. *Burmese and Thai newspapers, an international union list*. Chinese Materials and Research Aids Service Centre, 1972. 44 p.
Lists 30 newspapers published in Burma and 240 published in Thailand, stating locations and holdings. Index in Thai for Thai language newspapers, and list of 76 newspapers published in Burma for which there is no holdings information.

H 21 Trager, Frank N. *Burma, a selected and annotated bibliography*. New Haven, Human Relations Area Files Press, 1973. 356 p.
Revises and updates New York University, Burma Research Project *Annotated bibliography of Burma* (1956) and contains 2,086 entries for books, periodicals and articles arranged into nine major groups, bibliographies, books, articles, official publications, periodicals, Burmese-language sources, Russian-language sources, and dissertations. Author and topical indexes.

H 22 *Sa ne zin thamaing pya pwe lan hnyun* (Guide to the Exhibition of the history of newspapers, journals and magazines). Yangon, Sa bei biman poun hneit taik, 1975. 64 p.
Lists in chronological order of date of first issue 272 periodicals published 1879–1974, and 203 newspapers published 1839–1974. No official publications noted.

I. DEMOCRATIC KAMPUCHEA

In 1863 a French protectorate was proclaimed over the Kingdom of Cambodia, which became part of French Indochina. Cambodia regained its complete independence in 1955. Renamed Democratic Kampuchea in 1975.

HANDBOOK

I 1 American University, Washington, D.C. Foreign Area Studies. *Area handbook for the Khmer Republic*. Washington, U.S. Government Printing Office, 1973. 389 p.
A short country ssmmary is followed by four major sections, for social, political, economic affairs, and national security. The research was completed in 1972. 34-page bibliography and an index. Replaces 1963 edition.

DICTIONARIES

I 2 Pannetier, Adrien Louis Marie. *Lexique francaise-cambodgienne*, nouvelle edition. Phnom-Penh, 1922. 505 p.
An enlarged edition of the 1907 Avignon version, which is also suitable. A handy little dictionary for its time, but because of its date, couched in now obsolete orthography and represents a form of Cambodian current before the present Standard Cambodian came into being. There are many typographical errors. The edition contains 11,500 words.

I 3 Guesdon, Joseph. *Dictionnaire cambodgien-francais*. Paris, Plon, 1930. 2 v. (Ministere de l'Instruction Publique et des Beaux-arts, Commission Archeologique de l'Indochine).
Far more scholarly than Pannetier, and still the best Khmer-French dictionary. Because of its date, the orthography is obsolete, and very many modern technical terms are not included. Very few errors. Contains some 20,000 words.

I 4 *Vacanukram Khmer* Dictionnaire cambodgien. Phnom Penh, Editions de l'Institut Bouddhique, 1962. 2 v.
A standard Khmer-Khmer dictionary with some 20,000 words. The first volume covers K–M and the second Y–A. 1968 edition reported.

I 5 Jacob, Judith M. *A concise Cambodian-English dictionary*. London, Oxford University Press, 1974. 242 p.
Lists some 8,000 Cambodian words in Cambodian, with transliteration and equivalents in English. A dictionary designed to include modern usage, and valuable for beginners.

BIOGRAPHICAL DICTIONARY

I 6 *Personnalites du Cambodge*, edition 1963. Phnom-Penh, Realites cambodgiennes, 1963. 303 p.
Contains approximately 350 biographies, but these are not substantial, since the format of the volume is small, and there are many portraits.

GAZETTEER

I 7 U.S. Office of Geography. *Cambodia, official standard names gazetteer*, second edition, Washington, U.S. Government Printing Office, 1971. 392 p. (Gazetteer no. 74)
22,000 names for places and features, with their classification by type and longitude and latitude. Replaces 1963 edition.

CENSUS AND STATISTICS

I 8 Cambodia. Ministere du Plan. *Statistical yearbook of Cambodia, 1937/1957*. Phnom Penh, 1958. 214 p.
The official statistical yearbook but not published annually. Arranged under broad subject divisions, with the table of contents serving as an index. Population statistics may not be considered as reliable.

I 9 Cambodia. Direction de la Statistique et des Etudes Economiques. *Enquete demographique au Cambodge*. Phnom Penh?, 1959?-. 14 v.
A series of surveys of major towns and sample of villages, and covering the period 1958–60.

I 10 Cambodia. Ministere du Plan. *Annuaire statistique retrospectif du Cambodge*, 1958–61. Phnom-Penh, 1962? 184 p.
Written in French, with no explanations or introduction, and organized by broad subjects. The table of contents is the only key to the yearbook. Issues to 1968 noted.

BIBLIOGRAPHY

I 11 Dik Keam. *Catalogue des auteurs khmers et etrangers*. Phnom Penh, Association des ecrivains khmers, 1966. 24 p.
304 books mostly in Cambodian and on Buddhism form the first part of this bibliography. The second part contains an additional 380 Cambodian books arranged by author.

I 12 United Nations. E.C.A.F.E. Mekong Documentation Centre. *Cambodia, a select bibliography*. Bangkok, 1967. 101 p.
1,013 books, periodicals and periodical articles, emphasizing the

modern period and the social sciences, are arranged in classified order. The bibliography is based on the resources of the E.C.A.F.E. Library in Bangkok.

I 13 Fisher, Margaret L. *Cambodia, an annotated bibliography of its history, geography and politics since 1954.* Cambridge, Center for International Studies, Massachusetts Institute of Technology, 1967. 66p.

337 books and articles are arranged by subject and annotated. Index to authors, subjects and some titles.

I 14 Gelinas, Andre. *Books and serials on Cambodia.* Saigon, 1974. 30 p.

A list of 443 items arranged under 21 subjects, and mostly in Cambodian or French. Includes 19 periodicals, with annotation on their contents.

J. INDONESIA

The Dutch became established in Indonesia in the beginning of the 17th century, and maintained control of the area until 1949, when Indonesia became independent. From 1811 to 1816, and from 1942 to 1945, there were brief interludes of British and Japanese occupation respectively.

ENCYCLOPEDIAS, HANDBOOKS AND YEARBOOKS

J 1 Dutch East Indies. Departement van Landbouw, Nijverheid, en Handel. *Handbook of the Netherlands East Indies*. Buitenzorg, 1916–30. 4 v.
An official survey of the Netherlands East Indies, with some statistics, and covering population, government, finance, farming, industry, commerce and communications. Issued in 1916, 1920, 1924 and 1930. The 1916 and 1920 issues have title *Yearbook of the Netherlands East Indies*.

J 2 *Encyclopaedie van Nederlandsch-Indie*. 's Gravenhage, M. Nijhoff, 1917–39. 8 v.
The first four volumes were published from 1917 to 1921, and have been abridged in the *Beknopte encyclopaedie van Nederlandsch-Indie*. Volumes 5–8 are supplements to the first four volumes, and were published from 1927 to 1939. Scholarly in treatment, but lacking illustration and maps, this encyclopedia remains an excellent source for the Dutch period. In Dutch.

J 3 *Ensiklopedia Indonesia*. Bandung and The Hague, W. Van Hoeve, 1954–7? 3 v.
A general encyclopedia not restricted to Indonesia, but with an emphasis on Asia. The treatment is popular, with short articles, and black-and-white photographs and drawings. The value of this encyclopedia lies mostly in its information on Southeast Asia. For other areas it is often dated and less reliable. No index. In Indonesian.

J 4 *Indonesia handbook*, 1970–. Djakarta, Department of Information, Republic of Indonesia, 1971–.
A yearbook giving background information on Indonesian geography, history, government, and social and economic development, with key statistics. 1975 issue seen.

J 5 *Almanak Djakarta*. Jakarta, P. T. Pentja, 1971–.
One half of the yearbook is concerned with the growth of Jakarta, and the second half is a selected directory of official and semi-official organizations, followed by a directory arranged by major trades and professions. No. 4 for 1974–5 noted. In Indonesian.

J 6 *Ensiklopedi umum*. Jakarta, Penerbitan Jajasan Kanisius, 1973. 1,433 p.
The publication of this encyclopedia was initiated largely through the efforts of Franklin Book Publications, and is based on the *Columbia desk encyclopedia*, but it is not a direct translation, for considerable matter has been deleted, and a great deal of new information has been added. Materials on Indonesia now comprise one-fifth of the total publication. The compilation was aided by a board of Indonesian experts, and the encyclopedia is valuable for more recent data than that found in *Ensiklopedia Indonesia* (J3).

J 7 American University, Washington, D.C. Foreign Area Studies. *Area handbook for Indonesia*. Washington, U.S. Government Printing Office, 1975. 488 p.
A country summary is followed by a survey of social, political and economic affairs, and national security. Full bibliography and glossary of Indonesian terms and acronyms. Research completed in May 1974. Third edition and revision of 1970 edition.

DICTIONARIES

J 8 Pino, Elisabeth and Tamme Wittermans. *Kamus Inggeris*. Djakarta, J. B. Wolters, 1955. 2 v.
This dictionary is oriented towards general and school use in Indonesia. The English-Indonesian volume has over 80,000 words, and the Indonesian-English volume some 15,000 words. Examples of usage are given. An unrevised reprint of the 1953 edition.

J 9 Echols, John H. and Hassan Shadily. *An Indonesian-English dictionary*, second edition. Ithaca, Cornell University Press, 1963. 431 p.
A revision of the 1961 edition with some 12,000 words and intended for the reader of contemporary materials. Among its excellent features are numerous technical terms and examples of usage.

J 10 Poerwadarminta, W. J. S. *Kamus umum bahasa Indonesia*. Djakarta, Dinas Penerbitan Balai Pustaka, 1966. 2 v.
Regarded as the best of the Indonesian-Indonesian dictionaries, even rated better than Suta Muhammed Zain *Kamus moderen bahasa Indonesia*, with the exception that the latter has better treatment of Islamic words.

J 11 Echols, John M. and Hassan Shadilly. *An English-Indonesian dictionary*. Ithaca, Cornell University Press, 1975. 660 p.
Contains some 25,000 English words, with phrases and equivalents in Indonesian. Uses the new Indonesian orthography.

BIOGRAPHICAL DICTIONARIES

J 12 *Orang Indonesia jang terkemoeka di Djawa* (Notable Indonesians in Java). Tjetakan pertana (preliminary edition). Djakarta, Gunseikambu, 2603 (1943). 501 p.
Some 3,000 biographies are arranged into three groups, for government, business, and other activities. Limited to those persons holding major positions. Lists of abbreviations for schools, organizations, and government bodies. Alphabetical index. 1944 edition seen.

J 13 Roeder, O. G. *Who's who in Indonesia, biographies of prominent Indonesian personalities in all fields*. Djakarta, Gunung Agung, 1971. 544 p.
Contains nearly 1,000 biographies of living persons, with name, date of birth, education, career, publications. The compilation is based on replies to a questionnaire. Also contains a list of important acronyms and abbreviations.

J 14 Suryadinata, Leo. *Prominent Indonesian Chinese in the twentieth century*. Athens, Center for International Studies, Ohio University, 1972. 62 p. (Papers in International Studies, Southeast Asia series no. 23)
Lists some 260 Indonesian Chinese associated with leading Chinese political and social organizations, legislative bodies and political parties.

J 15 Kantor Bibliografi Nasional (Office of National Bibliography). *Names of Indonesian authors* Nama nama pengarang Indonesia. Jakarta, 1973. 128 p.
Lists 1,139 authors' names, usually with birthdates. Cross-references and publications are also given.

DIRECTORIES

J 16 *Directory of scientific institutions in Indonesia*. Djakarta, Council for Sciences of Indonesia, 1959. 80 p. (Madjelis ilmu pengetahuan Indonesia, Bulletin no. 1)
106 institutions are listed first by geographical area, then alphabetically by name, with information on address, objectives, name of director, publications, the library and a brief history. Subject index.

J 17 *Trade directory of Indonesia*, 1964/5–. Djakarta, 1965?–
A survey of the Indonesian economy, investment and taxation regulations is followed by lists of Indonesian importers, exporters and banks, and shorter directories of insurance, warehousing and shipping companies. No index. 1972/3 issue seen.

J 18 *Almanak negara R.I.* (Almanac of the Republic of Indonesia), 1970–. Djakarta, Menteri Negara Penjempurnaan dan Pembersihan Aparatur Negara Republic Indonesia, 1970–

Supersedes *Almanak organisasi negara Republik Indonesia*, 1960–, published by the Lembaga Administrasi Negara. A guide to the structure of the Indonesian government, with numerous organization charts.

J 19 Morzer Bruyns, A. *Kamus singatan dan akronim jang dipergunakan di Indonesia* Glossary of abbreviations and acronyms used in Indonesia. Djakarta, Ichitar, 1970. 1 v. (various pagings)

Containing some 9,600 abbreviations and acronyms, and regarded as the most comprehensive. Compiled from newspapers, periodicals and books published from 1925 to 1970. Elisabeth P. Wittermans *Dictionary of Indonesian abbreviations and acronyms* (Honolulu, East-West Center, 1970. 258 p.) contains some 5,000 examples compiled from materials published from 1965.

J 20 Lembaga Penelitian Pendidikan dan Penerangan Ekonomi dan Sosial (Institute of Research for Education and Economic and Social Information). *Buku petunjuk tentang perpustakaan 2 dibidang ekonomi dan ilmu sosial* Directory of libraries in the field of economic and social science. Djakarta, 1972. 58 p.

Replies from 58 libraries to a questionnaire circulated in June 1971, with comments. In English and Indonesian.

J 21 Lembaga Ilmu Pengetahuan Indonesia (Indonesian Institute of Science). *Directory of research institutes and related activities under ministries and non-ministerial bodies in Indonesia.* Djakarta, 1972. 114 p.

97 institutes are arranged by geographical area, and are listed with addresses, objectives, staff, and some with information on libraries. Index by major subject, then by title of institute.

J 22 Lembaran Perpustakaan. *Direktori perpustakaan Indonesia, 1970/71* (Directory of libraries in Indonesia, 1970/71). Jakarta, 1973? 434 p.

434 libraries, one to a page, are listed with address, information on collections, budget and staff. Index by place and by name of library.

ATLASES

J 23 *Atlas van tropisch Nederland.* Amsterdam, Koninklijk Nederlandsch Aardrijkskundig Genootschap, 1938. 79 maps, including historical maps.

Since this atlas covers the whole of the tropical Netherlands colonies, Surinam and Curacao are included with the East Indies. Maps show the sea, flora and fauna, rainfall, and administrative divisions. Each map has an explanatory note in German, French, Dutch, and English. The second revised edition of this publication originally issued in 1923. Alphabetical index.

J 24 Adinegoro. *Atlas semesta dunia*. Djakarta, Djambatan, 1952. 256 p.
A world atlas, but stressing Asia and Indonesia, with just over a third dealing with Asia, and with half of the Asia section on Indonesia. In addition to general maps for the whole of Indonesia covering flora and fauna, language, climate, geology, economy and population, there are large-scale physical maps for each province. The provincial boundaries have changed since 1952.

J 25 I Made Sandy. *Atlas Indonesia, buku pertama umum* (Atlas of Indonesia, first general volume). Jakarta, 1974. 42 l.
The first general volume of an Indonesia atlas, consisting of a series of provincial maps showing physical features, communications and place names. Geographical names index. The maps are coloured.

GAZETTEER

J 26 U.S. Office of Geography. *Indonesia and Portuguese Timor* . . ., second edition. Washington, U.S. Government Printing Office, 1968. 901 p. (Gazetteer no. 13).
60,000 place and feature names in Indonesia and 600 in Portuguese Timor in a separate list, with classification of the names and their longitude and latitude.

CENSUS AND STATISTICS

J 27 Dutch East Indies. Central Kantoor voor de Statistiek in Nederlandsch-Indie. *Statistisch jaaroverzicht van Nederlandsch-Indie*. Batavia, Landsdrukkerij, 1923–40.
A wealth of statistical tables surveying population, health, education, religion, law, economy, agriculture, trade and finance, and communications. From 1930, this yearbook appeared as part 2 of the *Indisch verslag*. For earlier statistical information on the Dutch East Indies, the best source is Netherlands, Departement van Kolonien, *Kolonial verslag*, 1849–1930 ('s Gravenhage, 1850–1930). In Dutch and English.

J 28 Dutch East Indies. Departement van Economische Zaken. *Volkstelling*, 1930. Batavia, 1933–6. 8 v.
Volumes 1–5 survey population, races, social conditions, literacy, religion and occupations, and are arranged by region. Volume 6 surveys Europeans, volume 7 Chinese and other Orientals, and volume 8 is a summary report. In Dutch and English. A census was also undertaken in 1905 and 1920. There was no census for 1940.

J 29 Indonesia. Biro Pusat Statistik (Central Bureau of Statistics). *Statistik Indonesia* Statistical pocket book of Indonesia, 1941–. Djakarta, 1947–.

Issued for 1941 and 1947, and has appeared annually since 1957. Organized under major subjects into some 300 tables, and compiled from data supplied by government bureaus, in particular the Statistical Bureau. Issues also contain a description of the statistics collection process in Indonesia. 1977/8 issue seen.

J 30 Nugroho. *Indonesia, facts and figures.* Djakarta, 1967. 608 p.
A comprehensive compilation of Indonesian statistics, based on official sources, with data ranging from 1950 to 1965. The section for population includes the census results for 1961. Other sections are for labour, social statistics, agriculture, manufacturing and power, trade and transport, and money and banking. An appendix describes statistical procedures in Indonesia.

J 31 Indonesia. Biro Pusat Statistik (Central Bureau of Statistics). *Sensus penduduk, 1971* Population census, 1971. Jakarta, 1972–.
Consists of a provincial series in 26 volumes, volumes for Java-Madura and Outer Java. Preliminary series A in five volumes principally covers households, Series B in three volumes gives preliminary population statistics, and Series C in one volume gives advance tables, Series D covers population, and a Series E in 24 volumes, population by major provinces. Series F covers housing.

J 32 Universitas Indonesia. Lembaga Demografi (Institute of Demography). *Demographic factbook of Indonesia.* Jakarta, 1973. 383 p.
Information is based on data available prior to the 1971 Population Census, and discusses population, fertility levels, death rates and geographical mobility.

J 33 Indonesia. Biro Pusat Statistik (Central Bureau of Statistics). *Statistik Indonesia* Statistical yearbook of Indonesia. Jakarta, 1976–.
The first issue (1,239 p.) surveys geography, climate, government, population and employment, social and cultural affairs, education, health, judiciary, agriculture, industry, trade, transportation, construction, finance, prices, and national income. Some tables give information as far back as 1963. In English and Indonesian. 1976 issue seen.

BIBLIOGRAPHY

Bibliography of Bibliographies

J 34 Indonesia. Department Pendidikan dan Kebudayaan (Department of Education and Culture). *Bibliografi tentang bibliografi Indonesia* (Indonesian bibliography of bibliographies). Jakarta, P. N. Balai Pustaka, 1977. 137 p.
740 bibliographies in book, report or periodical form, arranged by major subjects. Author and title index. Supersedes J. N. B. Tairas *Indonesia, a bibliography of bibliographies* (1974).

Bibliography to 1941

J 35 Chijs, Jacobus Anne van der. *Proeve eener Nederlandsch-Indische bibliographie (1659–1870)*. Batavia, Bruining, 1875. 325 p. (Bataviaasch Genootschap van Kunsten en Wettenschappen, Verhandelingen v. 37).
Approximately 3,000 books, mostly in Dutch, but with some in Japanese and Malay, are arranged chronologically by date of publication, with separate author-title and subject indexes. Lists of printers and publishers and of newspapers and periodicals are appended. Supplement I, published in 1880, appeared in Verhandelingen v. 39 and supplement II, published in 1903, in Verhandelingen v. 55.

J 36 Hooykaas, J. C. *Repertorium op de koloniale litteratuur of systematische inhoudsopgaaf van hetgeen voorkomt over de kolonien (beoosten de Kaap) in mengelwerken en tijdschriften, van 1595 tot 1865 uitgegeven in Nederland en zijne overzeesche bezittingen*. Amsterdam, P. N. Van Kampen & Zoon, 1877–80. 2 v.
Includes books, periodicals and other printed material published in the Netherlands and its colonies from 1595 to 1865. The first volume is divided into two parts, the first on the country and the second on the people; contains 10,500 items. The second volume has its first part on government, and its second on science; it contains 10,873 entries. Each part is further divided into more specific subjects, and many entries are annotated. There is a general index. Continued by, and bound in the same volume in the University of Hawaii copy, A. Hartmann *Repertorium op de litteratuur* (J 37).

J 37 Hartmann, A. and others. *Repertorium op de litteratuur betreffende de Nederlandsche kolonien, voor zoover zij verspreid is in tijdschriften en mengelwerken. Part I. Oost-Indie, 1866–1893. Part II. West-Indie, 1840–1893, met een alphabetisch zaak- en plaatsregister.* 's Gravenhage, M. Nijhoff, 1895. 454 p.
Some 12,000 books and periodical articles in Dutch, German, French, Latin and Italian, divided into two parts. The first and by far the greatest part on the East Indies is further divided into sections for country and people, history, government and economics. These sections are further subdivided. Subject and place-name index. There is an index to personal names, Dorothée Buur *Alfabetisch persoonsnamen: register behorende bij A. Hartman's Repertorium* . . . Leiden. (Koninglijke Instituut voor Taal-, Land-, en Volkenkunde, 1974). Continues J. C. Hooykaas *Repertorium op de koloniale litteratuur* (J 36). Supplements 1–8 for 1894 to 1932 were published from 1901 to 1934, with some 54,000 books and periodical articles, almost entirely on the East Indies, and arranged in subject order, with indexes.

J 38 Hague. Koloniale Bibliotheek. *Catalogus der Koloniale Bibliotheek van het Kon. Instituut voor de Taal-, Land-, en Volkenkunde van Ned. Indie en het Indische Genootschap.* 's Gravenhage, M. Nijhoff, 1908. 1,053 p.

Approximately 26,000 books, periodicals and newspapers are arranged geographically, subdivided into 78 broad subjects, and further divided chronologically. The books are in Dutch, French, German, Spanish, Indonesian and English. There is a subject and title index. Supplements were issued in 1915, 1927, 1937, 1966 and 1972, and are similarly arranged as the main work. The 1966 supplement includes acquisitions received through 1959, and the 1972 supplement covers 1960–9 acquisitions. The 1975 supplement covers 1970–2.

J 39 Ockeloen, G. *Catalogus van boeken en tijdschriften uitgeven in Nederlandsch Oost-Indie van 1870–1937.* Batavia, Kolff, 1940. 2 v.

Approximately 10,000 books published in the Netherlands East Indies from 1870 to 1937, and continuing Jacobus Anne van der Chijs *Proeve* (J 35).

Entries in volume 1 are mostly in Dutch, but with some English, French and German titles. Volume 2 contains titles in Indonesian. The bibliography is arranged by author and the lack of an index makes it difficult to locate material on a subject, unless the reader happens to know the authors in the field. An appendix to volume 1 lists some 500 Indonesian publishing houses and printing firms, arranged by location. Continued by G. Ockeloen *Catalogus* (J 40).

A 1856 announcement in the *Staatsblad van Nederlandsch-Indie* states that three copies of all publications were to be handed to the provincial government, two of these being retained ard one sent to the central government. In 1913 another announcement required that copies be sent to the Museum Library in Batavia. This practice continued to 1945. After 1945 deposit in the Museum Library was voluntary. Under the Republic official publications are deposited in the Museum Library.

J 40 Ockeloen, G. *Catalogus van in Nederlandsch-Indie verschenen boeken in de jaren 1938–1941 en enkele aanvullingen op de gestencilde catalogus verschenen in 1939.* Batavia, Kolff, 1942. 322 p.

An author catalogue of some 4,500 books, written almost entirely in Dutch. No index.

J 41 Coolhaas, Willem Ph. *A critical survey of studies on Dutch colonial history.* 's Gravenhage, M. Nijhoff, 1960. 144 p. (Instituut voor Taal-, Land-, en Volkenkunde, Bibliographical series 4).

Consists of six chapters, covering archives, journals, books of travel, the area covered by the Dutch East India Company (V.O.C.), the Netherlands East Indies after 1795, and the area covered by the charter of the West-indische Companie. Items cited are in Dutch, English, French and Spanish. Since this is in the form of a bibliographical essay, comments on materials will be found in the text. Personal names index.

J 42 Sudjatmoko. *An introduction to Indonesian historiography.* Ithaca, Cornell University Press, 1965. 427 p.
Soedjatmoko, the editor of this book, has long been concerned with the development of Indonesian history, and while this is primarily a book on historiography, it is also a valuable annotated and select bibliography, surveying Javanese, Malay, Dutch, Japanese, Chinese, English and Soviet sources. Individual articles are written by some of the outstanding scholars in the field.

Regional Bibliography

J 43 Joustra, M. *Litteratuur overzicht de Bataklanden.* Leiden, L. H. Becherer, 1907. 180 p.
Divided into six major geographical sections, then subarranged by a uniform subject division. Some 2,000 books and periodical articles, mostly in Dutch, are listed with some entries going back as far as 1826.

J 44 Lekkerkerker, Cornelius. *Bali en Lombok, overzicht der litteratuur omtrent deze eilanden tot einde 1919.* Rijswijk, Blankwaardt & Schoonhover, 1920. 456 p.
Over 800 books and periodical articles listed mostly in Dutch; divided into five parts, the first consisting of books, the second of periodical articles, the third of books and articles not exclusively concerned with Bali and Lombok, the fourth on government publications, and the fifth on maps. Each part is divided by subject. Author and subject index. Continued by G. Goris *Overzicht over de belangrijkste litteratuur betreffende Bali over het tijdvaak, 1920–1935* (31 p., with 247 entries for Bali).

J 45 Wellan, J. W. J. and H. L. Helfrich. *Zuid Sumatra, overzicht van de litteratuur der gewesten Bengkoelen, Djambi, de Lampongsche districten en Palembang.* 's Gravenhage, H. L. Smits, 1923–38.
Lists some 5,000 books, maps, periodicals and periodical articles, almost entirely in Dutch, and arranged by kind of publication, then by author. Volume 1 covers the period to the end of 1915, volume 2 from 1916–25. Annotated. Subject and author index.

J 46 Molukken Instituut, Amsterdam. *Overzicht van de literatuur betreffende de Molukken.* Amsterdam, 1928–.
Over 4,000 books and periodical articles have been compiled by W. Ruinen, the archivist of the Molukken Instituut. Divided into three parts, the first containing materials exclusively about the Moluccas, the second periodical articles, and the third books not exclusively dealing with the Moluccas. Each part is arranged chronologically, and the materials listed are in the Koloniale Bibliotheek, the Library of the Ministry of Colonial Affairs, or, if

not in these two, where stated. Entries are almost entirely in Dutch and annotated. Subject and title index.

J 47 Galis, Klaas Wilhelm. *Bibliographie van Nederlands-Nieuw Guinea*, 3e verbeterde en vemeerderde uitg. Den Haag, 1962. 275 p.
Some 6,300 books and periodical articles in Dutch, English, French, German and Indonesian, are arranged by alphabetical author order. The entries have been largely compiled from the collections of the Volkenkundig Instituut te Utrecht and the Koninklijke Instituut de Tropen te Amsterdam in Hollandia, and other bibliographies.

Bibliography after 1941

J 48 U.S. Library of Congress. General Reference and Bibliography Division. *Netherlands East Indies, a bibliography of books published after 1930, and periodical articles published after 1932, available in U.S. Libraries*. Washington, 1945, 208 p.
Some 2,700 books and periodical articles in Dutch and English are arranged in a detailed subject arrangement including geography, history, economics, social conditions, language and literature, the arts, religion, government and administration, law, and individual islands. Indexes for authors, anonymous works and titles. Supplements A. Hartmann *Repertorium op de litteratuur* (J 37) and supplements for 1894 to 1932, for periodical articles.

J 49 Ockeloen, G. *Catalogus dari buku-buku jang diterbitkan di Indonesia, 1945–54* (Catalogue of books published in Indonesia, 1945–54). Bandung, Gedung Buku Nasional, 1950–5. 4 v.
Dictionary-type arrangement, compiled by G. Ockeloen, who resigned as director of the Office of National Bibliography in 1954 and returned to the Netherlands in 1958. Later volumes may include books with earlier imprints which have not been previously reported. The bibliography depended on the voluntary cooperation of the publishers, and is not complete. Since not all books were personally inspected by the compilers some of the descriptions are bibliographically deficient. There are some 1,700 books noted in each volume. The first volume is partly superseded for 1945–9 imprints by John M. Echols *Preliminary checklist of Indonesian imprints, 1945–49, with Cornell University holdings* (J 54).

J 50 Indonesia. Kantor Bibliografi Nasional (Office of National Bibliography). *Berita bulanan dari Kantor bibliografi nasional*, 1953–62 (Monthly report of the Office of National Bibliography). Djakarta, 1953–62. 10 v.
The Office of National Bibliography was established in January 1953, and given the responsibility of compiling a listing of books, periodicals and government reports, and eventually a cumulated national bibliography. In 1956 it was transferred to the Jajasan

Lektur, where it remained for two years. It is now under the Ministry of Education. Although monthly publication was intended, it has appeared irregularly. Arrangement is according to the Dewey Decimal Classification. New periodicals and some non-confidential government reports are noted. No index. Since there is no legal deposit law in force in Indonesia, bibliographical reporting depends on the voluntary cooperation of the publishers. Less coverage than the *Berita bibliografi* (J 52). Continued by *Bibliografi nasional Indonesia*, 1963–5. Frequency was reduced in 1962, concluded in 1965, and resumed in 1970, covering one-quarter of the total output.

J 51 Stanford University. Hoover Institution on War, Revolution and Peace. *Indonesian language publications in the Hoover Library.* Stanford, California, 1953. 21 l.
Approximately 450 entries published from the 1940s to the early 1950s arranged alphabetically by author. No annotations. Important for locating Indonesian-language materials in the United States.

J 52 *Berita bibliografi*, 1955– (Bibliographical report, 1955–). Djakarta, Gunung Agung, 1955–.
Lists publications in Indonesian, published in Indonesia and elsewhere, together with some Malayan books. It was compiled and issued as a monthly, with annual cumulations, and later as a quarterly. Dewey Decimal Classification is used, with author and title indexes. The 1961 cumulative index lists some 3,700 entries. On manuscript and not published in 1967 and 1968. Continued by *Berita Idayu* [*dan*] *Bibliografi* from 1976. July 1978 last issue seen.

J 53 Echols, John M. *Preliminary checklist of Indonesian imprints during the Japanese period, March 1942 – August 1945, with annotations.* Ithaca, Modern Indonesia Project, Southeast Asia Program, Department of Asian Studies, Cornell University, 1963. 56 p. (Cornell University, Modern Indonesia Project, Bibliography series).
Lists 252 entries, of which 216 are monographs, 6 almanacs, 16 newspapers and 13 periodicals, mostly published in Java and Sumatra. Arranged first by form of material, then alphabetically by author or title. To compile the list, American libraries and the library of the Lembaga Kebudajaan Indonesia were searched. Only 139 of the entries cited are in Cornell University Library. Estimated that only one-half of the books published in this period are represented. Annotated. Subject, title, and proper name indexes.

J 54 Echols, John M. *Preliminary checklist of Indonesian imprints, 1945–1949, with Cornell University holdings.* Ithaca, Southeast Asia Program, Department of Asian Studies, Cornell University, 1965. 186 p. (Modern Indonesia Project, Bibliography series).
1,782 books in an author/title arrangement, with an index to

subjects, and to co-authors, editors, preface writers, and variant spellings. Some 750 of the entries represented in the Cornell University Library. Includes more than 300 titles not reported in G. Ockeleon *Catalogus dari buku-buku jang diterbitkan di Indonesia* (J 49) for same period.

J 55 *Bibliografi nasional Indonesia, kumulasi, 1945–1963*. Djakarta, P. N. Balai Pustaka, 1965. 2 v.
Some 8,700 publications are arranged by author, with subject and author indexes. The 1964–5 supplement contains 796 entries arranged by the Universal Decimal Classification. No annotation. Government publications are not included since these are to be found in Rusina Sjahrial-Pamuntjak *Daftar penerbitan pemerintah Republik Indonesia* (J 60).

J 56 Ikatan Penerbit Indonesia (Indonesian Publishers Association) (Ikapi) O. P. S. Penerbitan. *Daftar buku 20 tahun penerbitan Indonesia, 1945–1965* (List of books published in Indonesia in 20 years, 1945–1965). Djakarta, 1965. 416 p.
Some 12,000 entries in a classified arrangement, with official publications listed on pp. 373–416. Since this cumulated list was published before the coup in 1965, there are many omissions of important writers and their works. No annotations and no index.

J 57 Ikatan Penerbit Indonesia (Indonesian Publishers Association). *Daftar buku 1975* (Catalogue of books, 1975). Jakarta, 1975. 343 p.
Lists publications in print, arranged by 48 publishers, and prices are given. Directory of booksellers arranged by place in appendix. 1976 edition available and 1977 reported.

J 58 Inter Documentation Company AG (IDC) *Indonesian monographs on microfiche, 1945–1968*. Zug, 1975. 154 p.
7,000 monographs are arranged first by author, and then by a subject arrangement. The catalogue is based on the Indonesian-language holdings of Cornell University Library, the most extensive in the world.

Official Publications

J 59 Lev, Daniel S. *Bibliography of Indonesian government documents and selected indonesian writings on government in the Cornell University Library*. Ithaca, Southeast Asia Program, Cornell University, 1958. 58 p. (Cornell University, Southeast Asia Program, data paper no. 31).
424 items, mostly in Indonesian, but some in English. No Dutch materials are included. The entries are arranged by subject, and subarranged by issuing agencies. Holdings of periodicals are noted. No annotation other than translation of titles. No index.

J 60 Sjahrial-Pumuntjak, Rusina. *Daftar penerbitan pemerintah Republik Indonesia* (List of government publications of the

Republic of Indonesia). Djakarta, Perpustakaan Sedjarah Politik dan Sosial, 1964. 56 p.
1,159 books and periodicals, almost entirely in Indonesian are arranged by department. Author index.

J 61 Lembaga Ilmu Pengetahuan Indonesia. Pusat Dokumentasi Ilmiah Nasional (Indonesian National Scientific Documentation Center. Indonesian Institute of Sciences). *Bibliografi penerbitan badan badan pemerintah Indonesia, 1950–1969* (Bibliography of official publications of the Indonesian government, 1950–1969). Djakarta, 1971. 412 p.
Nearly 5,000 titles are arranged by department and by subdivisions, with locations in official libraries. The most complete listing available of Indonesian official publications. Classified publications have been included with the permission of the government.

J 62 Kantor Bibliografi Nasional (Office of National Bibliography). *Bibliografi penerbitan pemerintah Indonesia, 1945–1972* (Bibliography of Indonesian official publications, 1945–1972). Jakarta, 1973. 483 p.
4,298 titles of serial and monograph official publications are arranged by department and subarranged by major departmental divisions. Serials are listed with open entry, not issue by issue. No annotations, locations or index.

J 63 Kantor Bibliografi Nasional (Office of National Bibliography). *Penerbitan pemerintah Indonesia* Manual of Indonesian government publications. Jakarta, 1973. 87 p.
A list of publications arranged by department, and subarranged by departmental divisions. Index of titles.

Periodicals and Newspapers

J 64 Nunn, G. Raymond. *Indonesian newspapers, an international union list*. Taipei, Chinese Materials and Research Aids Service Center, 1971. 131 p. (Occasional series no. 14).
Holdings for approximately 1,000 newspapers published in Indonesia, and located in the Central Museum Library in Djakarta, in the Koninklijke Bibliotheek in The Hague, in the Koninklijk Instituut voor de Tropen Library in Amsterdam, and in major libraries in the United States. Index to newspaper titles.

J 65 *Daftar majallah dan surat kabar Indonesia* (Directory of Indonesian periodicals and newspapers). Jakarta, 1972. 145 p.
Gives directory information for some 650 current Indonesian periodicals and newspapers. Titles are arranged by localities. Subject and title indexes.

J 66 Museum Pusat (Central Museum). *Katalogus surat-kabar, 1810–1973* (Catalogue of newspapers, 1810–1973). Djakarta, Koleksi Perpustakaan Museum Pusat, 1973, 131 p.

1,261 newspapers are arranged alphabetically by title, with frequency and holdings of the Central Museum Library. This represents one of the most extensive collections of Indonesian newspapers in the world.

INDEXES

J 67 *Indonesian abstracts, containing abstracts of scientific articles appearing in Indonesia*, 1959–. Djakarta, Madjelis Ilmu Pengetahuan Indonesia (Council for Sciences of Indonesia), 1959–.
Each issue contains about 60 abstracts from about 20 Indonesian periodicals, covering all fields of science. The abstracts are in English, and are arranged according to the Universal Decimal Classification. No index. Science is widely interpreted and covers the whole field of knowledge. 1975 last issue noted.

J 68 *Index of Indonesian learned periodicals*, 1960–. Djakarta, Madjelis Ilmu Pengetahuan Indonesia (Council for Sciences of Indonesia), 1961–.
The 1967 issue listed 150 periodicals, and indexed over 454 articles with an emphasis on natural and applied science and the social sciences. The arrangement is by the Universal Decimal Classification. Title index to the periodicals, and author index to the articles. No annotation. First issued with title *Indeks madjalah ilmiah* Indonesian periodicals index. 1974 issue last noted.

J 69 Perpustakaan Sedjarah Politik dan Sosial (Library of Political and Social History). *Press index*. Djakarta, 1969–.
Indexes Djakarta editions of *Berita Yudha, El Bahar, Harian Kami, Nusantara, Operasi,* and *Sinar Harapan*. Arranged by detailed subjects. Personal name index and short subject index. Frequency varies, quarterly or semi-annual. Last issue seen for second quarter 1972.

J 70 Nagelkerke, G. A. *Bibliographisch overzicht uit periodieken over Indonesie* Bibliographical survey based on periodicals on Indonesia, 1930–1945. Leiden, Bibliotheek Koninklijk Instituut voor Taall-, Land- en Volkenkunde, 1974. 232 p.
3,159 articles indexed from 30 periodicals arranged by major geographical divisions of Indonesia. Subject index.

Theses

J 71 Kartosedono, Soekarman and Darlis Ismail. *Bibliografi skripsi beranotasi* (Annotated theses bibliography). Jakarta, Lembaga Perpustakaan Departemen P dan K, 1973. 622 p. (Indonesia, Lembaga Perpustakaan, seri penerbitan).
1,576 theses published from 1968 through 1971 are arranged under 20 disciplines, with annotations. Author and title indexes.

Subject Bibliography

SOCIAL SCIENCES

J 72 Sjahrial-Pamuntjak, Rusina. *Regional bibliography of social science publications, Indonesia*. Djakarta, Ministry of Education and Culture, National Bibliographical Centre, 1955? 65 p.
Lists 594 books and periodical articles in Dutch, English and Indonesian, with an emphasis on the latter, and published from 1945 through 1954. There is an index to authors and subjects, and a list of the 14 principal periodicals indexed. Arranged into 4 major sections.

J 73 Suzuki, Peter. *Critical survey of studies on the anthropology of Nias, Mentawei and Enggano*. 's Gravenhage, M. Nijhoff, 1959. 87 p. (Instituut voor Taal-, Land- en Volkenkunde, Bibliographical series 3).
Some 365 books and periodical articles in Indonesian, English and German. Arranged according to the three cultures, with a section for each. Items inspected by the compiler are annotated.

J 74 Jaspan, M.A. *Social stratification and social mobility in Indonesia, a trend report and annotated bibliography*. Djakarta, Seri Ilmu dan Masjarakat, Gunung Agung, 1959. 76 p.
139 articles, of which over half are in Indonesian, are arranged under six major categories showing aspects of social structure. 100 entries are annotated fully. The trend report describes the pre- and post-revolutionary periods.

J 75 Kennedy, Raymond. *Bibliography of Indonesian peoples and cultures*, revised and edited by Thomas W. Maretzki and H. Th. Fischer. New Haven, Southeast Asia Studies, Yale University, by arrangement with Human Relations Area Files, 1962. 207 p. (Behaviour science bibliographies).
Over 11,600 books and periodical articles, over half in Dutch, arranged by islands and island groups, then by peoples, tribes or tribal groups and entries are subdivided within these into Dutch and other languages. The emphasis is on anthropology and sociology, but administration, education, economics, history and geography, with some references to botany, zoology, and geology are included. An alphabetical key to islands, peoples, tribal groups and tribes assists in the use of the table of contents. At first books and articles in Yale University Library were marked with an asterisk, but in the revised edition only important items were so marked.

J 76 Hicks, George L. and Geoffrey McNicoll. *The Indonesian economy, 1950–1965, a bibliography*. Detroit, Cellar Bookshop, 1967. 248 p. (Yale University, Southeast Asia studies, Bibliography series no. 9).
1,270 books and periodical articles in Indonesian and English, with Australian and Indian imprints strongly represented, arranged under 27 subjects. The emphasis is on the post-war

situation, but there is some background material. Most entries are annotated. Author and subject indexes.

J 77 Hicks, George L. and Geoffrey McNicoll. *The Indonesian economy, 1950–1967, bibliographic supplement*. Detroit, Cellar Bookshop, 1967. 211 p. (Yale University, Southeast Asia studies, Bibliography series no. 10).

807 books and periodical articles in English and Indonesian supplement and update the authors' *The Indonesian economy, 1950–1965, a bibliography* (J 76). Two-thirds of the materials was published before 1965, and fills out the earlier bibliography. The remaining one-third was published in 1966 and 1967. Author and subject indexes.

J 78 Jankovec, Miloslav. *Zahranicni politika Indoneske republiky, 1945–1967, svazek III, bibliografie vyrbranych documentu.* Praha, Ustav pro mezinarodni politiku a ekonomii, 1968? 103 p.

952 entries in English and Indonesian for books, newspapers and periodical articles, arranged in classified order. No index or annotations.

J 79 Pusat Dokumentasi Ilmiah Nasional (Indonesian National Scientific Documentation Center). *Food in Indonesia, a bibliography, 1952–1967.* Djakarta, 1968. 104 p.

481 books and articles mostly in English and Indonesian and found in five major Indonesian libraries are arranged by subject. No annotations. Author index. Continues *Nutrition bibliography of Indonesia* (Honolulu, Hawaii University Press, 1955) with some 360 periodical articles, fully annotated and covering period to 1950.

J 80 The, Liang Gie. *Bibliografi ilmu administrasi dalam bahasa Indonesia* (Bibliography on administration in Indonesia). Jogjakarta, Balai Pembinaan Administrasi Universitas Gadjah Mada, 1968. 220 p.

Some 1,000 books, articles and reports, mostly in Indonesian, are arranged in detailed subject order. No index.

J 81 McNicoll, Geoffrey. *Research in Indonesian demography, a bibliographic essay.* Honolulu, East-West Center, 1970. 50 p. (Working Papers of the East-West Population Institute, Paper no. 6).

133 books and articles related to Indonesian population, about one-half being published in England, the United States and Australia. The bibliography is appended to a bibliographical essay.

J 82 Lembaga Penelitian Hukum dan Kriminologi. Universitas Padjadjaran (Institute of Legal and Criminological Research. Padjadjaran University). *Bibliografi hukum Indonesia, 1945–1971, daftar literatur hukum dalam bahasa Indonesia terbitan tahun 1945 S/D 1970* (Bibliography of Indonesian law, a list of the literature on law published in Indonesian from 1945 through 1970). Bandung, 1971. 352 p.

Some 5,000 books, articles and theses are arranged in a detailed subject order. Mostly in Indonesian.

J 83 Singaribum, Masri. *The population of Indonesia, a bibliography, 1930–1972*. Jogjakarta, Institute of Population Studies, Gadjah Mada University, 1974. 175 p.
A revision of the author's *The population of Indonesia, 1930–1968, a bibliography* (London, 1969), and including mention of the preliminary findings of the 1971 census. Some 1,400 entries for books, articles and reports, are arranged under 13 major subject and form headings. No annotations. Author index.

J 84 Siregar, Muchtaruddin. *Bibliografi masalah pengangkutan di Indonesia* (Bibliography on transportation in Indonesia). Jakarta, Lembaga Ekonomi dan Kemasyarakatan Nasional, Lembaga Ilmu Pengetahuan Indonesia, 1974. 53 leaves.
Some 500 books, articles and reports in English and Indonesia are arranged under general and five major subject headings. No index or annotations.

J 85 Koentjaraningrat, Raden Mas. *Anthropology in Indonesia, a bibliographical review*. The Hague, Nijhoff, 1975. 343 p. (Instituut voor Taal-, Land- en Volkenkunde, Bibliographical series 8).
A major survey of Indonesian anthropology is followed by an 85-page bibliography of over 900 books and articles arranged by author.

LANGUAGE AND LITERATURE

J 86 Voorhoeve, Petrus. *Critical survey of studies on the languages of Sumatra*. 's Gravenhage, M. Nijhoff, 1955. 55 p. (Instituut voor Taal-, Land- en Volkenkunde, Bibliographical series 1).
205 books and periodical articles are noted in the introduction to the linguistics and history of the languages of Sumatra, and at the end of the survey.

J 87 Cense, Ant. Abr. and E. M. Uhlenbeck. *Critical survey of studies on the languages of Borneo*. 's Gravenhage, M. Nijhoff, 1958. 82 p. (Instituut voor Taal-, Land- en Volkenkunde, Bibliographical series 2).
323 books and periodical articles are listed in the survey essay.

J 88 Teeuw, A. *Critical survey of studies on Malay and Bahasa Indonesia*. 's Gravenhage, M. Nijhoff, 1961. 82 p. (Instituut voor Taal-, Land- en Volkenkunde, Bibliographical series 5).
Some 1,000 books and periodical articles are listed by alphabetical author order. They serve as notes to the survey essay on the history, linguistics, and literature of the two languages and on the influence of the West.

J 89 Danandjaja, James. *An annotated bibliography of Javanese folklore*. Berkeley, University of California Press, 1972. 162 p.

(Centre for South and Southeast Asia Studies, Occasional papers no. 9).
Some 800 entries for books and articles arranged in subject groups, with annotation for each entry. Dutch is the major language represented. Author index.

J 90 Lembaga Bahasa Nasional (National Language Institute). *Almanak sastra Indonesia, daftar pustaka* (Bibliography on Indonesian literature). Djakarta, 1972. 233 p. (Bahasa dan Kesusastraan seri chusus no. 16).
Divided into two major sections, on classical and on modern literature, and subdivided by the type of literature or critical works. No annotations or index. Some 1,200 books and articles in the first section, and 1,100 in the second.

HISTORY

J 91 Van de Veur, Paul W. *The Eurasians of Indonesia, a political historical bibliography*. Ithaca, Cornell University, 1971. 115 p. (Southeast Asia Program, Modern Indonesia Project, Bibliography series).
964 entries are arranged in five major sections, for bibliographies and reference works, government documents, books and pamphlets, articles, and other sources. Most of the entries are in Dutch or Indonesian. Author and subject indexes.

J 92 Naim, Asma M. *Bibliografi Minangkabau, a preliminary edition*. Singapore, 1973. 253 p.
Over 4,000 books, articles, theses and dissertations are arranged in 15 major subject areas. No annotations. Author index.

J 93 Nagelkerke, G. A. *A selected bibliography of the Chinese in Indonesia, 1740–1974*. Leyden, Royal Institute of Linguistics and Anthropology, 1975. 89 p.
748 entries for books and articles from newspapers, periodicals, mostly in Dutch and found in the Institute's Library. Index.

K. LAOS

The Kingdom of Laos became a French protectorate in 1893, and formed part of French Indochina. Laos gained its full independence again in 1956.

HANDBOOKS

K1 Berval, Rene de. *Kingdom of Laos.* Saigon, France-Asie, 1959. 506 p.
An encyclopedic survey of the geography, history, arts, ethnography, religion, language and literature, folklore, education, economy and external relations of Laos, with many illustrations and a bibliography of some 500 books and articles, almost entirely in French. No index.

K2 American University, Washington, D.C. Foreign Area Studies. *Area handbook for Laos.* Washington, U.S. Government Printing Office, 1972. 337 p.
A survey of social, political and economic affairs and of national security for Laos, Bibliography, glossary and index. Research completed June 1971. Replaces 1967 edition.

DICTIONARIES

K3 Marcus, Russell. *English-Lao, Lao-English dictionary.* Bangkok, 1968. 415 p. Distributed by Tuttle, Rutland.
Contains some 10,000 English words with Lao equivalents, and 9,000 Lao words with English equivalents. No examples of usage.

K4 Kerr, Allen D. *Lao-English dictionary.* Washington, Catholic University of America Press, 1972. 2v
Some 25,000 entries, with examples of usage, and representing a thorough study of existing dictionaries, and 12 years research, ten of which were spent in Laos. Based on the Vientiane dialect.

BIOGRAPHICAL DICTIONARY

K5 Sithibourn, Sithat. *Biographies des personnalities du Royaume d' Laos.* Vientiane, Lao Presse, 1960. 1v. (unpaged).
75 full biographies, with portraits, giving positions held education and decorations, 74 pages.

GAZETTEER

K6 U.S. Board on Geographical Names. *Laos* . . . Washington, U.S. Government Printing Office. 1973. 348 p. (Gazetteer no. 69).
21,000 place and feature names, together with their classification and longitude and latitude. Second edition, revision of 1962 edition.

STATISTICS

K7 Laos (Kingdom). Ministere du Plan et de la Cooperation. Service national de la statistique. *Bulletin de statistiques*. Vientiane, 1951–.
Statistical tables for trade, transport, finance, industry and population. Quarterly issues noted for 1958, 1961 and 1968. Former title *Bulletin de statistiques du Laos. Annuaire statistique du Laos 1953/7* published in 1961, and noted as fourth in series which commenced in 1951. Errors in compilation and transcription noted.

K8 Laos (Kingdom). Bureau de la Statistique. *Population officiel du Laos*. Vientiane, 1956–9. 9v.
Results are available for the provinces of Vientiane (1958), Champassak (1958), Luang Prabang (1958), and Khammouane (1959). *Estimation de la population dans le circonscription administrative* have been issued for the provinces of Attopeu (1956), Saravane (1956), Sayaboury (1958), Savannakhet (1956), and Xg Khouang (1958).

K9 Halpern, Joel Martin. *Population statistics and associated data*. Los Angeles, University of California, Laos Project, 1961. 59 p.
76 tables on population, rate of population growth, death rates, and distribution of ethnic groups, compileed from 34 periodicals and books, mostly in English, and published from 1900 to 1960. Each table is footnoted and annotated with comments by the author on its reliability.

K10 *Population statistics on Laos, and names, locations of the country's administrative divisions. December 1968*. n.p., n.d. 12 1.
States number of villages in each district, and lists districts and istrict headquarters by province. Population estimated by province.

K11 Butler, Lucius. *Lao educational statistics*. Vientiane, University of Hawaii Contract Team, 1973. 172p.
Statistical tables with notes translated from the French originals in Laos. A detailed account distributed for checking purposes only, but valuable in view of the general absence of statistics for Laos.

BIBLIOGRAPHY

K12 Lafont, Pierre Bernard. *Bibliographie du Laos.* Paris, Ecole francaise d'Extreme Orient, 1964–78. 2 v. (Publications de l'Ecole francaise d'Extreme Orient v.50).
The first volume includes 1,867 books and periodical articles published from 1800 to 1962, mostly in French. There are, however, a few English and German titles, and a short section with Laotian, Vietnamese, Thai and Russian entries. 39 periodicals were surveyed. The bibliography is arranged by broad subjects, and one-sixth of the entries are annotated.
The second volume covers materials published from 1962–75 and includes 2931 entries for reports, books and periodical articles in a latin script, 99 newspapers and periodicals, 710 entries in Lao, 226 in Vietnamese, 41 in Thai and 79 in Russian. Author index.

K13 Laos (Kingdom). Bibliotheque Nationale. *Bibliographie Nationale, 1968.* Vientiane, 1969? 97p.
The first volume published by the National Library, but the third sponsored by the Asia Foundation. Separate sections for subject, author and title. Dewey Decimal Classification numbers given. 360 titles are noted. In Lao.

K14 Halpern, Joel Martin and James A. Hafner. *A preliminary and partial bibliography of miscellaneous research materials on Laos.* Bruxelles, Centre d'Etude du Sud-Est Asiatique et de l'Extreme Orient, 1971. 113 p. (Courrier de l'Extreme Orient III).
Nearly three-quarters of the entries relate to Laos, numbering some 700 items, listing books, reports, and periodical articles, mostly in English. Arrangement is under 23 subjects. The approach of this bibliography with contemporary and social scientific emphasis contrasts with Pierre Bernard Lafont *Bibliographie du Laos* (K 12), which is historical and anthropological and covers mostly the French literature.

K15 Butler, Lucius. *Laos education documents, a preliminary bibliography of documents in English concerning education in Laos.* Honolulu, University of Hawaii, College of Education, 1971. 13 p.
Notes some 250 entries for documents and books. No annotations or index.

K16 Mogenet, Luc. *Bibliographie complementaire du Laos 1962–1973.* Vientiane, Bibliotheque Nationale, 1973. 85 p.
Continues the work of Pierre Bernard Lafont *Bibliographie du Laos* (K 12) and includes 480 books and articles, arranged alphabetically by author, and 150 anonymous works, arranged by date of publication.

L. MALAYSIA
(Including SINGAPORE)

Britain established a foothold in Malaya at Penang in 1786, at Malacca in 1795, and at Singapore in 1819. These three areas became the Straits Settlements, severing their connection with India in 1867. In 1895 the four States of Negri Sembilan, Pahang, Perak and Selangor became the Federated Malay States with their capital at Kuala Lumpur. In 1909 the States of Kedah, Kelantan, Perlis and Trengganu were associated with the other Malay States. Johore did not have its status defined until 1914. The Malayan Union was established in 1946, but was replaced by the Federation of Malaya in 1948, which became independent in 1957. Singapore maintained a separate status as a Crown colony. In 1963 Malaysia was established, and included the former Federation of Malaya, Singapore, Sabah and Sarawak. Brunei remained independent. Singapore became an independent state in 1965.

HANDBOOKS

L 1 American University, Washington, D.C. Foreign Area Studies. *Area handbook for Malaysia*. Washington, U.S. Government Printing Office, 1977. 454 p.
Divided into four sections, on social, political and economic affairs, and on national security, preceded by a short summary statement. Bibliography and index. Supersedes 1970 edition.

L 2 American University, Washington, D.C. Foreign Area Studies. *Area handbook for Singapore*. Washington, U.S. Government Printing Office, 1977. 216 p.
A country summary is followed by a survey of history, social, political and economic affairs, and national security. Bibliography and index. Research completed December 1976.

YEARBOOKS

L 3 *Malaysia yearbook*, 1956–. Kuala Lumpur, Straits Times Press, 1956–.
A reference book similar to the *World almanac*, but covering Malaysia only. Almost all subjects, except science and literature, are included. Arranged in topical order, with the table of contents arranged alphabetically to serve as an index. Among the special features are maps of the States of Malaysia, a who's who of government officials, and a directory of national organizations.

Title to 1963 *Federation of Malaya yearbook*. 1972 issue does not include a who's who of government officials.

L 4 Malaysia. *Official yearbook*, 1961–. Kuala Lumpur, Ministry of Information and Broadcasting, 1961–.
In contrast to the *Malaysia yearbook* (L 3), this annual stresses economic and political affairs, with less materials on religion and customs. Divided into 22 chapters, with a detailed table of contents. Appendices contain valuable information on the government, statistics and the constitution. 1976 issue last noted.

L 5 *Singapore*, 1964–. Singapore, 1964–.
1969 issue, published 1970, surveys 1969 developments in political, social, economic, cultural, defence, science and health affairs. Continues *Singapore yearbook*, 1964–8. No issue for 1970. 1976 latest issue seen.

DICTIONARIES

L 6 Winstedt, Richard Olof. *An English-Malay dictionary (roman character)*. Singapore, Kelly and Walsh, 1951. 524 p.
Based on Richard James Wilkinson *Malay-English dictionary* (L 7), and is widely used, but is out of date.

L 7 Wilkinson, Richard James. *A Malay-English dictionary (romanized)*. London, Macmillan, 1957. 2 v.
Represents Malay usage throughout Western Malaysia, but now out of date. Reprint of the original edition, published 1932.

L 8 Iskandar, Tenku. *Kamus dewan*. Kuala Lumpur, Dewan Bahasa dan Pustaka, 1970. 1,352 p.
An authoritative and up-to-date Malay-Malay dictionary, giving examples of usage.

BIOGRAPHICAL DICTIONARY

L 9 *Who's who in Malaysia and guide to Singapore*. Kuala Lumpur, J. Victor Morais, 1956–.
In two parts: Malaysia and Singapore. Biographical information is short, includes addresses, but no publications. Many entries have portraits. Changes of title: *The leaders of Malaya and who's who* from 1956–62 and *Who's who in Malaysia* from 1963–79. 1977–8 latest issue seen.

DIRECTORIES

L 10 *Straits Times directory of Malaysia*, 1949–. Singapore, Straits Times, 1949–.

This directory emphasizes industry and business, but schools, churches, and professional societies are also covered, divided into nine regions, including Singapore, Sabah, Sarawak, Brunei, and Bangkok, and under each region entries are arranged alphabetically by firm. There is a subject directory and an alphabetical index to companies, agencies and individuals. Title to 1964 *Straits Times directory of Singapore and Malaya.* 1972 last issue noted. Continued in part by *New Straits Times Directory of Malaysia*, 1975 and *Straits Times Directory of Singapore*, 1974–. 1977/8 issue of *New Straits Times Directory of Malaysia* seen.

L 11 Sutter, John Orval. *Scientific facilities and information services of the Federation of Malaya and the State of Singapore.* Honolulu, published for the National Science Foundation by the Pacific Science Information Center, 1961. 43 p.
The first section deals with the history, culture and economy of the two countries. The second consists of a number of appendices, giving information on the facilities of the University of Malaya, listing museums, research institutions and laboratories. The third appendix lists 44 scientific journals published in Malaya and Singapore of 1959. There is an excellent subject, author and title index.

L 12 Keeth, Kent H. *A directory of libraries in Malaysia.* Kuala Lumpur, University of Malaya Library, 1965. 163 p.
Information is based on 66 replies to a questionnaire sent to 93 libraries in Malaysia and Singapore. Library collections, administration, staff, facilities, and publications are noted. Subject index to library collections.

L 13 Library Association of Singapore. *Directory of libraries in Singapore.* Singapore, 1975. 166 p.
Lists 138 educational, government, public and special libraries in Singapore. Revision of 1969 edition. Actually published in 1971.

ATLAS

L 14 Philip (George) and Son. *Philip's senior atlas for Malaysia and Singapore*, ninth edition. London, 1967. 64 p.
A world atlas, but one-third consisting of maps on Malaysia and Singapore, including large-scale maps of States and cities.

GAZETTEER

L 15 U.S. Office of Geography. *Malaysia, Singapore and Brunei.* Washington, U.S. Government Printing Office, 1970. 1,014 p. (U.S. Board on Geographic Names, Gazetteer no. 10).

62,000 names for places and features, arranged by political division under West Malaysia, Singapore, Sabah, Sarawak and Brunei. Longitude and latitude given for each name. Supersedes 1955 edition.

CENSUS

L 16 Straits Settlements. *A report on the 1931 census* . . . London, Crown Agents for the Colonies, 1932. 389 p.
One of a series of decennial census reports noted from 1901. This issue covers the Straits Settlements, the Federated and Unfederated Malay States, including Brunei. Arranged by subjects with the table of contents serving as an index to both the main body of the report and the tables.

L 17 Malaya (Federation). *A report on the 1947 census of population* . . . London, Crown Agents for the Colonies, 1949. 597 p.
The first part of the report discusses the census, while the second part consists of 127 tables. The distribution of population is also shown on maps. Among the appendices are population by community as recorded in past censuses, results of Japanese census taking, classification of population, classification of industries, and Malayan migration statistics for the period 1931–41.

L 18 Malaya (Federation). Department of Statistics. *Population census*, 1957. Kuala Lumpur, 1957–60. 14 v.
The first volume gives the distribution of the population of the Federation by race and sex for the States, districts, etc. The last two volumes also cover the Federation as a whole, with comments on the characteristics of the population and the changes that have taken place since 1947. The remaining volumes are each concerned with a single state, and give distribution of population by race and sex, and show age, place of birth, literacy, occupation, industry, etc.

L 19 Malaysia. Jabatan Perangkaan Malaysia (Department of Statistics Malaysia). *Banchi pendudok dan perumahan Malaysia, 1970* (Population and housing census of Malaysia, 1970). Kuala Lumpur, 1971. 26 v.
In two series, the first covers general housing tables divided by States, the second also covers general housing, with town and village breakdown.

STATISTICS

L 20 Malaya (Federation). Department of Statistics. *Malayan yearbook*, 1935–. Singapore, 1935–.
Arranged by subjects and divided by chapters, with an index

giving subject, chapter and page. A comprehensive one-volume guide on Malaya up to the end of the year prior to publication. Superseded the *Statistical summary* issued by the same department. 1939 issue last noted.

L 21 Singapore. Department of Statistics. *Monthly digest of statistics*. Singapore, 1946–.
Includes statistics for the whole of Malaya until January 1962.

L 22 Malaysia. Department of Statistics. *Annual bulletin of statistics, 1964–* Kuala Lumpur, 1965?–.
Based on the *Monthly statistical bulletin of West Malaysia* and the *Annual bulletin of statistics issued by Sabah and Sarawak*. The most comprehensive report available, but lacking information owing to some States' failure to submit statistics.

L 23 *Yearbook of statistics, Singapore*. Singapore, Chief Statistician, Department of Statistics.
The eighth edition, for 1975/6 surveys statistics from 1965 through 1975, and covers climate, demography, employment, agriculture, industrial production, utilities, housing, trade, transport, finance, education and health.

BIBLIOGRAPHY

L 24 Cheeseman, Harold R. *Bibliography of Malaya, being a classified list of books wholly or partly relating to the Federation of Malaya and Singapore*. New York, Longmans, 1959. 234 p.
A largely unannotated list of some 1,000 books and periodical articles in English arranged by subjects, including history, law, economics, peoples of Malaya, lists of newspapers and periodicals, religion, etc. Author index.

L 25 Tregonning, Kennedy G. *Malaysian historical sources, a series of essays on historical materials mainly in Malaysia and on Malaysia*. Singapore, University of Singapore, 1962. 130 p.
Bibliographical essays, with particular emphasis on early sources, archives and newspapers. No index.

L 26 Lim, Beda. 'Malaya, a background bibliography'. *Journal of the Malayan Branch of the Royal Asiatic Society*, v. 35, parts 2–3, 1962, pp. 1–199.
Some 3,400 books and periodical articles with little annotation and mostly in English, on the Federation of Malaya, the States of Singapore and Brunei, and the Colonies of Sarawak and North Borneo, and covering the period from the earliest Western accounts through 1956. Items are arranged alphabetically by author under eight main subject divisions, including bibliographies, description, history, government, and economic conditions. Materials on technical and scientific subjects are excluded, and also materials in Malay and other languages not using a romanized script. This bibliography is based on the

resources of the National Library of Australia. Published as a separate.

L 27 Cotter, Conrad Patrick. *Bibliography of English-language sources on human ecology, Eastern Malaysia and Brunei.* Honolulu, University of Hawaii, Department of Asian Studies, 1965. 2 v.

Over 7,300 periodical articles and books in English cover Sarawak, Sabah, Labuan and Brunei from the first Western accounts to 1964. In spite of its size it is still not claimed to be comprehensive, but it is easily the fullest bibliography of its kind, with entries arranged in alphabetical order by author and numbered. These numbers are given under a series of broad subjects in an index, but the size of the subjects makes the arrangement unwieldly. Much of the material listed is very difficult to secure. There is some annotation and library locations are also stated. Items not examined are indicated. The appendix contains a list of 1,114 papers of the British North Borneo Chartered Company. The much more limited University of Chicago *Bibliography of North Borneo* (New Haven, Human Relations Area Files, 1956), which lists only 125 items, is still useful since it is introductory and its entries are annotated.

L 28 Malaysia, Arkib Negara Malaysia, *Bibliografi regarea Malaysia* 1967– Malaysian national bibliography, 1967–. Kuala Lumpur, 1969–.

The first issue includes some 700 books and pamphlets whether published for sale or not, official publications, maps and music. A classified section, arranged by the Dewey Decimal Classification, is followed by an author and title index. 1975 issue published 1976. From 1975 issued quarterly as well as annually. 1977 issue seen.

L 29 University of Singapore. Library. *Catalogue of the Singapore/Malaysia collection.* Volume 1: Boston, G. K. Hall, 1968. Volume 2: Singapore, Singapore University Press, 1974.

Lists some 10,600 titles, mostly in English, referring to Singapore and Malaysia arranged in two sequences, the first according to a modified Library of Congress classification, and the second by author and title. The second volume covers 1968–72.

L 30 Singapore (City). National Library. *Singapore national bibliography*, 1967–. Singapore, 1969–.

Lists some 900 commercial and official publications and publications not for sale, and arranges these by a modified Dewey Decimal Classification. Author, title and subject index. 1976 issue published. Issued quarterly from 1977, with annual volume projected.

L 31 *Daftar buku2 terbitan Malaysia* (List of books published in Malaysia). Kuala Lumpur, Penerbitan Pustaka Antara, 1972. 390 p.

Some 2,000 books, published from 1960–71 and in Bahasa

Melayu, are arranged by author, and then by title. Prices given. Cover title *Bibliografi buku-buku Melayu yang diterbitkan di Malaysia, Singapura dan Brunei* (Bibliography of books in Malay published in Malaysia, Singapore and Brunei).

L 32 Tong, Sit Chee. *Bibliography of Penang*. Pulau Pinang, Perpustakaan Universiti Sains Malaysia, 1974. Unpaged.
Lists 1,311 items, including books, articles, and official publications on Penang. Unfortunately, far from comprehensive.

L 33 Ng, Aileen. *Books about Singapore, 1975*. Singapore, National Library, Reference Services Division, 1975. 71 p.
503 books and periodicals, arranged under broad subject headings, and each with a short annotation. All items are in the National Library. Author index.

Official Publications

L 34 Malaysia. National Archives. *Senarai penerimaan* (Accessions list, 1957–1967). Kuala Lumpur, Arkib Negara Malaysia, 1969?. 185 p.
Primarily a collection of records, but includes information on Malaysian and Singapore official publications held by the National Archives.

L 35 Roff, Margaret. *Official publications of Malaysia, Singapore and Brunei in New York libraries.* New York, Columbia University, Southern Asia Institute, 1971. 45 p. (Occasional bibliographic papers no. 1).
Based mainly on the holdings of the New York Public Library but great pains have been taken to go beyond the official catalogue record to more accurately note holdings.

L 36 *Majalah kini Malaysia, kerajaan* Current Malaysian serials, Government. Kuala Lumpur, Perpustakaan Negara Malaysia. 1974. 45 p.
Gives holdings and bibliographical information for 438 current official serials held by the National Library of Malaysia, and brings together and complements the information in the Malaysian national bibliography (L 28). Appendix has valuable list of department names in English, with Malay equivalents.

Periodicals and Newspapers

L 37 Lim, Patricia Pui Huen (Wang). *Newspapers published in the Malaysian area, with a union list of local holdings*. Singapore, Institute of Southeast Asian Studies, 1970. Pp. 157–98. (Occasional paper no. 2).
Divided into two sections, with 375 newspapers listed for Western Malaysia and Singapore and 70 for Eastern Malaysia and Brunei. In each section newspapers are subdivided by language, and arranged alphabetically. Lists all newspapers known to have been

published in the area, with holdings for major libraries, and for the British Museum, when local holdings cannot be located.

L 38 Roff, William R. *Bibliography of Malay and Arabic periodicals published in the Straits Settlement and Peninsular Malay States, 1876–1941.* London, Oxford University Press, 1972. 73 p.
Lists 197 newspapers and periodicals with holdings and locations, where known. Valuable introduction to the place of this literature in the intellectual history of Malaysia. Revision of the 1961 edition.

L 39 Ahmad, A. M. Iskandar Haji. *Persuratakhabaran Melayu, 1876–1968* (Newspapers in Malaysia, 1876–1968). Kuala Lumpur, Dewan Bahasa dan Pustaka, 1973. 190 p.
434 titles of newspapers and periodicals published in Malay, and 43 titles published in Malay and other languages, and issued in peninsular Malaysia and Singapore, are arranged by major chronological periods. For each entry there are annotations and publishing history. Continues William R. Roff *Bibliography of Malay and Arabic periodicals . . . 1876–1941* (L 38). By no means a comprehensive list. Index to personal names and titles.

L 40 Singapore (City). National Library. *Singapore periodicals index, 1969/70–*. Singapore, 1974–.
1971/2 issue, published in 1977, indexes 88 Singapore and 2 Brunei periodicals in Malay, Chinese and English, published during 1971 and 1972. Tamil and Jawi periodicals excluded. 3,477 entries are arranged by subject. Author and subject indexes Character index to Chinese names. Continues in part *Indeks majallah kini Malaysia Singapore dan Brunei, 1967–8*. 1973–4 issue seen.

L 41 Malaysia. Perpustakaan Negara Malaysia. *Indeks majalah Malaysia, 1973–* Malaysian periodicals index, 1973–. Kuala Lumpur, 1974–.
The 1975 issue, published in 1976, covers 95 Malaysian periodicals published in 1975, and in Chinese, Malay and English. In two sections, the first arranged by the Dewey Decimal Classification, and the second by author and title. Alphabetical index to subjects. Continues in part *Indeks majallah kini Malaysia, Singapore dan Brunei, 1967–8*. 1976 issue published 1977 seen.

L 42 *Majalah kini Malaysia, bukan kerajaan* Current Malaysian serials, non-government. Kuala Lumpur, Perpustakaan Negara Malaysia, 1976. 57 p.
Over 1,000 newspapers, including annuals and newspapers, are arranged in alphabetical order. Complements the information in the Malaysian national bibliography (L 28).

Theses and Dissertations

L 42a Fan, Kok-sim. *Dissertation materials in the University of Malaya*

Library, revised edition. Kuala Lumpur, University of Malaya Library, 1977. 223 p.
3,265 dissertations, theses and academic exercises in a detailed subject arrangement, including dissertations acquired outside Malaysia. Author and subject indexes. Revisions of 1974 edition.

L 42b University of Singapore. Library. Reference Department. *Dissertations, theses and academic exercises, 1947–1976.* Singapore, University of Singapore Library, 1977. 341 p.
Lists 690 masters' theses and doctoral dissertations arranged by subject field, and then by year, and 2,500 undergraduate academic exercises. Author and subject indexes.

Subject Bibliography

SOCIAL SCIENCES

L 43 Great Britain. Colonial Office. *An annotated bibliography on land tenure in the British and British protected territories in South East Asia and the Pacific*. London, Her Majesty's Stationery Office, 1952. 164 p.
Includes only material available in the United Kingdom and in English. Compiled from 1947 to 1950, and arranged geographically, further subdivided into legal sources, legislative proceedings, official statements and reports, and special studies.

L 44 Tilman, Robert O. and Peter L. Burns. *A guide to British library holdings of government publications relating to Malaysia in the field of the social sciences.* N.p., n.d. 67 l.
A preliminary working draft for limited circulation, listing some 469 items in nine libraries in London. It is arranged geographically then subarranged by subject. Includes annual reports and laws. All items are in English. No annotations.

L 45 Malaya (Federation). Division of Agriculture. *Publications, 1.* Kuala Lumpur, 1962. 139 p.
Index to the *Agricultural bulletin* of Straits and Federated Malay States, classified list of principal original articles in the *Agricultural bulletin,* and list of publications of the Department of Agriculture, Federation of Malaya.

L 46 Wang, Chen hsiu chin. *Education in Malaysia, a bibliography.* Singapore, University of Singapore Libraries, Reference Department, 1964. 35 p.
Arranged by country (Malaya, Sabah, Sarawak and Singapore) and then by type of education, and includes some 400 books, articles and reports. No annotations or index.

L 47 Challis, Joyce. *Annotated bibliography of economic and social material in Singapore, Part I, government publications.* Singapore, Economic Research Centre, University of Singapore, 1967. 78 p. (Research bibliography series no. 1).
Approximately 150 series and reports relating primarily to

Singapore and published from 1946, located in the University of Singapore Library, the Economic Research Centre special collection, the National Library, and libraries of government departments. Extensive annotations. Second edition 1969.

L 48 Challis, Joyce. *Annotated bibliography of economic and social material West Malaysia, part I, government publications.* Singapore, Economic Research Centre, University of Singapore, 1968. 152 p. (Research bibliography series no. 2).
Notes some 450 publications, most with full annotations, organized under 12 major headings, with further subdivision. Most entries published in Kuala Lumpur.

L 49 Challis, Joyce. *Annotated bibliography of economic and social materials in Sabah (North Borneo) and Sarawak, part I, government publications.* Singapore, Economic Research Centre, University of Singapore, 1969. 29 p. (Research bibliography series no. 4).
Some 90 publications are noted under ten headings each for Sabah and Sarawak.

L 50 Challis, Joyce. *Annotated bibliography of economic and social materials in Singapore and West Malaysia, non-government publications.* Singapore, Economic Research Centre, University of Singapore, 1969. 241 p. (Research bibliography series no. 3).
Some 1,200 publications are listed under 11 major headings, of which 10 are further subdivided. Entries are annotated. Author index.

L 51 *Development, a selected and annotated bibliography.* Kuala Lumpur, Malaysian Centre for Development Studies, Prime Minister's Staff, 1971? Annual?
Official and other reports, theses and dissertations, with annotations in English, or occasionally in Bahasa Melayu.

L 52 Yeh, Stephen H. K. and Margaret W. N. Leong. *Annotated urban bibliography of Singapore.* Singapore, Statistics and Research Department, Housing and Development Board and Economic Research Centre, University of Singapore, 1972. 94 p.
Some 300 articles and reports are arranged by subject and fully annotated.

L 53 Lim, Lena U Wen. *Physical planning in Singapore and Malaysia.* Singapore, Design Partnership, 1972. 137 p.
1,419 books, periodicals, articles and reports in English and published from 1945 to 1971 are arranged by major subjects. Author index.

L 54 Saw, Swee Hock. *A bibliography of the demography of Malaysia and Brunei.* Singapore, University Education Press, 1975. 103 p.
644 books, reports and articles in English are arranged by subject. No annotations. Author index.

L 55 Van Niel, Eloise and Yeoh Hoong Kheng. *Guide to reference sources on industrial development in Malaysia.* Pulau Pinang, MIDAS Unit, Universiti Sains Malaysia Library, 1976. 46 p.

122 entries listing annual reports, bibliographies, dictionaries and glossaries, handbooks, periodicals, registers and directories, statistics and yearbooks, and emphasizing current material.

L 56 Chen, Peter S. J. and Tai Ching-Ling. *Social development in Singapore, a selected bibliography.* Singapore, Chopmen Enterprises, 1976. 74 p.
662 numbered entries in English on social development in Singapore, including monographs, articles, dissertations, theses, papers, reports and periodicals. Entries are listed under 11 headings. No annotations. Author index.

LITERATURE

L 57 Goh, Thean Chye. *Modern Chinese literature in Malaysia and Singapore, a classified bibliography of books in Chinese.* Kuala Lumpur, University of Malaya Chinese Department, 1975. 354 p.
Entries include poetry, songs, essays, fiction, collections and criticism, and cover period from 1934 to 1975. Author index.

HISTORY AND GEOGRAPHY

L 58 Pelzer, Karl J. *West Malaysia and Singapore, a selected bibliography.* New Haven, HRAF Press, 1971. 394 p.
Some 4,500 entries for books and periodical articles are arranged in 12 sections, covering periodicals and conference proceedings cited, bibliographies, description, general history, physical geography, man and culture, economy, and Singapore. Author index refers only to the subject division, and not to the page, which is awkward. A revision of Karl Joseph Pelzer *Selected bibliography on the geography of Southeast Asia, part III, Malaya* (New Haven, 1956).

M. PHILIPPINES

The conquest of the Philippines archipelago commenced in 1564 with the Spanish expedition under Legazpi. Spanish rule continued until the 1898 cession of the islands to the United States. In 1946 the Philippines became independent.

ENCYCLOPEDIA AND HANDBOOKS

M 1 *Encyclopedia of the Philippines*, third edition. Manila, E. Floro, 1950–8. 20 v.
Arranged by broad subjects, with separate volumes for literature, biography, commerce and industry, art, education, religion, government and politics, science, history and general information. The last volume lists contents for the whole series. The encyclopedia aims at providing the essentials of Philippine culture, and is written to appeal to businessmen, those in the professions, students and teachers. Actually it is more introductory, and primarily suitable for school use. The contributors cannot be considered as authoritative. A first edition in ten volumes was published in 1935–6. The materials for a second edition were destroyed by fire in 1949, and much of the material in the third edition was copied directly from the first. Indexed in *ASLP Bulletin*, v. 15, no. 3, September 1969. A dated, but valuable encyclopedia survey, *El archipielago Filipino, coleccion de datos geograficos, estadisticos, cronologicos, y cientificos* . . . (1900. 2 v.), has its most important parts translated and included in Senate document 138, 56th Congress, 1st session, United States *Serial set*, no. 3885, v. 2 and 3. The subject matter is arranged in a classified order, with an index to each volume.

M 2 American University, Washington, D.C. Foreign Area Studies. *Area handbook for the Philippines*. Washington, U.S. Government Printing Office, 1976. 458 p.
A country summary is followed by a survey of social, political and economic affairs and national security. Bibliography and glossary of terms. Research completed January 1976. Revision of first edition published 1969.

M 3 Demetrio y Radaza, Francisco. *Directory of Philippine folk beliefs and customs*. Cagayan de Oro City, Xavier University, 1970. 4 v.
Arranged by major topics, notes beliefs and customs, quoting sources or locations.

M 4 Maring, Ester G. and Joel M. Maring. *Historical and cultural dictionary of the Philippines*. Metuchen, Scarecrow Press, 1973. 240 p. (Historical and cultural dictionaries of Asia, no. 3)

Some 1,800 entries refer to Philippine geography, history, economy, government and politics. Short select bibliography.

YEARBOOK

M 5 *Fookien Times yearbook*. Manila, The Fookien Times Yearbook Publishing Co., 1948–
An annual review of developments in the Philippines in the form of articles by authorities. 1976 issue seen.

DICTIONARIES

M 6 *An English-Tagalog dictionary*. Manila, Institute of National Language, 1960. 412 p.
Has some 10,000 entries, and is now being reissued with Jose V. Panganiban as compiler, and with the title *Tesaurong Ingles-Pilipino* (1965–) in mimeograph form.

M 7 Serrano Laktaw, Pedro. *Diccionario Hispano-Tagolog, Tagalog-Hispano*. Madrid, Ediciones Cultura Hispanica, 1965. 3 v. (in 2)
Volume 1 is a reprint of the 1889 edition; Volume 2, in two parts, was originally published in 1914. Regarded as the best Tagalog dictionary.

M 8 Panganiban, Jose V. *Talahulaganang Pilipino-Ingles*. Manila, Surian ng Wikang Pambansa, 1966. 362 p.
A current edition of the *National language-English vocabulary* (Manila, Institute of National Language, 1950) compiled by the director of the institute. This and *An English-Tagalog dictionary* (M 6) are far more complete than any other dictionary available at present. Over 10,000 entries.

BIOGRAPHICAL DICTIONARIES

M 9 Retana y Gamboa, Wenceslao Emilio. *Indice des personas nobles y otras de calidad que han estados en Filipinas desde 1521 hasta 1898*. Madrid, Libraria de Victriano Suarez, 1921. 84 p.
Identifies 789 personalities, giving brief information and some key dates.

M 10 *Who's who in the Philippines, a biographical dictionary of notable living men of the Philippine islands, volume 1*. Manila, McCullough Printing Company, 1937. 175 p.
Some 1,350 persons, including officials, professors, doctors, accountants, and Americans in the Philippines. There appears to be no criteria for the selection. Brief information is given on each,

such as place and date of birth, education, experience and present position. A considerable part is taken up with non-biographical material such as the Constitution of the Philippines.

M 11 Manuel, E. Arsenio. *Dictionary of Philippine biography.* Quezon City, Filipiniana Publications, 1955–70. 2 v.
This first volume contains the results of research completed before World War II and has a complete alphabetical sequence. It contains some 110 bibliographies of varying length, and each refers to a person of some prominence in Philippine history. The second volume, which is in a similar format, represents research completed before and after World War II.

M 12 *Tableau, encyclopedia of distinguished personalities in the Philippines.* Manila, National Souvenir Publications, 1957. 658 p.
565 biographies of contemporary personalities are written in a popular style that sometimes lacks important information. Length of article depends on the prominence of the personality.

M 13 Retizos, Isidro and D. H. Soriano. *Philippine who's who.* Quezon City, Capital Publishing House, 1957. 327 p.
Lists some 400 living residents of the Philippines, mostly Filipinos, compiled from interviews and other sources. Each biography is short, and gives information of place and date of birth, positions held, wife and children, and address. Intended to be issued annually, but the first is believed to be the only issue. Since over half is concerned with biographies of politicians and government officials, it lacks balance.

M 14 University of the Philippines. Library. *U.P. Biographical directory.* Quezon City, 1964. 190 p.
Lists nearly 1,900 present and former members of the academic staff of the University of the Philippines, giving name, present position, date and place of birth, degrees, previous positions, membership in professional organizations, and office and home addresses. No note of publications.

M 15 Garcia, Mauro. *Philippine pseudonyms, aliases, pen names, pet names, screen names and name aberrations.* Manila, UNESCO National Commission of the Philippines, 1965. 156 p. (Bibliographical Society of the Philippines, Occasional papers no. 4).
Some 1,500 forms are given under the form used, with references to the correct form. The second list lists forms used under the correct form, with a useful introduction quoting sources, forms used and reasons for use.

M 16 Valenzuela, Wilfredo P. *Know them, a book of biographies.* Manila, Dotela Publications, 1968. 316 p.
Some 150 contemporary biographies for leading political, business and other leaders of the Philippines. No index.

M 17 Zaide, Gregorio F. *Great Filipinos in history, an epic of Filipino greatness in war and peace.* Manila, Verde Book Stores, 1970. 675 p.
100 full biographies for major figures or groups of figures in

Philippine history, with an appendix containing a short bibliography for each biography.

DIRECTORIES

M 18 *Commercial and trade directory of the Philippines*, 1947–. Manila, Islanders Publishing Co., 1947–
Gives information on Philippine business, industry, trade, population, and the Constitution. It is divided into four parts: the first has a street directory of Manila and lists officials of the Republic, official holidays, labour unions, etc.; the second lists business organizations and professional persons; the third is a classified list of firms; the fourth lists residents arranged alphabetically, including their occupation and address. The 1961 edition included 15,000 firms. There have been a number of changes of title. It was first known as the *Commercial and trade directory of the Philippines*, in 1949 it became the *Commercial directory of the Philippines*, and in 1961 it was finally entitled the *AB Commercial directory of the Philippines* (1963/4 issue latest noted).

M 19 Philippines (Republic). Office of Public Information. *Republic of the Philippines official directory*, 1949–. Manila, 1949–.
Lists Philippine elected and appointed officials, arranging them by departments, and subdividing these by office or bureau. A selective, not a comprehensive listing of officials. No index. 1970 issue last noted.

M 20 Philippines (Republic). National Institute of Science and Technology. Division of Documentation. *Philippine libraries*. Manila, 1961–2. 2 v.
The first volume lists 935 libraries arranged by provinces and then by city, with indexes by place, type of library, and name. The second volume lists the main and branch libraries of 25 Philippine universities.

M 21 *Philippine corporations, financial directory, manufacturing, mining, financial firms*, 1965/6–. Makati, Philippine Economic Development Foundation, 1965–.
1968 edition, published 1969, lists some 1,800 firms arranged by type of activity, with addresses, officers, and financial data for each. Index to firms in each major group.

M 22 Philippines (Republic). Congress. Joint Local Government Reform Commission. *National government agencies, a directory of offices with functions relevant to local government*. Manila, 1971. 1 v. (unpaged)
Over 100 government bureaus are described, with their addresses. Although written for local government, it has much value as a general guide to Philippine central government agencies.

M 23 Dayrit, Marina G. *Directory of libraries in the Philippines.* Quezon City, University of the Philippines Library, 1973. 131 p.
Based on questionnaires sent to 932 libraries, of which 498 replied, and arranged under four main divisions by academic, special, public and government, and other libraries, including a list of extension libraries. An additional 450 'other' libraries are listed by name and their location is given. Index to some 500 librarians' names, and short subject index to libraries.

ATLASES AND GAZETTEERS

M 24 Hendry, Robert S. *Atlas of the Philippines.* Manila, Phil-Asian Publishers, 1959. 228 p.
Some 56 subject and provincial maps. For each provincial map there is a brief description and history, and a short list of places. In spite of the large format, the amount of information given is disappointing. The lack of an index is a major defect. Although very much older, P. Jose Algue *Atlas of the Philippine Islands* (Washington, Government Printing Office, 1900), a reprint of the 1899 *Atlas de Filipinas,* is still useful; it has 30 maps, and over 5,000 place names in its index.

M 25 U.S. Office of Geography. *Philippine Islands, preliminary NIS gazetteer.* Washington, Central Intelligence Agency, 1953. 2 v.
51,350 place and feature names, with classification and longitude and latitude.

M 26 Fund for Assistance to Private Education. *The Philippine atlas, a historical, economic and educational profile of the Philippines.* Manila, 1975. 2 v.
A well produced and colourful atlas, with coloured maps of the Philippines and provinces, with a substantial amount of text and diagrams covering population and economy. The second volume discusses education. Index.

CENSUS

M 27 Philippines (Commonwealth). Commission of the Census. . . . *Census of the Philippines, 1939.* Manila, Bureau of Printing, 1940–3. 4 v. (in 7)
The first volume consists of four parts, and gives the distribution of the population by municipalities and barrios, and the classification of inhabitants by sex, age and race, civil status, literacy, occupation, religion and employment. Each province section commences with a map of the province. The second volume is a summary for the Philippines of the statistics in the first volume, with a general report on the census. Volume 3 has a similar arrangement to volume 1, but is exclusively concerned

with agriculture. Volume 4 reports the result of an economic census for forestry, transport, fisheries, mining and electricity. Earlier censuses have been reported for 1818, 1876 and 1887, under Spanish rule. Censuses for 1903 (4 v.) and for 1918 (4 v. in 6) have been noted.

M 28 Philippines (Republic). Bureau of the Census and Statistics. *Census of the Philippines, 1948*. Manila, Bureau of Printing, 1951–4. 4 v. (in 12).
The Census appeared in four volumes, three of which appeared in parts. The first volume, in six parts, covers the population and is classified by city, municipality and barrio. The second, in three parts, is an agricultural census with information on area, land use, acreage, production and value of different crops and livestock by province and municipality. The third volume is a summary report in two parts, the first on agriculture, the second on population. The fourth volume is an economic census. The census was compiled principally through the help of schoolteachers, and its accuracy has been questioned since this was the first to be undertaken by the Republic and also since much of Central Luzon was unsettled politically.

M 29 Philippines (Republic). Bureau of the Census and Statistics. *Census of the Philippines, 1960. Population and housing*. Manila, Department of Commerce and Industry, 1962. 2 v.
A great advance on the accuracy of the 1948 Census. Questionnaires were pre-tested, and houses were enumerated before the census count. The first volume has 51 sections, one for each province. Information is given for sex, age, citizenship, literacy, school attendance, and language. Each provincial section is in two parts, the first on population, the second on housing.

M 30 Philippines (Republic). National Census and Statistics Office. *1970 census of population and housing*. Manila, 1974. 2 v.
Volume 1 is in 67 parts, with census information for each province, and volume 2 gives the national summary.

STATISTICS

M 31 Philippines Islands. Bureau of Commerce and Industry. *Statistical bulletin of the Philippine Islands*, nos. 1–12, 1918–29. Manila, Bureau of Printing, 1918–29.
Each volume has approximately 100–140 tables arranged by subject, and the information is compiled from official returns. There is no index except in the 1920 issue, and the detailed table of contents for each volume is an excellent guide.

M 32 Philippines (Republic). Bureau of the Census and Statistics. *Yearbook of Philippines statistics*, 1940–6. Manila, Bureau of Printing, 1941–7. 2 v.
These two volumes are valuable since they give statistical

information for the last year before World War II and the first two years of liberation. Arranged by major subject divisions, such as geography, population, education, vital statistics, agriculture, labour, industry, business, banking and finance, and domestic and foreign trade. Subsequent issues 1957, 1958, 1966. For 1969 issued as *Philippine statistics (1969) yearbook*.

M 33 Philippines (Republic). Bureau of the Census and Statistics. *Journal of Philippine statistics*. Manila, Bureau of Printing, 1941–.
Issued quarterly to give statistical information on social and economic conditions in the Philippines, and in each issue there are some 50–60 tables grouped by subject, and covering prices, labour, education, immigration, business, agriculture, transportation and trade. Lack of uniformity in treatment makes this publication of less value. Issues for 1969 last noted.

M 34 *Philippine yearbook*. Manila, National Economic and Development Authority, 1971–
Continues *Philippine statistics (1969) yearbook* (see under M32). Second issue is *Philippine yearbook*, 1975, which is the most up-to-date source for statistical and general information on the Philippines.

M 35 Philippines (Republic). Bureau of the Census and Statistics. *Statistical handbook of the Philippines*. Manila.
1971 issue, published in 1972, is the seventh in the series, and contains statistical tables and charts covering mostly the 1960s to 1970. Covers climate, population, employment, prices, education, industry, trade, agriculture, finance and health.

M 36 Philippines (Republic). National Economic and Development Authority. *NEDA statistical yearbook, 1974*. Manila, 1974–
Divided into 14 chapters on population, industry, finance, trade and education. Data coverage from the late 1940s to the early 1970s. 1975 and 1976 issues seen.

BIBLIOGRAPHY

Bibliography of Bibliographies

M 37 Bernardo, Gabriel A. *Bibliography of Philippine bibliographies, 1593–1961*. Quezon City, Ateneo de Manila University, 1968. 192 p. (Occasional papers of the Department of History, Bibliographical series no. 2)
1,160 books, articles and sections of books are arranged in chronological order. Author and selected subject index.

M 38 Houston, Charles O., Jr. *Philippine bibliography, I, an annotated preliminary bibliography of Philippine bibliographies, since 1900*. Manila, University of Manila, 1960. 60 p.
155 books and periodical articles in English published to the end

of 1957, and arranged in author order. Critical annotations. No index, and it is necessary to search through the whole bibliography to find a bibliography on a given subject. Not all entries were inspected by the compiler.

M 39 Saito, Shiro. *The Philippines, a review of bibliographies.* Honolulu, East-West Center Library, 1966. 80 p. (Occasional papers of the East-West Center Library no. 5)
Lists 215 bibliographies on the Philippines appearing as books and as periodical articles. Supplements Charles O. Houston *Philippine bibliography* (M 38), bringing his coverage down to 1965, and noting bibliographies published before 1957 and not listed by him. Bibliographies in the sciences have not been included. The principal part of this work is an essay, which has a subject arrangement and contains critical annotation. Author, subject and title index.

M 40 Hart, Donn V. *An annotated bibliography of Philippine bibliographies, 1965–1974.* De Kalb, Center for Southeast Asian Studies, Northern Illinois University, 1974. 160 p. (Occasional Papers no. 4)
283 bibliographies, appearing as periodical articles or books, are arranged alphabetically by author. Continues the work of Shiro Saito *The Philippines, a review of bibliographies* (M 39) and Charles Houston *Philippine bibliography* (M 38).

Bibliography to 1900

M 41 Bernardo, Gabriel A. *Philippine retrospective bibliography, 1523–1699.* Manila, Ateneo de Manila University Press, 1973. 160 p.
Lists 760 titles on the Philippines or published in the Philippines in two sections, the first 542 titles being published outside the Philippines, and the second 218 being Philippine imprints. Bibliographical descriptions are full, and there are notes on locations of the works in the Philippines and in major libraries in Europe and America.

M 42 Medina, Jose Toribio. *La imprenta en Manila desde sus origenes hasta 1810.* Amsterdam, N. Israel, 1964. 280, 203 p.
In two parts, the main work and a supplement. Each has a separate index. 565 books are arranged chronologically by date of publication and have full bibliographical descriptions and notes. A reprint of the 1896 Santiago de Chile edition.

M 43 Medina, Jose Toribio. *Bibliografia espanola de las Islas Filipinas, 1523–1810.* Santiago de Chile, Imprenta Cervantes, 1897. 556 p.
667 books in Spanish, Latin and other Western languages on the Philippines arranged chronologically. Each entry is annotated in Spanish, and its origins and relation to other works is explained. Author index.

M 44 Robertson, James Alexander. *Bibliography of the Philippine*

Islands, printed and manuscript, preceded by a descriptive account of the most important archives and collections containing Philippiniana . . . Cleveland, A. H. Clark Co., 1908. New York, Kraus Reprint, 1970. 437 p.

150 copies of the original publication issued as a separate from Emma Helen Blair and James Alexander Robertson *The Philippine Islands, 1493–1898*. The first part lists some 600 printed books in two sections, a bibliographical section, and a section for books published in the series in whole or in part. The second part, pp. 143–419, lists Philippine manuscripts. Well annotated.

M 45 Pardo de Tavera, Trinidad H. *Biblioteca filipina* . . . Washington, Government Printing Office, 1903. 439 p.

2,850 books on the Philippines, including Jolo and the Marianas, are arranged alphabetically by author for the most part, although some are arranged by subject. Most of the material is in Spanish, but English and French works are also included. It is almost complete for books published in the latter half of the 19th century. May be bound with A. P. C. Griffin *A list of books with references to periodicals on the Philippines in the Library of Congress* (M 47). Reprinted by Gale, Detroit.

M 46 Welsh, Doris Varner. *A catalogue of printed materials relating to the Philippine Islands, 1519–1900, in the Newberry Library.* Chicago, Newberry Library, 1959. 179 p.

A classified list of 1,868 books and periodical articles based on the Edward E. Ayer Collection in the Newberry Library. The entries are divided under a general heading and under history, with subdivisions for political, ecclesiastical, economic, social, cultural and local aspects. Author index.

M 47 Griffin, A. P. C. *A list of books with references to periodicals on the Philippines in the Library of Congress.* Washington, Government Printing Office, 1903. 397 p.

A classified list of some 2,700 books and 1,000 periodical articles and government reports. The entries are organized first by subject, and then chronologically. There is a separate author and subject index. In addition to the 265-page listing of books and articles, there is a 130-page section noting 860 maps on the Philippines in the Library of Congress. Particularly valuable for the early period of Philippine-American relations.

M 48 Retana y Gamboa, Wenceslao-Emilio. *Aparato bibliografico de la historia general de Filipinas*. Madrid, 1906. 3 v.

4,623 books, intended to include all books printed in the Philippines, about the Philippines, or published by Filipinos, are arranged chronologically, with the date of imprint noted in the margin. The first volume covers the period 1524–1800, the second 1801–86, and the third, which is in two parts, 1887–1905, with an added list of newspapers and periodicals for 1801–1905. The table of contents is divided into five parts listing principal subjects and anonymous works, periodical publications, collections of Oriental names and idioms, geographical places, and proper names; and items in the bibliography are referred to by number. A key work for the study of Philippine history, but difficult to use. Reprinted Manila, 1964.

Bibliography after 1900

M 49 U.S. Army. Office of the Chief of Counter Intelligence. Philippine Research and Information Section. *The Philippines during the Japanese regime, 1942–1945, an annotated list of the literature published in or about the Philippines during the Japanese occupation*. Manila, 1945. 52 p.
185 entries mostly in Tagalog or English, but with a few in romanized Japanese, divided into two sections. The first contains approved and official materials, and periodical articles, including 17 newspapers. The second contains documents of the Resistance movement, but most of these were published by the U.S. Army. Brief annotations, and subject arrangement. Author and title index.

M 50 Philippines (Republic). Bureau of Public Libraries. *Books copyrighted, published in the Philippines, 1945–1957*. Manila, 1957. 143 p.
An unannotated list of 1,447 books published and copyrighted in the Philippines from 1945 to 1957, and excluding non-copyrighted material. Usually arranged by author, but sometimes by publisher, under the year of copyright, and depends for its compilation on the materials actually in the Copyright Office of the Bureau of Public Libraries. It may be supplemented by the monthly list of books and periodicals registered for copyright purposes and appearing in the *Official Gazette*. By no means a complete record of Philippine publications.

M 51 Eggan, Frederick Russell. *Selected bibliography of the Philippines, topically arranged and annotated, preliminary edition*. New Haven, Human Relations Area Files, 1956. 138 p. (Behaviour science bibliographies).
Some 620 books and periodical articles, mostly in English, arranged under 23 subject headings, including modern history, social and political structure, education, religion, fishing, and industry. Annotated. Author index.

M 52 Lopez Memorial Museum. *Catalogue of Filipiniana materials in the Lopez Memorial Museum*. Pasay City, 1962–71. 5 v.
Total of 7,908 entries. Each volume has a similar subject arrangement, and its own author and title index.

M 53 University of the Philippines. Interdepartmental Reference Service. *Union catalogue of Philippine materials of sixty-four government agency libraries of the Philippines*. Manila, 1962. 718 p.

10,277 books, pamphlets, reprints, microfilms and theses on the Philippines, or by Philippine authors and arranged by author. Location symbols show where entries may be found. Subject index. Includes items noted in the University of the Philippines Library *Classified list of Filipiniana and pamphlets in the main library, University of the Philippines as of December 1958 (Quezon City, 1959)* and *Books copyrighted, published in the Philippines, 1945–1957* (M 50).

M 54 University of the Philippines. Library. *Philippine bibliography, 1963–*. Diliman, Rizal, 1965–.
Lists non-governmental and governmental publications on the Philippines, published in the Philippines or elsewhere. First issues of periodicals are included, but music and school textbooks are excluded. Entries held by the University of the Philippines Library are noted. List of Philippine printers and publishers appended. Subject and title index. 1968/9 issue reported.

M 55 University of the Philippines. Library. *Filipiniana 68*. Quezon City, 1969. 2 v.
Representing the holdings of the University of the Philippines with some 9,843 entries for official and non-official books. Items are arranged into detailed subject groups, and subarranged by author. Author-title index and subject index.

M 56 Ferrer, Maxima Magsanoc. *Union catalog of Philippine materials*. Quezon City, University of the Philippines Press, 1970–6. 2 v.
Lists 20,920 books, theses, reprints, and microfilms on the Philippines, giving locations in 201 Philippine Libraries in December 1964. An enlarged edition of *Union catalogue of Philippine materials of sixty-four government agency libraries of the Philippines* (M 53), which it supplements but does not supersede. The most comprehensive list of Filipiniana.

M 57 Taimson, Alfredo T. *Mindanao-Sulu bibliography, containing published, unpublished manuscripts, and works-in-progress, a preliminary survey and W. E. Retana's Bibliografia de Mindinao (1894)*. Davao City, Ateneo de Davao, 1970. 344 p.
Lists some 3,760 entries arranged by author. Indexes by province-subject and general subject.

M 58 University of the Philippines. Library. *Filipiniana on microfilm 1970*. Diliman, 1970. 186 p. (Research guide no. 15).
Lists 1,271 titles of books, theses, manuscripts and serials in the University of the Philippines Filipiniana microfilm collection at the end of 1969. Separate title, joint author and subject indexes.

M 59 *Select*. Cagayan de Oro City, Xavier University Library, 1971–.
A bibliographical journal aimed at assisting Philippine college and university libraries. Each issue lists some 50 Philippine books, and gives a full review. In addition there are excellent articles on Philippine bibliography. Annual cumulative index. January 1977 issue seen.

M 60 Maloles, Leticia R. *The National Library, a finding guide to the Picture Collection of the Filipiniana Division*. Manila, National Library, 1971. 203 p. (TNL Research guide series no. 2).
Lists 1,580 captioned items covering period through the 1920s. Titles of pictures are arranged alphabetically by subject.

M 61 Medina, Isagani R. *Filipiniana materials in the National Library*. Quezon City, University of the Philippines Press, 1971. 353 p.
2,524 titles, including 38 newspapers and periodicals, being principally those in the Tabacalera collection.

M 62 Far Eastern University, Manila. *Classified list of Filipiniana books and pamphlets in the Filipiniana Research Section of the Far Eastern University Library*, revised edition. Manila, Far Eastern University, 1971. 287 p.
3,011 books and reports arranged by the Library of Congress classification, with an author, title and subject index.

M 63 Philippines (Republic). National Library. *Catalog of copyright entries, 1964–68*. Manila, National Library, Bibliography Division, 1972. 2 v. (TNL Research guide series nos. 5, 6).
Volume 1 notes 2,925 entries arranged by author, with an author and title index. Approximately one-half of the entries are United States publications. Contains a directory of printers and publishers represented in the catalogue. Volume 2 contains 1,578 entries for musical scores.

M 64 Tubangui, Helen R. *A catalog of Filipiniana at Valladolid*. Quezon City, Ateneo de Manila University Press, 1973. 364 p. (Occasional papers of the Department of History, Bibliographical series no. 4).
Consists for the most part of printed materials published from 1585, but over nine-tenths of these date from the mid-19th century to the 1950s.

M 65 American Historical Research Collection, Manila. *Classified listing of books, government documents, pamphlets, periodicals, serials, etc. of the American Historical Research Collection, Manila.* Manila, 1973. 340 p.
Some 5,000 titles, mostly relating to 20th-century Philippines and in English, are arranged by Library of Congress classification. No index. Represents a major Filipiniana collection with materials often not locatable elsewhere.

M 66 De Guzman, Abraham C. *Bibliography of materials in Philippine vernacular languages*. Manila, National Library, Bibliography Division, 1973. 914 p. (TNL Research guide series no. 7).
3,761 entries for publications in Philippine languages are arranged by author, with a title, author and subject index. The catalogue is based on the holdings of the National Library Filipiniana Division until December 1970, but does not include rare Philippine language material to be found in Isagani R. Medina *Filipiniana materials in the National Library* (M 61).

M 67 Saito, Shiro. *Philippine research materials and Library resources, an overview*. Honolulu, Asian Studies Program, University of Hawaii, 1973. 63 p. (Southeast Asian Studies working paper no. 3).
Intended as a bibliographical guide to the researcher in Philippine studies, and divided into two main parts, the first being concerned with resources in the United States and the second with those in the Philippines. A bibliography at the end notes 93 titles.

M 68 Philippines (Republic). National Library. *Philippine national bibliography*. Manila, 1974–.
Filipiniana publications registered under the copyright law are arranged by form of publication, with a title, author and subject index. Issued bimonthly, with some 250 items in each issue. Volume 3, nos. 1 and 2, January–April 1976, and annual volumes for 1974 and 1975 seen.

M 69 *Philippine union catalog*. Quezon City, University of the Philippines Library, 1974. v. 1–.
The union catalog will be issued quarterly and in annual cumulations, and will replace *Philippine bibliography* (M 54) and the *Filipiniana union catalog 1968–73*, which was itself a continuation of *Filipiniana 1968*. The first annual issue for 1974 contains 2,558 entries, arranged by author. Subject and title index.

Official Publications

M 70 Elmer, Emma Osterman. *Checklist of publications of the government of the Philippine Islands, September 1, 1900 to December 31, 1917*. Manila, Philippine Library and Museum, 1918. 288 p.
A comprehensive listing of some 3,000 government publications arranged under the categories of legislative, executive, judiciary, University of the Philippines, provinces, boards and committees, and then by offices, departments and bureaus. Materials are subarranged by form, including bulletins, reports, gazettes and other publications. Reports are arranged by chronological order. Index to government authors and subject index.

M 71 University of the Philippines. Library. *Checklist of Philippine government documents, 1917–1949*. Quezon City, 1960. 817 p.
This is a continuation of Emma Osterman Elmer *Checklist of publications* (M 70). The materials are arranged by government departments, and the index lists names of authors, titles, subjects, and government departments in one sequence. Documents appearing under the Japanese administration are included under a separate heading. Altogether 6,469 entries. A smaller bibliography of 755 items, U.S. Library of Congress *Checklist of Philippine government documents, 1950* (Washington, Library of Congress, 1953. 62 p.), continues this list.

M 72 University of the Philippines. Institute of Public Administration. Library. *List of Philippine government publications*. Manila, 1958–.
The 1961 issues were quarterly, and listed only those official publications in sufficient numbers of copies for gift or exchange. 1962, 1963, and 1964 issues were annual. The 1965/6 issue lists 1,431 publications, and asterisks those items available for exchange. 1972/73 issue seen.

Periodicals and Newspapers

M 73 University of the Philippines. *Index to Philippine periodicals*, 1955–. Quezon City, 1955–.
Indexes 114 Philippine periodicals, and 34 foreign titles. Strong emphasis on the social sciences, agriculture and science, but some literary material is also included. Author and subject arrangement, except that entries under subjects are not repeated. Volume 20, covering 1975 and published 1977, the latest noted. Foreign titles have been included for their coverage of the Philippines.

M 74 Saito, Shiro. *Philippine newspapers in selected American libraries, a union list*. Honolulu, East-West Center Library, 1966. 46 p. (Occasional papers of the East-West Center Library, no. 6).
199 newspapers published in English, Spanish, Philippine, Japanese and Chinese languages, arranged by place of publication. Information on frequency, language of publication, title changes, and holdings by library. Title index.

M 75 University of the Philippines. Library. *Index to Philippine periodical literature, 1946–67*. Quezon City, 1972. 5 v. (Research guide no. 10).
Over 500 periodical titles published in the Philippines or about the Philippines and received in the Filipiniana Section of the University of the Philippines Library from 1946–67. Omits articles on non-Philippine subjects. Lists of periodicals indexed, followed by index arranged alphabetically by subject.

M 76 Baylon, Conception S. *Philippine serials on microfilm*. Manila, Philippine and Asia Division, 1973. 73 p. (TNL Research guide series)
Lists 111 serial titles in the National Library on microfilm, and arranges these alphabetically. Copy inspected in typescript.

M 77 University of the Philippines. Library. *Manila Times index, 1946–1969*. Quezon City, 1973–4.
A microfilm of the 60,000 index slips held by the University of the Philippines Library for the period 1946–68, and for the year 1969. 1969 was covered in much greater detail than the previous years, but marks the concluding year of the compilation.

M 78 Golay, Frank H. and Marianne H. Hauswedell. *An annotated*

guide to Philippine serials. Ithaca, Southeast Asia Program, Department of Asian Studies, Cornell University, 1976. 131 p. (Data paper no. 101)
Some 1,300 titles, annotated and arranged in two major lists, non-governmental and government. Index to each list. Cornell holdings are given. Supersedes the 1962 edition.

M 79 Philippines (Republic). National Library. Filipiniana and Asian Division. *Checklist of rare Filipiniana serials.* Manila, 1976–
To be issued in two parts. The first part was published in 1976, and covers 271 periodicals and newspapers published 1811–1944, giving holdings in the National Library.

Theses and Dissertations

M 80 Nemenzo, Catalina A. *Graduate theses in Philippine universities and colleges, 1908–1969.* Manila, Philippine Center for Advanced Studies, University of the Philippines System, 1974. 4 v. (PCAS Bibliography series 1974)
Lists 8,375 theses and dissertations of which over 60% are annotated, and over 90% deal with the Philippines. Items are arranged by subject. Author index and subject-title index.

Maps

M 81 Quirino, Carlos. *Philippine cartography (1320–1899)*, second revised edition, with introduction by R.A. Skelton. Amsterdam, N. Israel, 1963. 140 p.
A lengthy introduction with many reproductions is followed by a chronological list of major published maps from 1320 to 1899. Annotations, locations and sources given. Bibliography and index.

M 82 Philippines (Republic). National Library. *A guide to the Map Collection of the Filipiniana Division, part 1, 1482–1899.* Manilla, National Library, Bibliography Division, 1971. 36 p. (TNL Research guide series no. 1)
71 maps listed, with author, subject and title index.

Subject Bibliography

SOCIAL SCIENCES

M 83 University of the Philippines. Social Science Research Center. *An annotated bibliography of the Philippines social sciences, 1956–60.* Quezon City, 1956–60. 3 v.
Based on the materials in the Filipiniana section of the University of the Philippines Library. Volume 1 (1956) is on economics, including 2,895 books, periodical articles, laws, proclamations and reports arranged under 31 subject headings; it covers the

period from the end of the Spanish occupation and has an author-title index. Volume 2, part 1 (1957) is on sociology, and has 268 books and reports. Volume 3, part 1 (1960) is on political science, and has 1,321 books, periodical articles and executive orders.

M 84 Philippines (Republic). Office of Statistical Coordination and Standards. *An annotated bibliography of official statistical publications of the Philippine government.* Manila, 1963. 25 p.
56 Philippine official publications issued by ten government agencies, and with statistical information. Annotations give publisher and frequency, and describe contents.

M 85 Cordero, Felicidad V. *An annotated bibliography on community development in the Philippines from 1946–1959.* Diliman, Rizal, Community Development Research Council, University of the Philippines, 1965. 2 v.
The first volume lists 2,292 books, periodical articles and reports arranged by subject. Books are given a descriptive annotation. The second volume lists the same materials, arranged by author.

M 86 Manuel, E. Arsenio. *Philippine folklore bibliography, a preliminary survey.* Quezon City, Philippine Folklore Society, 1965. 125 p. (Philippine Folklore Society paper no.1)
An author list of some 1,100 books and periodical articles, almost entirely in English, and mostly Philippine publications. The works of each author arranged by date. Classified ethnographic index.

M 87 Virata, Enrique T. *Agrarian reform, a bibliography.* Diliman, Quezon City, Community Development Research Council, University of the Philippines, 1965. 239 p.
1,013 books, unpublished reports and periodical articles, some with extensive annotations, show development of government policy on land reform. Index to authors and subjects.

M 88 Collantes, Augusto L. *A bibliography on taxation in the Philippines.* Manila, Joint Legislative Executive Tax Commission, 1968. 38 p.
Some 500 entries, divided into books, articles and sources, and with the first two parts further divided by topic. No index or annotations.

M 89 University of the Philippines. Institute of Planning. *An annotated bibliography of Philippine planning.* Manila, 1968. 203 p.
1,114 entries are arranged by form into books and pamphlets, government publications, periodical and newspaper articles, and theses. Entries are annotated. Author index.

M 90 Mercado-Tann, Filomena C. *Philippine libraries and librarianship, a bibliography.* Manila, 1969. 58 p.
574 entries for books and articles on librarianship and the development of libraries in the Philippines. Arranged by topic.

M 91 Edralin, Josefa S. and Vicenta C. Rimando. *Local government in the Philippines, a classified, annotated bibliography.* Manila, Joint Local Government Reform Commission, 1970. 236 p.

Major divisions are for historical background, then for problems in local government. Each section is further divided into books, official publications, periodical articles, and theses and dissertations. Laws, orders, regulations and local history are excluded. 1,797 entries. Author-subject index.

M 92 Community Development Research Council. *An annotated bibliography on rural Philippines*, v. 1–. Diliman, Quezon City, 1969–.
The first volume of 289 entries is divided into books, articles, masters theses, Ph.D. dissertations and bachelors' theses. Subject Index. Volume 1 only seen.

M 93 Angeles, Belen and Rachel Cabato. *A bibliography of periodicals and statistical sources on the Philippines economy*. Quezon City, Institute of Economic Development and Research, School of Economics, University of the Philippines, 1970. 65 p.
246 serials are arranged by subject, and well annotated. Title and subject indexes. The serials are to be found in the University of the Philippines School of Economics Library. *Supplement, 1973 . . .* (1974) lists another 67 serials, with author and title indexes.

M 94 Saito, Shiro. *Philippine ethnography, a critically annotated and selected bibliography*. Honolulu, University Press of Hawaii, 1972. 512 p.
4,328 books and articles, almost entirely in English, arranged primarily by cultural linguistic groups, and then by subject. Many entries are graded by specialists. Author index.

M 95 Walsh, Tom. *Martial law in the Philippines, a research guide and working bibliography*. Honolulu, Southeast Asian Studies Program, University of Hawaii, 1973. 130 p. (Southeast Asia working paper no. 4)
Consists of two main parts. The first is concerned with the general problem of bibliographical searching for research materials published in and outside the Philippines. The second is a list of about 1,000 titles, including official publications, books, periodicals and periodical articles. The list is arranged under 17 major subjects. No annotations or index.

M 96 Bulatao, Rodolfo A. and others. *Philippine population studies, a preliminary bibliography with selected annotations*. Diliman, Quezon City, Social Research Laboratory, University of the Philippines, 1974. 435 p.
The main part consists of some 2,300 books, articles, reports, theses and dissertations, arranged by author, and then by subject.

M 97 De Jesus, Emilinda Y. *Mass communications in the Philippines, an annotated bibliography*. Singapore, Asian Mass Communication Research and Information Centre, 1976. 335 p. (Asian Mass Communication bibliography series 4)
1,221 entries for books, articles and reports in English, arranged under 21 subjects. Excludes unpublished material written before 1960. Author and title index.

APPLIED SCIENCES

M 98 Teves, Juan S. *Bibliography of Philippines geology, mining and mineral resources*. Manila, Bureau of Printing, 1953. 155 p.
2,846 books, reports and periodical articles covering the period 1574–1952 are arranged by author. No annotations or subject index.

LANGUAGE AND LITERATURE

M 99 Welsh, Doris Varner. *Checklist of Philippine linguistics in the Newberry Library*. Chicago, Newberry Library, 1950. 176 p.
1,154 entries, mostly for books, arranged by language. Author index.

M 100 Yabes, Leopoldo Y. *Philippine literature in English, 1898–1957, a bibliographical survey*. Quezon City, University of the Philippines. 1958. pp. 343–434.
386 periodicals and some 900 books and pamphlets in English are arranged alphabetically in two parts, the first for periodicals, and preceded by a short bibliographical essay. The term literature is used broadly, and includes Philippine writing in history. No subject index. Reprinted from *Philippine social sciences and humanities review*, v. 22, December 1957.

M 101 Florentino, Alberto S. *Midcentury guide to Philippine literature in English*. Manila, Filipiniana Publishers, 1963. 96 p.
Some 150 books in English are arranged in a number of sections, but nearly all material is literary or is related to Philippine literature in English. Not systematic, but quite valuable.

M 102 Ward, Jack H. *A bibliography of Philippine linguistics and minor languages, with annotations and indices based on works in the Library of Cornell University*. Ithaca, Southeast Asia Program, Department of Asian Studies, Cornell University, 1971. 539 p. (Data paper no. 83)
4,500 books and periodical articles, mostly published in the 20th century, are arranged by author. Indexed by language to code numbers in entries. Based on the libraries at Cornell University, University of the Philippines, Philippine National Library, Ateneo de Manila, and Philippine Normal College. Emphasizes the minor languages.

M 103 Asuncion-Lande, Nobleza C. *A bibliography of Philippine linguistics*. Athens, Ohio University, Southeast Asia Program, 1971. 147 p. (Southeast Asia series 20)
1,977 books, articles and theses arranged by author, with major and minor language indexes. Collections in Philippine and American libraries, with the exception of Cornell University, have been examined. No annotations. Emphasizes the eight major languages, and over half on Tagalog.

GEOGRAPHY

M 104 Pelzer, Karl J. *Selected bibliography on the geography of*

Southeast Asia, part II, the Philippines. New Haven, Yale University, Southeast Asia Studies, Bibliography series)
Some 1,100 books, periodical articles, and theses, mostly in English, are arranged under ten broad subject headings. Most entries are not annotated. The term geography is interpreted broadly, and the bibliography is intended to supplement John F. Embree *Peoples and cultures of mainland Southeast Asia* (G9). Location of entries in Yale University libraries noted.

M 105 Huke, Robert E. *Bibliography of Philippine geography, 1940–1963, a selected list.* Hanover, Department of Geography, Dartmouth College, 1964. 84 p. (Geography publications at Dartmouth no. 1)
Some 1,200 books and periodical articles, almost entirely in English, are arranged in a subject order, with author index. Practically no entries are dated before 1939, and almost all after 1950, thus supplementing Karl J. Pelzer *Selected bibliography on the geography of Southeast Asia, part II, The Philippines (M 104).*

HISTORY

M 106 Philippines (Republic). Bureau of Public Libraries. Research and Bibliography Division. *Manuel L. Quezon, a bio-bibliography.* Manila, 1962. 170 p.
Some 3,000 entries compiled from periodical indexes and newspapers. The first section consists of President Quezon's works and addresses, the second of works and articles by other authors, and the third and major section of newspaper accounts.

M 107 Miravite, Rosalina S. *Philippine Muslims, a preliminary history and bibliography.* Honolulu, 1967. 111 p.
Introduction is followed by 501 entries in English and Spanish, arranged by author, followed by chronological index by date of publications, with a major section on history and politics, and smaller sections on literature, art, music and linguistics.

M 108 Philippines (Republic). National Historical Commission. *Preliminary bibliography on Emilio Aguinaldo.* Manila, 1969. 76 p.
Books, official papers and articles published 1897–1969 are arranged chronologically.

M 110 Tantoco, Daniel W. *A selected bibliography for Philippine prehistory.* Manila, National Museum, 1970. 59 p.
157 books, 348 articles and 59 unpublished manuscripts are arranged by author. No annotations and no subject index.

M 111 See, Chinben. *A bibliography of the Chinese in the Philippines.* Cagayan de Oro City, Xavier University, 1970. 97 p.
Some 1,100 books, articles and reports in English are arranged under 15 major divisions. The bibliography includes materials published through the first half of 1970. No index. Reprinted 1972.

M 112 Netzorg, Morton J. *The Philippines in World War II and to independence (December 8, 1941 – July 4, 1946), an annotated bibliography*. Ithaca, Cornell University, 1977. 222 p. (Cornell University, Department of Asian Studies, Southeast Asia Program, Data paper no. 105)

Approximately 2,600 entries arranged by author, and with most entries annotated. Mostly books, but with some periodical articles. Coverage is to 1974, and is valuable for a period not well documented

N. THAILAND

The historical foundations of Thailand go back to the mid-13th century with the expulsion of the Thai from Southwest China by the Mongols. Their kingdom was consolidated in the Lower Menam River basin. In recent times territorial adjustments were made in 1941 at the expense of Cambodia, and in 1943 at the expense of Malaya and Burma. These areas were restored to their former countries in 1946. In 1949 the official name of the country was changed from Siam to Thailand.

ENCYCLOPEDIA AND HANDBOOKS

N1 *Saranukrom Thai, chabap Ratchabandit sathan* (Encyclopedia Thai, Royal Institute edition). Phranakhon (i.e. Bangkok), Ratchabandit sathan, B.E. 2498/9– (1956–).
Compiled by a commission of Thai scholars, with approximately one-half of the contents relating to Thailand. Articles are signed, but have no bibliography. Volume 14, through 'th' of the Thai alphabet, published 1978.

N2 American University, Washington, D.C. Foreign Area Studies. *Area handbook for Thailand.* Washington, U.S. Government Printing Office, 1971. 413 p.
A country summary is followed by a survey of social, political and economic affairs, and of national security. There is a 62-page bibliography and a glossary of terms. Research completed November 1970. Replaces 1968 edition.

N3 Smith, Harold E. *Historical and cultural dictionary of Thailand.* Metuchen, Scarecrow Press, 1976. 213 p. (Historical and cultural dictionary of Asia series no. 6).
Some 800 entries reflect all aspects of Thai cultural, social, economic and historical backgrounds. A short bibliography is appended.

YEARBOOKS

N4 *Thailand yearbook,* 1964/5–. Bangkok, Temple Publicity Services, 1964?–.
Contains sections on the government of Thailand, banking, social services, income tax, population, international organizations related to Thailand and social welfare services; a listing of temples; and a directory of individuals arranged alphabetically. Indexed. 1975/6 issue noted.

N5 *Thailand official yearbook,* 1964–. Bangkok, Government House Printing Office, 1964?–.

Review of the history, geography, politics, economy and religion of Thailand, and intended to be issued only on an occasional basis. 1968 issue noted. Index.

DICTIONARIES

N 6 McFarland, George Bradley. *Thai-English dictionary.* Stanford, Stanford University Press, 1956. 1,019 p.
A reprint of the 1941 Bangkok edition, including some 16,000 Thai words, with their transliterated and English equivalents and examples of usage.

N 7 Haas, Mary Rosamond. *Thai-English student's dictionary.* Stanford, Stanford University Press, 1964. 638 p.
Some 8,000 Thai words in the 1950 official spelling are transliterated and given English equivalents, with detailed examples of usage. More up to date but less extensive than George Bradley McFarland *Thai-English dictionary* (N 6).

N 8 Sethaputra, So. *New model Thai-English dictionary,* library edition. Samud Prakan, So Sethaputra's Press, 1965. 2 v.
Thai words with English equivalents and ample illustrations as to usage. A companion work is *New model English-Thai dictionary* (Samud Prakan, So Sethaputra's Press, 1961. 2 v.).

BIOGRAPHICAL DICTIONARIES

N 9 Thammasat Mahawitthayalai. Khana Rathaprasasanasat (Thammasat University. Institute of Public Administration. *Khrai pen khrai nai Prathet Thai 2506* (Who's who in Thailand, 1963). Phranakhon, B.E. 2506 (1963). 2 v.
6,000 questionnaires were sent out to prominent persons in government and other fields. Of these 3,204 replied, but 52 could not be used, and the remaining 3,152 are mostly government employees, and some quite prominent people are not included. The only modern Thai biographical dictionary available. Accounts are full, with degrees, date and place of birth, positions held, address, education, specialty and publications.

N 10 *Who's who in Thailand.* Bangkok, Advance Publications, 1973–.
Issued in monthly parts, with some 20–30 biographies in each issue. 1977 latest issue noted.

DIRECTORIES

N 11 *The Siam directory,* 1878–. Bangkok, 1878–.
Lists the Royal family, members of the government, and the foreign diplomatic corps, and includes the text of the Constitu-

tion. Also listed are universities, newspapers and business firms. Short index. 1880 edition seen. 1978/9 issue last noted.

N 12 U.S. Operations Mission to Thailand. Public Administrative division. *Organizational directory to the government of Thailand.* Bangkok, 1960?–.
The main part is a directory of government organization, arranged by department, with important officials. This is preceded by two lists, a subject index and a name index. The second part is a directory of provincial officials. 1968/9 issue latest noted.

N 13 Thailand. Sapha Wichai haeng Chat (National Research Council). *Directory of natural and social scientific institutions in Thailand.* Bangkok, 1963. 1 v.
Has been brought up to date and supplemented by the National Research Council *Directory of natural scientific institutions in Thailand, 1964* (Bangkok, Government House Printing Office, 1965. 10 p.) and Jacques Amyot and Robert W. Kickert *Directory of the social sciences in Thailand, 1963* (Bangkok, Faculty of Political Science, Chulalongkorn University, 1963? 100 p.).

N 14 Allison, Gordon H. and Aurati Smarnond. *Thailand's government, including dictionary locator.* Bangkok, Siam Security Brokers, 1972. 155 p.
A concise outline of the Thai government structure is followed by an index of English forms of names of government bodies, with their Thai equivalents.

GAZETTEERS

N 15 *Akkaranukron phumisat Thai chabap Ratchabandit Sathan* (Geographical Dictionary of Thailand). Phranakhon, Ratchabandit Sathan, B.E. 2506–9 (1963–9). 4 v.
The first volume is a general geography of Thailand. The second and third list geographical names in Thai alphabetical order, with descriptions, history, archaeology, resources, economic conditions and statistics. The fourth volume is an appendix arranged by *changwad,* and then by place, with a map of each *changwad.*

N 16 U.S. Office of Geography. *Thailand* . . . Washington, U.S. Government Printing Office, 1966. 675 p. (Gazetteer no. 97).
45,500 entries for place and feature names in Thailand, with longitude and latitude, and classification.

CENSUS AND STATISTICS

N 17 Thailand. Samnakngan Sathiti haeng Chat (National Office of Statistics). *Statistical yearbook,* 1915/6–. Bangkok, 1916–.
Arranged by broad subjects such as general information, meteorology, population, public health, education, justice,

agriculture, forestry, mining and external trade. Annually to 1930/1, biennially 1931/5 to 1939/44, and then annually again. In English, or in English and Thai. No. 31 for 1974/5 seen.

N 18 Thailand. Samnakngan Sathiti haeng Chat (National Office of Statistics). *Thailand population census, 1960. Changwad series.* Bangkok, 1961–2. 71 v.
Carried out with the aid of the U.S. Technical Assistance Program, and shows the number of inhabitants, their personal, educational and economic characteristics, and has information on fertility. Arranged alphabetically, with a volume for each *changwad* or district. An additional volume, *Thailand population census, 1960. Whole kingdom* (Bangkok, 1962. 57 p.), brings together the information found in the 71 *changwad* volumes. A 1947 census (7 v. in 10) reported. In Thai.

N 18a Thailand. Samnakngan Sathiti haeng Chat (National Office of Statistics). *1970 population and housing census* (Bangkok) 1972?–76 v.
The first volume contains results for Thailand as a whole, followed by results for each of the four major regions. The remaining volumes are for each of the 71 *changwads.* A detailed census in Thai and English.

BIBLIOGRAPHY

Thai Language

N 19 Cornell University Libraries. *Catalogue of Thai-language holdings in the Cornell University through 1964,* compiled by Frances A. Bernath. Ithaca, Southeast Asia Program, Department of Asian Studies, Cornell University, 1964. 235 p. (Data paper no. 54).
4,921 entries for the Cornell Thai collection. Full bibliographical information for library purposes. Author arrangement.

N 20 Ajia Keizai Kenkyujo, Tokyo (Institute of the Developing Economies). *Tai-go bunken sogomokuroku* (Union catalogue of Thai materials). Tokyo, 1972. 2 v.
Some 5,000 titles in the Tokyo University of Foreign Studies, Osaka University of Foreign Studies, the Toyo Bunko, and the private libraries of five individual scholars are arranged in two volumes. The first contains materials on general subjects and the social sciences, and the second on social sciences and the humanities. Also published in one volume.

Western Languages

N 21 Sharp, Lauriston. *Bibliography of Thailand, a selected list of books and articles.* Ithaca, Cornell University, 1956. 64 p.

(Cornell University, Southeast Asia project, Data paper no. 20).
An annotated bibliography of some 315 books and periodical articles, with a stress on sociology. A number of subjects such as history, economy, politics and government, public health and welfare, education, religion, art, literature, language and ethnic groups are covered, but none in great depth. Most entries are in English, but some Thai titles are transliterated and translated. Subject arrangement, but no index.

N 22 Mason, John Brown and H. Carrol Parish. *Thailand bibliography.* Gainesville, University of Florida Libraries, 1958. 247 p. (University of Florida Libraries, Bibliographical series no. 4).
Over 2,300 books and periodical articles on Thai history, government, archaeology, geography, sociology, education, art and natural sciences. Although nine languages are represented, most of the entries are in English. Arranged into two major sections, one for books and the other for articles, both in author order. Some entries are annotated. Also contains a useful list of English-language newspapers and periodicals published in Thailand.

N 23 Chulalongkon Mahawitthayalai. Hong Samut (Chulalongkorn University Library). *Bibliography of materials about Thailand in Western languages* . . . Bangkok, B.E. 2503 (1960). 325 p.
Over 4,400 books, periodical articles, microfilms and films on Thailand are arranged by subject, and then by author, with Thai authors being entered by first name. Philosophy, religion, social sciences, language and literature, science, art, history, travel and biography are included. Compiled from the catalogues of the principal libraries in Thailand and from other bibliographies. No index and no annotation, but easily the most comprehensive bibliography on Thailand.

Official Publications

N 24 Pandayankun, Yim. *Saraban khon r'uang lem l nai nangsu'phim cak ton chabap khon Ho samut haeng chat, B.E. 2444 thu'ng B.E. 2470* (An index of works published by the National Library, B.E. 2444 to 2470 (April 1901 – March 1927)). Phranakhon, Krom Sinlapakon, B.E. 2484 (1941). 289 p.
In three parts. The first, pp. 1–68, is a chronological list of publications; the second, pp. 69–230, is a subject index; and the third, pp. 232–89, is an author index. Includes all the cremation (i.e. commemorative or memorial) volumes published by the National Library in this period. Since the cremation volumes contain obituary notices, they provide an important source for biographical information also.

N 25 Thailand. Hong Samut haeng Chat (National Library). *List of Thai government publications covering the years 1954, 1955, 1956.* Bangkok, 1958. 31 p.

Some 750 publications, including serials, are arranged by ministry, then by bureau. Titles cited in English, representing the official translation of the Thai title, but only 10% of the publications are actually in English or in English and Thai.

N26 Thammasat Mahawitthayalai. Khana Rathaprasasanasat (Thammasat University. Institute of Public Administration). *List of Thai government publications.* Bangkok, 1958. 43 p.
Continues the *List of Thai government publications covering the years 1954, 1955, 1956* (N 25) with some 1,200 publications arranged by ministry and then by bureau. The titles of publications in Thai, as well as those in English, are all given in English.

N27 Samakhom Hong Samut haeng Prathet Thai (Thai Library Association). *Bannanukrom singphim khong ratthaban Thai* (Bibliography of Thai government publications). Phranakhon, B.E. 2505– (1962–).
Does not include the publications of the Department of Fine Arts and Ministry of Culture. Important since it does not provide titles in English translation only, and retains the original Thai, making it possible to more readily identify items described. The first volume, containing some 1,500 entries, is the only one noted. Materials are organized by departments, and there are separate author-title indexes for Thai and English language publications.

N28 U.S. Operations Mission to Thailand. Bangkok. *A compilation of reports and publications.* Bangkok, 1965. 95 p.
Some 300 entries are arranged in broad subjects. A key, unfortunately for one country only, of the principal reporting literature overseas, connected with American programs. Author index, English film index and Thai title index.

N29 Pandayangkun, Yim. *Saraban khon ru'ang nai nangsu'thi krom Sinlapakon Chat phim, B.E. thu'ng B.E. 2510, lem 2* (An index of works published by the Fine Arts Department, B.E. 2471 to B.E. 2510, volume 2). Phranakhon, Krom Sinlapakon, B.E. 2512 (1969). 4, 119, 427, 73 p.
Lists some 3,000 publications issued from March 1928 to 1967, divided into three parts, the first being a chronological list of publications, the second a subject index and the third an author index. Publications include the cremation (i.e. commemorative or memorial) volumes issued by the National Library.

Periodicals and Newspapers

N30 *Rainam nangsuphim khao sung ok pen raya nai Prathet Sayam* (List of newspapers published in Siam). Phranakhon, Ratchabandit Sapha, B.E. 2474 (1931). 22 p.
363 newspapers and periodicals in the National Library, mostly in Thai, but with some in English and Chinese. This is a cremation (i.e. commemorative or memorial) volume compiled by the Royal Society, and the only source for noting dates of commencing and

ceasing publication and frequency for these newspapers and periodicals.

N31 Thailand. Krom kanfukhat khru (Teacher Training Department). *Datchani nittayasan Thai* Index to articles in Thai periodicals. Phranakhon, B.E. 2500– (1957–). v.1–.
Compiled by the Teacher Training Department of the Ministry of Education, each volume contains some 6,000 entries from some 30 periodicals. Entries are arranged in each volume by author, title and subject headings. Volume 5, covering 1968, noted.

N32 Thailand, Sathaban Bandit Phatthanaborihansat (National Institute of Development Administration). *Datchani warasan Thai*, B.E. 2503- Index to Thai periodical literature, 1960–. Phranakhon, B.E. 2507–.
The first volume was published by the Institute of Public Administration of Thammasat University. The second, by its successor, the National Institute of Development Administration, contains over 4,000 periodical articles. 1975 volume, published 1978, seen.

N33 Thailand. Sathaban Bandit Phatthanaborihansat (National Institute of Development Administration). *Detchani nangsuphim Thai* Index to Thai newspapers, 1964. Phranakhon, B.E. 2511 (1965). 710 p.
Some 14,000 entries from three newspapers published in 1964 are arranged by subject. 1970–2 volume, published 1974, noted.

N34 Thailand. Hong Samut haeng Chat (National Library). *Warasan lae nangsu'phim nai prathet Thai su'ng ti phim nawang . . . bannanukrom* Periodicals and newspapers printed in Thailand . . . a bibliography. Phranakhon, B.E. 2515–17 (1970–2) 2 v.
The first volume includes 928 periodicals, newspapers and official publications published from 1844–1934, and the second 1305, published from 1935–71. Supplement for 1972–3. An associated bibliography: *Chinese periodicals and newspapers, printed in Thailand, history and bibliography* (1976) lists 95 periodicals and newspapers in Chinese.

N35 Nunn, G. Raymond. *Burmese and Thai newspapers, an international union list.* Taipei, Chinese Materials and Research Aids Service Centre, 1972. 44 p. (Occasional series no. 13).
Entries for 30 Burmese and 240 Thai newspapers, with holdings in Australian, British, Japanese and American libraries and the National Library of Thailand, are arranged by place of publication. Index to Thai newspapers in Thai.

Subject Bibliography

SOCIAL SCIENCES

N36 Thailand. Samnakngan Sathiti haeng Chat (National Statistical Office). *Statistical bibliography.* Bangkok, National Statistical Office, 1961–.

Issued in 1961, 1964, 1966 and 1974. The 1966 issue noted 308 publications, with over half in English, or in Thai and English, arranged by issuing office. Each entry is annotated. Thai version of 1966 issue, *Bannanukrom sathiti Ph.S* (1969. 133 p.), seen. 1974 issue in English, but listing material mostly in Thai.

N37 Amyot, Jacques. *Provisional paper on changing patterns on social structure in Thailand, 1851–1965, an annotated bibliography with comments.* Delhi, U.N.E.S.C.O. Research Centre, 1965. 171 p.
621 books and periodical articles, mostly in English, but with a few in Thai and French. Most entries are not annotated. The bibliography is arranged in three sections. The first is divided topically, covering geography, history, people, economy, social organization, religion, education and government. The second section is a list arranged alphabetically by author, giving full citations for the materials listed topically under the first section, with a few annotations. The third section evaluates the materials from the standpoint of the social sciences.

N38 Raksasataya, Amara. *Thailand, social science materials in Thai and Western languages.* Bangkok, The National Institute of Development Administration, 1966. 378 p.
1,300 books and periodicals in Western languages are arranged in author order. However the most significant section is a 245-page section of Thai-language books on the social sciences, arranged by the Thai alphabet, with some 2,300 entries. The third section lists 109 Thai-language periodicals. Social science is widely interpreted and includes much history.

N39 Thrombley, Woodforth G., William J. Siffin and Pensri Vayavananda. *Thai government and its setting, a selective annotated bibliography.* Bangkok, National Institute of Development Administration, 1967. 513 p.
In two parts. The first, in 93 pages, contains some 500 books and periodical articles in English, in a subject arrangement, with an author index. The second part, in 420 pages, contains some 2,000 items in Thai, and is also arranged by subject with an author index. Annotations are in Thai, but titles are translated into English.

N40 Thrombley, Woodworth G. and William J. Siffin. *Thailand, politics, economy and socio-cultural setting, a selective guide to the literature.* Bloomington, Indiana University Press, 1972. 148 p.
A revision of the English-language section of the authors' *Thai government and its setting, a selective annotated bibliography* (N 39). Some 800 books and articles are arranged by broad subjects and items are annotated. The authors have long experience in the field of Thai government. Indexed.

N41 U.S. Operations Mission to Thailand. Bangkok. Technical Library. Document Section. *USOM–Thailand Technical Library*

Document Section card catalog. Bangkok, 1967. 580 p.
An author-title and subject catalogue of some 5,000 items collected as background materials for projects, and reports written by advisers. Relevant to Thailand's social and economic development, the catalogue represents the complete holdings of the Library. *Supplement* (1970) contains some 1,800 additional entries.

N42 Bitz, Ira. *A bibliography of English-language source materials on Thailand in the humanities, social and physical sciences.* Washington, Center for Research in Social Systems, American University, 1968. 272 p.
Some 2,500 entries for books, articles and reports arranged in a detailed classification with a strong social science emphasis.

N43 Gray, Audrey W. *Bibliography in Thai education.* Bangkok, Thailand Information Center; Research and Development Center, Thailand; Advanced Research Projects Agency, 1970. 396 p.
Lists 792 reports arranged by date of acquisition from June 1967 to September 1970. Annotated. Subject key.

N44 O'Hara, Michael N. *Some bibliographical resources on development in Thailand.* Los Angeles, Academic Advisory Council for Thailand, University of California, 1970. 45 p. (Report no. 2–1790 for U.S. Operations Mission to Thailand).
Lists some 400 reports, books and articles in a number of Agency for International Development Libraries, in the International Monetary Fund Library and other collections.

N45 Chapman, Valerie. *Food and nutrition in Thailand, medical, social and technological aspects, 1950–1970.* Bangkok, National Institute of Nutrition and Food Science, 1972. 103 p.
340 articles are listed with full annotations. Subject and author index.

N46 East-West Center. East-West Population Institute. *Population research in Thailand, a review and a bibliography.* Honolulu, 1973. 123 p.
A valuable introduction is followed by a bibliography of 634 articles, reports and books, arranged by author, with a subject index. Entries are in English, but one-fifth of the items are in Thai, some with English summaries. The Thai version, published by the Institute of Population Studies, Chulalongkorn University, contains citations for Thai items in Thai.

HISTORY

N47 Ishii, Yoneo, Yoshikawa Toshiharu and Akagi Osamu. *A selected Thai bibliography on the reign of King Chulalongkorn.* Osaka, Osaka University of Foreign Studies, 1972. 44 p.
Some 450 books, articles and manuscripts in Thai published from 1868 to 1910, and including King Chulalongkorn's own writings, biographies and genealogies of prominent persons, and important works and documents on the reign.

O. VIETNAM

French influence was first established in Indochina in 1787, but it was not until 1862–7 that Cochin China became a French colony. Cambodia became a French protectorate in 1863. In 1883 a French protectorate was proclaimed over Annam and Tongking, and in 1893 over Laos. Indochina was governed as one political unit from 1887. In 1954 the independent Democratic People's Republic of Vietnam was established in North Vietnam, the Republic of Vietnam in South Vietnam. Cambodia became independent in 1955, and Laos in 1956. North and South Vietnam were united in 1975.

REFERENCE WORKS

O1 Cotter, Michael. *Vietnam, a guide to reference sources.* Boston, G. K. Hall, 1977. 272 p.
Lists some 1,400 books, articles and periodicals in English, French and Vietnamese, in a detailed subject arrangement, with extensive annotations for each entry, and sometimes for each section. Covers humanities, social sciences, and the pure and applied sciences. Author-title and subject index.

ENCYCLOPEDIA AND HANDBOOKS

O2 *Viet-Nam bach-khoa tu-dien co bo chu chu Han, va Anh, do Dao-dang-Vy* Dictionnaire encyclopedique vietnamien, avec annotations en chinois, francais et anglais. Vietnamese encyclopedic dictionary with annotations in Chinese, French and English. Saigon, 1960–1. v. 1–3, A–Ch.
The greater part (some 60%) is concerned with the anthropology, history, geography, literature and archaeology of Vietnam. A further fifth is concerned with religion and philosophy, and the final fifth with science, technology and medicine. Articles are not signed, and no bibliography is given.

O3 American University, Washington, D.C. Foreign Area Studies. *Area handbook for North Vietnam.* Washington, U.S. Government Printing Office, 1967. 510 p.
Divided into four major sections, for social, economic and political affairs and for national security, covering research completed December 1966. Includes a lengthy 62-page bibliography. Index. Revision of *Area handbook for Vietnam* (1962).

O4 American University, Washington, D.C. Foreign Area Studies.

Area handbook for South Vietnam. Washington, U.S. Government Printing Office, 1967. 510 p.
A survey of social, political and economic affairs, and of national security. 36-page bibliography and glossary. Research completed 1966.

O 5 Whitfield, Danny J. *Historical and cultural dictionary of Vietnam*. Metuchen, Scarecrow Press, 1976. 369 p. (Historical and cultural dictionaries of Asia series no. 7).
Approximately 1,500 entries cover all aspects of Vietnamese history and culture. A dynastic chronology and series of historical maps included. Select bibliography, including works in Vietnamese.

DICTIONARIES

O 6 Nguyen, Van-Khon. *English-Vietnamese dictionary*. Anh-Viet tu dien, In lan thu hai. Saigon, Khai-tri, 1955. 1,741 p.
Over 50,000 English words, with their Vietnamese equivalents, together with examples of usage are given.

O 7 Dao, Duy-Anh. *Phap-Viet tu dien, Chu them chu Han* Dictionnaire francais-vietnamien . . . Saigon, Truong-thi xuat ban, 1957. 1,958 p.
Some 60,000 French words, with their equivalents in Chinese characters and Vietnamese, are given with examples of usage.

O 8 Gouin, Eugene. *Dictionnaire vietnamien chinois francais*. Saigon, Imprimerie d'Extreme Orient (Ideo), 1957. 1,606 p.
Gives some 15,000 key entries, with approximately 150,000 compounds, and their translation into French. Chinese characters for the entries are given where appropriate. Character index.

O 9 Nguyen, Dinh-hoa. *Vietnamese-English Student dictionary*. Carbondale, Southern Illinois University Press, 1971. 675 p.
Contains some 45,000 entries, approximately double the size of the 1959 edition. Examples of usage given. Reprint of the 1967 Saigon edition.

O 9a Vien Ngon Ngu Hoc (Institute of Linguistics) *Tu dien Anh-Viet* (English-Vietnamese dictionary) Hanoi, Khoa Hoc Xa Hoi, 1975. 1959 p.
60,000 entries, with numerous examples of usage, and Vietnamese equivalents. Valuable also for contemporary Communist vocabulary and usage in Vietnamese.

DIRECTORIES

O 10 Sutter, John Orval. *Scientific and information services of the Republic of Vietnam*. Honolulu, Pacific Science Information

Center, for National Science Foundation, 1961. 236 p. (Pacific Science Information no. 3).

The first part describes the geographical, political and economic situation in Vietnam in relation to science, and then goes on to discuss scientific manpower and training, research institutions and information activities. The appendices describe science teaching and research at the University of Saigon and the University of Hue. Lists ten research institutes, 21 scientific publications, and seven societies.

O 11 *A.E.C. Viet-Nam, annuaire industriel et commercial* Industrial and commercial directory, 1962–3. Saigon, Trinh-Hung and Co., 1963? 1 v. Various paging.

A directory of organizations, firms, importers, exporters and agencies, and some directory-type information for the provinces. Altogether some 28,000 entries.

O 12 *Principal institutions and personalities of North Vietnam.* Bangkok, printed by S. Chai Charoen, 1969. 180 l.

Map and historical introduction followed by a 40-leaf section on principal institutions and mass organizations, and by a major section listing some 800 North Vietnamese personalities.

O 13 Hoi Thu-vien Viet-Nam (Vietnamese Library Association). *Nien-giam thu-vien* Directory of libraries. Saigon, 1970. 62 p.

Lists 62 libraries in Saigon and Cholon, with their name, address and information on collections, including languages. The information is based on replies to a questionnaire. Indexed by type of collection.

BIOGRAPHICAL DICTIONARIES

O 14 Indochina, French. Government-General. Service-Information Propaganda Press. *Souverains et notabilities d'Indochine, notices par ordre alphabetique.* Hanoi, Edition du Gouvernement General de l'Indochine, 1943. 112 p.

Lists some 450 persons, including the reigning families of Annam, Cambodia and Luang Prabang (Laos), with photographs. There is an emphasis on Cochin China. The index is not a true index, but a contents lists.

O 15 U.S. Department of State. Interim Research and Intelligence Service. Research and Analysis Branch. *Biographical information of prominent nationalist leaders in French Indochina.* Washington, 1945. 90 p. (R and A no. 3336).

A list of 63 social and nationalist leaders in Vietnam in 1945, including cabinet members of the provisional Vietnam Republic, the General Vietnam Council, and the provisional executive committee of South Vietnam.

O 16 Nguyen, Huyen-Anh. *Viet-Nam danh nhan tu dien* (Vietnam biographical dictionary). Saigon, Khai-tri, 1967? 559 p.

A dictionary of some 1,200 persons prominent in the history of Vietnam. Dates of birth and death, when known, are given, together with short accounts. Revision of 1960 edition.

O 17 *Gendai Betonamu minshu kyowakoku jimmei jiten* Who is who in Democratic Republic of Vietnam. Tokyo, Ajia kenkyujo, 1967. 433 p.
The first section contains some 840 biographies, arranged by the Japanese syllabic system. The second section lists persons by their organization, and over half of the book consists of documents relating to North Vietnam.

O 18 Tran, Van Giap, Nguyen Tuong Phuong, Nguyen Van Phu and Ta Phong Chau. *Luoc truyen cac tac gia Viet Nam* (Brief sketches of Vietnamese authors). Hanoi, Nha Xuat Ban Khoa Hoc Xa Hoi, 1971–2. 2 v.
The first volume lists 735 historical figures arranged by historical periods, and the second 116 late-19th-century authors. Index of titles and authors.

O 19 *Who's who in Vietnam.* Saigon, Vietnam Press, 1974. 968 p.
Lists some 800 personalities, holding elected positions, high-ranking government officials and other outstanding individuals. All listed were alive at the beginning of 1974. For each name, place and date of birth, education, positions held, publications and address given. Latest issue of a publication previously published in 1967, 1968 and 1972.

GAZETTEERS

O 20 U.S. Office of Geography. *Northern Vietnam . . .* Washington, U.S. Government Printing Office, 1964. 311 p. (Gazetteer no. 79).
22,250 place and feature names are listed with their classification and longitude and latitude.

O 21 U.S. Office of Geography. *South Vietnam, official standard names approved by the United States Board on Geographic Names,* second edition. Washington, U.S. Government Printing Office, 1971. 337 p. (Gazetteer no. 58).
23,500 place and feature names for South Vietnam and a second list of 500 names for the South China Sea, with classification of the name, longitude and latitude. Vietnamese diacritical marks given. Supersedes 1961 edition.

CHRONOLOGICAL TABLES

O 22 Nguyen, Nhu-lan. *200 nam duong-lich va am-lich doi chieu* Calendrier solaire lunaire pour 200 ans, 1780–1980. Saigon, Khai-tri, n.d. 240 p.

Gives Vietnamese calendar years, months and days and their Gregorian calendar equivalents.

O 23 American University, Washington, D.C. Counter Insurgency Information Analysis Center. *A U.S./Vietnamese calendar of holidays and celebrations in Vietnam.* Washington, Special Operations Research Office. American University, 1964. 1 v. (various paging).
Describes U.S./Vietnamese calendar of holidays and celebrations in Vietnam for the years 1955–64, the Vietnamese lunar calendar, the Cambodian lunar calendar and holidays, and Laotian holidays.

CHRONOLOGY

O 24 Great Britain. British Information Services. *Vietnam, Laos and Cambodia, chronology of events, 1945–68.* London, 1968. 152 p.
Lists major events, with dates and some annotation.

CENSUS AND STATISTICS

O 25 Indochina, French. Service de la Statistique Generale. . . . *Annuaire statistique de l'Indochine, 1913–48.* Hanoi, 1927–48.
Issued irregularly, and presenting departments and aspects of Indochina. Each issue may cover from one to as many as eight years, and was usually published one or two years after the date of the statistics it includes. Alphabetical index.

O 26 Vietnam. Vien Quoc-gia Thong-ke (Institut national de la statistique). *Nien-giam thong-ke Viet-Nam,* 1949– Vietnam statistical yearbook, 1949–. Saigon, 1949–.
Compiled with the co-operation of government and private agencies, and may cover one or two years, with a delay of one or two years in publication. The statistics are presented in tabular form under 14 main subjects. Published in three languages, Vietnamese, French and English. Indexed. 18th issue for 1972 noted. Not regarded as highly reliable from 1962.

O 27 Vietnam. Vien Quoc-gia Thong-ke (Institut national de la statistique). *Enquetes demographiques au Vietnam en 1958.* Saigon, 1960. 122 p.
A special study of the population statistics of Vietnam in 1958, based on a census taken in that year. There are 16 headings under which information is given. The data on population is in much greater detail than that in the *Annuaire statistique* (O 25).

O 28 Vietnam. Vien Quoc-gia Thong-ke (Institut national de la statistique). *Theo Don-vi Hanh-chanh Trong Nam, 1965* (Population, 1965, village, district and provinces). Saigon?, n.d.

Detailed population estimates for provinces, districts and villages. In Vietnamese.

BIBLIOGRAPHY

O 29 Boudet, Paul and Remy Bourgeois. *Bibliographie de l'Indochine francaise* . . . Hanoi, Imprimerie d'Extreme Orient, 1929–67. 4 v. in 5.
Continues the work of Henri Cordier *Biblioteca Indosinica* (G 8) from 1913, and includes books and periodical articles in French on Indochina only. The first volume, published in 1929, covers the period 1913–26. There are 4,500 entries, and more periodical articles than books. Of the 30 most cited periodicals, 11 are published in Indochina, and the remaining 14 in France. It has an alphabetical subject arrangement, with entries listed by author under each subject. The second section is an alphabetical index to authors, and to titles with anonymous authors. The second volume, published in 1931, covers the period 1927–9 and has 2,500 entries. The third, published in 1933, covers 1930. The fourth volume is in two parts: the first part, *Ordre alphabetique,* was published in Hanoi in 1943, and the second, *Matieres,* in Paris in 1967. Volume 3 and the first part of volume 4 reported. Legal deposit of publications is noted in *Liste des imprimes deposes a la Regie du Depot Legal a Hanoi,* 1922–44, 1946–9.

O 30 Brebion, Antoine. *Dictionnaire de bio-bibliographie general ancienne et moderne de l'Indochine francaise* . . . Paris, Societe d'Editions Geographiques, Maritimes et Coloniales, 1935. 446 p. (Academie des Sciences coloniales tome 8).
Summaries of the lives of 1,600 persons prominent in the history of Indochina from 1859 to the 1930s, together with their publications. A subject approach to the persons listed is provided.

O 31 U.S. Library of Congress. Reference Department. *Indochina, a bibliography of the land and people.* Washington, 1950. 367 p.
1,850 entries in Western, Vietnamese and Russian languages, published for the most part after 1930. Most entries are annotated to show relationship to other entries and to give additional information. The bibliography is arranged first by language, then by subject. Library locations are given. Indexed. Reprinted by Greenwood Press, Westport, 1970.

O 32 Hanoi. Thu-vien Quoc-gia (National Library). *Muc-luc xuat ban pham* (Catalogue of published works). Hanoi, 1957–.
Lists books and other published materials received by the National Library on legal deposit. 2,850 titles of books, and 220 newspapers and periodicals were noted in the 1963 issue. Books are arranged by subject. There are separate sections for music, posters, maps, gramophone records, newspapers and periodicals.

Indexes of authors, translators, and titles for books entered under title. Issue for 1972 reported.

O 33 Saigon. Hoc-vien Quoc-gia Hanh-chanh Thu-vien (National Institute of Administration Library). *Ban thong ke phan-loai sach thu vien* Classified catalogue of books in the Library. Saigon, 1960. 606 p.

A classified catalogue of books in the Library, together with a list of its periodical holdings. There are two subject indexes, one in English and the other in Vietnamese. Approximately 8,000 entries, of which 60% are in English, 20% in French and 20% in Vietnamese.

O 34 Michigan. State University of Agriculture and Applied Science, East Lansing. Vietnam Advisory Group, Saigon. *What to read on Vietnam, a selected annotated bibliography.* New York, Institute of Pacific Relations, 1960. 73 p.

Lists some 300 books and periodical articles, mostly in English for the period from 1955 to the end of 1959, divided into two parts, the first to November 1958, and a supplement. There is in addition a valuable listing of periodicals, the first part for current publications and the second for periodicals no longer published.

O 35 Vietnam. Nha Van Kho va Thu Vien Quoc-gia (Directorate of National Archives and Libraries). *Sach moi* Nouvelles acquisitions, 1962–8. Saigon, 1962–8.

A monthly list recording in a subject arrangement approximately 100 books, periodicals and newspapers in Vietnamese and other languages received by the National Library through legal deposit, exchange with other countries, purchases and donations. Author index. The directorate is a division of the Ministry of Information.

O 36 Keyes, Jane Godfrey. *A bibliography of North Vietnamese publications in Cornell University Library.* Ithaca, Southeast Asia Program, Department of Asian Studies, Cornell University, 1962. 116 p. (Data paper no. 47)

Contains some 800 works in English and French on North Vietnam from 1945 to 1960. The materials are arranged into nine major subjects, and each of these has been divided into a pre-1954 and a post-1954 period. Materials translated by the Joint Publications Research Service have been annotated. The table of contents has to serve in place of an index, and since there are no cross-references, the user will have to check all subjects which appear to be relevant. Supplemented by the author's *A bibliography of Western-language publications concerning North Vietnam in the Cornell University Library* (O 40).

O 37 Vietnam. Nha Van Kho va Thu Vien Quoc-gia (Directorate of National Archives and Libraries). *Tin-tuc thu-tich luoc ke cac loai sach moi nhan duoc* (News of bibliography, with listing of new publications received). Saigon, 1964–.

A listing of publications received by the Ministry for censorship purposes, and arranged in classified order. In latest issue noted, no. 53, published in February 1969, 220 items are listed. Copy in National Library, Saigon.

O 38 Auvade, R. *Bibliographie critique des oeuvres parus sur l'Indochine francaise, un siecle d'histoire et d'enseignement.* Paris, Maisonneuve, 1965. 153 p.
150 entries are fully annotated and arranged by 13 subjects. An additional unannotated list of 80 entries is appended. Author index.

O 39 Vietnam. Nha Van Kho va Thu Vien Quoc-gia (Directorate of National Archives and Libraries). *Thu-muc* (Catalogue of books). Saigon, 1965–.
Each annual issue notes some 1,500 books, mostly in Vietnamese and mostly current imprints. Entries are arranged by the Dewey Decimal Classification. Author index. Last issue seen for 1968. 1972 issue reported

O 40 Keyes, Jane Godfrey. *A bibliography of Western-language publications concerning North Vietnam in the Cornell University Library.* Ithaca, Southeast Asia Program, Department of Asian Studies, Cornell University, 1966. 280p. (Data paper no. 63).
2,500 books and serials in Western languages and Russian are arranged in two parts. The first has a subject arrangement covering description, culture, biography, economic conditions, social conditions, politics and government, and foreign relations. The second part, over half of the book, consists of Joint Publications Research Service translations from Vietnamese. Supplements but does not replace the author's *A bibliography of North Vietnamese publications in Cornell University Library* (O 36).

O 41 Vietnam. National Commission for U.N.E.S.C.O. *Thu-muc chu giai ve van hoa Viet-nam* (Commented bibliography on Vietnamese culture). Saigon, 1966. 226 p.
229 entries for books, periodicals and periodical articles on anthropology, language and writing, technology, and arts, in French and Vietnamese, with annotations. There is in addition a list of 153 books published in France from 1945–54 on Vietnam. No index.

O 42 United Nations. E.C.A.F.E. Mekong Documentation Centre. *Vietnam, a reading list.* Bangkok, 1966. 119 p.
1,251 books and articles, nearly all in French and English, subdivided into a large number of subjects. No index

O 43 Vietnam. Nha Van Kho va Thu Vien Quoc-gia (Directorate of National Archives and Libraries). *Thu tich quoc-gia Viet-Nam* National bibliography of Vietnam, 1967–. Saigon, 1968–.
Intended to be a quarterly publication, listing new publications arranged by the Dewey Decimal Classification, with author and title indexes. Official publications and serials are excluded. A combined issue, no. 17–18 for 1972, noted

O 44 Oey, Giok Po. *A checklist of the Vietnamese holdings of the Wason Collection, Cornell University Libraries as of June 1971.*

Ithaca, Southeast Asia Program, Cornell University, 1971. 377 p. (Data paper no. 84).
5,707 Vietnamese-language books acquired by the Wason Collection since 1959 are arranged alphabetically by author or title, with a broad subject index referring to the entries by serial number. The first appendix lists 354 Vietnamese-language periodicals. The second appendix lists 118 South Vietnamese and four North Vietnamese newspapers, with short annotations for the former. Neither appendix states holdings.

O 45 Vietnam. Nha Van Kho va Thu Vien Quoc-gia (Directorate of National Archives and Libraries). *Thu-tich hoi-to quoc-gia Viet-Nam* Retrospective national bibliography of Vietnam, 1963–7. Saigon, 1971. 389 p.
2,409 entries, mostly in Vietnamese, arranged in broad subject categories, based on books deposited in the Legal Deposit Bureau. Periodicals, phonorecords and maps are excluded. Author and title indexes.

O 46 Chen, John H. M. *Vietnam, a comprehensive bibliography.* Metuchen, Scarecrow Press, 1973. 314 p.
2,331 books almost entirely in English, and including a very high proportion of materials not related to Vietnam or not on Vietnam. Subject and title index.

Official Publications

O 47 Vietnam. Nha Van Kho va Thu Vien Quoc-gia (Directorate of National Archives and Libraries). *Thu-tich ve an pham cong Viet-Nam* Bibliography on Vietnamese official publications, 1960–9. Saigon, 1970. 134 p.
717 titles, almost entirely in Vietnamese, are arranged by bureau. Title and author index.

Periodicals and Newspapers

O 48 Tran, Thi Kimsa. *Muc-luc phan-tich tap-chi Viet-ngu, 1954–1964* A guide to Vietnamese periodical literature, 1954–1964. Saigon, Hoc-vien Quoc-gia Hanh-chanh, 1965. 318 p.
1,976 articles in Vietnamese from seven periodicals, arranged by subject and not limited to materials on Vietnam. Author index.

O 49 Tran, Thi Kimsa. *Bibliography on Vietnam, 1954–1964* Thu tich ve Viet-Nam, 1954–1964. Saigon, National Institute of Administration, 1965. 255 p.
Some 3,000 books and articles from over 100 periodicals in French, Vietnamese and English, but mostly in English, published in Vietnam and elsewhere, arranged by subjects. Author index.

O 50 Vietnam. Tong-bo Van-hoa Xa-hoi (Ministry of Cultural and Social Affairs). *Muc-luc bao-chi Viet-ngu, 1865–1965* (Catalogue

of newspapers and periodicals published in Vietnamese, 1865–1965). Saigon, 1966. (182) p.
1,280 newspapers and periodicals are arranged in order of date of first publication, with dates of ceasing publication also noted. There is some annotation of entries. Alphabetical index to titles.

O 51 Vietnam. Bo Thong Tin, Nha Van Kho va Thu Vien Quoc-gia (Ministry of Information, Archives and Libraries). *An pham dinh ky quoc noi, 1968–* (Comprehensive list of Vietnamese serials, 1968–). Saigon, 1969–.
Lists 186 newspapers and periodicals published in South Vietnam in 1968, noting publisher, editor and address. Entries are arranged in order of frequency of publication. Title index. 1969 and 1970 issues seen.

O 52 Nunn, G. Raymond and Do Van Anh. *Vietnamese, Cambodian and Laotian newspapers, an international union list.* Taipei, Chinese Materials and Research Aids Service Center, 1972. 104 p. (Occasional series no. 12).
Notes 142 newspapers published in Cambodia and 41 in Laos, with holdings and locations for most of these newspapers. Holdings and locations for 764 newspapers published in Vietnam are also noted. These are for the Bibliotheque Nationale in Phnom Penh, the National Library and the General Library in Saigon, the Bibliotheque Nationale in Paris, and for major U.S. collections. Index to newspapers published in Vietnam.

Maps

O 53 U.S. Department of the Army. Engineer Agency for Resources Inventories. *Vietnam, subject index maps.* Washington, 1970. 182 p.
182 black and white copies of maps of Vietnam are arranged in 24 subject groups. List of sources given. No index

Subject Bibliography

RELIGION AND THOUGHT

O 54 Vietnam. Nha Van Kho va Thu Vien Quoc-gia (Directorate of National Archives and Libraries). *So-thao muc-luc thu-tich Khong-giao o Viet Nam* A bibliography on Confucianism in Vietnam. Saigon, 1967. 41 p.
253 books and articles, but mostly articles in Vietnamese, arranged by author.

O 55 Vietnam. Nha Van Kho va Thu Vien Quoc-gia (Directorate of National Archives and Libraries). *So-thao muc-luc thu-tich ve thien chua-giao o Viet-Nam* A bibliography on Christianity in Vietnam. Saigon, 1967. 81 p.
634 books and articles arranged by author. Presumably call

numbers cited are for the National Library. No subject approach. No annotations

SOCIAL SCIENCES

O 56 Ti, Tang-Ti. *Muc-luc phan-tich tap-chi khoa-hoc xa-hoi Viet-Nam, 1958–62* Index to Vietnamese social science periodicals, 1958–62. Saigon, Hoc-vien Quoc-gia Hanh-chanh, 1961–3. 2 v.
The first volume covers 1958 to 1960, the second 1961 and 1962. Only four periodicals are indexed, and entries are arranged by subject. Each volume has an author index.

O 57 U.S. Department of the Army. Engineer Agency for Resources Inventories. *Vietnam, subject index catalog.* Washington, 1970. 288 p.
Arranges some 4,000 reports and books, a high proportion of which originate from the Agency for International Development, in broad subject groups

O 58 U.S. Department of the Army. Engineer Agency for Resources Inventories. *Vietnam, a selected annotated bibliography, agriculture.* Washington, 1970. 58 p.
Some 300 annotated entries, largely reports from U.S. official sources on agriculture in contemporary Vietnam.

O 59 Ng, Shui-meng. *Demographic materials on the Khmer Republic, Laos and Vietnam.* Singapore, Institute of South East Asian Studies, 1974. 54 p.
510 books, articles, reports and theses in English, French and Vietnamese are arranged under 20 main divisions and subdivisions. Author index.

O 60 Nguyen, Hung-cuong. *Thu-tich ve khoa hoc xa hoi tai Viet-Nam* (A bibliography of social science materials published in Vietnam, 1947–67). Saigon, Phu Quoc vu Khanh dac-trach Van hoa Nha Van kho va Thu vien Quoc gia, 1970. 246 p.
1,247 selected books and articles. The articles are from nine periodicals; locations are given in the National Library, General Library and Library of the National Institute of Administration. Arranged under 14 major sections. Author index. Materials cited are mostly in Vietnamese, but some are in French and English.

O 61 Phan, Thien Chan. *Vietnamese communism, a research bibliography.* Westport, Greenwood Press, 1975. 359 p.
3,467 entries for books, articles and reports in English, French and Vietnamese, and published to June 1974, are arranged in a detailed subject classification. The bibliography concentrates on North Vietnam. Author and title indexes.

O 62 Nguyen Phuong-Khanh. *Vietnamese legal materials, 1954–75, a selected, annotated bibliography.* Washington, Library of Congress, 1977. 74 p.
460 entries for books and periodical articles, mostly published in South Vietnam and mostly in Vietnamese, but with some articles in French and English, are arranged in broad subject classifica-

tion. Some annotation. Most of materials cited are in the Library of Congress. Author index.

NATURAL AND APPLIED SCIENCES

O 63 Grimes, Annie E. *An annotated bibliography on the climate of the Republic of Vietnam.* Silver Springs, Environment Data Service, 1967. 122 p.
The sources on the climate of Vietnam are arranged with abstracts, by date of publication. Author index and list of stations in Vietnam.

LANGUAGE AND LITERATURE

O 64 Vietnam. Nha Van Kho va Thu Vien Quoc-gia (Directorate of National Archives and Libraries). *So-thao muc-luc thu-tich ve ngon-ngu Viet Nam* Reading list on Vietnamese language. Saigon, 1967. 29p.
Lists 243 books and periodical articles mostly in Vietnamese. No annotation and no index.

O 65 Baruch, Jacques. *Bibliographie des traductions francaises des litteratures du Vietnam and du Cambodge.* Bruxelles, Editions Thanh-Long, 1968. 62 p.
256 entries for Vietnam, 16 for the Montagnards and 36 for Cambodia, each section in author order. Index to translators.

O 66 Nha-Trang, Cong-Huyen Ton-Nu. *Vietnamese folklore, an introductory and annotated bibliography.* Berkeley, University of California, Center for South and Southeast Asian Studies, 1970. 33 p.
199 entries for books and periodical articles in French and Vietnamese, with annotations. Arranged by categories, and with a lengthy introduction to the subject. Author index.

HISTORY

O 67 Brebion, Antoine. *Bibliographie des voyages dans l'Indochine francaise du IX au XIX siecle.* New York, Burt Franklin, 1970. 289 p.
Reprint of a 1910 publication listing some 500 books arranged chronologically and annotated. Indexes to authors, travellers and titles of anonymous works.

O 68 Jumper, Roy. *A bibliography on the political and administrative history of Vietnam, 1802–1962.* Saigon, Michigan State University, Vietnam Advisory Group, 1964. 115 p.
964 books and periodical articles in French, English and Vietnamese, of which about one-half are on historical subjects. The materials are arranged under broad subjects, some of which are further sub-divided. Brief annotations. Author index.

O 69 Vietnam. Nha Van Kho va Thu Vien Quoc-gia (Directorate of National Archives and Libraries). *Thu-muc ve su hap-thu van-hoa tay-phuong tai Viet-Nam* A bibliography on the acceptance

of Western cultures in Vietnam. Saigon, Ministry of Culture, Directorate of National Archives and Libraries, 1967. 35 p.
In four parts. The first notes archive sources, the second bibliographies, the third lists dictionaries and works translated into Vietnamese, and the fourth is on the relation of Western culture to Vietnam.

O 70 Nguyen, The-Anh. *Bibliographie critique sur les relations entre le Viet-Nam et l'Occident, ouvrages et articles en langues occidentales.* Paris, Maisonneuve and Larose, 1967. 310 p.
1,635 books and archive sources, almost entirely in French are arranged in a classified order, with an index to authors and personal names.

O 70a Desire, Michel. *La campagne de l'Indochine, 1945–1954, bibliographie.* Vincennes, 1971– v. 1–.
A detailed chronology to December 1954, and pre-1940 Indochina and Indochina from 1940–5 are included in the first volume. Succeeding volumes will cover geography, economics, politics, diplomacy and the military campaigns.

O 71 Leitenberg, Milton and Richard Dean Burns. *The Vietnam conflict, its geographical dimensions, political traumas and military developments.* Santa Barbara, ABC-Clio, 1973. 164 p. (War/Peace Bibliography series 3).
2,367 books, periodicals and articles systematically arranged with principal divisions for Vietnamese history and politics, U.S. participation, and military operations. No annotations. Author-subject index. Short introduction, with a chronology of U.S. involvement.

P. EAST ASIA

The East Asia area in this guide will include China, with Chinese Central Asia, Japan, Korea and Mongolia.

HANDBOOK

P 1 Edmunds, William. *Pointers and clues to the subjects of Chinese and Japanese art*. London, Sampson Low, Marston and Co., 1934. 725 p.
An encyclopedia of Japanese and Chinese art symbolism, with references in the Chinese and Buddhist sections to the Japanese forms of names. For Japanese art more recent and superior to Henri L. Joly *Legend in Japanese art* (R 11).

BIBLIOGRAPHY

P 2 Kerner, Robert J. *Northeastern Asia, a selected bibliography*. Berkeley, University of California Press, 1939. 2 v.
13,884 books, periodicals and periodical articles cover the whole of East Asia, including Eastern Siberia, but excluding Southeast Asia. The materials cited are in Chinese, Japanese, Korean, Russian and Western Languages, and all the titles are translated. Two-thirds of the entries are in non-Western languages. After an initial regional and country division, there is a classified subject arrangement. The best key to the bibliography is a detailed table of contents. There are no annotations. Small subject index. Reprinted by Burt Franklin, New York, 1968.

P 3 Beardsley, Richard K. *Bibliographic materials in the Japanese language on Far Eastern archeology and ethnology*. Ann Arbor, University of Michigan Press for Center of Japanese Studies, 1950. 74 p. (University of Michigan, Center of Japanese Studies, Bibliographical series no. 3).
1,063 books and periodical articles published after 1900 have been arranged by country and subdivided by topic. The annotations are usually brief. Library locations are noted. No index.

P 4 Teng, Ssu-yu. *Japanese studies on Japan and the Far East*. Hong Kong, Hong Kong University Press, 1961. 485 p.
Over 4,200 books and periodical articles by 775 living Japanese scholars arranged in subject order. For each scholar there is a short introduction, followed by a list of their books and then their articles. Many older and well-known scholars have been omitted, and also writings before 1942. Authors' names are indexed by character. General index.

P5 Harvard University. Library. *China, Japan and Korea.* Cambridge, Harvard University Library (distributed by Harvard University Press), 1968. 494 p. (Widener Library shelflist 14).
In the first two parts, Western-language books on China, Japan and Korea are arranged in a classified order. The third part is an author and title index, and the fourth a chronological listing by date of publication. The shelflist represents a rich collection on East Asia of some 15,300 books and periodicals.

P6 California. University. Berkeley. East Asiatic Library. *Author-title catalog.* Boston, G. K. Hall, 1968. 13 v.
Some 190,000 reproductions of catalogue cards are arranged in radical order in eleven volumes and in a two-volume *hangul, kana* and alphabetical supplement. An accompanying six-volume *Subject catalog* (1968) contains some 90,000 entries. There is a two-volume first supplement to the *Author-title catalog* and a two-volume first supplement to the *Subject catalog,* both supplements were published in 1973.

P7 Gillin, Donald G., Edith Ehrman and Ward Morehouse. *East Asia, a bibliography for undergraduate libraries.* Williamsport, Bro-Dart, 1970. 130 p.
2,066 books in English. Not annotated but with references to annotations in other bibliographies and to reviews. Arranged by country, then by a detailed subject division. Author index.

P8 Imon, Hiroshi. *Taiheiyo sensoshi bunken kaidai* (Annotated bibliography of the history of the Pacific war). Tokyo, Shin Jimbutsu Oraisha, Showa 46 (1971). 330 p.
Books and articles in Japanese are arranged by major war theatres, excluding the Chinese theatre, but including Manchuria and Mongolia. Sketch maps are useful for identifying place names in *katakana.* Author index.

P9 U.S. Library of Congress. Division of Orientalia. *Far Eastern languages catalog/Library of Congress.* Boston, G. K. Hall, 1972. 22 v.
Contains 332,000 printed Library of Congress cards for 121,000 Chinese, Japanese and Korean books and serials catalogued from 1958, with author, title and subject entries in one alphabet. Notes some 55,000 Chinese, 55,000 Japanese and 11,000 Korean books. 80% of the materials are post–World War II publications.

P10 Yang, Theresa Shu-yi, Thomas C. Kuo and Frank Joseph Shulman. *East Asian resources in American libraries.* New York, Paragon Book Gallery, 1977. 143 p.
A useful directory of East Asian library collections in U.S. and Canada, with an extensive bibliography comprising over half the publication.

Q. CHINA

In the modern period China lost major portions of her territory. After the Sino-Japanese war in 1895. Taiwan was seized by Japan. As a result of the 1911 Revolution, Outer Mongolia became independent. In 1932 the Japanese established Manchoukuo, and in 1937 they invaded China proper, and the Nationalist government moved to Chungking. After World War II both Manchuria and Taiwan were recovered. The latter remained in Nationalist hands after 1949, when the Chinese People's Republic was established on the mainland.

REFERENCE WORKS

Q1 Berton, Peter and Eugene Wu. *Contemporary China, a research guide*. Stanford, Hoover Institution, Stanford University, 1968. 695 p. (Hoover Institution bibliographical series, v. 31).
2,226 general reference works, documentary materials, periodicals, and dissertations in English, Chinese, Japanese and Russian, cover mainland China from 1949, Hong Kong and Taiwan from 1945, and concentrate on social science and humanities aspects. Materials are arranged by topics, with full and critical annotations. There are subject and author-title indexes. A definitive reference work for China from 1949 to 1963, when systematic collection of materials for this work was completed.

Q2 Teng, Ssu-yu and Knight Biggerstaff. *An annotated bibliography of selected Chinese reference works,* third edition. Cambridge, Harvard University Press, 1971. 250 p. (Harvard-Yenching Institute studies 2).
Some 700 selected reference works in Chinese have a classified arrangement, and is an extensive revision of the second edition. The preface states that it is concerned with China before 1949, but there are reference works relating to post-1949 China. This book is orientated to the Western student of China, and each entry is helpfully and fully annotated. Combined author, title index and glossary.

Q3 Ying, Yu-k'ang and Hsieh Yun-fei. *Chung wen kung chu shu chih yin* (Guide to Chinese reference works). Taipei, Lan-t'ai Shu chu, 1975. 442 p.
1,371 reference works, almost entirely in Chinese, are arranged under 11 headings, which are further subdivided. All entries are annotated. Mainland Chinese publications are not included. Title index by strokes.

ENCYCLOPEDIAS AND HANDBOOKS

Q4 *Ku chin t'u shu chi ch'eng* (The Chinese encyclopedia). Shanghai, Shang-hai T'u shu chi ch'eng Cheng chu, Kuang-hsu 10 (1884). 1,628 v.
This, the greatest of all encyclopedias, was compiled under imperial sponsorship and presented to the Chinese throne in 1725. It contains 10,000 *chuan* or chapters. 6,109 items are arranged according to a classified order, and sources are noted. There is an index and description in Lionel Giles *An alphabetical index to the Chinese encyclopedia* (London, British Museum, 1911), which translates headings and lists the section and *chuan* in which they can be found. Published in a number of editions. A reduced facsimile reprint of Yung-chang palace bronze movable-type edition published in Taiwan 1965 in 100 volumes.

Q5 Brunnert, Ippolit Semenovich. *Present-day political organization of China*. Shanghai, Kelly and Walsh, 1912. 572 p.
A valuable guide to official positions and organization under the Ch'ing dynasty (1644–1911). To be preferred to William F. Mayers *The Chinese government, a manual of Chinese titles . . .* (1886). For a fuller treatment of this topic, Yorozu Orita *Shinkoku gyosei ho* (Administrative law of China) (Tokyo, Daian, 1965–6) is a standard reference.

Q6 Couling, Samuel. *Encyclopedia sinica*. Shanghai, Kelly and Walsh, 1917. 633 p.
A one-volume dictionary of Chinese works, persons and places, mostly written by Samuel Couling but with some articles from other authorities. Each article is short. Some bibliographical references are given. No index. Reprinted by the Chinese Materials and Research Aids Center, Taipei, 1965.

Q7 Ball, James Dyer. *Things Chinese, or notes connected with China*. Shanghai, Kelly and Walsh, 1925. 766 p.
Another one-volume encyclopedia of China, but with lengthier articles and fuller lists of references than the *Encyclopedia sinica* (Q 6). There is an excellent index. The work has a Southeast China bias. The 1925 edition is the fifth, and was revised by Edward Theodore Chalmers Werner.

Q8 Werner, Edward Theodore Chalmers. *A dictionary of Chinese mythology*. New York, Julian Press, 1961. 627 p.
An important reference work for understanding many terms and words which appear in Chinese history and literature. Information is given on gods and goddesses, myths and superstitions. There is an index to myths which refers to related articles, but not to pages. A reprint of an earlier edition, and except for the preface, little different from the 1932 edition.

Q9 Williams, C. A. S. *Encyclopedia of Chinese symbolism and art motives, an alphabetical compendium of legends and beliefs as reflected in the manners and customs of the Chinese throughout*

history. New York, Julian Press, 1960. 468 p.
Consists of articles of varying length arranged alphabetically. The Chinese characters are given for each item, and sources are frequently noted. The book is illustrated and there is an index. Originally published as *Outlines of Chinese symbolism and art motives* (Shanghai, Kelly and Walsh, 1932). Reprinted again by Tuttle, Rutland, 1974.

Q10 Soothill, William Edward and Lewis Hodous. *A dictionary of Chinese Buddhist terms with Sanskrit and English equivalents.* London, Kegan Paul, Trench, Trubner and Co., 1937. 510 p.
8,000 Buddhist terms are arranged in character stroke and then by radical order, and definitions given. There is a Sanskrit and Pali index. Important for reading Chinese Mahayana texts. Reprinted by Buddhist Cultural Service, Taipei, 1962.

Q11 Girard, Marcel. *Nagel's encyclopedia-guide, China.* New York, Cowles Educational Corporation, 1968. 1,504 p.
First published in French in 1967, and the product of a team of young French sinologists. The first section, in 393 pages, is an introduction to Chinese civilization, surveying geography, language, history, thought, literature, art, the economy, modern culture, games and cooking. The second section, consisting of over two-thirds of the book, is a guide covering the whole of China, with much detail and over 120 maps. Short index.

Q12 American University. Washington, D.C. Foreign Area Studies. *Area handbook for the Republic of China.* Washington, U.S. Government Printing Office, 1969. 435 p.
A survey of the background and current situation in social, political, economic and security fields. Research completed November 1967.

Q13 American University. Washington, D.C. Foreign Area Studies. *Area handbook for the People's Republic of China.* Washington, U.S. Government Printing Office, 1972. 729 p.
A survey of social, political and economic affairs and of national security. Bibliography and glossary. Research completed October 1971.

Q14 Wu, Yuan-li. *China, a handbook.* New York, Praeger, 1973. 915 p.
Consists of 30 chapters, each dealing with an aspect of contemporary China, and written by authorities. Each chapter has a bibliography, and there is a general bibliography in the concluding chapter on information.

YEARBOOKS

English Language

Q15 *China year book,* 1912–39. Shanghai, North China Daily News, 1912–39.

Published by E. P. Dutton, New York from 1912–19, by the Tientsin Press, Tientsin from 1921–9, and by the *North China Daily News* from 1931–9. No issues for 1915, 1917 and 1918. The first yearbook to be published in China, each issue contains much valuable information on social, political and economic conditions. From the second issue, a biographical dictionary and lists of newspapers and periodicals were included. Later issues reflect the Japanese occupation in China. Indexed.

Q16 *Chinese year book,* 1935/6–1944/5. Shanghai, Daily Tribune Publishing Co., 1935–45. 7 v.
Published by the Commercial Press from 1935–41, Thacker in Bombay for 1943, and by the *Daily Tribune* for the 1944/5 issue. No issue for 1942. Was written by outstanding Chinese contributors, and has historical, economic and directory-type information, with lists of central and local Chinese government officials. No biographical section. Indexed. Reprinted by Kraus Reprint Corporation, New York.

Q17 *China annual,* 1943-4. Shanghai, Asia Statistics Co., 1943–4. 2 v.
Only two issues noted. An encyclopedic survey of Chinese history and contemporary political, economic and regional conditions. Includes the texts of laws of the Wang Ching-wei National Government of China established by the Japanese in Nanking. Indexed.

Q18 *China yearbook,* 1937–. Taipei, China Publishing Co., 1943–.
Earlier issues were published by Macmillan, New York; the 1950 issue was published by Rockport Press, New York; and from 1951 issues were published from Taipei. With the 1957/8 issue, the title was changed from *China handbook* to *China yearbook.* Surveys political, economic, social and cultural affairs, and has a section on the Chinese Communist regime. An extensive biographical section lists some 1,500 personalities. Appendices include the Constitution of the Republic of China, important laws passed during the previous year, and other official documents. Indexed. 1978 last issue seen.

Q19 *Communist China,* 1955–. Hongkong, Union Research Institute, 1956–.
Each issue contains a number of commentaries and essays on such subjects as the Communist Party, finance, education and political development. Based on documentation from Chinese Communist newspapers. 1971 issue last seen.

Japanese Language

Q20 *Chugoku nenkan* China yearbook. Tokyo, Toa Dobunkan, 1908?–.
Compiled by the Toa Dobunkan (East Asia cultural alliance), and provided a detailed survey of population, government, finance.

foreign relations, defence, economy, communications and trade. 1908 edition reported, but first issue seen 1911, and latest 1926. Reprinted in Taiwan.

Q21 *Shina nenkan,* 1916–42 (China yearbook, 1916–42). Tokyo, Toa Dobunkan, Taisho 5 – Showa 17 (1916–42). 7 v.
An encyclopedic yearbook, the 1942 issue having 1,210 pages, surveying China's geography, peoples, cities and villages, economy, politics and government, foreign relations, communications, the Chinese Communist Party, and Overseas Chinese. Detailed table of contents, but not indexed.

Q22 *Chugoku nenkan,* 1955–60 (China yearbook, 1955–60). Tokyo, Ishigaki Shoten, Showa 30–5 (1955–60).
Relies heavily on the *Jen min shou ts'e* (People's handbook) published in Peking. Stresses foreign relations of Communist China, Sino-Japanese relations and trade. Arrangement is by subject, with sections for geography, foreign relations, economics, culture, politics and education. Appendices contain texts of laws, lists of organizations and statistics. Subject and names indexes arranged by the Japanese syllabary. Continued by the *Shin Chugoku nenkan* (New China yearbook) (Q 23).

Q23 *Shin Chugoku nenkan,* 1962– (New China yearbook, 1962–). Tokyo, Kyokuto Shoten, Showa 37– (1962–).
Arranged by subject, and includes foreign relations, land and people, politics and government, economy, social affairs, culture and statistics. Detailed table of contents, and subject and name indexes. 1978 issue seen.

Q24 Ajia Chosakai, Tokyo. *Chugoku soran,* 1971 nempan (China survey, 1971). Tokyo, Showa 46 (1971). 1,139 p.
A survey of the Cultural Revolution, Chinese government foreign policy, the economy, culture, education and society. Appendixes contain important documents, a detailed chronology for the years 1966 through 1969, selected biographies for 320 persons, and a glossary of terms. 1978 issue seen.

Chinese Language

Q25 *Shen pao nien chien,* Min kuo 22–33 (Shen pao yearbook, 1933–44). Shanghai, Shen pao, Min kuo 22–33 (1933–44). 6 v.
Arranged by subject, and including population, home and foreign events, politics and government, finance, industry, labour, education and transportation, and based on information from official and other publications. Laws and regulations are included. Statistical information is frequently unreliable. Available on microfilm from Center for Chinese Research Materials, Washington, D.C.

Q26 *Jen min shou ts'e,* 1950– (People's handbook, 1950–). Peiching, Ta kung pao, 1950–.
Contents are largely compiled from the Peking *Jen min jih pao*

(People's Daily) and are arranged by subject, frequently stressing the most outstanding topic of the previous year. The 1964 issue, for example, stresses Sino-Soviet relations. Other subjects include population, government, foreign relations, finance, culture and sports. No issue for 1954. 1965 issue last noted. 1955 issue contains 1953 census results.

Q27 *Chung hua min kuo nien chien,* 1951– (Yearbook of the Republic of China, 1951–). Tai-pei, Chung hua min kuo nien chien she, Min kuo 40– (1951–).
Records political, economic, education, social and general events for the previous financial year, from July 1 to June 30, and gives some coverage for events on the China mainland. Detailed table of contents, but not indexed. 1975 issue last noted.

DICTIONARIES

Q28 Mathews, Robert. *Chinese-English dictionary,* revised American edition. Cambridge, Harvard University Press, 1956. 1,226 p.
Arranged by romanization, with an index to some 7,800 characters arranged by radicals. This dictionary is rich in compounds, but less consistent than others in its romanization. A revision of the 1931 edition. Reprinted by the Cheng wen shu chu, Taipei, 1964. There is also the *Chinese-English dictionary*, revised English index (Cambridge, Harvard University Press, 1954. 186 p.), which is valuable as an abridged key to some 20,000 English words in the dictionary.

Q29 Fenn, Courtenay. *The five thousand character dictionary.* Cambridge, Harvard University Press, 1966. 696 p.
Arranged by romanization, with an index in radical order. Useful for establishing a consistent romanization, but has fewer compounds than others. A reprint, without revision, of the 1940 edition.

Q30 *Kuo yu tzu tien* (Dictionary of the national language). T'ai-pei, Shang wu Yin shu kuan, Min kuo 42 (1953). 4 v.
The first comprehensive and scholarly dictionary to include spoken language forms, and arranged by the *Chu yin fu hao,* a Chinese phonetic alphabet, which was first published in 1918. Each character also has an accompanying *Gwoyeu romatzyh* romanization which represents both pronunciation and tones through spelling. The first volume was originally published in 1937. A revised and abridged edition, *Han yu tz'u tien* (Dictionary of the Chinese language) (Pei-ching, Shang wu yin shu kuan, 1957), omits the *Gwoyeu romatzyh.*

Q31 Chung wen Ta tz'u tien Pien tsuan Wei yuan hui. *Chung wen ta tz'u tien* (Encyclopedic dictionary of the Chinese language). T'ai-pei, Min kuo 51–7 (1962–8). 40 v.
Based on Tetsuji Morohashi *Dai Kanwa jiten* (R 21). With some

supplementation and changes, and with definitions in Chinese. Certainly the most comprehensive dictionary of Chinese now available.

Q32 Shu, Hsin-ch'eng. *Tz'u hai* (Chinese encyclopedic dictionary). T'ai-pei, Chung hua Shu chu, Min kuo 51 (1962). 2 v.
Arranged by stroke order, with brief but excellent definitions. No index. In the second volume a number of appendices give the Constitution of the Republic of China, a world chronology to 1962, a listing of mainland administrative units, and Western proper names in the dictionary. George Kennedy *ZH Guide* (New Haven, 1953. 185 p.) is a useful guide to this dictionary. New Peking edition reported, volumes 1 and 10, 1961–.

Q33 *Chinese-English dictionary of modern Communist usage,* second edition. Washington, Joint Publications Research Service, 1963. 845 p. (JPRS 20,904 OTS 63-31674).
A valuable and more official guide to current usage translated from *Chinesisch-deutsches Worterbuch* (Han te tz'u tien) (Peiching, Shang wu yin shu kuan, 1960. 789 p.), with 35,000 words and phrases arranged alphabetically in the *p'inyin* romanization officially employed in Mainland China, with characters and translation into English. There is a Wade-Giles and *p'inyin* conversion table.

Q34 *Modern Chinese-English technical and general dictionary.* New York, McGraw-Hill, 1963. 3 v.
Includes most of Robert Mathews *Chinese-English dictionary* (Q 28), and other dictionaries, but is twice the size of Mathews, with 212,000 entries, of which 80% are scientific and technical. The third or main volume is arranged in the *p'inyin* romanization, with characters noted as in the standard telegraphic code. The first two volumes are concerned with tables showing characters and their telegraphic code equivalents.

Q35 Huang, Yen-kai. *Chung hua ch'eng yu tz'u tien* A dictionary of Chinese idiomatic phrases. Hongkong, Eton Press, 1964. 1,291 p.
Arranged in romanized order, according to the Wade-Giles system, this dictionary lists 30,000 phrases with some 4,700 initial characters. The phrase is first given in characters, followed by the romanization, then its translation and source when known. Unfortunately only the title of the work is given and this is usually insufficient to locate the context. The romanization contains many errors.

Q36 Yale University. Institute of Far Eastern Languages. *Dictionary of spoken Chinese.* New Haven, Yale University Press, 1966. 1,071 p.
A revised edition of the U.S. War Department Technical Manual TM 30-933, *Dictionary of spoken Chinese* (Washington, 1945), and for use by students of the colloquial language at the intermediate level. In two parts: the first, Chinese-English, arranged by the Yale system of romanization, with some 3,000

entries; and the second, English-Chinese. Characters and examples of usage are stated. Index from Wades-Giles romanization to the *p'inyin* and Yale system.

Q37 Aichi Daigaku, Toyohashi, Japan. Chu-Nichi Daijiten Hensanjo. *Chu-Nichi daijiten* (Chinese-Japanese dictionary). Toyohashi-shi, Chu-Nichi Daijiten Kankokai, 1968. 1,947 p.
Contains 11,000 single characters and 130,000 compounds, and is excellent for contemporary, colloquial and classical Chinese usage, and for pronunciation.

Q38 Doolin, Dennis J. and Charles Price Ridley. *A Chinese-English dictionary of Communist Chinese terminology*. Stanford, Hoover Institution Press, 1973. 569 p. (Hoover Institution publications 124).
17,000 entries for Chinese words and phrases arranged in order of radicals, and designed for the reader of contemporary Chinese documents.

Q39 *Hsin Ying-Han tz'u tien* (A new English-Chinese dictionary). Hsiang-kang, Sheng huo Tu shu Hsin chih San lien Shu tien Hsiang-kang fen tien, 1976. 1,688 p.
50,000 entries and derivatives equal some 80,000 words, and in addition there are 14,000 idioms. A contemporary and comprehensive dictionary reflecting present-day Chinese.

BIOGRAPHICAL DICTIONARIES

Q40 Giles, Herbert. *A Chinese biographical dictionary*. Taipei, Literature House, 1962. 2 v. (in case).
A reprint of the 1898 edition containing 2,579 entries for prominent persons in Chinese history, and arranged in alphabetical order, with the names followed by characters and dates of birth and death, which are sometimes unreliable. Biographies are usually short. A number of revisions have been suggested by Paul Pelliot and others but these are ignored in this reprint. Also reprinted by Burt Franklin, New York, 1966.

Q41 Fang, I. *Chung-kuo jen ming ta tzu tien* Cyclopedia of Chinese biographical names. Shang-hai, Shang wu Yin shu kuan, Min kuo 27 (1938). 1,808 p.
Over 40,000 persons are listed by stroke order of the Chinese characters, and covering the period from earliest times to 1912, but with weaker representation from 1644. Persons included are those mentioned in the official histories, and others important for literacy or classical studies. Non-Chinese associated with Chinese history are also included, but legendary names are not. The annotation includes the dynasty in which the person lived, his home town, various names by which he was known, and a brief biography. The dating by dynasty is often not helpful, since a

single dynasty may cover a number of centuries. Reprinted in Taiwan, 1966.

Q42 Liu, Ping-li. *Chung wai jen ming tz'u tien* (Biographical dictionary of Chinese and foreigners). Shang-hai, Chung hua Shu chu, Min kuo 29 (1940). 1,300 p.
Useful for identification of non-Chinese names found in Chinese texts. Arranged in stroke order, with an alphabetical index for some 5,000 Western names, representing one-third of the entries.

Q43 Tan, Cheng-pi. *Chung-kuo wen hsueh chia ta tzu tien* (Biographical dictionary of Chinese literary figures). Shang-hai, Kuang ming Shu chu, Min kuo 30 (1941). 1,746 p.
Lists 6,848 authors who lived to about 1940. The arrangement is chronological. For each his various names, home area, dates of birth and death, and biographical and bibliographical information are given. There is an index in stroke order. Reprinted in Taiwan, 1967.

Q44 Shang, Ch'eng-tsu. *Chung-kuo li tai shu hua chuan k'o chia tz'u hao so yin* (Dictionary of Chinese anonyms and pseudonyms). Pei-ching, Jen min Mei shu Chu pan she, 1960. 2 v.
The first volume arranges the pseudonym forms of the names by stroke order, and adds the correct name, place, dynasty, field of specialty, and other notes. The second volume lists by the correct name, and gives the pseudonym. Some 16,000 personal names are represented.

Q45 Chen, Charles K. H. *A biographical and bibliographical dictionary of Chinese authors.* New York City, Oriental Society, 1971–6. 3 v.
Consists of an initial volume and a two-volume supplement. Authors' names are romanized according to the Wade-Giles system, and arranged alphabetically, with dates and a short biographical note and list of works for each. In Chinese.

Sung Dynasty 960–1279

Q46 Franke, Herbert. *Sung biographies.* Wiesbaden, Franz Steiner, 1976. 4 v. (Munchener Ostasiatischen Studien, Band 16, 1–4).
500 biographies for persons living in the Sung dynasty are arranged alphabetically, with the exception of painters who are arranged separately in the fourth volume. Over half the biographies are in English. Most of the remainder are in French, and nine are in German. No index.

Ming Dynasty 1368–1644

Q47 Association for Asian Studies. Ming Biographical History Project Committee. *Dictionary of Ming biography, 1368–1644,* edited by L. Carrington Goodrich and Fan Chao-ying. New York, Columbia University Press, 1976. 2 v.

Some 650 signed biographies with extensive bibliographical notes. Names, book and subject indexes.

Ch'ing Dynasty 1644–1911

Q48 U.S. Library of Congress. Asiatic Division. *Eminent Chinese of the Ch'ing period,* edited by Arthur Hummel. Washington, 1943–4. 2 v.
800 biographies of Ch'ing dynasty personalities, excluding all who died after 1912. In addition to the sources quoted, personal impressions from Western residents in China have been used.

Republican China 1912–

Q49 *Who's who in China,* 1918–50. Shanghai, China Weekly Review, 1918–50. 6 v. and 3 supplementary volumes.
Short biographies of several thousand of China's prominent business, political and professional men, with information gathered from questionnaires, newspapers and interviews. Names are listed alphabetically, followed by characters. Character indexes. Reprinted in five volumes by Ryukei shosha, Tokyo, 1973.

Q50 *Chung hua min kuo jen shih lu* (Biographical dictionary of the Republic of China). T'ai-pei, Chinese Science Commission, Min kuo 42 (1953). 470 p.
Lists some 4,500 men and women, with names arranged in stroke order, and who were living at the time of publication. Communists are excluded. Accounts are short, and include the popular name if used, age, place of birth, schools attended, occupation, and membership in the Kuomintang. More recent, in English, but more selective is the biographical listing in the *China yearbook* (Q 18) with some 1,000 entries.

Q51 Perleberg, Max. *Who's who in modern China.* Hong Kong, Ye Olde Printerie, 1954. 428 p.
Max Perleberg lived in China for 25 years as a scholar and translator, compiled this biographical dictionary of 2,019 biographies of persons prominent in the period from 1911 to the end of 1953. Useful appendices include a history of Chinese political parties and a description of the government organization in mainland China and Taiwan.

Q52 Boorman, Howard L. and Richard C. Howard. *Biographical dictionary of Republican China.* New York, Columbia University Press, 1967–71. 4 v.
Lists over 600 persons prominent in China from 1911–49, including some still living. Biographies are scholarly and substantial in length. It continues *Eminent Chinese of the Ch'ing period,* edited by Arthur Hummel (Q 48).

Q 53 Chu, Pao-liang. *Twentieth-century Chinese writers and their pen names.* Boston, G. K. Hall, 1977. 366 p.
Some 7,500 pen names are listed for over 2,500 writers. The pen names and writers' names are listed in one sequence. The list is very valuable also for identifying the characters and dates for writers, many of whom are obscure. Stroke count index.

People's Republic 1949–

Q 54 U.S. Department of State. Bureau of Intelligence and Research. *Directory of Chinese Communist officials.* Washington, 1966. 621 p.
The latest of a series with previous issues appearing in 1960 and 1963 with similar titles. It is based on published information available at the end of February 1966. In the first part (464 pages) officials are listed according to their positions, and the second part is an alphabetical index of approximately 1,000 names. Through its arrangement the work also provides a valuable guide to the organization of the Communist Party, Chinese central and local government, the mass organizations, armed forces, diplomatic and consular corps, and scientific institutions. Continued by *Directory of officials of the People's Republic of China* (Q 60).

Q 55 Kazan-kai, Tokyo. *Gendai Chugoko jimmei jiten,* 1966 nemban (Biographical dictionary of modern China, 1966 edition). Tokyo, Gaiko Jihosha, Showa 41 (1966). 1,209 p.
A revision of *Gendai Chugoku, Chosenjin meikan* (Biographical dictionary of modern China and Korea) (1953), which appeared in revised editions in 1957 and 1962 as *Gendai Chugoku jimmei jiten.* 15,000 personalities are arranged in the Japanese syllabic order, with a Wade-Giles romanization and character key. The date and place of birth, personal history, occupation and present position are noted. Persons who died before 1960 are excluded unless their names are still very prominent. Overseas Chinese are included. The previous editions are still important since they include less prominent persons now dead and not included in the current publication. 1972 issue seen.

Q 56 Ajia Kenkyujo, Tokyo (Asia Research Institute). *Genshoku, shin Chugoku jimmei jiten,* 1968 nemban (New China biographical dictionary, with official positions, 1968 edition). Tokyo, Sawa shoten, Showa 43 (1968). 491 p.
The main text is arranged by Japanese syllabic order, giving names and present official positions. Wade-Giles index. Lists some 11,000 names for Mainland China, as of December 1967.

Q 57 U.S. Department of State. Bureau of Intelligence and Research. *Directory of Chinese Communist officials, provincial, municipal and military.* Washington, 1969. 211 p.
Some 2,100 officials, identified between January 1967 and

January 1969, are arranged under their respective provincial offices, by selected municipal revolutionary committees and by miliary organs. Personal names index.

Q58 Yu lien yen chiu so, Hongkong (Union Research Institute). *Who's who in Communist China.* Hongkong, 1969–70. 2 v.
Over 3,000 personalities are included. Some of those noted have died recently, but none who died before 1949 are included. The date for last inclusion of entries for volume 1 was September 1968, and for volume 2 was May 1969. Character index. Revision of 1966 edition.

Q59 Klein, Donald W. and Anne B. Clark. *Biographic dictionary of Chinese Communism, 1921–1965.* Cambridge, Harvard University Press, 1971. 2 v.
Contains 433 substantial biographies, and includes all persons who have held a prominent role in the Chinese Communist Party from 1921 to 1965. Connections with the revolutionary parties, and location before 1949 are given.

Q60 U.S. Central Intelligence Agency. *Directory of officials of the People's Republic of China. China, a reference aid.* Washington, 1978, 325 p.
Notices some 5,000 officials identified through March 1978. Since the officials are arranged by their organization, the directory forms an organization manual of the Chinese government at all major levels, including provincial and military leadership. Alphabetical index to officials. Continues *Directory of Chinese Communist officials* (Q 54).

DIRECTORIES

Q61 Chuang, Wen-ya (W. Y. Chyne). *Handbook of cultural institutions in China,* Shanghai, Chinese National Committee on Intellectual Cooperation, 1936. 282 p.
Lists some 450 organizations, mostly with a research function, giving for each their history, finances, activities and publications. A classified index lists organizations in broad subject categories, and then alphabetically. Each entry in the index is followed by the organization's name in characters. Reprinted by the Chinese Materials and Research Aids Service Center, 1967.

Q62 Kun, Joseph C. *Higher educational institutions of Communist China, 1953–1958, a cumulative list.* Cambridge, Massachusetts Institute of Technology, Center for International Studies, 1961. 50 p.
227 institutions are listed by field of study, and then by the six major geographical divisions of China. Each entry lists the latest name in English, followed by the characters. Other earlier names are noted. Not all institutions are noted, and this list is becoming increasingly dated. Indexed.

Q 63 Wang, Chi. *Mainland China organizations of higher learning in science and technology and their publications, a selected guide.* Washington, U.S. Government Printing Office, 1961. 104 p.
Some 700 societies, organizations, universities, institutes and libraries are grouped into sections, and information is given on their officials, location, activities and publications. There are indexes by romanized title to the organizations, to English titles of organizations, and to serial publications.

Q 64 Chung yang T'u shu kuan, Taipei (National Central Library). *Directory of the cultural organizations of the Republic of China.* Taipei, 1963. 142 p.
Some 260 learned societies, libraries, museums, universities, colleges, research institutions and research departments of official and commercial organizations are arranged by type of institution. For each body the name is listed, followed by the name in characters, address, officers, publications, and if a library, the size of the collection. First published in 1961. No index. Continued by *Directory of the Chinese cultural organizations of the Republic of China, fourth edition* (Q 68).

Q 65 Ajia Kenkyujo, Tokyo (Asia Research Institute). *Chugoku kogyo kojo soran* (Guide to industry and factories in China). Tokyo, 1965. 1,200 p.
Lists some 4,000 factories in China, arranged by product and subdivided by province. The source for the information is cited. Alphabetical index giving the name of the factory in *p'inyin* romanization, with kind of factory stated in English.

Q 66 Nielsen, Robert R. *Academic and technical research organizations of mainland China, a selective listing, revised.* Washington, Aerospace Technology Division, Library of Congress, 1966. 172 p.
Consists of four lists, each arranged by name of organization in the Wade-Giles romanization. The romanized name is followed by the characters and translation. Some 1,260 organizations, including libraries are listed, but 220 of these are affiliated with the Chinese Academy of Sciences. Index in the *p'inyin* romanization. First published 1965.

Q 67 Surveys and Research Corporation, Washington. *Directory of selected scientific institutions in mainland China.* Stanford, Hoover Institution Press, for National Science Foundation, 1970. 469 p.
Contains entries for 490 scientific institutions, with detailed information on their location, personnel, structure and publications. An additional 1,127 institutions, colleges and societies are listed. Useful for a survey of scientific activity in mainland China, but no mention of the supporting library apparatus.

Q 68 *Directory of the cultural organizations of the Republic of China, fourth edition.* Taipei, National Central Library, 1972. 353 p.
Lists 440 organizations arranged by field of activity, with an

alphabetical index to organizations. For organizations, the address, Chinese title, date of establishment, membership, activities and publications are given; for libraries, the size of collection; and for colleges, size of student body and faculty. Continues *Directory of the cultural organizations of the Republic of China* (Q 64).

Q 69 Kan, Lai-bing. *Library services in Hong Kong, a new directory.* Hong Kong, Hong Kong Library Association and Chinese University of Hong Kong, 1975. 228 p.
Provides detailed information for 88 general libraries, 45 official libraries, 119 school libraries, 21 college libraries, 36 special libraries, and eight others. A revision of the 1963 edition.

Q 70 Swannack-Nunn, Susan. *Directory of scientific research institutions in the People's Republic of China.* Washington, National Council for U.S.–China Trade. 1977–8. 3 v.
Some 1,800 institutes are arranged by technological field with information on organizations, recent acquisitions and publications. Selected abstracts of scientific papers follow institute descriptions. Each volume has separate index to institutes listed in it.

ATLASES

Q 71 Herrmann, Albert. *An historical atlas of China.* Chicago, Aldine Publishing Co., 1966. 88 p.
A revision by Professor Norton Ginsburg of the *Historical and commercial atlas of China* originally published 1935 and reprinted in 1964 in Taipei. 64 pages of maps, mostly coloured, are arranged chronologically, commencing with prehistoric sites and extending down to the contemporary period (for which there are also a number of valuable subject maps). Appendices contain a selected bibliography of some 300 items, an index of geographical and proper names, and a list of Chinese characters.

Q 72 U.S. Central Intelligence Agency. *China, provisional atlas of Communist administrative units.* Washington, 1959. 14 p.
Contains 29 maps, of which 25 are reproductions of the provincial maps appearing in the *Chung-kuo fen sheng ti t'u* (Provincial atlas of China) (1956). The first four maps depict China as a whole, with administrative units as of March 1959. Chinese characters are romanized, and there is an index to administrative names. Valuable for showing changes in administrative areas in mainland China.

Q 73 *National atlas of China.* Taipei, National War College in cooperation with Chinese Geographical Institute, 1959–62. 5 v.
Written in Chinese and English. The first volume is concerned with Taiwan, the second with the border areas, the third with North China, and the fourth with South China; the fifth covers China as a whole, with maps of population, topography, climate, forestry, etc. Only the first four volumes have an index. Useful for locating places and administrative units noted in Nationalist

publications, but does not recognize the various changes that have taken place on the mainland since 1949. Volumes 2 and 3 have title *Atlas of the Republic of China.* Some volumes issued in revised edition.

Q74 *Rand McNally illustrated atlas of China.* Chicago, Rand McNally, 1972.
Consists of 35 coloured maps, with five at a scale of 1:4 million, and others showing major administrative divisions, population, ethnic groups, communications, climate, agriculture, minerals, fuel and power, industry and Peking. Maps have introductions. Over 2,000 names in the Index.

Q75 Hsieh, Chiao-min. *Atlas of China.* New York, McGraw-Hill, 1973. 282 p.
273 maps and explanatory text surveying China's physical, cultural, economic and regional features. The regional section has many town plans and is the most extensive. Taiwan is included.

Q76 *Chung hua jen min kung ho kuo feng sheng ti t'u chi* (A provincial atlas of the People's Republic of China). Peking, Ti t'u Ch'u pan she, 1974. 251 p.
The latest edition of an atlas, the most recent previous available edition being the 1964 edition republished in Taiwan in 1966
Maps for each province. Radical index and romanized index.
for each province. Radical index and romanized index.

Q77 *The Times atlas of China,* edited by P. J. M. Geelan and D. C. Twitchett. New York, Quadrangle/New York Times Book Co., 1974. 144 p.
Includes historical and physical maps, maps of provinces and major cities. For each map there is an introduction and list of place-names in characters and romanized forms. Tables provided for conversion of Wade-Giles, *p'inyin* and Chinese Post Office systems. Index of provincial place-names.

GEOGRAPHICAL DICTIONARIES AND GAZETTEERS

Q78 Playfair, G. H. M. *The cities and towns of China, a geographical dictionary,* second edition. Shanghai, Kelly and Walsh, 1910. 582 p.
Over 9,000 entries for place-names, many of which are references, arranged in alphabetical order, stating locations. Lists of cities are also arranged by provinces. There is an index arranged by radicals. Both contemporary names and historical names are included. The second edition has added rivers and lakes, and claims to have eliminated inaccuracies of the first edition. Reprinted by Literature House, Taipei, 1965.

Q79 Liu, Chun-jen. *Chung-kuo ti ming ta tz'u tien* (Chinese geographical names dictionary). T'ai-pei, Wen hai Ch'u pan she, Min kuo 56 (1967). 1,118 p.
Some 16,000 place-names are arranged by stroke order, with a

romanized form for each entry. Indexed by the Chinese Post Office romanization system. Some duplication with Li-ho Tsang *Chung-kuo ku chin ti ming ta tz'u tien* (Q 80). The 1930 edition has similar pagination.

Q 80 Tsang, Li-ho. *Chung-kuo ku chin ti ming ta tz'u tien* (Chinese historical geographical dictionary). Shang-hai, Shang wu Yin shu kuan, Min kuo 20 (1931). 1,410 p.
Lists over 40,000 place-names, including mountains and rivers, arranged in stroke order. For modern names, reference is given to older forms. For about half of the places sources are cited; location is often difficult owing to lack of detail. Reprinted in Taiwan 1966.

Q 81 U.S. Office of Geography. *China* . . . Washington, U.S. Government Printing Office, 1968. 2 v. (Gazetteer no. 22).
108,000 place and feature names. For each name its classification, longitude and latitude are given. The introduction warns of variations of as much as a degree in these coordinates. Second edition, revision of 1956 edition, and covers whole of People's Republic of China, Hong Kong and Macao.

Q 82 Tien H. C. *Gazetteer of China.* Hong Kong, Oriental Book Co., 1961. 237 p.
2,457 localities are listed, and of these 1,963 are *hsien* (county) names. Older names in use are also noted. For each place-name its Chinese Post Office romanization, romanization according to the Wade-Giles system, Chinese characters, province or region, longitude and latitude are given. An index by stroke order lists characters in place-names.

Q 83 U.S. Office of Geography. *Mainland China, administrative divisions and their seats* . . . Washington, U.S. Government Printing Office, 1963. 253 p. (Gazetteer no. 70).
Divided into three parts, a general list of about 11,900 entries for administrative divisions at the province, sub-province and *hsien* (county) level, the names of Communist and Nationalist seats, with Nationalist names and conventional names cross-referenced to Communist names. The second part has 2,560 names for administrative seats, and the third part 2,156 province, sub-province and *hsien* level administrative areas. Both parts are divided by the 28 provinces and major city areas. Taiwan is excluded. Communist names are based on the *Chung hua jen min kung ho kuo hsing cheng ch'u hua chien ts'e* (Administrative divisions of the People's Republic of China) (Pei-ching, 1960). Locations for names are stated by longitude and latitude.

Q 84 U.S. Board on Geographic Names. *Republic of China* . . . Washington, U.S. Government Printing Office, 1974. 789 p.
25,000 entries for place and feature names, with their classification, longitude and latitude given. Refers to Taiwan and off-shore islands under the control of the Republic of China.

CHRONOLOGICAL TABLES

Q85 Moule, Arthur Christopher. *The rulers of China, 221 B.C. – A.D. 1949* . . . London, Routledge and Kegan Paul, 1957. 131 p.
The most useful and detailed guide to Chinese chronology in English. W. Perceval Yetts has written an introductory section on the earlier rulers, c. 2100–249 B.C. Indexes to year titles, and to emperors by their temple titles, memorial titles, styles and family names.

Q86 U.S. Immigration and Naturalization Service. *Chinese-American calendar for the 40th through the 89th year of the Chinese Republic, February 6, 1951 to January 23, 2001,* compiled by Windon Chandler Welch. Washington, 1957. 50 p.
The only English-language source which gives years, months and days in the Chinese calendar and the corresponding years, months and days in the Gregorian calendar. A continuation of the same compiler's *Chinese-American calendar for the 102 Chinese years commencing January 24, 1849 and ending February 5, 1951* (Washington, U.S. Government Printing Office, 1928. 102 p.).

Q87 Chung-kuo Ko hsueh yuan. Tzu-chin-shan T'ien wen tai (Chinese Academy of Sciences. Purple Mountain Observatory). *1821–2020 nien erh pai nien li piao* (Chronological tables for two centuries, 1821–2020). Pei-ching, K'o hsueh Ch'u pan she, 1959. 477 p.
A comparative Western and Chinese calendar, making possible the rapid conversion of Chinese and Western dates.

Q88 Tung, Tso-pin. *Chung-kuo nien li tsung p'u* Chronological tables on Chinese history. Hong Kong, Hong Kong University Press, 1960. 2 v.
An exhaustive collection of tables enabling conversion of dates from the Chinese to Western systems. The first volume emphasizes the period 2674–1 B.C., the second A.D. 1 onwards. There are indexes to the tables in both stroke and alphabetical order. A knowledge of Chinese is required to use these volumes.

Q89 Cheng, Peter. *A chronology of the People's Republic of China, from October 1, 1949.* Totowa, Rowman and Littlefield, 1972. 347 p.
A detailed chronology covering to the end of 1969 with a subject index. Useful for establishing dates as a lead to examining newspapers and other sources. Particularly strong for foreign relations.

Q90 Association of Research Libraries. Center for Chinese Research Materials. *Chung kuo ta shih chi* A chronology of twentieth-century China, 1904–49. Washington, 1973. 6 v.
Based on the chronology section of the *Tung fang tsa chih* (The Eastern miscellany), but since the latter did not cover the final year of takeover and did not publish a chronology section for November 1941 to December 1946, four other sources have been reproduced in volume 6.

Q91 *Hsin hua yueh pao kuo nei wai ta shih chi* New China monthly chronology of national and international events of significance. Washington, Center for Chinese Research Materials, Association of Research Libraries, 1972. 3 v.
Published from November 1949 to May 1966, and included in each issue a chronology, which was grouped by major topics from the end of 1958.

STATISTICS

Q92 China. Chu chi ch'u (Directorate General of Budget, Accounts and Statistics). *Chung hua min kuo t'ung chi t'i yao* Statistical abstract of the Republic of China. T'ai-pei, Min kuo 24– (1935–).
There are four kinds of statistical data in this yearbook. The first concerns China as a whole, the second refers to the achievements of the National government, the third to Taiwan province, and the fourth to recent surveys. The 1972 edition has 318 tables and 45 charts, and most of the information covers a ten years' span when there are changes to report. Current issues are in Chinese and English, but some explanatory matter only in Chinese. First appeared in 1935 in Nanking. 1974 edition seen.

Q93 China (People's Republic of China, 1949–). Kuo chia T'ung chi chu (State Statistical Bureau). *Ten great years, statistics of the economic and cultural achievement of the People's Republic of China.* Peking, Foreign Languages Press, 1960. 223 p.
A series of official statistical tables for the period 1949 to the end of 1958 showing growth of population, development of socialist reorganization of industry and agriculture, capital construction, industrial production, growth of agricultural production, transportation, commerce, and cultural and educational affairs.

Q94 Aird, John Shields. *The size, composition and growth of the population of mainland China.* Washington, U.S. Department of Commerce, 1961. 100 p.
An evaluation of the 1953 Chinese census, concentrating on a narrative analysis of techniques used for collection and reporting data. 17 tables and a short bibliography of Chinese and English sources are provided.

Q95 Chen, Nai-Ruenn. *Chinese economic statistics, a handbook for mainland China.* Chicago, Aldine Publishing Co., 1967. 539 p.
Includes the economic data from *Ten great years, statistics of the economic and cultural achievement of the People's Republic of China* (Q 93) and supplements these from a wide variety of Chinese Communist sources. Over 600 tables cover area and population, national income, capital formation, industry, agriculture, communications, trade, prices and living standards, public finance and employment. Statistics are restricted to the

period 1949–59. More recent economic statistical estimates may be found in U.S. Joint Economic Committee *An economic profile of mainland China* (Washington, U.S. Government Printing Office, 1967). 2 v.

Q96 China. Chu chi chu (Directorate General of Budget, Accounts and Statistics). *Statistical yearbook of the Republic of China, 1975–*. Taipei, 1976–.
The 1976 volume, entirely in English, contains 210 statistical tables relating to the economy, social conditions and cultural development of Taiwan. 1977 issue seen.

BIBLIOGRAPHY

Chinese Language

BIBLIOGRAPHY OF BIBLIOGRAPHIES

Q97 Tsien, Tsuen-hsuin. *China, an annotated bibliography of bibliographies*. Boston, G. K. Hall, 1978. 604 p.
Over 2,500 bibliographies, in Chinese, Japanese, English and other Western languages, published in 1977, in book, article and report form. Organized in a detailed form and subject arrangement. Author, title and subject indexes.

PRE-1912 PUBLICATIONS

Q98 Chi, Yun and others. *Ssu k'u ch'uan shu tsung mu, ch'in ting* (Catalogue of the collection of the Four Libraries). Shang-hai, Ta tung shih yin, Min kuo 19 (1930). 44 v.
The *Ssu k'u ch'uan shu* was a collection of over 10,000 Chinese books, of which 3,461 were reprinted, and another 6,793 were extant when it was compiled, but not part of it. The catalogue is annotated, but difficult to use, and for this reason Ping-yao Yu and I. V. Gillis *Title index to the Ssu k'u ch'uan shu* (Peiping, 1934. 420 p.) is useful.

Q99 Liu, I-cheng. *Chiang-su sheng li kuo hsueh t'u shu kuan tsung mu* (Catalogue of the Kiangsu Provincial Sinological Library). Nanching, Min kuo 22–4 (1933–5). 24 v.
Lists 37,002 titles in 198,222 volumes, and arranged in the traditional Chinese book classification. Three additional sections were added for gazetteers, maps and collectanea. Each section is further divided. No annotations and no index. The . . . *Pu pien* (. . . Supplement) published in 1937 (6 v.) adds another 18,000 entries, but these are principally contents of collectanea. Books listed now reported to be part of the Nanking Library.

Q100 Wang, Chung-min. *Kuo hui t'u shu kuan ts'ang Chung-kuo shan pen shu lu* Descriptive catalogue of rare Chinese books in the Library of Congress. Washington, Library of Congress, 1957. 2 v.

1,777 works are listed, of which all but 70 are pre-Ch'ing. The books are arranged in the traditional Chinese book classification, and there are separate author and title indexes. The entries are annotated. Rarity is defined as being published before the Ch'ing dynasty, or having been proscribed in the Ch'ing dynasty. Does not include the rare books of the National Library of Peking which are available from the Library of Congress on microfilm.

Q 101 Ch'u, Wan-li. *A catalogue of the Chinese rare books in the Gest Collection of the Princeton University Library*. Taipei, Yee Wen Publishing Company, 1974. 584 p.
Lists over 1,100 titles in 30,500 *ts'e* published before 1644, and represents the richest collection of Chinese rare books outside China and Japan. The books are arranged in the traditional Chinese bibliographical classification, and entries are fully annotated.

REPUBLICAN AND CONTEMPORARY PUBLICATIONS

Q 102 Tohogakkai, Tokyo (Institute of Eastern Culture). *Kin hyaku nen rai Chugoku bun bunken genzai shomoku* (Catalogue of books published in Chinese in the past century and located in Japanese libraries). Tokyo, Showa 32 (1957). 838 p.
Some 20,000 books and periodicals published from 1851 to 1954, and in major Tokyo libraries, are arranged in Japanese syllabic order, with bibliographical and location information. No character index, making use of the list difficult for non-Japanese readers.

Q 103 Yang, Chai-lo. *T'u shu nien chien* (Book yearbook). Nan-ching, Chung kuo T'u shu Ts'u pen chi kuan, Min kuo 22 (1933). 2 v. (Chung kuo t'u shu ta tz'u tien pai chung ti 67 chung).
The first volume contains sections on Chinese bibliography, library and publication law, libraries in China arranged by province, and a list of publishing firms. The second lists some 9,000 books published between 1912 and 1933, first by subject, then alphabetically by title. No publication dates are given, and there is no index. The entries are annotated. In the copy noted the two volumes were bound in one. Available on microfilm from Center for Chinese Research Materials, Washington, D.C.

Q 104 P'ing Hsin. *Sheng huo ch'uan kuo tsung shu mu* (Sheng huo cumulated catalogue of Chinese publications). Shang-hai, Shanghai Sheng huo Shu tien, Min kuo 24 (1935). 716 p.
20,000 titles published in China from 1912 to 1935 are arranged by subjects. Title, author and price given, but no date of publication. The original title and author of books translated into Chinese noted. Four corner index to titles.

Q 105 *Quarterly bulletin of Chinese bibliography*. Shanghai, Chinese National Committee on Intellectual Cooperation, 1934–47.
A quarterly list of selected periodical articles and books compiled originally from the holdings of the National Library of Peiping.

Divided into sections for Chinese books, Western-language books, Chinese periodical articles and Western-language articles. The sections are subdivided by subject. Characters and romanization are given for all Chinese entries, and each issue contains about 300 articles and 150 books. No mention of the basis of selection. Volumes 1–4 were issued from 1934 to 1937, and a new series commenced in 1939 and continued to volume 7 in 1947. The Chinese edition *T'u shu chi k'an* has a different content, and only the 1934 issues were combined. Reprinted by Kraus Reprint Corporation, New York.

Q106 *Philobiblon, a quarterly review of Chinese publications,* nos. 1–7, June 1946 – September 1948. Nanking, 1946–8.
Each issue is a classified listing of books and periodicals issued during the three months under review. Chinese author names are transliterated and titles translated. From December 1946, extremely select with annotations. The issue for July 1947, the last noted, contains some 180 books and periodicals. Reprinted by Kraus Reprint Corporation, New York.

Q107 *Ch'uan kuo hsin shu mu,* 1950– (National catalogue of new books, 1950–). Pei-ching, Wen hua pu Ch'u pan shih yeh Kuan li chu, 1951–.
The most continuous bibliographical record for mainland Chinese publications from 1950, arranged by broad subjects and giving full bibliographical information, and sometimes a short annotation. Books in minority and Western languages are cited by their Chinese titles. Original titles and authors of books translated into Chinese noted. Issued on an annual basis for 1950 (published 1951); semi-annually for 1951 to 1952; annually for 1953; and monthly from 1954 to August 1958 when its frequency changed to three times a month. Then appearing semi-monthly, discontinuing publication in 1966. Translations of nos. 8–11, May and June 1965, published as *National bibliography of new books, selected issues* (Honolulu, East-West Center Research Translations, 1966. 2 v.). Resumed publication July 1972. No. 1 (n.s.) is no. 287 of the cumulated sequence (no. 286 was published July 1966), and has 440 items noted as published from March to first part of May 1972. Publication reported as restricted since 1975.

Q108 *Revue bibliographique de sinologie,* v. 1–, 1955–. Paris, Mouton, 1957–.
Selected books and periodical articles on China in the social sciences and the humanities, and not restricted to materials in Chinese, are arranged by subject and reviewed in English or French. There is a list of periodicals from which articles have been analyzed, and an author index. A gap of several years now exists between the publications and the date of their review, reducing the value of this bibliography. Volume 10 for 1969 published 1973. Volume 11 for 1965 published 1977.

Q109 *Ch'uan kuo tsung shu mu,* 1949/1954– (National cumulated catalogue of books, 1949/1954–). Pei-ching, Wen hua pu Ch'u pan shih yeh Kuan li chu, 1956–.

Arranged by a detailed subject classification based on the People's University Classification system. The first volume covers publications for the period 1949–54, but includes, presumably, only those still in print in 1954. Succeeding volumes are for publications issued in 1955, 1956, 1957 and 1958, the last noted, and listing 26,414 books. These annual volumes are more than a cumulation of the *Ch'uan kuo hsin shu mu,* since they contain 40% more titles. A wide range of publications are included such as periodicals, textbooks, books for the blind, books in minority and Western languages. There is an index of titles. An outstanding bibliographical achievement, which appears to have ceased publication with the volume for 1958. Available on microfilm from Datamics, New York.

Q110 Kuo li Chung yang T'u shu kuan, Taipei (National Central Library). *Select bibliography of the Republic of China.* Taipei, 1957. 59 p.

1,200 titles, judged to be the most important published from 1947 to 1957, but mostly from 1952 to 1956, are divided into eight major subject divisions. Titles are translated into English. No index.

Q111 Kuo li Chung yang T'u shu kuan, Taipei (National Central Library). *Monthly list of Chinese books,* v. 1–, 1960–. Taipei, 1960–.

A select list of current Chinese publications arranged by subject. Authors and titles are romanized, and the title translated into English. Author index to the issues of the previous year. Basis of selection not stated, and lagging badly in its coverage. Publication suspended in July 1967 and resumed in 1969 with title *Kuo-li chung yang t'u shu kuan hsin shu mu lu.*

Q112 Fairbank, John King and Kwang-ching Liu. *Modern China, a bibliographical guide to Chinese works, 1898–1937.* Cambridge, Harvard University Press, 1961. 608 p.

1,500 annotated entries are arranged in a subject order, covering historical materials, government and law, foreign affairs, economic data, social problems, culture and education and intellectual and literary history. All books are to be found in the Harvard-Yenching Institute. Noted that "some corrections have been made to the 1950 edition, but this work is not noted as revised". Index to authors, compilers, titles and subjects.

Q113 Kuo li Chung yang T'u shu kuan, Taipei (National Central Library). *Chung hua min kuo ch'u pan t'u shu mu lu hui pien* (Catalogue of publications of the Republic of China). T'ai-pei, Min kuo 53 (1964). 2 v.

14,500 books received through copyright deposit at the National Central Library from 1949 to 1963 and published in Taiwan, Hong Kong and Macao. Most books are in Chinese, but some are in English. Entries are arranged by subject, and full bibliographical information is given. No index. The most complete statement we have for Taiwan publications. Supplement *Chung hua min kuo ch'u pan t'u shu mu lu hui pien hsu chi* published in 1970 in two volumes. The supplement lists 14,000 titles, almost all in Chinese, and published from 1964 to 1968, and has author and title index.

Q114 Ajia Keizai Kenkyujo, Tokyo (Institute of the Developing Economies). *Gendai Chugoku kankei Chugokugo rombun sogo mokuroku* (Union catalogue of Chinese literature on modern China). Tokyo, 1967–8. 8 v.

36,000 different titles, based on 110,000 cards from 22 Japanese libraries, cover the period from 1912 to 1965, are arranged in six volumes, the first three on the social sciences, the fourth on the natural sciences, and the fifth and sixth on the humanities. Volume 7 is an index by authors, and volume 8 an index in three sections (Chinese romanization, Japanese romanization and stroke). The Japanese *toyo kanji,* or simplified standard characters, have been used even when this has meant a departure from the original. Older characters are used only when these are not listed in the *toyo kanji.* Supplement 1 and 2 published 1971.

Q115 Stanford University. Hoover Institution on War, Revolution and Peace. *Library catalogs of the Hoover Institution on War, Revolution and Peace. Catalog of the Chinese Collection.* Boston G. K. Hall, 1969. 13 v.

Reproduces 202,000 cards in the catalogue of the Chinese-language collection, representing one of the strongest U.S. libraries for post–World War II China.

Q116 Tang, Raymond N. *Source materials on Red Guards and the Great Proletarian Cultural Revolution.* Ann Arbor, University of Michigan, University Library, 1969. 332 p.

In two parts, the first listing over 550 Red Guard newspapers and circulars and 150 notices, and the second a chronological listing of some 4,000 articles selected from these newspapers and circulars.

Q117 Skinner, G. William. *Modern Chinese society, an analytical bibliography.* Stanford, Stanford University Press, 1973. 3 v.

Without question a bibliographical landmark for the study of modern China. The first volume includes publications in Western languages for the period 1644 to 1972, the second for those in Chinese from 1644 to 1969, and the third for those in Japanese from 1644 to 1971. The three volumes contain together 31,443 entries for books and periodical articles. Only published secondary sources are included. Entries in each volume are arranged by subject, and there are analytical indexes, the first being an historical one, arranged principally by period, then by subject, a second index lists by geographical area, then by subject, while a third lists by geographical area, then by type of social system. There are also in each volume conventional indexes for subjects and authors. Further each item is coded to indicate its source, assisting in the evaluation of the material.

Q118 China, Hsing cheng yuan. Hsin wen chu. *Chung hua min kuo tu shu tsung mu lu* General catalogue of books published in the Republic of China. T'ai-pei, Min kuo 63 (1974). 693 p.
30,000 books still in print are arranged in 100 subject categories, giving title, author, price and publisher, but unfortunately no date of publication. There are short sections for children's literature and books in Western languages. An appendix lists publishers and their addresses.

Q119 Yu, Ping-kuen. *Research material on twentieth-century China, an annotated list of CCRM publications.* Washington, Center for Chinese Research Materials, Association of Research Libraries, 1975. 273 p. (Bibliographical series, no. 15).
976 titles for newspapers, periodicals and books are listed, of which 926 have been reproduced or published by the Center. Full annotations are provided for each item. Titles which have been reproduced by the Center are available permanently on film or xerox copies. Index.

Q120 McMullen, D. L. *Concordances and indexes to Chinese texts.* San Francisco, Chinese Materials Center, 1975. 204 p.
282 indexes and concordances to Chinese texts published to 1900. The indexes have been arranged under seven main headings: concordances; standard histories; historical, geographical and administrative texts; philosophical, religious, critical and literary texts, title and heading indexes; and miscellaneous indexes. Index to texts.

OFFICIAL PUBLICATIONS

Q121 Kuo li Chung yang T'u shu kuan, Nanking (National Central Library). *Kuo li chung yang t'u shu kuan ts'ang kuan shu mu lu, ti i chung* (Catalogue of official publications in the National Central Library, first part). Nanching, Min kuo 23 (1934). 318 p.
Includes some 2,000 central and local official publications in the National Central Library. The main text lists publications issued from 1926 to 1932, and an appendix lists publications issued from 1911 to 1925. Arrangement follows the Chinese government structure. Chinese title and Western-language index.

TRANSLATIONS

Q122 Kuo li Chung yang T'u shu kuan, Taipei (National Central Library). *Chin pai nien lai Chung i shi shu mu lu* (Bibliography of translations from Western languages into Chinese in the past hundred years). T'ai-pei, Chung hua wen hua Ch'u pan chih yeh Wei yuan hui, Min kuo 47 (1958). 328 p.
Lists 5,047 books translated into Chinese from 1867 to 1956, based on eight major bibliographies and catalogues. In addition to information on the Chinese edition, information concerning

the author, and the Western titles is also given. The entries are arranged under ten major subject headings. No index.

PROHIBITED BOOKS

Q 123 Yao, Chin-kuang. *Ch'ing tai chin hui shu mu ssu chung* (Catalogue of books prohibited in the Ch'ing dynasty, 1644–1911). Shang-hai, Shang wu Yin shu kuan, Min kuo 26 (1937). 180 p. (Wan yu wen k'u 2 chi 700 chung).
Many of the approximately 2,500 entries, in addition to title, size and statement of contents, have short critical comments. No index.

PERIODICALS AND NEWSPAPERS

Q 124 *China publishers' directory, a practical guide to newspapers and periodicals for China advertisers*. Shanghai, Commercial Advertising Agency, 1934. 123 p.
Some 540 newspapers and periodicals, with an emphasis on those in Chinese, are listed by province, noting their date of establishment, frequency of publication, circulation, format and size. Supplementary list (4 p.) includes another 35 newspapers.

Q 125 Ssu-ch'uan Sheng ko T'u shu kuan, Chengtu (Szechwan Provincial Library). *Ssu-ch'uan sheng ke t'u shu kuan kuan ts'ang Chung wen chiu ch'i k'an lien ho mu lu (shao kao) 1884–1949* (Union catalogue of Chinese-language periodicals in libraries in Szechwan (first draft) 1884–1949). n.p., 1959. 4 v. and index volume.
Lists 9,788 periodicals in 19 libraries, and is important since only two of these libraries are surveyed in the *Ch'uan kuo Chung wen ch'i k'an lien ho mu lu, 1833–1949* (Q 126), and includes wartime publications not noted elsewhere.

Q 126 *Ch'uan kuo Chung wen ch'i k'an lien ho mu lu, 1833–1949* (National union catalogue of Chinese-language periodicals, 1833–1949). Pei-ching, Pei-ching T'u shu kuan, 1961. 1,522 p.
19,115 periodicals in 50 major Chinese libraries are arranged by stroke order of titles. Information given is full, including the date of first issue, frequency of publication, publisher, library locations and holdings. When periodical has ceased publication, this is noted.

Q 127 Hsien tai Wen hsueh Ch'i k'an Lien ho tiao ch'a hsiao tsu. *Chung-kuo hsien tai wen hsueh ch'i k'an mu lu, shao kao* Contemporary Chinese literature, a list of periodicals, 1902–1949. Shang-hai, Shang-hai Wen i Chu pan she, 1961. 110 p.
Some 1,700 periodicals are arranged in broad chronological periods, with some periodicals further subdivided. For each, dates of commencing and ceasing publication, frequency, editors, place of publication and publisher are given. Holdings in the Shanghai Library are also noted. Many of the periodicals noted are not listed in any other bibliography, including the *Chuan kuo Chung wen ch'i k'an lien ho mu lu, 1833–1949* (Q 126). Title index.

Reprinted by the Center for Chinese Research Materials, Association of Research Libraries, Washington, 1968.

Q128 Yu lien Yen chiu so, Hongkong (Union of Research Institute). *Catalogue of mainland Chinese magazines and newspapers held by the Union Research Institute*, third edition. Hongkong, 1968. 149 p.
Divided into two parts, the first containing 716 periodicals, with romanized title, characters, translation of title, frequency and holdings, and the second with similar information for 426 newspapers. Copies of materials listed available from the Institute of microfilm.

Q129 Yu lien Yen chiu so, Hong Kong (Union Research Institute). *Hung wei p'ing tzu liao mu lu* Catalogue of Red Guard publications (Chinese edition) held by URI. Chilun, 1970. 70 p.
58 titles of pamphlets and periodicals; 561 newspapers in 1,814 issues are listed. Other materials include 211 items. Mostly published in 1967 and 1968.

Q130 Herzer, Christine. *Die Volksrepublik China, eine annotierte Zeitschriften-bibliographie, 1960–1970.* Wiesbaden, Otto Harrosowitz, 1971. 346 p. (Band 31 der Schriften des Institut fur Asienkunde, Hamburg).
In two parts, the first with some 900 periodicals published in the People's Republic, and the second another 150 also published in the People's Republic. Titles, dates of publication when known and extensive annotations are given. No indication of locations.

Q131 Irick, Robert L. *Annotated guide to Taiwan periodical literature, 1972.* Taipei, Chinese Materials and Research Aids Service Center, 1972. 174 p.
1,070 periodicals are listed in alphabetical order by the romanized form of their titles, with notes on frequency, dates of first issue, subscription cost and short annotation. The Chinese character title follows the romanized form. Updates the 1966 edition, which has 519 titles. Character index by strokes and general subject index. Short list of English and bilingual publications.

Q132 Cheng, Heng-hsiung. *Chuan kuo tsa chih chih nan* Guide to Chinese periodicals. T'ai-pei, Min kuo 61 (1972). 160 p.
1,189 periodicals listed in a detailed subject classification, stating frequency, date of establishment, address. Chinese- and English-language title indexes. Appendices lists Chinese periodical and newspaper indexes published since 1912, reprinted Chinese periodicals, new periodicals appearing from 1970–2, and those ceasing publication in 1970–2.

Q133 Cheng, Paul P. W. *Annotated guide to current Chinese periodicals in Hong Kong*. Taipei, Chinese Materials and Research Aids Service Center, 1973. 71 p.
Lists 173 periodicals in Chinese or Chinese and English, giving address, subscription rate and annotation. Subject index, stroke count index and English title index.

Library Holdings outside the People's Republic

Q 134 Nunn, G. Raymond. *Chinese periodicals, international holdings, 1949–1960.* Ann Arbor, 1961. 85 p.
Lists over 1,700 Chinese periodicals in an attempt to compile a comprehensive listing. For each entry the romanized form of the title, the characters, translation of the title and location of library holdings are stated. The emphasis is on U.S. holdings. *Indexes and supplement* (1961. 107 p.) lists additional holdings, and provides Wade-Giles and *p'inyin* indexes.

Q 135 Shih, Bernadette P. N. *International union list of Communist Chinese serials, scientific, technical and medical, with selected social science titles.* Cambridge, Massachusetts Institute of Technology Libraries, 1963. 75 p.
A later list than G. Raymond Nunn *Chinese periodicals, international holdings, 1949–1960* (Q 134), and notes only 874 titles, with holdings for 601. Entries for 100 selected social science titles.

Q 136 Toyo Bunko, Tokyo. Chugoku Kenkyu Iinkai (Oriental Library. Seminar on Modern China). *Chugoku-bun shimbun zasshi sogo mokuroku. Nihon shuyo kenkyu kikan toshokan shozo* (Union catalogue of newspapers and periodicals in Chinese, in libraries of important Japanese research institutions). Tokyo, Showa 34 (1959). 171 p.
Some 3,000 newspapers and periodicals are located in 23 Japanese libraries. Holdings stated.

Q 137 U.S. Library of Congress. *Union card file of Oriental vernacular serials. Chinese, Japanese and Korean. Chinese file.* Washington, 1966.
Contains 27,479 cards and is available on microfilm, or on electrostatic enlargement in card size from the Library of Congress. 17 major Chinese collections in the U.S. made their serial records available for microfilming in 1964 and 1965, and are represented.

Q 138 London. University. Contemporary China Institute. *A bibliography of Chinese newspapers and periodicals in European libraries.* Cambridge and New York, Cambridge University Press, 1975. 1,025 l. (Contemporary China Institute publications).
Important since it replaces many publications on Chinese-language periodicals in Europe by one comprehensive bibliography. Holdings for approximately 6,000 titles in European libraries, including those in the Soviet Union. Arranged by *p'inyin* romanization. Index to Western-language subtitles. *Interim supplement: acquisitions by British Libraries, 1972–1977,* London, SOAS for China Library Group, 1978, reported.

Q 139 Goodman, David S.G. *Research guide to Chinese provincial and regional newspapers.* London, Contemporary China Institute, School of Oriental and African Studies, University of London, 1976. 140 p. (Research notes and studies no. 2).
Lists 39 provincial and regional Chinese newspapers found in

microfilm copies outside the United Kingdom, in the Library of Congress and the Hoover Institution on War, Revolution and Peace in the U.S., and in the Union Research Institute in Hongkong. Detailed holdings in these institutions are given.

Q140 U.S. Library of Congress. *Chinese periodicals in the Library of Congress*. Washington, 1978. 521 p.
Over 6,400 titles, with holdings representing the largest collection of Chinese serials outside China, and covering the period 1868–1975. Alphabetical arrangement under Chinese titles, with references from English titles. Chinese legal serials in the Library's Law Division are excluded.

Indexes

Q141 T'an, Cho-yuan. *Chung wen tsa chih so yin* (Index to Chinese periodicals). Kuang-tung, Ling-nan Ta hsueh T'u shu kuan, Min kuo 24 (1935). 2 v.
105 periodicals published from the beginning of the Republic to 1929 are indexed in a similar system to that of the *Readers' guide to periodical literature,* and under each heading titles of articles, author's name, periodical, volume, issue, pagination and date are given. Although only a small number of the total number of periodicals for the period are covered, this is a most valuable source.

Q142 Columbia University. East Asian Library. *Index to learned Chinese periodicals*. Boston, G. K. Hall, 1963. 215 p.
Contains 4,500 entries from 13 Chinese periodicals published for the most part from the mid-1920s to 1950. The first part is arranged by author, and the second by subject. Titles are translated, but not romanized. No index.

Q143 *Jen wen yueh k'an* (Humanities monthly), v. 1–8, 1930–7, v. 9, 1947. Shang-hai, Jen wen yueh k'an she, Min kuo 19–36 (1930–47). 9 v.
Articles from 250 Chinese periodicals are indexed by subject. Entries give title, author's name, periodical, volume, page and date. New books are listed in a book section. For volume 9, issues 1–3 only noted, published in 1947 after a break of ten years. These monthly supplements to the *Jen wen yueh k'an* have been cumulated for volumes 1–8, 1930–7 in *Jen wen yueh k'an tsa chin yao mu so yin* (Taipei, T'ien i ch'u pan she, 1975).

Q144 *Ch'i k'an so yin* The current Chinese magazine essays index, v. 1–8. Nan-ching, Nan-ching Chung-shan Wen hua Chiao yu kuan, Min kuo 22–6 (1933–7). 8 v.
More comprehensive than the *Jen wen yueh k'an* (Q 143). Volume 5 indexes some 450 periodicals. A number of subject arrangements are used. Volume 5 uses the Dewey Decimal Classification system.

Q145 *Jih pao so yin* The leading Chinese newspapers index, a book of record, v. 1–7. Shang-hai, Chung-shan Wen hua Chiao yu kuan, Min kuo 23–6 (1934–7). 7 v.

12 leading Chinese newspapers are indexed in a detailed classified arrangement. Each monthly issue contains some 12,000 entries.

Q 146 *Jen min jih pao so yin* (Index to the People's Daily), 1950–. Pei-ching, Jen min jih pao, 1950–.

A monthly subject index to the *Jen min jih pao*. Other newspapers such as the *Kuang ming jih pao* (Enlightenment Daily) and *(Ta kung pao* (L'Impartiale) published monthly indexes. Newspapers are also indexed in the *Ch'uan kuo chu yao pao k'an tzu liao so yin* (Q 147). Issue for September 1971 seen. Reprinted by Center for Chinese Research Materials, Washington with coverage for 1948–70 in 23 volumes.

Q 147 *Ch'uan kuo chu yao pao k'an tzu liao so yin* (National index to materials in important periodicals and newspapers), nos. 1–38, 1955–8. Shang-hai, Shang-hai shih Pao k'an T'u shu kuan, 1955–8. 38 nos.

Arranged by subjects, then by the newspaper and periodical title in which the article appeared. Date of publication, name of author, pagination and volume are stated. A representative issue will cite some 5,000 articles from some 40 newspapers and 260 periodicals. In 1959 divided into two sections: *Che hsueh she hui k'o hsueh pu fen* (Philosophy and social sciences section), no. 39–, 1959– and *Tzu jan chi shu k'o hsueh pu fen* (Natural and applied sciences section), no. 1–, 1959–. Available on microfilm, including nos. 39–57 of *Che hsueh she hui k'o hsueh pu fen* and nos. 1–12 of *Tzu jan chi shu k'o hsueh pu fen.*

Q 148 Kuo li T'ai-wan Ta hsueh, Taipei (National Taiwan University). *Chung wen ch'i k'an lun wen fen lei so yin* Classified index to Chinese periodicals. T'ai-pei, Min kuo 49– (1960–).

The number of periodicals indexed has increased from the original 30 for the period 1945–57 to 75 for 1961 (in the third issue). The third issue also contains a list of some 450 periodicals published in Taiwan, and arranged in classified order. Subject arrangement. 1977 issue, series 12 seen. Title varies.

Q 149 Kou li Chung yang T'u shu kuan, Taipei (National Central Library). *Chung hua min kuo chi k'an lun wen so yin* Index to Chinese periodicals. T'ai-pei, Min kuo 49– (1960–).

From January 1971 science and technology section only. Former title *Chi k'an lun wen so yin* through 1968, and published by the Chung kuo min kuo Kuo fang Yen chiu yuan T'u shu kuan. July–December 1976 issue seen.

Q 150 Yu lien Yen chiu so, Hongkong (Union Research Institute). *Index to the material on Communist China held by the Union Research Institute.* Hongkong, 1962. 197 p.

Microfilm copies of the files of the Union Research Institute's newspaper clippings are now held at three U.S. centres: the Center for Research Libraries; the Center for Chinese Studies, University of California, Berkeley; and the University of Hawaii Library. The index is a key to these files, which are particularly valuable for the period from 1956.

Q151 Cheng chi Ta hsueh, Taipei. She hui K'o hsueh tzu liao Chung hsin (Chengchi University. Social Science Materials Centre). *Chung wen pao chih lun wen fen lei so yin* Classified index to Chinese newspapers, 1962–. T'ai-pei, Min kuo 52– (1963–). Annual.
Each issue contains some 7,000 entries for articles from Taiwan and Hong Kong newspapers, arranged in a detailed subject order. 1975 issue seen.

Q152 Cheng chi Ta Hsueh. She hui Ko hsueh tzu liao Chung hsin (Chengchi University. Social Sciences Materials Centre). *Chung-wen chi k'an jen wen chi she hui k'o hsueh lun wen fen lei so yin* Classified index of humanities and science to Chinese periodicals. T'ai-pei, Min kuo 58– (1969–).
1966 issue published in 1969, and 1968 issue published in 1971. The 1967 issue contains some 6,000 periodical articles selected from 74 periodicals, and arranged in a classified subject order.

Q153 Kuo li Chung yang T'u shu kuan, Taipei (National Central Library). *Chung kuo chin erh shih nien wen shih che lun wen fen lei so yin* (Classified index to articles on literature, history, and philosophy, written in the past twenty years). T'ai-pei, Min-kuo 59 (1970). 852 p.
23,626 articles are entered in a detailed subject arrangement, with an author index and list of some 300 periodical sources.

Q154 Kuo li Chung yang T'u shu kuan, Taipei (National Central Library). *Chung hua min kuo chi k'an lun wen so yin* Index to Chinese periodicals. T'ai-pei, Min kuo 59– (1970–).
Some 3,000 entries are cited each month, and are divided into a humanities and social science section covering 340 periodical titles, and a science and technology section covering 140 periodicals.

Q155 *Hsin hua yueh pao pao k'an ts'an k'ao tzu liao so yin* New China monthly index to reference materials in newspapers and periodicals. Washington, Center for Chinese Research Materials, Association for Research Libraries, 1972. 3 v.
The *Hsin hua yueh pao* was a leading periodical in China from November 1949 to May 1966, and from February 1951 included this index of materials from Chinese newspapers and periodicals.

Q156 Chang, Chin-lang. *Chung wen pao chih wen shih che lun wen so yin* Index to articles on the humanities in Chinese newspapers, 1936–1971. T'ai-pei, Cheng chung Shu chu, Min kuo 62 (1973). 2 v.
Index to articles on the humanities published in twenty Chinese newspapers between 1936 and 1971. Volume 1 with 6,593 entries indexes the *Chung yang jih pao* (Central Daily News), and volume 2 with 5,534 entries indexes the 19 other newspapers. Author index and subject heading index in each volume.

COLLECTANEA OR CHINESE SERIES

Q 157 *Chung-kuo ts'ung shu tsung lu* (Comprehensive bibliography of Chinese series). Shang-hai, Chung hua Shu chu, 1959–62. 3 v.

A Chinese collectanea or *ts'ung shu* is to be distinguished from a publisher's series where books may continue to be added from time to time. The collected works of a writer is one form of *ts'ung shu,* but the emphasis may be on works concerning a family or an area. The first of these series was issued in 1202, and this form of publication has led to the preservation of possibly over one-half of early Chinese works, which would otherwise have been lost. Chinese bibliographies of *ts'ung shu* date from 1799, but this is the most comprehensive, listing more *ts'ung shu* and more individual titles than others which it now supersedes. The first volume is a classified arrangement of 2,797 collectanea published by 1842, giving their locations among 41 mainland Chinese libraries. the second arranges 38,891 titles found in these *ts'ung shu* in a similar traditional order of classics, history, philosophy and belles lettres. The third indexes titles and authors by the four corner system. Buddhist collectanea and collectanea published after 1842 are not included. Editions are noted, and the more reliable indicated. Conversion tables as key to the four corner system included.

Q 158 Wang, Pao-hsien. *T'ai-wan ko t'u shu kuan hsien ts'un ts'ung shu tzu mu . . . shu ming so yin* Title and author index to *ts'ung shu* in Taiwan libraries. San Francisco, Chinese Materials Center, 1975. 3 v. (Chinese Materials and Research Aids Service Center, Research aids series no. 7).

An index to over 40,000 titles of works, and 30,000 authors, located in some 1,000 collectanea in libraries in Taiwan, and published from earliest times to the present. Complements the *Chung-kuo ts'ung shu tsung lu* (Q 157).

ESSAY BIBLIOGRAPHY

Q 159 Kyoto Daigaku. Toyoshi Kenkyukai (Kyoto University. Oriental History Society). *Chugoku zuihitsu sakuin* (Index to Chinese essays). Tokyo, Nihon Gakujutsu Shinkokai, Showa 29 (1954). 1,018 p.

The tables of contents of 157 collections of Chinese essays are indexed in the Japanese syllabic order. Stroke index.

Q 160 Saeki, Tomi. *Chugoku zuihitsu zatcho sakuin* Index to Chinese essays and miscellaneous writings. Kyoto, Kyoto Daigaku Toyoshi Kenkyukai, Showa 35 (1960). 1,144 p. (Toyoshi kenkyu sokan 7).

A supplement to the *Chugoku zuihitsu sakuin* (Q 159), indexing the tables of contents of an additional 46 collections.

THESES AND DISSERTATIONS

Q 161 Chung yang T'u shu kuan, Taipei. *Chung hua min kuo po shih*

shuo lun wen so yin (Catalogue of Chinese doctoral dissertations and masters' theses). T'ai-pei, Min kuo 59 (1970). 272 p. (Kuo li Chung yang T'u shu kuan mu lu ts'ung kan ti 3 chi).
Lists 18 doctoral dissertations and 2,650 masters' theses published from 1949–68 in Taiwan. These are arranged by subject, and note title of thesis, date of publication, and institution where it was published. Index to authors.

Western Languages

Q 162 Cordier, Henri. *Bibliotheca sinica, dictionnaire bibliographique des ouvrages relatifs a l'Empire chinois.* Paris, E. Guilmoto, 1904–8. 4 v. *Supplement et index.* Paris, Geuthner 1922–4.
Some 26,000 books, periodicals and periodical articles in Western languages, and published from the 16th century to 1924. Cordier's French annotations are critical and reflect his great knowledge of China. The main work is divided into five parts. The first part deals with China as a whole, and comprises the first two and a half volumes; the second deals with foreigners in China; the third with relations between China and foreigners; the fourth with Chinese in foreign countries; and the fifth with tributary countries of China. Reprinted by the Cheng wen Publishing Co., Taipei, 1966. Difficult to use since there is no comprehensive index, a need partly met by the *Author index to the Bibliotheca sinica of Henri Cordier* (New York, East Asiatic Library, Columbia University Libraries, 1953. 84 p.) which lists 7,700 author entries with page references. A key bibliography of China for Western-language materials, but contains much that is now superseded.

Q 163 Toyo Bunko, Tokyo (Oriental Library). *Catalogue of the Asiatic Library of Dr. G. E. Morrison, now a part of the Oriental Library, Tokyo, Japan.* Tokyo, 1924. 2 v.
Dr. G. E. Morrison was once adviser to the President of China and Peking correspondent of the London *Times*. From 1892 to 1917 he collected all available books on China and adjacent areas. The collection contains some 13,530 books in many Western languages, but nearly two-thirds are in English and one-sixth is in French. Entries are arranged in author order, and there is no annotation and no subject index. Since a large proportion of these entries are to be found in Henri Cordier *Bibliotheca sinica* (Q 162), the principal importance of this catalogue is the location of an extant copy.

Q 164 Yuan, T'ung-li. *China in Western literature, a continuation of Cordier's Bibliotheca sinica.* New Haven, Far Eastern Publications, Yale University Press, 1958. 802 p.
Dr. T. L. Yuan was Director of the National Library of Peiping from 1926 to 1948. He has listed some 18,000 books in English, French, German and Portuguese published between 1921 and

1957 in broad subject divisions, with detailed breakdown. There are divisions for areas as Manchuria, Mongolia, Tibet, Sinkiang, Taiwan, Hong Kong and Macao, which are treated separately. It is not annotated, and all items have been examined by the compiler. Author index. Since books only are included, John Lust *Index sinicus* (Q 172), which includes periodical articles and excludes books, supplements this bibliography.

Q 165 Hucker, Charles O. *China, a critical bibliography.* Tucson, University of Arizona Press, 1962. 125 p.
A selected annotated list of 2,285 books, periodical articles and sections of books on traditional and modern China. Many entries are repeated. The bibliography has a subject arrangement and within each subject division the compiler has grouped his materials from the most authoritative to the less, and the more general in scope to the more narrow. Entries are mostly in English, although there are some French and German items. Each subject division has a short introduction. Author index. A valuable introductory bibliography.

Q 166 Sinor, Denis. *Introduction a l'etude de l'Eurasie centrale.* Wiesbaden, Otto Harrassowitz, 1963. 371 p.
A bibliographical essay, with 4,403 entries, mostly periodical articles published in the 20th century to 1961, with only a few in English. Important since it is concerned with a number of peoples on China's borderland where they have often played a major role in Chinese history. Author index to pages, not items.

Q 167 Leslie, Donald and Jeremy Davidson. *Author catalogues of Western sinologists.* Canberra, Department of Far Eastern History, Research School of Pacific Studies, Australian National University, 1966. 257 p. (Guide to bibliographies on China and the Far East).
Some 500 Western writers on China and related areas are arranged in alphabetical order, with references to sources where listing of their works may be found. Altogether 286 periodicals, nearly all of them Western, were analyzed. A further 100 are noted as not being analyzed. Short subject index.

Q 168 Ling, Scott K. *Bibliography of Chinese humanities, 1941–1972, studies on Chinese philosophy, religion, history, geography, biography, art and literature.* Taipei, Liberal Arts Press, 1975. 645 p.
A compilation based mainly on the annual *Bibliography of Asian studies* (A 17), and following the subject arrangement of its G. K. Hall compilation, lists books, articles and theses in Western languages.

TRANSLATIONS

Q 169 Wang, Erh-min. *Chung-kuo wen hsien hsi i shu mu* (Bibliography of Western translations of Chinese works). Taipei, T'ai-wan Shang wu Yin shu kuan, 1975. 761 p.

Lists translations of some 3,000 Chinese books and articles mainly into English, French and German, arranged under 14 subjects. Title, original author and translator indexes.

PERIODICALS AND NEWSPAPERS

Q170 King, Frank H. H. and Prescott Clarke. *A research guide to China-Coast newspapers, 1833–1911.* Cambridge, Harvard University Press, 1965. 235 p. (Harvard East Asia monographs 18).

235 newspapers are listed, with information on holdings for 125 in 46 libraries. In addition to the listing there is a great deal of information concerning the development of the China-Coast newspaper. Japanese newspapers published in China are quoted in an appendix. This account can be brought down to 1930 by Thomas Min-heng Chao *The foreign press in China* (Shanghai, China Institute of Pacific Relations, 1931. 114 p.).

Q171 Birch, Garnett Elmer. *Western-language periodical publications in China, in 1828–1949.* Honolulu, 1967. 166 p.

Master's thesis at the University of Hawaii, 1967. 861 periodicals issued from 1828 to 1949 are listed in alphabetical order. The most comprehensive listing available. Holdings not stated. Chronological index to periodicals by date of first issue. The main part of the text is a discussion of the development and distribution of Western-language periodical publishing in China.

Indexes

Q172 Lust, John. *Index sinicus, a catalogue of articles relating to China in periodicals and other collective publications, 1920–1955.* Cambridge, Heffer, 1964. 663 p.

Supplements T'ung-li Yuan *China in Western literature* (Q 164), and has 19,734 Western-language articles in periodicals, memorial volumes, symposia and congress proceedings. Some 840 periodicals, 150 collective works and 25 congresses were surveyed to make the compilation. The subject arrangement of Dr. Yuan's work is followed. All items were personally examined by the contributors.

Q173 Sorich, Richard. *Contemporary China, a bibliography of reports on China published by the United States Joint Publications Research Service.* New York, prepared for the Joint Committee on Contemporary China of the American Council of Learned Societies and the Social Science Research Council, 1961. 99 p.

The reports on China published from the end of 1957 to July 1960 are listed by JPRS number. The contents of each number is stated. Subject index.

Q174 Kyriak, Theodore E. *China, a bibliography,* v. 1, nos. 1–12, v. 2, July 1962–June 1964. Annapolis, Research and Microfilm Publications, 1962–4.

After a break from August 1960 to the end of June 1962, this new indexing of JPRS reports continues the work of Richard Sorich *Contemporary China* (Q 173), but with the same defect of not indexing the individual articles within each report. Subject index. Continued by *China, bibliography—index to U.S. JPRS Research translations,* v. 3, nos. 1–12, July 1963 – June 1965, and *China and Asia (exclusive of Near East) bibliography—index to U.S. Research translations,* v. 3, July 1965–, itself continued by *Transdex, bibliography and index to the United States Joint Publications Research Service (JPRS) translations.* Issues of *Transdex* seen through 1978

DISSERTATIONS

Q 175 Gordon, Leonard H. D. and Frank J. Shulman. *Doctoral dissertations on China, a bibliography of studies in Western languages, 1945–1970.* Seattle, University of Washington Press, 1972. 317 p. (Association for Asian Studies, Reference series no. 1).
2,217 dissertations are listed in a detailed subject arrangement. Nearly two-thirds of the dissertations are from the U.S. The Soviet Union, Great Britain, Germany and France are also well represented. Nearly one-third of the book is given over to author, subject and institutional indexes, and a note on availability.

Q 176 Shulman, Frank J. *Doctoral dissertations on China, 1971–1975, a bibliography of studies in Western languages.* Seattle, University of Washington Press, 1978. 329 p.
1,802 dissertations are arranged by a detailed subject order, with references where abstracts may be found, publication as a book, and in most cases a short annotation. Continues the author's and Leonard H. D. Gordon *Doctoral Dissertations on China, a bibliography of studies in Western languages, 1945–1970* (Q 175). Author, institutional and modified subject indexes. Note on the availability of the dissertations. Includes as an appendix a list of dissertations completed between 1945 and 1970, and omitted in the parent volume. First in a series of five-year supplements.

MAPS

Q 177 Williams, Jack F. *China in maps, 1890–1960, a selective and annotated cartobibliography.* East Lansing, Asian Studies Center, Michigan State University, 1974. 365 p.
An extensive introduction surveys the mapping of China and is followed by a list of available maps with locations arranged by country publishing: China, France, Germany, Britain, Japan, Russia and U.S.

FILMS

Q 178 Ching, Eugene. *Audio-visual materials for Chinese studies.* New York, American Association of Teachers of Chinese Language and Culture, 1974. 171 p.

The materials are arranged by type, such as films. Subject and general indexes and addresses of distributors and producers.

Q 179 Posner, Arlene. *China, a resource and curriculum guide,* second edition revised. Chicago, University of Chicago Press, 1976. 317 p.
Designed to support instruction in Chinese studies. In two parts, the first is concerned with teaching on China, and the second is a well-annotated bibliography of materials on China, including audio-visual materials, arranged by subject. Author and title index. Revision of the 1973 edition.

Japanese Language

Q 180 Fairbank, John King and Masataka Banno. *Japanese studies of modern China, a bibliographical guide to historical and social science research on the 19th and 20th centuries.* Cambridge, Harvard University Press, 1971. (Harvard-Yenching Institute studies 26).
Lists over 1,000 Japanese books and periodical articles on modern China, arranging them by major subjects in modern Chinese history, and then by author. Critical annotations, with notes on the existence of book reviews have been added. The index lists authors and titles in one sequence. There is a character index to authors. Originally published by Tuttle, Tokyo, 1953.

Q 181 Kamachi, Noriko, John K. Fairbank and Chuzo Ichiko. *Japanese studies of Modern China since 1953, a bibliographical guide to historical and social science research on the nineteenth and twentieth centuries, supplementary volume for 1953–1969.* Cambridge, East Asian Research Center, Harvard University, 1975. 603 p. (Harvard East Asian monographs 60).
Supplements John King Fairbank *Japanese studies of modern China, a bibliographical guide to historical and social science research on the 19th and 20th centuries* (Q 180), and lists some 2,500 Japanese books and articles on modern China up to 1949, published between 1953 and 1969, and a small number of books published from 1970 to 1973. General index to authors and titles.

Russian Language

Q 182 Skachkov, Petr. Emelianovich. *Bibliografiia kitaiia.* Moskva, Izdaltelstvo Vostochnoi Literaturi, 1960. 690 p.
19,951 books and periodical articles published in Russian up to 1957, and covering the period 1730 to 1957, are arranged under 25 broad subjects and further divided into books and articles. A revised edition of the 1932 bibliography which contains only 10,000 entries. Ideally the two should be used together to avoid missing material not in the second edition. Articles include

reviews of major books in Russian, listed by the title of the book. The second edition has an author index only, where the first has both an author and subject index.

Q183 Yuan, T'ung-li. *Russian works on China, 1918–1960, in American libraries.* New Haven, Yale University, Far Eastern Publications, 1961. 162 p.

1,348 entries are divided into the main geographical areas of China Proper, Manchuria, Mongolia, Sinkiang, Tibet and Taiwan, and are further subdivided by subjects. Only the latest edition is cited, with earlier editions noted in brief annotations. While this bibliography is small compared with Petr. Emelianovich Skachkov's *Bibliografiia kataiia* (Q 182), it is important for locating materials.

Q184 Efimov, Gerontii Valentinovich. *Istoriko-bibliografischeskoe obozrenie istochnikov i literatury po novoi istorii Kitaia.* Leningrad, 1965–72. 3 v.

In three volumes, the first covering historiography and archives in China, the second on Chinese studies in Russia, and the third on Chinese studies in Europe, the United States and China. In bibliographical essay form. No index.

Subject Bibliography

RELIGION AND THOUGHT

Q185 Pfister, P. Louis. *Notices biographiques et bibliographiques sur les Jesuites de l'ancienne Mission de Chine, 1552–1773.* Changhai, Imprimerie de la Mission Catholique, 1932–4. (Varietes sinologiques nos. 59–60).

Lists 463 Jesuits arranged in chronological order, and commencing with St. Francis Xavier, with their biographies and publications. In addition there is a short bibliography of some 250 entries. Detailed subject and name index.

Q186 Wylie, Alexander. *Memorials of Protestant missionaries to the Chinese, giving a list of their publications and obituary notices of the deceased with copious indexes.* Shanghai, American Presbyterian Mission Press, 1867. 330 p.

338 missionaries are listed in chronological order, with a short account of their lives and lists of their publications in Chinese and English. Index to missionaries and to titles of Chinese and English publications. Reprinted in Taipei 1967.

Q187 Chu, Clayton H. *American missionaries to China, books, articles and pamphlets extracted from the subject catalogue of the Missionary Research Library.* Cambridge, Harvard University Press, 1960. 509 p. (Research aids for American Far Eastern policy studies no. 2).

Some 7,000 entries for materials in English, published to 1959, but with a stress on publications issued before 1941. The entries are arranged under 464 subject headings, following the arrangement in the Missionary Research Library. Author and organization index.

Q188 Chan, Wing-tsit. *Chinese philosophy, 1949–1963, an annotated bibliography of mainland China publications.* Honolulu, East-West Center Press, 1965. 290 p.
Divided into two sections, the first containing 213 books, and the second 756 periodical and newspaper articles. Each section subdivided chronologically by period. Authors' names in romanization and characters, and titles in romanization, character and translation. Brief annotations. Name index to authors and to persons cited.

Q189 Chan, Wing-tsit. *An outline and an annotated bibliography of Chinese philosophy.* New Haven, Far Eastern Publications, Yale University, 1969. 220 p.
Revises earlier bibliographies published in 1955 and in 1959. In two parts, an introduction where brief author and title entries are arranged in a syllabus order, and an annotated bibliography arranged by author, containing some 700 titles in Western languages.

Q190 Thompson, Laurence G. *Studies of Chinese religion, a comprehensive and classified bibliography of publications in English, French and German through 1970.* Encino, Dickenson Publishing Co., 1976. 190 p.
Some 5,000 entries for books and periodical articles published to 1970 are grouped under two major categories, Chinese Buddhism and Chinese religion exclusive of Buddhism. Both are further subdivided into over 40 headings. Index to authors, editors, translators and compilers.

Q191 Eu, Charles Wei-hsun and Wing-tsit Chan. *Guide to Chinese philosophy.* Boston, G. K. Hall, 1978. 262 p.
Intended as a teaching and research guide, limited mostly to English-language material and listing over 1,000 books and articles in a detailed subject arrangement. Annotated. Author and title index.

SOCIAL SCIENCES

Q192 U.S. Bureau of the Census. *Bibliography of social science periodicals and monographs series, mainland China, 1949–1960.* Washington, U.S. Government Printing Office, 1961. 32 p. (Foreign social science bibliographies series P-92 no. 3).
107 periodicals and 35 monograph series in the Library of Congress are arranged under 14 social science fields and bibliography. Separate subject and title indexes.

Q193 U.S. Bureau of the Census. *Bibliography of social science periodical and monograph series, Republic of China, 1949–1961.* Washington, U.S. Government Printing Office, 1962. 24 p. (Foreign social science bibliographies P-92 no. 4).
57 periodicals and 27 monograph series are arranged into 15 social

science fields. Annotation covers frequency, contents and holdings of the Library of Congress. Separate indexes to subjects, titles, authors and issuing agencies.

Economics

Q 194 Wu, Yu-chang. *Chung-kuo ho tso wen hsien mu lu* (Bibliography on cooperation in China). Shang-hai, Nan-ching Chung-kuo Ho tse she, Min kuo 25 (1936). 110 p.
840 books and periodicals, almost entirely in Chinese on co-operation in China and elsewhere, arranged by publisher and including both official and commercial publications. No annotation and no index.

Q 195 U.S. Bureau of the Census. *Population and manpower of China, an annotated bibliography.* Washington, U.S. Government Printing Office, 1958. 132 p. (International population statistics reports series P-90 no. 8).
Some 650 books and serials in Chinese, Japanese and Western languages are arranged in subject order, with annotations. Author index. Reprinted by Greenwood Press, Westport.

Q 196 Chen, Nai-ruenn. *The economy of mainland China, 1949–1963, a bibliography of materials in English.* Berkeley, Committee on the Economy of China, Social Science Research Council, 1963. 297 p.
Contains 10,000 entries for materials published between 1949 and July 1963, including translations. Approximately 160 periodicals were surveyed. The first part (pp. 1–256) includes materials originating in mainland China, and consists mainly of translations from the American Consulate-General in Hong Kong. The second part (pp. 257–97) is for materials originating outside mainland China, mostly from the United States and Hong Kong. There are 297 subject divisions.

Q 197 Yuan, K'un-hsiang. *Ching-chi lun wen fen lei so yin* A classified index to articles on economics, 1945–1965. Taipei, 1967. 2 v. (Chinese Materials and Research Aids Service Center, Research aid series).
Index to 37,083 periodical articles on economic matters appearing in Taiwan and Hong Kong periodicals. Author index.

Q 198 Hall, W. P. J. *A bibliographical guide to Japanese research on the Chinese economy.* Cambridge, East Asian Research Center distributed by Harvard University Press, 1972. 100 p.
250 books and articles are arranged by subject order, with rankings as to significance. Author and subject indexes.

Q 199 Bell, Bella Zi. *An annotated bibliography of materials on the population of the People's Republic of China in the Resource Materials Collection of the East-West Population Institute, as of June 1972.* Honolulu, East West Population Institute, 1972. 65 p.
Over 200 reports, books, articles and clippings. Author index.

Q 200 Chang, Henry C. *Taiwan demography, 1946–1971, a selected,*

annotated bibliography of government documents. Minneapolis, Center for Population Studies, University of Minnesota, 1973. 60 p.
149 entries in Chinese, arranged by subject, and fully annotated. Author and title index.

Q201 Chinese Center for International Training in Family Planning. *Annotated Taiwan population bibliography.* Taichung, 1974. 115 p.
Some 300 books, reports and articles in English, arranged by subject, with annotations. No index.

Q202 Emerson, John Philip. *The Provinces of the People's Republic of China, a political and economic bibliography.* Washington, U.S. Department of Commerce, 1976. 734 p. (International population statistics reports, series P-90-25).
Some 6,000 entries, mostly published from 1954 to 1961, have been arranged by province. Material selected has been guided largely by the Chinese indexes to periodicals and newspapers. Translations are noted, where available. Author index.

Q203 Blair, Patricia. *Development in the People's Republic of China, a selected bibliography.* Washington, Overseas Development Council, 1976. 94p. (Occasional paper no. 8).
413 entries for books and articles in English published between 1970 and 1976 are arranged under 27 sections, each with a short introduction. Introductory essay by A. Doak Barnett. Some annotation. Author index.

Political Science and Law

Q204 Jiang, Joseph. *Chinese bureaucracy and government administration, an annotated bibliography.* Honolulu, Research Translations, East-West Center, 1964. 157 p.
561 Chinese books and periodical articles, published since 1911, of which only one-half have been inspected and annotated. Divided by subjects, and has author and subject indexes.

Q205 Lin, Fu-shun. *Chinese law, past and present, a bibliography of enactments and commentaries in English text.* New York, East Asian Institute, Columbia University, 1966. 419 p.
Divided into two sections: the first on Communist Chinese law occupies some two-thirds of the book; the second is on non-Communist Chinese law. Altogether there are 3,500 books, periodical articles, statutes, documents and newspaper articles surveying Chinese law from earliest times. Author index. No annotations.

Q206 Hsia, Tao-t'ai. *Guide to selected legal sources of mainland China, a listing of laws and regulations and periodical legal literature with a brief survey of the administration of justice.* Washington, Library of Congress, 1967. 357 p.
The first part consists of a translation of two statutory collections, the *Chung yang jen min cheng fu fa ling hui pien*

(Collections of laws and decrees of the Central People's Government) (v. 1–5, 1952–5) and the *Chung hua jen min kung ho kuo fa kuei hui pien* (Collections of laws and regulations of the People's Republic of China) (v. 1–13, 1956–64). The second part consists of 940 legal articles from some 58 mainland Chinese periodicals, with titles in translated form only. The second part has an author index and a 71-page introductory survey of the mainland Chinese legal system.

Q207 *Preliminary union list of materials on Chinese law.* Cambridge, Harvard Law School, 1967. 919 p. (Studies in Chinese law no. 6).
A union list of approximately 9,000 items, mostly in Chinese and located in 19 libraries, 17 of which are in the United States. The principal section is arranged by subject, and is followed by a list of some 100 periodicals, and a listing of statutory materials.

Q208 Ho, Paul. *The People's Republic of China and international law, a selective bibliography of Chinese sources.* Washington, Far Eastern Law Division, Library of Congress, 1972. 45 p.
632 books and articles published in the People's Republic. Arrangement is by topic, and then by country.

Q209 Chang, Wei-jen. *Chung-kuo fa chih shih shu mu* An annotated bibliography of Chinese legal history. Tai-pei, Chung yang Yen chiu yuan, Li shih yu yen cho, Min-kuo 65 (1966). 3 v. (Chung yang yen chiu yuan, Li shih yu yen cho 67).
2,433 books in Chinese located in 14 major libraries in Taiwan, and covering the Chinese legal system to 1911, arranged by subject. Books listed include law collections, and survey institutions, theory and practice of Chinese law. Author index and title index.

Q210 Cho, Sung Yoon. *Japanese writings on Communist Chinese law, 1946–1974, a selected annotated bibliography.* Washington, Library of Congress, 1977. 223 p.
1,083 books and articles selected from 200 periodicals are arranged in detailed subject arrangement. Author index.

Education, Libraries and Mass Communication

Q211 Kuo li Taiwan Shih fan Ta hsueh T'u shu kuan, Taipei (National Taiwan Normal University. Library). *Chiao yu lun wen so yin* Education index to periodical literature. T'ai-pei, Min kuo 46– (1957–)
Arranged by topics. Ninth series for 1970 published 1972 seen. First series has title: *Chiu shih nien chiao yu lun wen so yin.*

Q212 Pei-ching T'u shu kuan (National Library of Peking). *T'u shu kuan hsueh lun wen so yin* (Index to library science articles). Pei-ching, Shang wu Yin shu kuan, 1959. 2 v.
Divided into two parts, the first covering materials published from the end of the Ch'ing Dynasty to September 1949 and comprising 5,359 entries, and the second from 1949 to December 1957

with 2,037 entries. Each volume arranged by a detailed subject order, with separate author indexes.

Q213 Fraser, Stewart E. and Kuang-Liang Hsu. *Chinese education and society, a bibliographic guide.* White Plains, International Arts Science Press, 1972. 204 p.
Arranged into sections for books, periodical articles and unpublished materials, and covering the period 1966–72. Most of the entries are in Chinese or English.

Q214 Yang, Shou-Jung. *Mass communications in Taiwan, an annotated bibliography.* Singapore, Asian Mass Communication Research and Information Centre, 1977. 65 p. (Bibliography series 5).
308 entries for books, pamphlets, reports, theses and periodicals, mostly in Chinese, under 17 headings. No Chinese-language titles given, making it almost impossible to search for items cited. Author index.

NATURAL AND APPLIED SCIENCES, MEDICINE

Q215 Manshu Ika Daigaku, Mukden (Manchurian Medical University). *Chugoku igaku shomoku* (Catalogue of Chinese medical books). Hoten (i.e. Mukden), Showa 6–16 (1931–41). 2 v.
Some 2,800 books are arranged in classified order, with a title and author index by strokes for each volume. Full bibliographical information and contents note for each entry.

Q216 Taki, Mototane. *Chung-kuo i chi k'ao* (Chinese medical books). Peiching, Jen min Wei sheng Chu pan she, 1956. 1,404 p.
3,800 books on traditional Chinese medicine are arranged in subject order, and entries are fully annotated. There is a list of titles in the expanded table of contents, and an index to titles by stroke order. Reprint of a Tokugawa period Japanese bibliography.

Q217 Chao, Chi-sheng. *K'o hsueh chi shu ts'an kao shu t'i yao* (Essentials of scientific and technical reference books). Pei-ching, Shang wu Yin shu kuan, 1958. 539 p.
1,554 books in Chinese, mostly published since 1950, are arranged in a classified order, and with the exception of a few items in the initial general section, all are concerned with the natural and applied sciences. Under each subject books are arranged according to their form, and entries are annotated. Separate title and author indexes arranged by stroke.

Q218 Pei-ching K'uang yeh Hsueh yuan, T'u shu kuan (Peking Mining Engineering Academy, Library). *Chung-kuo k'uang yeh ch'i k'an lun wen so yin* (Index to periodical articles on Chinese mining engineering). Pei-ching, Ko hsueh Ch'u pan she, 1960. 366 p.
Over 8,000 articles from 102 periodicals published from 1917 to 1959, on mining engineering and associated fields, are arranged in detailed subject order.

Q219 U.S. Library of Congress, Reference Department. Science and

Technology Division. *Chinese scientific and technical serial publications in the collections of the Library of Congress,* revised edition. Washington, 1961. 107 p.
Some 1,900 entries, mostly from mainland China, are divided into seven major topic groups, and further subdivided. Entries give the romanized title, characters, translation of title, former titles and Library of Congress holdings. There are romanized and Western-language title indexes.

Q220 Lee, Amy C. and D. C. Dju Chang. *A bibliography of translations from mainland Chinese periodicals in chemistry, general science and technology published by the U.S. Joint Publications Research Service, 1957–1966.* Washington, National Academy of Sciences, 1968. 161 p.
Identifies some 2,000 reports translated into English by the JPRS, with an emphasis on the sciences. These reports are not indexed in detail through any other source.

Q221 Dean, Genevieve C. *Science and technology in the development of modern China, an annotated bibliography.* London, Mansell, 1974. 265 p.
944 entries for books, dissertations, unpublished reports and articles in Western and Japanese languages published to 1972, but mostly in English. Entries are arranged in five major sections. Author indexes.

Q222 Akhtar, Shahid. *Health care in the People's Republic of China, a bibliography with abstracts.* Ottawa, International Development Research Centre, 1975. 182 p.
560 books, articles and reports, with full annotations are arranged by subject. Author and subject indexes.

AGRICULTURE

Q223 Kuo, Leslie Tse-chiu. *Communist Chinese monographs in the U.S.D.A. Library.* Washington, U.S. Department of Agriculture Library, 1961. 87 p. (Library list no. 71).
Some 900 monographs are arranged in a detailed subject order, and nearly all entries are annotated. Author index.

Q224 Kuo, Leslie Tse-chiu and Peter B. Schroeder. *Communist Chinese periodicals in the agricultural sciences.* Washington, U.S. Department of Agriculture, National Agricultural Library, 1963. 33 p. (Library list no. 70 revised).
132 periodicals arranged in alphabetical order, with holdings in the National Agricultural Library. 19 new titles have been added to the 1960 edition. Title, publisher and subject indexes.

Q225 Logan, William J. C. *Chinese agricultural publications from the Republic of China since 1947.* Washington, U.S. Department of Agriculture, National Agricultural Library, 1964. 55 p. (Library list no. 81).
58 periodicals and 257 monographs published in Taiwan since

1947 are arranged by major subjects. For most entries there are brief annotations. Author and title indexes.

Q226 Wang, Yu-hu. *Chung-kuo nung hsueh shu lu* (Catalogue of books on Chinese agriculture). Pei-ching, Nung yeh Ch'u pan she, 1964. 351 p.
Some 500 books on traditional Chinese agriculture are arranged in chronological order with annotations. Separate subject, title and author indexes.

Q227 Logan, William J. C. *Publications on Chinese agriculture prior to 1949.* Washington, U.S. Department of Agriculture, National Agricultural Library, 1966. 148 p. (Library list no. 85).
888 books and 186 periodicals in Chinese, Japanese and Western languages are arranged in subject order. Many entries have brief annotations. The materials are in the National Agricultural Library. Author and title indexes.

Q228 Chi-ling Ta hsueh, Nanking. Nung hsueh Yuan. Nung yeh ching chi hsi. Nung yeh li shih tsu (University of Nanking. College of Agriculture and Forestry. Department of Agricultural Economics. Division of Agricultural History). *Nung yeh lun wen so yin* Agricultural index to periodicals and bulletins in Chinese and in English principally published in China. T'ai-pei, Min kuo 60 (1971). 3 v. (Min kuo tzu liao ts'ung k'an 13).
Indexes 312 Chinese periodicals and eight bulletins in Chinese and 36 English-language periodicals and bulletins, with some 30,000 Chinese and 6,000 English entries covering the period 1858–1931. Added title: *Chung kuo nung yeh lun wen so yin* (Index to articles on Chinese agriculture).

CHINESE ART

Q229 Lovell, Hin-cheung. *An annotated bibliography of Chinese painting catalogues and related texts.* Ann Arbor, Center for Chinese Studies, 1973. 141 p.
Compiled as a companion to John C. Ferguson *Li tai chu lu hua mu,* reviewing the 108 catalogues used by him, and adding another 22 not used. The location of catalogues is stated. Name index.

Q230 Chan, Kam-po. *Chung-kuo i shu k'ao ku lun wen so yin, 1949–1966* Chinese art and archaeology, a classified index to articles published in mainland China periodicals, 1949–1966. Hong Kong, University of Hong Kong, Centre of Asian Studies, 1974. 361 p.
5,922 entries in Chinese on Chinese art and archaeology published in 155 mainland Chinese journals and newspapers from 1949 to 1966, arranged under a detailed subject division. Author index.

Q231 Vanderstappen, Harrie A. *The T. L. Yuan bibliography of Western writings on Chinese art and archaeology.* London, Mansell, 1975. 606 p.
2,278 books and 8,954 articles are arranged in two separate

detailed subject sequences. The editor has contributed one-half of the total work, covering materials published between 1956 and 1965. Index to authors, and index to collectors and collections. A major standard reference bibliography in the fields of Chinese art and archaeology.

CHINESE LANGUAGE

Q232 Teng, Maurice H. *Recent Chinese publications on the Chinese language.* New Haven, Yale University, Institute of Far Eastern Languages, 1961. 45 p.
110 books are arranged into seven major sections, and in the sections by title according to the Yale Romanization system. Brief annotations for all entries. No index.

Q233 Yang, Winston L. Y. and Teresa S. Yang. *A bibliography of the Chinese language.* New York, American Association of Teachers of Chinese Language and Culture, 1966. 171 p.
Some 1,500 books, periodical articles and theses in Western languages are arranged under 18 major subject groups. Author index. No annotation.

Q234 Chiu, Rosalie Kwan-Wai. *Language contact and language planning in China (1900–1967), a selected bibliography.* Quebec, Presses de l'Universite Laval, 1970. 273 p.
Divided into four sections, each covering dialects, standardization, minority languages and loan words. 510 books and periodical articles in Chinese are listed. Author index.

Q235 Yang, Paul Fu-mien. *Chinese linguistics, a selected and classified bibliography.* Hongkong, Chinese University at Hong Kong, 1974. 292 p.
3,257 books, dissertations and articles in English, French, Chinese and Japanese, with English translation of the titles of Chinese and Japanese articles, in a detailed subject arrangement, with comprehensive coverage, but with the exclusion of dialects. Most publications issued from 1900 to the present. Book reviews also noted.

Q236 Hixson, Sandra and J. Mathias. *A compilation of Chinese dictionaries.* New Haven, Far Eastern Publications, Yale University, 1975. 87, 37 p.
Over 1,000 dictionaries are listed in two sections. The first consists of dictionaries arranged under 163 subjects, and the second of general dictionaries arranged by titles. The most complete listing of Chinese dictionaries available.

Q237 Dunn, Roberts. *Chinese-English and English-Chinese dictionaries in the Library of Congress, an annotated bibliography.* Washington, Library of Congress, 1977. 140 p.
569 dictionaries are arranged by subject, and full annotations are given. Author index, titles index and Chinese character author and title list arranged in the sequence of the list.

CHINESE LITERATURE

Q238 Davidson, Martha. *A list of published translations from Chinese into English, French and German.* Ann Arbor, J. W. Edwards for American Council of Learned Societies, 1952–7. 2 v.
The first part contains 1,493 entries, arranged under subjects. Novels, drama and folktales included, but not poetry. The second part, with entries numbered 1494 to 5391, covers poetry arranged by dynasty, then by author, to the end of the Sung dynasty.

Q239 Hightower, James Robert. *Topics in Chinese literature, outlines and bibliography,* revised edition. Cambridge, Harvard University Press, 1953. 128 p. (Harvard-Yenching Institute studies v. 3).
A select bibliography arranged under 17 different literary styles. Each section has an introduction, followed by short bibliographies, divided into authorities and translations. Index to authors and to Chinese titles.

Q240 Sun, K'ai-ti. *Chung-kuo t'ung su hsiao shuo shu mu* (Catalogue of Chinese popular novels). Pei-ching, Tso chia Ch'u pan she, 1957. 323 p.
Some 800 novels are arranged in a broad classified order, and indexed by the *chu yin fu hao* system. For most entries annotations and locations are given, but some are noted as not having been inspected by the compiler.

Q241 Fu-chien Shih fan Hsueh yuan, Foochow. Chung wen hsi. *Chung-kuo hsien tai wen hsueh tso chia tso pin p'ing lun tz'u liao so yin* (Index to articles on modern Chinese literature, authors and works). Tokyo, Daian, 1967. 234, 275 p.
Reprint of edition in two parts, published in 1961–2. Articles are mostly from newspapers and are arranged by the literary author.

Q242 Schyns, Joseph. *1500 modern Chinese plays and novels.* Hong Kong, Lungmen Bookstore, 1966. 484 p. (Scheut editions, Series 1, Critical and literary studies, v. 3).
Summarizes the contents of 1,500 modern plays and novels, with special attention to their moral content. There are sections for fiction, present-day drama, drama translated into Chinese and ancient drama. There is also a biographical section for 202 writers, giving information on birth date, education and works. Stroke index. Reprint of the 1948 edition published by Catholic University Press, Peiping.

Q243 Li, Tien-yi. *Chinese fiction, a bibliography of books and articles in Chinese and English.* New Haven, Far Eastern Publications, Yale University, 1968. 356 p.
Some 2,000 books and periodical articles, mostly in Chinese, are arranged into sections for reference works, general studies, traditional fiction, divided by period, then by work, and modern fiction, arranged by author. No annotations. Index to authors and translators.

Q244 Paper, Jordan D. *Guide to Chinese prose.* Boston, G. K. Hall, 1973. 137 p. (Asian literature bibliography series).

141 books are listed in this short selected introduction. Full annotations. Index.

Q245 Bailey, Roger B. *Guide to Chinese poetry and drama.* Boston, G. K. Hall, 1973. 100 p. (Asian literature bibliography series).
A short selective introductory bibliography noting 112 books, each with full annotations. Index.

Q246 Gibbs, Donald A. *A bibliography of studies and translations of modern Chinese literature, 1918–1942.* Cambridge, East Asian Research Center, Harvard University, 1975. 239 p. (Harvard East Asian monographs 61).
A short bibliography of sources and studies is followed by the main body of the work arranged by author. No annotation.

Q247 Wang, Kai-chee, Pung Ho and Shu-leung Dang. *A research guide to English translations of Chinese verse (Han dynasty to T'ang dynasty).* Hong Kong, Chinese University Press, 1977. 368 p.
2,953 entries are arranged by dynasty and subarranged by poet. There are indexes to the title of the English translations, to poets by their name in Chinese characters, and to poets arranged alphabetically.

Q248 Yang, Winston L. Y., Peter Li and Nathan K. Mao. *Classical Chinese fiction, a guide to its study and appreciation. Essays and bibliographies.* Boston, G. K. Hall, 1977. 302 p.
Over half of this guide is an annotated bibliography of 904 books, articles and periodicals, nearly all in English. A glossary of Chinese authors, titles and terms gives Chinese character equivalents. Short index.

CHINESE DRAMA

Q249 Huang, Wen-ying. *Ch'u hai tsung mu t'i yao* (Bibliography of Chinese drama). Shang-hai, Ta tung Shu chu, Min kuo 19 (1930). 19 v.
Over 770 entries arranged by title, with little information other than a synopsis of the plot, and date of publication and publisher. If drama is extant or not is not mentioned. No index. Supplemented by Pei Ying *Ch'u hai tsung mu t'i yao yu pien* (Supplement to the Bibliography of Chinese drama) (Pei-ching, Jen min ch'u pan she, 1959. 298 p.), which adds another 72 dramas and makes a large number of corrections to the original work. The supplement contains a title index to the original work by stroke order.

Q250 Fu, Hsi-hua. *Yuan tai tsa chu ch'uan mu* (Catalogue of Yuan Northern drama). Pei-ching, Tso chia Ch'u pan she, 1957. 429 p. (Chung-kuo ku ten hsi chu tsung lu chih 3).
737 entries, of which 550 are identified with authors, are arranged under a broad period order. Annotated. Author and title indexes.

Q251 Fu, Hsi-hua. *Ming tai tsa chu ch'uan mu* (Catalogue of Ming Northern drama). Peiching, Tso chia Ch'u pan she, 1958. 328 p. (Chung-kuo ku ten hsi chu tsung lu chih 4).

523 entries, of which 349 are identified with authors, are arranged in broad period order. Annotated. Indexes for authors and titles.

Q252 Fu, Hsi-hua. *Ming tai ch'uan ch'i ch'uan mu* (Catalogue of Ming dramatic romances). Pei-ching, Jen min Wen hsueh Ch'u pan she, 1959. 580 p. (Chung-kuo ku ten hsi chu tsung lu chih 5).
950 Ming dramatic romances, of which 618 are identified with authors, are listed with full annotations. Indexes to authors and titles.

Q253 Fu, Hsi-hua. *Pei-ching ch'uan t'ung ch'u i tsung lu* A bibliography of folk literature in the Peking tradition. Pei-ching, Chung hua Shu chu, 1962. 1,008 p.
Arranged by type of literature, and with short annotations for each item. Four corner index.

Q254 Lo, Chin-t'ang. *Chung-kuo hsi ch'u tsung mu hui pien* A comprehensive bibliography of Chinese drama. Hsiang chiang, Wan yu T'u shu kung ssu, 1966. 368 p.
A comprehensive listing by types of drama, and excluding Peking opera. Includes a useful list of translations into Japanese and Western languages. No index.

Q255 Yang, Daniel Shih-p'eng. *An annotated bibliography of materials for the study of the Peking theatre.* Madison, University of Wisconsin, 1967. 98 p.
162 reference books and plays, mostly in Chinese, and partly representing material held by the University of Wisconsin. Annotated. Index to personal names, titles and terms.

CHINESE MUSIC

Q256 Yuan, T'ung-li. *Chung-kuo yin yueh shu p'u mu lu* Bibliography on Chinese music. T'ai-pei, Chung hua Kuo yueh hui, Min kuo 45 (1956). 24, 49 p.
Reproduces the eleventh instalment of Richard A. Waterman *Bibliography of Asiatic Musics* (A 45) and adds another 56 entries. The remainder of the bibliography consists of 323 books in Chinese. Not annotated.

Q257 Chung yang Yin yueh Hsueh yuan, Tientsin. Chung-kuo Yin yueh Yen chiu so (Central Academy of Music. Chinese Music Institute). *Chung kuo ku tai yin yueh shu mu* (Catalogue of books on early Chinese music). Peiching, Yin yueh Ch'u pan she, 1962. 142 p.
Some 1,400 books of Chinese music from earliest times to 1840 are listed in three major groups: extant works, possibly extant works and lost works. Entries are subarranged by categories. Title index in alphabetical order.

Q258 Lieberman, Fredric. *Chinese music, an annotated bibliography.* New York, Society for Asian Music, 1970. 157 p.
The first section covers bibliography and discography, with 29 entries; the second section, on Chinese music, and dance and drama, has 1,454 entries for books and periodical articles in

Western languages arranged in author order; and the final section is a topic outline and selected readings, this time restricted to Chinese music.

GEOGRAPHY

Q259 Wang, Yung and Mao Nai-wen. *Chung-kuo ti hsueh lun wen so yin* (Index to articles on Chinese geography). Pei-p'ing, Kuo li Pei-p'ing Shih han Ta hsueh, Min kuo 23–5 (1934–6). 4 v.
11,000 articles selected from 180 Chinese periodicals published from 1902 to 1935, arranged in a detailed subject order in 2 two-volume sections. Each section has a separate place-name index. Citations do not give dates of publication or page number. Reprinted in Taiwan 1970.

Q260 *Translations on the geography of mainland China.* Washington, U.S. Department of Commerce, Joint Publications Research Service, 1968. 232 p. (Translations on Communist China, no. 10, Bibliography of Joint Publications Research Service, JPRS 45,174).
The first section is arranged by topic and the second by area. Approximately 1,500 entries, many of which are entered under both topic and area.

HISTORY

Q261 Sun, I-tu(Jen) and John DeFrancis. *Bibliography of Chinese social history, a selected and critical list of Chinese periodical sources.* New Haven, Institute of Far Eastern Languages, Yale University, 1952. 150 p.
176 periodical articles are arranged under 14 subjects. Each entry has a full citation, together with an annotation. Author and subject entry index.

Q262 *Chung-kuo shi hsueh lun wen so yin* (Index to articles on Chinese history). Pei-ching, K'o hsueh Ch'u pan she, 1957. 2 v. (in 4).
Over 30,000 articles on Chinese history from 1,300 Chinese periodicals published from 1900 to 1937, and arranged in four major subject divisions, further subdivided. Based on the *Kuo hsueh lun wen so yin* (Index to articles on Chinese studies), 1928–36 in 4 parts, and containing some 12,000 articles. The revision is largely based on additional material located in Peking libraries. No author index, but an index of subjects and proper names. Pagination not cited in entries.

Q263 Hua tung Shih fan Ta hsueh, Shanghai. Li shi hsi (East China Normal University. History Department). *Chung kuo ku tai chung chi shih chi pao k'an lun wen tzu liao so yin* (Index to newspaper and periodical articles on early and medieval Chinese history). Shang-hai, 1959. 197 p.
Approximately 6,000 articles from periodicals and newspapers published from 1949 to 1959. Divided into two parts, the first by subject, and the second by dynasty to the end of the Ch'ing

dynasty, then subdivided by subjects. Date of issue of article given, but no pagination. No index.

Q264 Yu, Ping-kuen (Yu Ping-chuan). *Chinese history, index to learned articles, 1902–1962, compiled by the Fung Ping Shan Library, University of Hong Kong*. Hong Kong, East Asia Institute, 1963. 572 p.

10,325 articles selected from 355 periodicals, covering Chinese history to the end of the Ch'ing dynasty. Articles are arranged by author to show evolution of his ideas and interests. Index by stroke order giving subjects referred to in the text. Only one-third of the number of entries of *Chung-kuo shi hsueh lun wen so yin* (Q 262), but bibliographical information more detailed. The same author's *Chinese history, index to learned articles, volume 2, 1904–1964* (Cambridge, Harvard-Yenching Library, Harvard University, 1970. 690 p.) has 25,000 articles selected from 599 periodicals, published from 1904–64, and is based on collections in American and European libraries.

To the End of the Ming Dynasty

Q265 Frankel, Hans Herman. *Catalogue of translations from the Chinese histories, for the period 220–960*. Berkeley, University of California Press, 1957. 295 p.

Over 2,000 translations which may be extensive or may be only a few lines, arranged in the order of the Po-na edition of the Chinese dynastic histories, citing locations. Index to subjects and translators.

Q266 Yamane, Yukio. *Mindai-shi kenkyu bunken mokuroku* (Catalogue of research materials on the Ming dynasty). Tokyo, Toyo Bunko Mindai shi Kenkyushitsu, 1960. 258 p.

2,373 periodical articles and 128 books in Japanese and Chinese are arranged in detailed classified order covering Japanese-Ming relations, biography, social, economic, political, religious, intellectual, literary, art and science history. Indexes to authors' names and prominent Chinese and non-Chinese of the Ming period.

Q267 Hartwell, Robert. *A guide to sources of Chinese economic history, A.D. 618–1368*. Chicago, University of Chicago, Committee on Far Eastern Civilizations, 1964. 257 p.

1,119 entries referring to collected works for the T'ang through Yuan dynasties, but emphasizing the Sung dynasty. Annotated. Index for place-names and personal names, and general index.

Q268 Franke, Wolfgang. *An introduction to the sources of Ming history*. Singapore and Kuala Lumpur, University of Malaya Press, 1968. 397 p.

Over 800 major works are annotated and arranged in chapters for historical works, biographies, memorials, political institutions, foreign affairs and military organization, geographical works and local histories, economics, technology, encyclopedias and collectanea. Locations of copies noted in many cases.

Ch'ing Dynasty 1644–1911

Q269 Irick, Robert L., Yu Ying-shih and Liu Kwang-ching. *American-Chinese relations, 1784–1941, a survey of Chinese-language materials at Harvard.* Cambridge, Harvard University Press, 1960. 296 p. (Research aids for American Far Eastern policy studies no. 3).
Some 2,800 entries are arranged in a detailed subject order, under reference works and surveys, documentary collections, periodicals, libraries and archives, economic and cultural relations, missions, education, social reform and diplomatic relations. Intended to be a practical guide for students. Author index.

Q270 Feuerwerker, Albert and Cheng S. *Chinese Communist studies of modern Chinese history.* Cambridge, East Asian Research Center, Harvard University, 1961. 287 p. (Chinese economic and political studies, Special series).
430 books and 18 periodicals are arranged in a classified order, with most entries fully and critically annotated. Each major subject division has a lengthy introduction. The principal divisions are: General, Ming and Chi'ing dynasties, the Republic, economic history, intellectual and cultural history, and reference works. Author, subject and title index. Includes a short essay on Chinese Communist historiography.

Q271 Teng, Ssu-yu. *Historiography of the Taiping rebellion.* Cambridge, East Asian Research Center, Harvard University distributed by Harvard University Press, 1962. 180 p. (Harvard East Asian monographs)
A bibliographical essay surveying T'aiping, Ch'ing, Japanese, Western and Russian sources. Titles are noted in the index-glossary.

Q272 Liu, Kwang-ching. *Americans and Chinese, a historical essay and a bibliography.* Cambridge, Harvard University Press, 1963. 211 p.
Lists over 1,500 sources for the study of American non-governmental relations with China. Materials are in English, and are arranged under manuscripts, archives, biography, memoirs and published letters, newspapers and periodicals, and reference works. Preceded by a short historical essay on American Chinese contacts.

Republican China and People's Republic

Q273 Mote, Frederick W. *Japanese sponsored governments in China, 1937–45, an annotated bibliography compiled from materials in the Chinese collection of the Hoover Library.* Stanford, Stanford

University Press, 1954. 68 p. (Hoover Institution and Library, Bibliographical series 3).
383 annotated entries for books, periodicals and newspapers divided into seven sections: reference and general background, books published in areas under puppet governments, non-puppet publications, prominent puppet leaders, postwar publications, serials and newspapers. Annotations are brief and descriptive. Author and title index.

Q274 Wu, Eugene. *Leaders of twentieth-century China, annotated bibliography of selected Chinese works in the Hoover Library.* Stanford, Stanford University Press, 1956. 106 p. (Hoover Institution and Library, Bibliographical series 4).
More than 500 entries with descriptive annotations are arranged in eight parts, for collective biography, political, military, intellectual, industrialist and businessmen biographies, overseas Chinese, school yearbooks and serials. Index for authors, titles and biographies.

Q275 Israel, John. *The Chinese student movement, 1927–1937, a bibliographical essay on the resources of the Hoover Institution.* Stanford, Stanford University Press, 1959. 29 p. (Hoover Institution, Bibliographical series 6).
46 books and 81 newspapers and periodicals are discussed.

Q276 Uchida, Naosaku. *The overseas Chinese, a bibliographical essay based on the resources of the Hoover Institution.* Stanford, Hoover Institution on War, Revolution and Peace, Stanford University, 1959. 134 p. (Hoover Institution, Bibliographical series 7).
679 books and periodicals are discussed under the following subjects: Amoy merchants, Kongsi system, coolie trade, anti-Chinese immigration policies, assimilation policies, social institutions, economic problems, the Communist Chinese and the overseas Chinese. Half the book an essay on overseas Chinese. No index.

Q277 Hsueh, Chun-tu. *The Chinese Communist movement.* Stanford, Hoover Institution, 1960–2. 2 v. (Hoover Institution, Bibliographical series 8, 11).
359 books and periodicals in the first volume cover the period from 1921 to 1937, and 863 in the second volume from 1937 to 1949. Entries are annotated and arranged by subject. Each volume has its own title and author index.

Q278 Chou, Ts'e-tsung. *Research guide to the May Fourth movement, intellectual revolution in modern China, 1915–1924.* Cambridge, Harvard University Press, 1963. 297 p. (Harvard East Asia series 13).
1,479 books, periodicals and periodical articles are arranged into three major parts. The first is a listing of periodicals and newspapers, mostly established from 1915 to 1923, arranged by year and annotated; the second is a bibliography of books and

periodical articles in Chinese and Japanese; and the third is a bibliography of periodical articles in Western languages. Index to authors, titles and terms.

Q279 Liu, Chun-jo. *Controversies in modern Chinese intellectual history, an analytical bibliography of periodical articles, mainly of the May Fourth and post-May Fourth era.* Cambridge, Harvard University Press, 1964. 207 p.
Over 500 articles in Chinese from 17 periodicals are arranged in classified order with full annotations. Author and subject index.

Q280 Rhoads, Edward J. M. *The Chinese Red Army, 1927–1963, an annotated bibliography.* Cambridge, Harvard University Press, 1964. 188 p. (Harvard East Asian monographs 16).
Some 600 books, periodical articles, mimeographed papers, and unpublished manuscripts, mostly in Chinese and English, arranged under 19 subject headings and annotated. The choice of Chinese-language materials is selective, attempting to avoid Communist and nationalist bias. Author index.

Q281 Young, John. *The research activities of the South Manchurian Railway Company, 1907–45, a history and bibliography.* New York, East Asian Institute, Columbia University, 1965. 730 p.
The first part is a study of South Manchurian Railway research activities, and the second consists of 6,284 books, studies or periodicals arranged in 46 categories. Each entry is entered under title, which is romanized and translated. Library locations stated. No index.

Q282 U.S. Department of the Army. Army Library. *Communist China, a bibliographic survey.* Washington, U.S. Government Printing Office, 1971. 252 p. (DA PAM 550-9).
The greater part of this work consists of books and articles in English, arranged by subject with full annotations and relating to the present situation in China. Appendices contain maps and other data.

Q283 Shu, Austin C. W. *On Mao Tse-tung, a bibliographical guide.* East Lansing, Asian Studies Center, Michigan State University, 1972. 78 p.
800 books and articles on Mao Tse-tung in Chinese, English and Japanese, arranged by subject. Library locations given. Author index.

Q284 Wang, James C. F. *The Cultural Revolution in China, an annotated bibliography.* New York, Garland Publishing, 1976. 246 p. (Garland reference library of social science v. 16).
361 books and articles, written by Western scholars and analyzing the Cultural Revolution, are arranged by major topics. Fully annotated. Author index.

Q285 U.S. Army. *China, an analytical survey of literature, 1978 edition.* 231 p. (DA pamplet nȯ. 550-9-1).
Some 500 entries in English cover the period from 1971 to 1976, and are arranged by topic. A number of appendices indicate

Chinese economic and military potential. This is a revision of a similar publication *Communist China, a bibliographic survey* (Q 282) issued in 1971. No index.

Local History

A valuable guide to bibliographies and library catalogues, referring to Chinese local gazetteers, is Donald Leslie and Jeremy Davidson *Catalogues of Chinese local gazetteers* (Canberra, Department of Far Eastern History, Research School of Pacific Studies, Australian National University, 1967. 125 p.) in which 111 items are described. Only the seven most important bibliographies and catalogues are listed here. For important American holdings outside the Library of Congress, the reader is referred to Ch'iu K'ai-ming *A classified catalogue of Chinese books in the Chinese-Japanese Library of the Harvard-Yenching Institute at Harvard University* (Cambridge, 1938–40. 3 v.) for a list of 1,200 local gazetteers. Another important holding of over 1,400 local gazetteers is to be found in the East Asian Library of Columbia University, New York, but this and other American collections have yet to be recorded in a union list.

Q286 Tan, Ch'i-hsiang. *Kuo li Pei-p'ing t'u shu kuan fang chih mu lu* (Catalogue of local histories in the Peiping Library). Pei-ching, Pei-ching T'u shu kuan, Min kuo 22 (1933–), 1957. 6 v.
Volumes 1–4 contain some 5,200 gazetteers in 3,800 different editions arranged by province, with a stroke order index to places. Volume 5, which is noted as Supplement II, was published in 1936, and lists 862 gazetteers acquired from 1933 to 1936. Volume 6, or Supplement III, contains an additional 2,357 titles.

Q287 Chu, Shih-chia. *Kuo hui t'u shu kuan ts'ang Chung-kuo fang chih mu lu* Catalogue of Chinese local histories in the Library of Congress. Washington, U.S. Government Printing Office, 1942. 552 p.
Nearly 3,000 local gazetteers are arranged by province. Gazetteers in *ts'ung shu* are included. Romanized and stroke order index to places. Does not include gazetteers published in the Ming period and earlier among the rare books of the National Library of Peking, and microfilmed by the Library of Congress.

Q288 Hervouet, Yves. *Catalogue des monographes locales chinoises dans les bibliotheques d'Europe*. Paris, Mouton, 1957. 100 p. (Le monde d'outre-mer, passe et present, 4 serie, Bibliographies 1).
2,590 local histories in 1,434 different editions are arranged by province, with locations in 25 libraries. Index to names of places. Not exceptional in numbers of gazetteers, and useful only in terms of stating availability.

Q289 Kuo li Chung yang T'u shu kuan, Taipei (National Central Library). *T'ai-wan kung ts'ang fang chih lien ho mu lu* (Union catalogue of local histories in public libraries in Taiwan). T'ai-pei, Sheng chung Chu chu, Min kuo 46 (1957). 107 p.
Some 3,300 gazetteers, published to 1954, arranged by provinces.

Includes the holdings of 11 libraries. But excludes useful modern gazetteers for Taiwan.

Q290 Chu, Shih-chia. *Chung-kuo ti fang chih tsung lu tseng ting pen* (Catalogue of Chinese local histories, revised edition). Shang-hai, Shang wu Yin shu kuan, 1958. 318 p.
A union list of the holdings of 22 libraries noting some 7,000 gazetteers, an increase of approximately 1,000 over the 1935 edition. Bibliographical information given is slight, with title, date and edition only noted. Arranged by province, with a stroke order index for personal names and for titles.

Q291 Lowe, Joseph Dzen-hsi. *A catalogue of the official gazetteers of China in the University of Washington.* Zug, Inter Documentation Co., 1966. 72 p.
882 gazetteers are listed by province, including a number which are found in Chinese collectanea. Nearly all were published in the Ch'ing dynasty.

Q292 Chicago. University. Far Eastern Library. *Chinese local histories.* Chicago, University of Chicago Bookstore, 1969. 139 p.
Lists 1,840 titles of Chinese local histories in the Far Eastern Library, arranged by administrative areas. The collection is strongest for Kiangsu, Hopei, Shantung and Shansi.

Q293 Kuo, Thomas C. T. *The Chinese local history, a descriptive holding list.* Pittsburgh, East Asian Library, University of Pittsburgh, 1969. 87 p.
276 titles of Chinese local histories are arranged by province. No annotations and no index. The holdings of the East Asian Library at the University of Pittsburgh.

Q294 Kokuritsu Kokkai Toshokan, Tokyo. Sankoshoshibu (National Diet Library. Reference and Bibliography Division). *Chugoku chihoshi sogo mokuroku, Nihon shuyo toshokan, kenkyujo shozo* Union catalogue of Chinese local gazetteers in 14 major libraries and research institutes in Japan. Tokyo, Showa 44 (1969). 344 p.
Some 3,000 different Chinese local gazetteers in 5,600 copies held in Japanese libraries are arranged by province, with note as to locations. Title index according to the Japanese syllabary. Wade-Giles index.

Q294a Morton, Andrew. *Union list of Chinese local histories in British libraries.* Oxford, China Library Group, 1979. 140 p.
Lists 2,505 gazetteers, arranged by province, with *p'in-yin* and character indexes for place-names. Locations are given in seven British libraries.

Hong Kong

Q295 U.S. Bureau of the Census. *Bibliography of social science periodicals and monograph series, Hong Kong, 1950–61.* Washington, 1962. 13 p. (Foreign social science bibliographies series P-92 no. 7).

27 periodicals and 22 monograph series in the Library of Congress are arranged under 14 social science fields and bibliography. Each entry is annotated. Separate title and subject indexes.

Q 296 Berkowitz, Morris I. *Hongkong studies, a bibliography.* Hong Kong, Department of Extramural Studies, Chinese University of Hong Kong, 1969. 137 p.
Lists some 1,300 books and periodicals on Hongkong in the historical and social sciences. No annotations or index.

Q 297 Ip, David Fu-keung. *Hong Kong, a social sciences bibliography.* Hong Kong, Centre for Asian Studies, University of Hong Kong, 1974. 355 p. (Centre for Asian Studies bibliographies and research guides no. 7).
Approximately 3,000 books, reports and articles are arranged by subject, with some annotation. Subject and author indexes.

Q 298 Rydings, H. Anthony. *A Hong Kong catalogue, works relating to Hong Kong in Hong Kong libraries.* Hong Kong, Centre for Asian Studies, University of Hong Kong, 1976. 2 v.
5,000 books, mostly in English or Chinese, are arranged by subject, with romanized and Chinese character author and title indexes.

Q 299 Yu, Timothy L. M. *Mass communication in Hong Kong and Macao, an annotated bibliography.* Singapore, Asian Mass Communication Research and Information Centre, 1976. 30 p. (Asian mass communication bibliography series 3).
122 entries for books, articles and reports in English and Chinese on mass communication in Hong Kong and Macao under 18 subject headings. Author and title index.

Q 300 Saw, Swee Hock. *A bibliography of the demography of Hong Kong.* Singapore, University Education Press, 1976. 112 p.
An unannotated list of 704 items in English, including books, pamphlets, reports, articles and ordinances under 17 broad headings, such as census reports, population laws, urbanization, fertility, family planning, etc. Author index.

Manchuria

Q 301 Berton, Peter. *Manchuria, an annotated bibliography.* Washington, Library of Congress, Reference Department, 1951. 187 p.
843 books and periodicals in English, Russian, Chinese and Japanese, but mostly in Japanese, arranged in a classified order, with an author and subject index. Annotated. Highly selective since the Library of Congress has over 2,000 titles in Western languages, and over 10,000 books in Japanese on Manchuria.

Sinkiang

Q 302 Yuan, T'ung-li and Watanabe Hiroshi. *Shinkyo kenkyu bunken mokuroku, 1866–1962, Nihon Bun* Classified bibliography of

Japanese books and articles concerning Sinkiang. Tokyo, 1962. 92 p.
1,166 books and periodical articles are arranged in a classified order, with separate author and subject indexes. No annotation.

Taiwan

Q 303 Cordier, Henri. *Bibliographie des ouvrages relatifs a l'ile Formose.* Chartres, Imprimerie Durand, 1893. 59 p.
Some 300 books, periodical articles and maps are arranged in a broad subject order, represent the earlier Western literature on Taiwan. No table of contents or index.

Q 304 T'ai-wan Sheng li T'ai-pei T'u shu kuan, Taipei (Taiwan Provincial Taipei Library). *T'ai-wan wen hsien tzu liao mu lu* (Catalogue of materials on Taiwan). T'ai-pei, Min kuo 47 (1958). 172 p.
Some 6,000 titles in Japanese are arranged by subject and in addition 120 entries for books in Western languages published before 1937.

Q 305 *T'ai-wan wen hsien fen lei so yin, Min kuo 48 nien–* Classified index to Taiwan materials, 1959–. T'ai-pei, T'ai-wan sheng Wen hsien Wei yuan hui, Min kuo 49– (1960–). Annual.
Bibliography of articles from some 200 newspapers and periodicals, arranged by a detailed subject classification. No index. 1974 issue noted.

Q 306 Chung-kuo Wen hua hsueh yuan, T'ai-wan Yen chiu so (China Cultural Council, Taiwan Institute). *T'ai-wan wen hsien mu lu* (Bibliography of materials on Taiwan). T'ai-pei, Min kuo 54 (1965). 264 p.
Some 4,000 books and reports in Japanese and Chinese in a detailed subject arrangement. No index. 1969 edition published 1971 seen.

Tibet

Q 307 Hsu, Ginn-tze (Hsu, Chin-chih). *A bibliography of the Tibetan highland and its adjacent districts* Ch'ing kang tsang kao yuan chi pi lien ti ch'u hsi wen wen hsien mu lu. Peking, Science Press, 1958. 462 p.
The compiler claims that this bibliography of some 5,000 articles from 384 Western- and Russian-language periodicals comprises approximately four-fifths of the total published literature. Arranged under broad subject headings as geology, seismology, history, general works, climatology, maps, languages, and geographical areas as Himalayas, Pamirs, Kashmir and Nepal. Author and subject index

Q 308 Smith, E. Gene. *University of Washington Tibetan catalog.* Seattle, University of Washington, 1969. 2 v.
Catalogue of the holdings of the University of Washington Far Eastern Library holdings, with indication of location of original copy from which microfilm was made. The second part consists

of a series of indexes, including personal names arranged by Tibetan consonants, list of titles in Tibetan, titles and subjects in English and romanization of Sanskrit, Tibetan short titles and subjects, and editions in Tibetan. No table of contents, and poorly paginated.

Q309 Vostrikov, Andrei Ivanovich. *Tibetan historical literature.* Calcutta, Indian Studies, Past and Present, 1970. 278 p. (Soviet Indology series no. 4).
Translation of *Tibetskaia istoricheskaia literatura,* a definitive study of Tibetan historical bibliography, consisting of an essay with extensive bibliographical footnotes.

Q310 Chaudhuri, Sibadas. *Bibliography of Tibetan studies, being a record of printed publications mainly in European languages.* Calcutta, Asiatic Society, 1971. 232 p.
Over 2,000 books and articles, mostly in Western languages, are arranged by author. Based mainly on the books and periodicals in the Library of the Asiatic Society. Subject index.

R. JAPAN

The first step of territorial expansion for modern Japan was in 1875, with the acquisition of the Kurile Islands. In 1879 the Ryukyus became Okinawa Prefecture. In 1895, following the Sino-Japanese War, Japan acquired Taiwan, and in 1906 the Liao-tung peninsula in Manchuria and Southern Sakhalin. Korea formally became a part of the Japanese Empire in 1910. In 1945 the territory of Japan was once again restricted to the four main islands. In 1953 the northern islands of the Ryukyus were returned to Japan, in 1968 the Bonins, and in 1972 the remaining islands of the Ryukyus.

REFERENCE WORKS

R1 *Guide to Japanese reference books (Nihon no sanko tosho). Chicago, American Library Association, 1966. 303 p.*
A translation into English of *Nihon no sanko tosho, kaitei ban* (Japanese reference books, revised edition) (Tokyo, 1965). 2,475 books and periodicals published to September 1964 have been cited, but older and out-of-print materials have been excluded to a large extent from the selection. Divided into four parts: general works, humanities, social sciences, and science and technology, with about one-third of the entries in the last part. In spite of translation, this is still a book designed for the Japanese audience, a bibliography of books published in Japan, and almost entirely in Japanese. Important Western reference works on Japan have been ignored, even when superior to Japanese works cited. Nevertheless this is a major step forward in the development of reference literature.

R2 Nihon no Sankotosho Henshuiinkai. *Nihon no sanko tosho* (Guide to Japanese reference books). Tokyo, Nihon Toshokan Kyokai, 1972. 379 p.
Some 1,600 books, almost entirely in Japanese and all published in Japan, are arranged by subject. Arranged by topic, on similar lines to earlier editions, and the key work in its field. Extensively annotated. Indexes for authors, titles and subjects.

ENCYCLOPEDIAS AND HANDBOOKS

Traditional Encyclopedias

R3 Jingu Shicho, Tokyo (Office of the Great Shrine). *Koji ruien*

(Encyclopedia of ancient matters). Tokyo, Yoshikawa Kobunkan, Showa 42–6 (1967–71).
A reprint of the 51-volume edition. Each volume or group of volumes represents a major subject such as astronomy, government, law, etc., and consists of collections of sources from diaries, records and myths, published to the end of the Tokugawa period. Volume 51 is a table of contents and an index in the order of the Japanese syllabary. A valuable collection for the student of Japanese cultural history.

R4 Mozume, Takami. *Kobunko* (Comprehensive anthology). Tokyo, Kobunko Kankokai, Showa 2 (1927). 20 v.
Collection of texts from Japanese and Chinese books noted in the *Gunsho sakuin* (Index to Japanese classical literature). Texts are arranged by subject and emphasize literature, but since the number of selections listed in the *Gunsho sakuin* is five times greater than those in the *Kobunko,* reference should be made to the latter source for fuller treatment of a subject. Traditional *kana* spelling is used. Each volume has its own table of contents.

General and Subject Encyclopedias

R5 Mochizuki, Shinko. *Bukkyo daijiten* (Buddhist encyclopedia dictionary). Kyoto, Sekai Seiten Kanko Kyokai, Showa 29–38 (1954–63). 10 v.
The main body consists of some 15,000 entries in volumes 1–5, and while it refers to Buddhism in general, there is an emphasis on Japan. Each entry has a bibliography, and is arranged by the Japanese syllabary. Volume 6 is a chronological table of Buddhism, indexed for personal names, dynastic reigns and book titles. Volume 7 is an index, with separate parts for Japanese and Chinese terms, Pali terms and Sanskrit terms. One unnumbered volume published in 1956 is a supplement to the first five volumes. The index for Japanese and Chinese terms is arranged by the Japanese syllabary and has an index by characters as a key to the Japanese pronunciation. Volumes 8–10, published 1958–63, are supplements and contain approximately 3,000 additional entries. First edition published 1909–31.

R6 *Nihon rekishi daijiten* (Encyclopedia dictionary of Japanese history). Tokyo, Kawade Shobo, Showa 43–5 (1968–70). 10 v. and 2 supplementary volumes.
A broad and objective coverage, reflecting post–World War II research, including foreign persons and subjects when related to Japan. Entries are signed and arranged in Japanese syllabic order. Volume 10 is supplementary and also contains names, place and subject indexes. The supplementary volumes are *Nihon rekishi nempyo* (Chronological table of Japanese history) (1960. 373 p.) and *Nihon rekishi chizu* (Japanese historical atlas) (1969).

R 7 Heibonsha. *Sekai daihyakka jiten* (World encyclopedia). Tokyo, Showa 39–43 (1964–8). 26 v.
A major encyclopedia with world-wide coverage where only 25% of the 80,000 items refer to Asia, and only one-half of these refer directly to Japan. Articles are signed, but have no bibliographies. The first atlas volume is for Japan, and has 114 maps and an index for some 60,000 place-names. The second atlas volume covers the rest of the world. Revision of the 1955–63 edition.

Handbooks

R 8 Chamberlain, Basil Hall. *Things Japanese.* London, Kegan Paul, Trench, Trubner, 1939. 584 p.
The author was Emeritus Professor of Japanese and Philology at Tokyo University. This is a combination of a brief introduction to Japanese culture, an encyclopedia and a dictionary. Treatment is popular and the number of revisions since 1890 is a reflection of changing times and attitudes in Japan. Reprinted by Tuttle, Rutland, 1970 with title: *Japanese things.*

R 9 Papinot, Edmond. *Historical and geographical dictionary of Japan.* New York, Ungar, 1964. 2 v.
A reprint of the 1910 translation of the 1906 French edition. A dictionary of historical and geographical names, including historical geographical names, together with considerable information on the customs, feasts and other aspects of Japanese culture. Useful lists appended include tables of provinces and departments, tables of fiefs, lists of emperors, genealogical tables, tables for computation of years, months and days, and tables of weights and measures. Reprinted by Tuttle, Rutland, 1972 in one volume.

R 10 Kobata, Atsushi. *Dokushi soran* (Handbook of Japanese history). Tokyo, Jimbutsu Oraisha, Showa 41 (1966). 1,864 p.
A valuable and entirely new guide to Japanese historical studies, with a topical arrangement, and a first name index in Japanese syllabic order. All aspects of history are well covered, the emphasis however being on illustration and tables rather than description. Chronology and genealogy well developed.

R 11 Joly, Henri L. *Legend in Japanese art.* Rutland, Tuttle, 1967. 623 p.
Over 1,118 entries, of which over 300 are cross-references, referring to the history, legend, folklore and religion in the art of Japan, with over 700 illustrations. Less reliable than William Edmunds *Pointers and clues to the subjects of Chinese and Japanese art* (P 1). Reprint of the 1908 edition.

R 12 Japan, Mombusho. Nihon Yunesuko Kokunai Iinkai. *Japan, its land, people and culture.* Tokyo, University of Tokyo Press, 1973. 702 p.
An encyclopedic survey of Japanese history, physical features, the

Japanese people, language, mass communication, Japanese thought and religion, education, social sciences, natural sciences, literature, fine arts, dance and music, theatre, manners and customs, recreation and amusement, and tourism. Major detailed index. Revision of the 1964 edition.

R 13 American University, Washington, D.C. Foreign Area Studies. *Area handbook for Japan.* Washington, U.S. Government Printing Office, 1974. 672 p.
A survey of social, political and economic affairs is followed by one on national security. 50-page bibliography and a glossary. Index. Research completed 1973. Replaces 1969 edition.

YEARBOOKS

R 14 *The Japan yearbook,* 1905–31. Tokyo, Japan Year Book Office, 1905–31.
Arranged by subject, with a detailed table of contents, and indexed from the 1926 issue. Later issues have a biographical section. Becomes: *The Japanese Empire, yearbook of Japan,* 1932, 1 v.; *The Japan Times year book,* 1933, 1 v.; *The Japan-Manchoukuo year book,* 1934, 1935, 1937, 1938–41; and the *Orient yearbook,* 1942. Issues for 1908–9, 1919–20, 1921–2 and 1924–5 were combined.

R 15 *Asahi nenkan,* 1925– (Asahi yearbook, 1925–). Tokyo, Asahi Shimbunsha, Taisho 13– (1924–).
The finest general yearbook for Japan, arranged by subjects, with sections on world affairs and Japanese affairs, including land and people, law, labour, economy, statistics, transportation, local affairs and culture. 1979 issue seen.

R 16 *The Japan yearbook,* 1933–52. Tokyo, Foreign Affairs Association, 1933–52.
Arranged by subject, with a detailed table of contents and excellent index. Coverage of not only prewar years, but of wartime Japan and Japan under the occupation. Criticized for attempting too much and lacking in reliability.

R 17 *The Japan annual,* 1954–8. Tokyo, Japan Annual Publications, 1954–8. 3 v.
Each issue has four parts, on national affairs, international affairs, the economy, and social and cultural affairs, further subdivided by subjects. The 1954 and 1955 issues have tables of contents and indexes, but the 1958 issue lacks both. Information supplied by government and private industry, and written by authorities.

R 18 *Japan almanac,* 1972–. Tokyo, Mainichi newspapers, 1972–.
Surveys all aspects of Japanese culture and contemporary Japan, and includes a short directory to the Japanese government, diplomatic missions, organizations, major companies, univer-

sities and colleges. A who's who section contains some 2,200 entries. Statistical summary. 1976 issue noted.

DICTIONARIES

R 19 Shimmura, Izuru. *Kojien* (Comprehensive dictionary). Tokyo, Iwanami Shoten, Showa 30 (1955). 2,359 p.
A standard one-volume dictionary representative of many similar works of this kind, with some 100,000 words covering a wide range of Japanese culture and arranged in the Japanese syllabic order. Entries are followed by characters and meanings in Japanese. Short index by stroke order to characters difficult to read.

R 20 Nihon Daijiten Kankokai. *Nihon kokugo daijiten* (Dictionary of the Japanese language). Tokyo, Shogakukan, Showa 47–51 (1972–6). 20 v.
Contains some 500,000 words and 2,000,000 quotations, including archaic and contemporary words, place-names, personal names, proper nouns, and technical terms.

Japanese Character Dictionaries

R 21 Morohashi, Tetsuji. *Dai Kanwa jiten* (Great Chinese-Japanese dictionary). Tokyo, Taishukan Shoten, Showa 30–5 (1955–60). 13 v.
50,000 different characters, with some 500,000 compounds, arranged in radical order, then by strokes. Characters given in variant forms, with both early and modern Chinese and Japanese pronunciation stated. The dictionary is based on a number of Chinese sources as the classical dictionary *Pei wen yun fu* and the *K'ang hsi tz'u tien* (K'ang hsi dictionary) and has been developed for the Japanese sinologist. Volume 13 has stroke indexes, Japanese readings and four corner indexes. A major work now published in a Chinese edition as *Chung wen ta tz'u tien* (Q 31).

R 22 Ueda, Kazutoshi. *Daijiten* (Great dictionary). Tokyo, Kodansha, Showa 38 (1963). 2,821 p.
A standard one-volume dictionary, important for the large number of characters represented, totalling some 15,000. These are arranged in radical order. For each pronunciation is given, and meaning stated in Japanese. Indexes arrange characters by stroke and by Japanese pronunciation, and a useful select list of characters in grass style or *sosho* forms. Widely known through its 1942 reprint by Harvard University Press.

Japanese-English, English-Japanese Dictionaries

R 23 Takahashi, Morio. *Romanized English-Japanese, Japanese-English dictionary*. Tokyo, Taiseido, 1958. 457, 1,226 p.

One of the few, and certainly one of the most comprehensive, modern Japanese dictionaries giving romanized Japanese equivalents for English words. The first part is for English-Japanese with 10,000 English words and phrases, and the second has 50,000 Japanese words and phrases. The entries in both parts have been selected on the basis of their usefulness for daily use. Japanese characters follow the romanized forms.

R24 *Kenkyusha's new English-Japanese dictionary on bilingual principles* (Kenkyusha shin Ei-Wa daijiten). Tokyo, Kenkyusha, 1960. 2,204 p.
Contains over 190,000 words, including abbreviations and proper names, with their Japanese equivalents in characters. No romanization of the Japanese since this is intended for the Japanese reader.

R25 *Kenkyusha's new Japanese-English dictionary* (Kenkyusha shin Wa-Ei diajiten). Tokyo, Kenkyusha, 1962. 2,136 p.
Some 85,000 works, with character equivalents and numerous examples of use in Japanese, followed by translations in English. Fourth edition, 1974 reported.

R26 Nelson, Andrew. *Modern reader's Japanese-English character dictionary*. Rutland, Tuttle, 1963. 1,048 p.
Now replacing as a standard dictionary the older Arthur Rose-Innes *Beginners' dictionary of Chinese-Japanese characters.* 5,446 characters, including 671 variants, arranged in radical order, and with readings and translations followed by some 70,000 compounds with translation. Valuable appendices, including a list of Japanese standard characters or *toyokanji.*

BIOGRAPHICAL DICTIONARIES

R27 Haga, Yaichi. *Nihon jimmei jiten* (Japan biographical dictionary). Tokyo, Ogura shoten, Taisho 3 (1914). 1,174 p.
Some 50,000 historical figures are arranged by their personal names in the order of the Japanese syllabary. Each entry has characters for the name, and a brief identifying biographical note. Two indexes, the first arranged by strokes for the characters of the personal name, and the second by the Japanese syllabic order for the family name. A valuable and extensive one-volume listing.

R28 Heibonsha. *Dai jimmei jiten* (Biographical dictionary). Tokyo, Showa 28–30 (1953–5). 10 v.
Volumes 1–6, list some 50,000 Japanese, and volume 9 8,000 living Japanese. Volumes 7–8 list 8,000 foreigners, of whom very few live in Japan. Volume 8 has an alphabetical index. Volume 10 is an index in stroke order. Earlier edition with title *Shinsen dai jimmei jiten* (Tokyo, 1937–41. 9 v.).

R29 *Seiyo jimmei jiten* (Biographical dictionary of Westerners). Tokyo, Iwanami Shoten, Showa 31 (1956). 1,962 p.

A greatly expanded revision of the 1932 edition, important for giving notice to Westerners and Asians prominent in Japanese history, but otherwise not noteworthy. Some 20,000 persons are listed in Japanese syllabic order, with indexes to names in their original spelling. No Chinese or Koreans included.

R 30 *Japan biographical encyclopedia and who's who,* 1964–5. Tokyo, Rengo Press, 1965. 2,377 p.
The third edition, the first being published in 1958, lists 15,730 names, including prominent persons in Japanese history, from Jimmu Tenno, whose dates are given as 711–585 B.C., to the present day, where the range of selection is wide, including important public and business personalities. All cabinet officials from 1885 are included. Each entry is followed by the family name, personal name, Japanese characters, a one-word classification, and an account varying from five lines to one-and-a-half columns. Principal works of the biographee noted. An inconvenience is the arrangement of names in one major and two minor alphabetical sequences, but the names index is cumulated.

R 31 Hisamatsu, Sen'ichi. *Biographical dictionary of Japanese literature.* Tokyo, International Association for Educational Information, 1976. 437 p.
Some 350 authors are arranged by major period, then alphabetically. A number of charts show major literary schools, and there is a glossary of literary terms, a bibliography and a full index.

R 32 Roberts, Laurance P. *A dictionary of Japanese artists, painting, sculpture, ceramics, prints, lacquer.* Tokyo and New York, Weatherhill, 1976. 299 p.
Lists some 2,800 Japanese artists, born before 1900 or died before 1972, giving information on additional forms of their names, biography, public collections where the artist's works can be found, and identifying works where the artists' works are reproduced. Appendices include lists of collections, art organizations, bibliography, index of alternate names, and character index.

R 33 Iwao, Seiichi. *Biographical dictionary of Japanese history.* Tokyo, International Society for Education Information, 1978. 655 p.
Some 500 biographies are grouped by major period and then alphabetically, with nearly one-half on the period since 1868. Appendices include maps, lineages and bibliography. Full index to the biographies.

Contemporary Biography

R 34 *Nihon shinshiroku* (Japan who's who). Tokyo, Kojunsha, Meiji 22– (1889–).
Recent issues list some 80,000 Japanese prominent in politics,

business, government, education and culture, and arranged in the Japanese syllabic order. Information includes occupation, place and date of birth, education, address and telephone number. Lists many persons not found in other collective biography sources. Appendices include directories of major firms, public offices and educational institutions. 1977 issue seen.

R 35 *Jinji koshinroku* (Japan who's who). Tokyo, Jinji Koshinjo, Meiji 36– (1903–).
Appears irregularly every two or three years and is the most comprehensive listing of prominent Japanese. The 24th issue published in 1968 lists some 80,000 and gives personal information as date and place of birth, education, address, and a brief account, about twice the length of that found in the *Nihon shinshiroku* (R 34). The entries are arranged in the Japanese syllabic order and there is a character key. 29th issue for 1977 seen.

R 36 *Who's who in Japan,* 1912–1940/1. Tokyo, Who's Who in Japan Publishing Office, 1912–40. 21 v.
Lists some 6,000 living persons with a short bibliographical note on their ages, educations, careers and addresses. Prominent foreigners in Japan are also noted. Becomes *Who's who in Japan and Manchoukuo,* 1941/2, noted as the 21st annual edition with some 4,800 names.

R 37 *Japan who's who and business directory,* 1948–51. Tokyo, Tokyo News Service, 1948–51. 2 v.
The 1950/1 volume contains some 3,200 biographies of living Japanese, some 1,200 more than in the 1948 edition, and is based on questionnaires.

R 38 Nihon Chosakuken Kyogikai (Japanese Copyright Council). *Bunkajin meiroku* (Who's who in culture). Tokyo, Showa 26– (1951–).
A classified arrangement of some 45,000 copyright holders, compiled from questionnaires distributed to authors. The author index is arranged by characters. Useful for identifying the correct pronunciation of an author's name, and also for brief summaries of the salient facts of his life, with important works. Title on spine *Chosakuken daicho* (Register of copyright holders) regarded by compilers as the correct name for this directory. 17th edition for 1977 seen.

R 39 *The Japan Times foreign residents, business firms, organizations, directory,* 1951–. Tokyo, Japan Times, 1951–.
An annual directory originally issued with title *Directory of foreign residents.* Arranged by cities, then alphabetically. Some 8,000 entries, including information on firms arranged by kind of business.

R 40 Nihon Yunesuko Kokunai Iinkai, Tokyo (Japan. National Commission for Unesco). *Who's who among Japanese writers.* Tokyo, 1957. 140 p.
Includes some 300 contemporary literary authors still actively

engaged in writing. For each author his name, special field, background and education, and description of his principal works noted. Appendices contain lists of literary organizations and prizes.

NAMES DICTIONARIES

R 41 O'Neill, P. G. *Japanese names, a comprehensive index by characters and readings*. New York, John Weatherhill, 1972. 357 p.
In two parts, the first giving the readings of 3,025 characters, and the second rendering the character forms of 5,000 readings of mainly personal and family names.

DIRECTORIES

R 42 *Zenkoku kakushu dantai meikan* (National directory of organizations). Tokyo, Zenkoku Kakushu Dantai Rengokai, Showa 46 (1971). 985 p.
Some 9,000 organizations are arranged by a detailed subject order, with information on date established, objects, area of interest, publications, membership and officials. Index arranged by the Japanese syllabary. First edition published 1966. Sixth edition listing 11,760 organizations published in 1976.

R 43 Kraft, Eva. *Japanische Institutionen, Lexikon der japanischen Behorden, Hochschulen, wissenschaftlichen Institute und Verbande. Japanisch-englisch, Englisch-japanisch*. Berlin, Staatsbibliothek Preussischer Kulturbesitz, 1972. 597 p. (Veroffentlichungen der Staatbibliothek Preussischer Kulturbesitz, Band 11).
Some 4,000 institutions are arranged alphabetically by their romanized Japanese names. Equivalents to the names are given in English translation and in characters. There is a small section for institutes forming part of larger institutions.

Official

R 44 *Shokuinroku,* Meiji 19– (Register of civil officials, 1886–). Tokyo, Okurasho Insatsukyoku, 1886–.
A directory of official organizations in Japan, listing officials by name under the appropriate departments and bureaus. The first part is concerned with the national officialdom, the second with that of the prefectures and local governments. Many valuable charts show the relationship of government organizations, but it contains no index to officials by name. Earlier issues from 1886 to

1943 and 1946 have now been published on microfilm by Yushodo, Tokyo. 1978 issue seen.

R 45 U.S. Embassy. Japan. *The government organization of Japan, with names of bureau, division and section chiefs, as of November 20, 1962.* Tokyo, Translation Services Branch, Political Section, American Embassy, 1962. 232 p.
An issue of a list published from time to time by the U.S. Embassy and valuable since it gives a comprehensive survey of English-language equivalents to Japanese official names. A shorter and even more dated list may be found in *Kenkyusha's New Japanese-English dictionary* (Tokyo, 1954), pp. 2,116–21, (see R 24).

R 46 *Nihon kankai meikan* (Who's who—Japanese officials). Tokyo, Nihon Kankai Johosha, Showa 50 (1975). 991 p.
Some 19,000 officials are listed in order of the Japanese syllabary, giving their present position, career and home address. 1952 edition noted.

R 47 Japan. Sorifu. Gyosei kanricho (Prime Minister's Office. Administrative Management Agency). *Table of organization of the Government of Japan, January 1976.* Tokyo, 1976. 136 p.
Tables of organization of the Japanese government, lists of Councils, public corporations and information on the organization and function of the government, including laws and the Japanese Constitution. No index. No Japanese forms given. For a detailed statement in Japanese of Japanese government organization see *Shokuinroku* (R 44).

Commercial

R 48 *Kaisha nenkan, jojo kaishahan* (Nikkei, annual corporation reports). Tokyo, Nihon Keizai Shimbunsha, Showa 29– (1949–).
1,727 corporations listed on the Stock Exchange are arranged by type of economic activity, with addresses, officials and financial information given. Name index. 1979 issue seen.

R 49 *Nihon shokuinroku,* Showa 22– (Japan who's who in government, schools, organizations, banks and companies, 1947–). Tokyo, Jinji Koshinjo, Showa 22– (1947–).
More a directory to some 30,000 firms and organizations than a who's who. There are four parts for government organization, universities, academic and professional associations, and business and industrial firms. Large stockholders and principal officers noted for commercial firms. No index. 13th edition published in 1970 in three volumes.

R 50 *Standard trade index of Japan,* 1950–. Tokyo, Japan Chamber of Commerce and Industry, 1950–.
An index to commodities and services in the 1967/8 issue lists over 28,000 items and identifies 8,600 Japanese firms which deal with these commodities. Short informative notes are given for each

company including address, date of establishment and kind of business. Index to companies. Title varies with 1950, 1955 and 1956 issues: *Japan register of merchants, manufacturers and shippers*. 1977/8 last issue noted.

R 51 *Kaisha soran, mijojo kaishahan* (Corporation yearbook, corporations not listed on the Stock Market). Tokyo, Nihon Keizai Shimbunsha, Showa 50 (1975). 2,318 p.
Nearly 7,000 corporations are listed with financial information, officials and addresses, arranged by economic activity. Name and place index.

Academic

R 52 National Committee of Japan on Intellectual Cooperation. *Academic and cultural organizations in Japan*. Tokyo, Kokusai Bunka Shinkokai, 1939. 525 p.
Lists some 600 organizations as academic and cultural societies and institutions of higher learning at the end of 1938, giving addresses, officers, year of establishment, membership, objects, history, expenditures and publications. Organizations are listed in their romanized form, followed by the form in characters and translation into English.

R 53 Japan. Mombusho. Daigaku Gakujutsukyoku (Ministry of Education. Higher Education and Science Bureau). *List of universities and colleges in Japan, natural and applied sciences*. Tokyo, Japan Society for the Promotion of Science, 1963. 107 p. (Directory of research institutions in Japan, Natural and applied sciences v. 3).
Some 140 universities are arranged in alphabetical order, and under each there is a listing of science departments and institutes. There is an index of institutes and laboratories under eight major headings, and list of periodical publications also arranged under broad subject headings.

R 54 Japan. Mombusho. Daigaku Gakujutsukyoku (Ministry of Education. Higher Education and Science Bureau). *Directory of research institutions and laboratories in Japan*. Tokyo, Japan Society for the Promotion of Science, 1964. 379 p. (Directory of research institutions in Japan, Natural and applied sciences v. 2).
1,326 research institutions are listed in alphabetical order, with addresses, statement of research objectives, and publications, where applicable. University institutes are not included, the list being restricted to official, other non-profit organizations and industrial firms. Title index to periodicals and a subject index to research activities included.

R 55 *Japanese universities and colleges, 1965–6, with national research institutes*. Tokyo, Japan Overseas Advertiser Co., 1965. 475 p.
Arranged in five sections. The first surveys scientific research in Japan, the second lists 324 universities and colleges arranged by

region, the third lists junior colleges, the fourth 67 research institutes attached to national universities, and the fifth 75 national research institutes arranged by ministry. Information is given on publications, staff, background and activities for each institution.

R 56 Nihon Gakujutsu Kaigi, Tokyo (Science Council of Japan). *Zenkoku gaku kyokai soran* Directory of the learned societies in Japan. Tokyo, Okurasho Insatsukyoku, Showa 41 (1966). 337 p.
1,061 learned societies are arranged by subject, with information noted for membership, background and publications. Index to English forms of journal and society names.

R 57 Nihon Gakujutsu Shinkokai (Japan Society for the Promotion of Science). *Directory of Japanese learned societies, 1970.* Tokyo, 1970. 133 p.
Lists 412 societies, giving the title in English, followed by the romanized title in Japanese, name of president, year of establishment, membership and publications. The societies are arranged by subject areas, and the index is by the English form of the society name. Revision of 1962 edition.

R 58 *Zenkoku kenkyukikan soran* Directory of the research institutes and laboratories in Japan. Tokyo, Nihon Gakujutsu Kaigi Jimukyoku, 1974. 1,112 p.
2,320 institutes and laboratories arranged under government research institutes, other public research institutes, university research institutes, and community research institutes. Detailed information given, including address, name if available in English, publications, research and objectives. Japanese name index arranged by Japanese syllabary, Western-language name index, and English index by research subject. Supersedes 1967 edition.

R 59 *A guide to colleges and universities in Japan.* Tokyo, Saikon Publishing Co., 1975–.
Issued in unnumbered parts in two looseleaf binders. 411 colleges and universities listed in ‘Colleges and universities in Japan, 1975,’ and additional parts entitled: ‘Research institutes attached to colleges and universities in Japan, 1975,’ ‘Undergraduate courses in Japan, 1975’ and ‘Graduate courses in Japan, 1975.’ Brief directory-type information given in English. No characters. The second binder has fuller descriptions of 36 universities.

R 60 Japan. Mombusho. Daigakukyoku Daigakuka. *Zenkoku daigaku ichiran* (Survey of Japan’s universities). Tokyo, Bunkyokyokai, Showa 50 (1975). 372 p.
160 universities and schools arranged by type: national, public and private, with directory-type information for each, including academic subdivisions, administration and addresses. Index to universities by the Japanese syllabary.

ATLASES

R 61 Zenkoku Kyoiku Tosho Kabushiki Kaisha. *Nihon keizai chizu* The economic atlas of Japan. Tokyo, Showa 29 (1954). 166 p.
An atlas of economic activity in Japan, data as of the 1950s, which has been made more accessible to the non-Japanese reader by Norton Ginsburg and John D. Eyre *The economic atlas of Japan* (Chicago, University of Chicago Press, 1959), which translates the Japanese-language sections of the atlas. Physical geography, land use and farming, mineral resources, industry, communications, and urban and regional development are shown under 61 major coloured maps. Dated, but still useful.

R 62 Zenkoku Kyoiku Tosho Kabushiki Kaisha. *Nihon rekishi chizu* (Historical atlas of Japan). Tokyo, Showa 31 (1956). 482 p.
A valuable atlas of Japanese history arranged in chronological order and containing 75 principal coloured maps, and many insets. Type on maps and in introductions rather small but clear. Place-name index. Republished in 1966.

R 63 Teikoku shoin, Tokyo. *Teikoku's complete atlas of Japan.* Tokyo, 1969.
Place-names are in the standard modified-Hepburn system of romanization and text is in English. Most of the maps are large, clear and coloured physical maps of parts of Japan, and show railroads. Additional maps for this revision of the 1964 edition show the centre of Tokyo, administrative boundaries, and four small-scale historical maps. Nearly 5,000 place-names noted in index.

R 64 *Atlas of Japan.* Tokyo, International Society for Educational Information, 1974. 64 p.
73 coloured maps on 48 plates, based on the 1960 census and later information. Maps cover physical, economic and cultural aspects of Japan, and the text is in English, French and Spanish. 1974 edition uses modified-Hepburn romanization instead of *Kunreishiki* system in 1971 edition. No index.

R 65 *Nihon bunken chizu chimei soran* (Prefectural atlas and place-name guide for Japan). Tokyo, Jimbunsha, Showa 53 (1978).
A section of general maps is followed by 47 prefectural sections, each with maps showing roads, tourism, physical features and major towns. Place-names guide in each prefectural section.

GEOGRAPHICAL DICTIONARIES AND GAZETTEERS

R 66 Gerr, Stanley. *A gazetteer of Japanese placenames.* Cambridge, Harvard University Press, 1942. 269, 225 p.
4,500 place-names are listed, and over one-third are for physical features. The area covered includes Japan, Korea, Formosa and mandated territories, but excludes China. In two parts, the first

arranged by radicals and the second alphabetically. Approximate longitude and latitude given.

R 67 U.S. Office of Geography. *Japan* . . . Washington, U.S. Government Printing Office, 1955. 731 p. (Gazetteer no. 12).
Approximately 28,700 places and physical features are listed in alphabetical order, with their longitude and latitude. The Ryukyus are included, and the Kuriles excluded.

R 68 Japan. Jichicho. Gyoseikyoku (Local autonomy Office. Administrative Bureau). *Zenkoku shichoson yoran*, 39 nemban The national directory of cities, towns and villages. Tokyo, Dai ichi hoki, Showa 39 (1964). 361 p.
3,398 local administrative units are arranged in regional order, with name of unit, population, date of establishment, and changes, including former names. Prefectural maps show location of units. Index. Issued annually from 1956 to 1966. No issue for 1965.

R 69 *Nihon chimei daijiten* (Place-name dictionary of Japan). Tokyo, Asakura Shoten, Showa 42–4 (1967–9). 7 v.
Place-names are arranged in Japanese syllabic order under major regions, and this dictionary reflects the important changes that have taken place in Japan since World War II. 14,000 places are listed with description.

CHRONOLOGICAL TABLES

R 70 Tsuchihashi, Yachita. *Japanese chronological tables from 601 to 1872 A.D.* Tokyo, Sophia University Press, 1952. 128 p. (Monumenta Nipponica monographs no. 11).
Tables permit conversion into the Western date of the first day of each Japanese month. Appendices contain tables for counting days of the year and for computing cyclical characters. The author has compiled a list of errors appearing in William Bramsen 'Japanese chronological tables . . . ' *Transactions of the Asiatic Society of Japan,* v. 37, no. 3, 1910, p. 1–131, and in Tsuji Zennosuke *Dai Nihon nempyo* (1941).

CHRONOLOGY

R 71 Nishioka, Toranosuke. *Shin Nihon nempyo* (New Japanese history chronological tables). Tokyo, Chuo koronsha, 1955. 633 p.
A chronology of Japanese history from 48 A.D. to 1955, with a comparative column for world history. Japanese era, Western calendar, Chinese sexagenary cycle dates are also noted. Appendices contain a chronological table for archaeology, and chronological tables for local rulers in Japan. Index.

R 72 Hioki, Shoichi. *Kokushi dai nempyo* (Japanese history chronology). Tokyo, Heibonsha, Showa 10–12 (1935–7). 7 v.
A detailed chronology of Japanese history, emphasizing political events and arranged by era names, with no indications of the Western date. Volumes 1–3 cover the period to 1868; volumes 4–6 from 1868 to 1934; and volume 7 is an index in two parts, the first dealing with names, the second with events.

R 73 Toyo Keizai Shimposha. *Sakuin seiji keizai dainempyo* The economic and political chronology of Japan, with index. Tokyo, Showa 46 (1971). 4 v.
The first volume with index covers the period 1840 to 15 August 1945, and the second from 16 August 1945 to the end of 1955. Both chronology and index are very detailed. A thorough revision and extensive supplementing of the 194[illegible] edition.

CENSUS

Annual estimates of the population of Japan may be found in the *Nihon teikoku tokei nenkan* (R 77) for the period from 1872 to 1897. For following years figures were based on the quinquennial registration of the population from 1903 to 1918. From 1920 a new quinquennial series commenced which has continued to the present day.

R 74 Japan. Naikaku. Tokeikyoku (Bureau de la statistique imperiale). *Taisho kyunen kokusei chosa hokoku* (Report on the 1920 census). Tokyo, Taisho 13 – Showa 4 (1923–9). In four parts, the fourth in 47 prefectural volumes.
Taisho juyonen kokusei chosa hokoku (Report on the 1925 census). Tokyo, Taisho 14 - Showa 10 (1925–35). In four parts, the last in 47 prefectural volumes.
Showa gonen kokusei chosa hokoku (Report on the 1930 census). Tokyo, Showa 6–10 (1931–5). In five parts, the third in two sections, and the fourth in 47 prefectural volumes.
Showa junen kokusei chosa hokoku (Report on the 1935 census). Tokyo, Showa 11–14 (1936–9). In two parts, the second in 47 prefectural volumes.
These pre–World War II censuses were of high quality, but were written completely in Japanese, making them less accessible than the postwar series. The mid-decade censuses in 1925 and 1935 were less complete than the decennial censuses. All available on microfilm from the Library of Congress.

R 75 Japan. Sorifu. Tokeikyoku (Prime Minister's Office. Statistical Bureau). *1940 population census of Japan* Showa 15-nen kokusei chosa hokoku. Tokyo, 1961–2. 2 v.
The first volume covers total population, sex, age, marital status, race and nationality, and the second industry and employment status.

R76 Japan. Sorifu. Tokeikyoku (Prime Minister's Office. Statistical Bureau).
Population census of 1950 Showa 25-nen kokusei chosa hokoku. Tokyo, 1951–5. Appeared in eight volumes, with volume 3 in two parts and volume 7 divided into 46 prefectural divisions.
1955 population census of Japan Showa 30-nen kokusei chosa hokoku. Tokyo, 1956–9. In five parts, of which the fifth was divided by prefectures.
1960 population census of Japan Showa 35-nen kokusei chosa hokoku. Tokyo, 1961–4. In four parts, of which the fourth was divided by prefectures.
1965 population census of Japan Showa 40-nen kokusei chosa hokoku. Tokyo, 1966–7. In six parts, of which the fourth was divided into 46 prefectural volumes.
1970 population census of Japan Showa 45-nen kokusei chosa hokoku. Tokyo, 1971–5. In eight parts, each divided into a number of volumes. Part 3 contains 46 prefectural volumes.
1975 population census of Japan Showa 50-nen kokusei chosa hokoku. Tokyo, 1977– Projected in five parts. The third part in 47 prefectural volumes. Parts 1–3 seen.
There are two subseries, the large scale decennial census and the simplified mid-decade census. An extremely reliable and valuable census, improved over the excellent pre–World War II series. In English and Japanese.

STATISTICAL YEARBOOKS

R77 Japan. Naikaku. Tokeikyoku (Bureau de la statistique imperiale). *Nihon teikoku tokei nenkan* (Statistical yearbook for the Japanese Empire). Tokyo, Tokyo Tokei Kyokai, Meiji 15 – Showa 26 (1882–1951). 59 v.
Covers the period from 1868 to 1940, and based on reports from ministries. Each volume consists of a large number of tables arranged by subject. Index to subjects by the Japanese syllabic system. Entirely in Japanese. Available on microfilm. An abstract in Japanese and French is entitled *Resume statistique de l'empire du Japon* Nihon teikoku tokei tekiyo, 1887–1940.

R78 Japan. Sorifu. Tokeikyoku (Prime Minister's Office. Statistical Bureau). *Nihon tokei nenkan,* Showa 24-nen– (Japan statistical yearbook, 1949–). Tokyo, Showa 24– (1949–).
Continues the pre–World War II statistical annual series, but differs in offering data in both English and Japanese. The first volume covers statistical information from 1941. Data is collected from official and private agencies, and the tables are grouped by subjects, and explanations and remarks accompany each table. The data cover land, climate, population, labour force, agriculture, forestry, fisheries, mining, manufacturing, construc-

tion, utilities, transportation, trade, finance, prices, wages, housing, elections, education, religion, health and justice. 1978 issue noted.

BIBLIOGRAPHY

Japanese Language

BIBLIOGRAPHY OF BIBLIOGRAPHIES

R 79 Amano, Keitaro. *Hompo shoshi no shoshi* (Bibliography of Japanese bibliographies). Osaka, Mamiya Shoten, Showa 8 (1933). 370 p.
Divided into two sections. The first contains 177 bibliographies published before 1858 arranged in chronological order, and the second 4,373 arranged by subject. Most of the bibliographies, which include materials published separately as books and also in books and periodicals, are in Japanese. Separate indexes for subjects and authors arranged in the Japanese syllabic order. The most comprehensive listing of Japanese bibliographies.

BOOKS PUBLISHED TO 1890

R 80 Samura, Hachiro. *Kokusho kaidai,* zotei kaihan (Bibliography of Japanese books, revised edition). Tokyo, Rikugokan, Taisho 15 (1926). 2 v.
Some 25,000 books published in 1867, arranged in the Japanese syllabic order, with author, subject, stroke and collected work indexes. Short and excellent descriptive annotations often include biographical information on the authors. A list of all collected works published up to 1926 is appended.

R 81 Iwanami Shoten, Tokyo. *Kokusho somokuroku* (Catalogue of Japanese books). Tokyo, Showa 38–51 (1963–76). 9 v.
A union catalogue of 500,000 extant books published before 1868 in some 450 public and private libraries. It is arranged in the Japanese syllabic order, with the title in Japanese characters, with subject classification, author, date of publication, and whether manuscript or printed. Printed books represent some 40% of the titles. Library locations also stated. Volume 8 includes a major section on *sosho* or Japanese series, with contents lists. Volume 9 is an author index. Since the basic compilation was carried out before World War II many of the locations stated have now changed.

R 82 Kokuritsu Kokkai Toshokan, Tokyo (National Diet Library). *Meiji-ki kanko tosho mokuroku* (Catalogue of books published in the Meiji period). Tokyo, Kinokuniya Shoten, 1971–6. 6 v.
Volumes 1–5 contain some 120,000 titles arranged in a detailed subject classification. Books published outside Japan and official publications are included. Volume 6 is a title index.

TRADE BIBLIOGRAPHY

R 83 Tokyo Shosekisho Kumiai, Tokyo. *Tokyo Shosekisho Kumiai tosho somokuroku* (Tokyo Booktrade Association catalogue of books in print). Tokyo, Meiji 26 – Showa 15 (1893–1940). 9 v.
Includes only the materials listed in the catalogues issued by the members of the association, but easily the most comprehensive trade listing available. Catalogues were issued in 1893, 1898, 1906, 1911, 1918, 1923, 1929, 1933, and 1940, with the number of entries increasing. A very valuable supplement to the catalogues of the Imperial Library (R 87–9).

R 84 *Shuppan nenkan,* Showa 5–16 nemban (Publication yearbook, 1930–41). Tokyo, Tokyodo, Showa 5–16 (1930–41). 12 v.
Tokyodo was a major Tokyo book wholesaler before World War II and this yearbook is based on its monthly *Tokyodo geppo* (1927–41). The most significant section consists of a catalogue of books published in the previous year arranged by subject, with full bibliographical description and short annotation. Other sections list deposits at the Naimusho (Ministry of Home Affairs) other than those in section three, and classified lists of periodicals. There is no index which makes the location of a particular title difficult. Compared to the Tokyo shosekisho kumiai *Shuppan nenkan,* Showa 4–15 nemban, coverage was as much as one-third more complete and the classification was also more complete.

R 85 *Shoseki nenkan,* Showa 17 nemban (Book yearbook, 1942). Tokyo, Kyodo Shuppansha, Showa 17 (1942). 1,426 p.
Supersedes the Tokyodo *Shuppan nenkan* (R 84) and supplements a yearbook for periodicals, the *Zasshi nenkan* (R 107), follows in general the arrangement of contents of the Tokyodo yearbook, except that all book titles were brought together in one sequence. There is no index, and only part of the entries are annotated. For the 1943 issue there was a title change to *Nihon shuppan nenkan,* Showa 17 nemban (1,260 p.); periodicals are again included. The 1944–6 and 1947–9 issues were published by the Nihon Shuppan Kyodo Kabushiki Kaisha, and neither issue included annotations and indexes.

R 86 *Shuppan nenkan,* 1951 nemban– (Publication yearbook, 1951–). Tokyo, Shuppan Nyusu-sha, Showa 26– (1951–).
Similar in contents to the Tokyodo *Shuppan nenkan* (R 84), which it regards as its direct predecessor, with the exception that the listing of books is now arranged according to the Nihon Decimal Classification. Indexing of author, titles and subjects commences from the 1952 issue. Periodicals also listed. 1978 issue seen.

IMPERIAL LIBRARY CATALOGUES

R 87 Teikoku Toshokan, Tokyo (Imperial Library). *Teikoku Toshokan wakan tosho bunrui mokuroku* (Classified catalogue of the Japanese and Chinese books in the Imperial Library). Tokyo, Meiji 33–40 (1900–7). 9 v.

The Imperial Library received one of the two copies of all Japanese publications deposited at the Ministry of Home Affairs. Each volume covers a major subject field, which is further subdivided, and has its own index to titles. Continued by the *Teikoku toshokampo* (Imperial Library bulletin) issued from 1908 to 1944, which has a subject arrangement and was issued first as a quarterly and then as a monthly from 1931.

R 88 Teikoku Toshokan, Tokyo (Imperial Library). *Teikoku Toshokan wakan tosho shomei mokuroku* (Title catalogue of the Japanese and Chinese books in the Imperial Library). Tokyo, Meiji 32 – Showa 37 (1899–1962). 12 v.

Series 1 covers accessions 1875–93; series 2 1894–9; series 3 1900–11; series 4, in three volumes, 1912–26; series 5, in four volumes, 1927–35; and series 6, in two volumes, 1936–40. Each series is arranged by title. Series 7, covering 1941–9 and published in 1966, seen.

R 89 Kokuritsu Kokkai Toshokan, Tokyo (National Diet Library). *Teikoku Toshokan Kokuritsu Toshokan wakan tosho bunrui mokuroku,* Showa 16-nen 1-gatsu – 24-nen 3-gatsu (A classified catalogue of Japanese and Chinese books in the Imperial Library, January 1941 – March 1949). Tokyo, Showa 39 (1964). 1,144 p.

32,890 entries are arranged by the Nihon Decimal Classification. No index.

NATIONAL DIET LIBRARY CATALOGUES

R 90 Kokuritsu Kokkai Toshokan, Tokyo (National Diet Library). *Zen Nihon shuppambutsu somokuroku,* Showa 23 nemban (Japanese national bibliography, 1948–). Tokyo, Showa 26- (1951–).

An annual cumulation with issues after 1955 based on the National Diet Library's *Nohon shuho* (weekly accessions report) (1955–), but with wider coverage. It includes trade publications, central and local official publications, periodicals, newspapers and Western-language materials published in Japan. Publications issued from 1948 are covered, and official publications were included from 1959, at first in separate volumes, but are now incorporated in the single annual volumes. Arranged by type of publication, and subdivided by the Nihon Decimal Classification. 1974 last volume noted, published 1976.

R 91 Kokuritsu Kokkai Toshokan, Tokyo (National Diet Library). *Kokuritsu Kokkai Toshokan zosho mokuroku,* Showa 23–33 nen (National Diet Library catalogue, 1948–58). Tokyo, Showa 34–43 (1960–8). 6 v. (in 7).

140,000 titles acquired by the Library from 1948 to 1958, of which nearly 100,000 are in Japanese, and are arranged in four volumes by the Nihon Decimal Classification. Each volume has an alphabetical author index. Volume 5 in two parts has over 40,000 non-Japanese books and periodicals, arranged by the Dewey Decimal Classification, with an author index in the second part. A title index to volumes 1–4 was published in 1968. Continued by the same title *Kokuritsu Kokkai Toshokan zosho mokuroku* (R 92).

R 92 Kokuritsu Kokkai Toshokan, Tokyo (National Diet Library). *Kokuritsu Kokkai Toshokan zosho mokuroku* National Diet Library catalogue. Tokyo, Showa 45–51 (1970–6). 4 parts (in 9 v.).
Continues the previous publication with the same title (R 91), and covers the years 1959–68. Each volume arranged by subject, with author index.

OFFICIAL PUBLICATIONS

R 93 Japan. Naikaku Insatsukyoku (Cabinet Printing Office). *Kancho kanko tosho mokuroku,* Showa 2–12 (Catalogue of government publications, 1927–37). Tokyo, Showa 2–12 (1927–37).
Includes both central and local official publications, together with publications from Taiwan and Korea, and arranged in two sequences, the first by issuing body, and the second by subject. Continued by *Kanko kancho tosho geppo,* Showa 13–18 nen (Government publications monthly, 1938–43) (Tokyo, Showa 13–188 (1938–43)).

R 94 Kokuritsu Kokkai Toshokan, Tokyo (National Diet Library). *Kancho kankobutsu sogo mokuroku* (Catalogue of official publications). Tokyo, Showa 27–35 (1952–60). 8 v.
Bibliography of central government publications issued from 1945 to 1958, published annually from 1953. From 1959 recording of official publications was continued by *Zen Nihon shuppambutsu mokuroku* (Japanese national bibliography) as separate volumes for 1959 and 1960, and from the 1961 issue incorporated in the main volume. Each volume is arranged by the Nihon Decimal Classification, and indexed by issuing agency.

R 95 Kokuritsu Kokkai Toshokan, Tokyo (National Diet Library). *List of Japanese government publications in European languages,* revised and enlarged edition. Tokyo, 1959. 82 p.
Includes Japanese government publications issued from August 1945 to December 1958, and materials published by the Supreme Commander of the Allied Powers to 1952. The publications are almost entirely in English, although some are bilingual in Japanese and English, and are arranged by ministry and bureau. There are approximately 1,200 government publications and 270 Supreme Commander of the Allied Powers materials. A revision of the 1956 edition.

R 96 Kokuritsu Kokkai Toshokan, Tokyo (National Diet Library). *Koku ga henshu, kanshu shi seifu kankei dantai, shuppansha ga hakko shita Kankobutsu ichiran, miteiko* List of the publications compiled by or under supervision of the Government of Japan, and published by extra-departmental organizations or commercial publishers, preliminary edition. Tokyo, Showa 44 (1969). 175 p. Lists some 1,800 publications by issuing organization. No index. Publications issued by extra-departmental organizations are of great interest since they are not listed in any other Japanese bibliographical source.

SELECTED BIBLIOGRAPHY

R97 Michigan. University. Center for Japanese Studies. *Bibliographical series,* no. 1–. Ann Arbor, 1950–.

The following bibliographies have been issued in this series, with the number of entries stated in parentheses:

1. *Political science,* second edition, 1961. 210 p. (1,759).
2. *Japanese dialects,* 1950. 75 p. (995).
3. *Far Eastern archeology and ethnology,* 1950. 74 p. (1,063).
4. *Japanese history,* 1954. 165 p. (1,551).
5. *Japanese economics,* 1956. 91 p. (1,191).
6. *Japanese geography,* 1970. 128 p. (1,486).
7. *Japanese religion and philosophy,* 1959. 212 p. (1,248).
8. *Japanese literature of the Showa period,* 1959. 212 p. (1,248).
9. *Japanese language studies in the Showa period,* 1961. 153 p. (1,473).
10. *Japanese sociology and social anthropology,* 1970. 276 p. (approximately 1,700).

Bibliographies of Japanese-language materials, arranged in detailed subject classification. Entries are selected and annotated, and each subject group will commence with an introduction to the subject and its materials. Numbers 1, 6 and 9 have author indexes. All have detailed tables of contents. These are excellent introductory guides to the Japanese literature of the fields represented. The inconsistency in providing indexing of authors and titles makes it difficult to determine whether or not a given book has been included.

R98 Kokusai Bunka Shinkokai, Tokyo (Society for International Cultural Relations). *K.B.S. bibliography of standard reference books for Japanese studies, with descriptive notes.* Tokyo, 1959–.

The following bibliographies have been issued in this series:

1. *Generalia,* 1959. 110 p.
2. *Geography,* revised edition. 1973. 224 p.
3. *History and biography. Part I,* 1963, 197 p. *Part II,* 1964, 218 p. *Part III,* 1965, 236 p.
4. *Religion,* 1963. 181 p.

5a. *History of thought. Part I,* 239 p. *Part II,* 1965. 167 p.
5b. *Education.* 1966. 186 p.
6a. *Language,* revised edition. 1972. 217 p.
6b. *Literature. Part I,* 1962, 122 p. *Part II,* 1966, 249 p. *Part III,*

1967, 150 p. *Part IV, Modern period,* 1967, 153 p. *Part V, Modern period II,* 1968, 252 p.

7a. *Traditional art and architecture,* revised edition. 1971. 167 p.

7b. *Theatre, dance and music.* 1960. 182 p.

8. *Manners, and customs and folklore.* 1961. 101 p.

9a. *Politics.* 1970. 178 p.

9b. *Law. Part I,* 1968, 165 p. *Part II,* 1970, 242 p.

10. *Economics. Part I,* 1969, 165 p. *Part II,* 1969, 196 p.

The term reference books has been used in a wider sense than usual and refers to standard works in the subject field. Annotations are critical and descriptive. All volumes have further subject divisions, but no indexes. A number of volumes have added listings of materials in Western languages. Valuable as an introduction to the Japanese-reading Western student. Publisher varies.

TRANSLATIONS

R99 Kokuritsu Kokkai Toshokan, Tokyo (National Diet Library). *Meiji, Taisho, Showa honyaku bungaku mokuroku* (Catalogue of translated literature from 1868 to 1955). Tokyo, Kazama Shobo, Showa 34 (1959). 779 p.

A bibliography of Japanese translations of Western-and Russian-language literary works listed in two parts. The first part, includes 26,600 entries published 1912–55, arranged by the original authors in Japanese transliteration and in the Japanese syllabic order. The second part has 3,200 translations and adaptions published 1911–68, arranged in order of date of publication. Two author indexes, one for 1,895 Western authors, and the other for 294 Russian authors.

R100 Fukuda, Naomi. *Meiji, Taisho, Showa hoyaku Amerika bungaku shomoku* A bibliography of translations, American literary works into Japanese. Tokyo, Hara Shobo, 1968. 239 p.

Some 2,300 American literary titles translated into Japanese are arranged by author. Based on information extracted from *Meiji, Taisho, Showa honyaku bungaku mokuroku* (R 99), which covered works published in 1955. To this has been added translations from 1955 to 1967, and other additional materials located in the National Diet Library and elsewhere. Textbook and other non-literary material has been excluded.

PROHIBITED PUBLICATIONS

R101 Saito, Shozo. *Gendai hikka bunken dai nempyo* (Chronological listing of banned modern materials). Tokyo, Suikodo, Showa 7 (1932). 432 p.

Lists over 5,000 periodical and newspaper issues and books which have been banned during the Meiji and Taisho periods (1868–1926). Index in the Japanese syllabic order.

R102 Japan. Mombusho. Shakai Kyoikukyoku (Ministry of Education.

Social Education Bureau). *Rengokokugun soshireibu kara bosshu o meizerareta senden-yo kankobutsu somokuroku* (Catalogue of propaganda publications whose confiscation was ordered by the Supreme Commander of the Allied Powers). Tokyo, 1948. 418 p.
Over 7,700 books arranged by title in the Japanese syllabic order. Author, publisher and date of publication given for each title.

R 103 Odagiri, Hideo and Seikichi Fukuoka. *Showa shoseki zasshi shimbun hakkin nempyo, jo* (Chronological tables of books, periodicals and newspapers prohibited in the Showa period, volume 1). Tokyo, Meiji Bunken, Showa 40 (1965). 676 p.
Some 8,300 entries for materials published through 1933, arranged by chronological order and divided into books, newspapers and periodicals and non-Japanese publications. The reason for prohibition is stated.

PERIODICALS AND NEWSPAPERS

R 104 Tokyo Teikoku Daigaku. Hogakubu (Tokyo Imperial University. Department of Law). *Totenko, Meiji shimbun zasshi bunko shozo mokuroku* (Totenko, catalogue of the Meiji newspaper and periodical library). Tokyo, Naigai Tsushinsha Shuppambu, Showa 5–16 (1930–41). 3 v.
Some 4,000 Japanese newspapers and periodicals published from 1868 to 1912 arranged by the Japanese syllabic order in each volume. Entries give title, issuing body, subject, date of first issue, frequency and holdings. Index by prefecture, then by date. Reprinted by Meiji Bunken, Tokyo, 1974.

R 105 Kokusai Bunka Shinkokai (Society for International Cultural Relations). *Catalogue of periodicals written in European languages and published in Japan.* Tokyo, 1936. 51 p.
Lists some 450 periodicals arranged by subject and annotated. Title index.

R 106 Teikoku Toshokan, Tokyo (Imperial Library). *Teikoku Toshokan zasshi shimbun mokuroku, Showa 10-nen matsu genzai* (Catalogue of the periodicals and newspapers in the Imperial Library at the end of 1935). Tokyo, Migensha, Showa 12 (1937). 157 p.
The newspaper section lists 240 Japanese-language newspapers, a few of which were published outside Japan, and the periodical section some 2,800 Japanese-language periodicals. Information given on publisher and holdings of the Imperial Library. Both sections arranged in the Japanese syllabic order. *Teikoku Toshokan zasshi shimbun zoka mokuroku, Showa 23-nen 6-gatsu matsu genzai* (Catalogue of the periodicals and newspapers in the Imperial Library, supplemented, at the end of June 1948) continues the coverage.

R 107 *Zasshi nenkan,* Showa 14–17 nen (Periodical yearbook, 1939–42). Tokyo, Kyodo Shuppansha, Showa 14–17 (1939–42). 4 v.

Some 2,400 to 3,000 general periodicals arranged under a large number of headings, with some annotations, together with lists such as yearbooks and other categories. The 1942 issue records Japanese periodicals published overseas, periodicals published in East Asia, local and academic periodicals. Index to titles in Japanese syllabic order.

R 108 *The Japanese press,* 1949–. Tokyo, Nihon Shimbun Kyokai, 1949–.
The most bibliographically significant section is one-tenth of the publication, and the 1977 issue lists over 156 newspapers with circulation, address and brief notes.

R 109 Nihon Shiryo Kenkyukai, Tokyo (Japan materials research society). *Nihon nenkanrui somokuroku* (Catalogue of Japanese yearbooks). Tokyo, Seiwado, Showa 39 (1964). 236 p.
Based on the *Sengo Nihon nenkanrui somokuroku,* but with 600 additional titles. The 2,477 current titles are arranged by the Nihon Decimal Classification. Bibliographical information is given, but no annotation. Where possible the latest issue has been examined. Title index in the Japanese syllabic order.

R 110 U.S. Library of Congress. *Union card file of Oriental vernacular series, Chinese, Japanese and Korean. Japanese file.* Washington, 1966.
45,242 holdings cards have been microfilmed from the periodical checklists of the principal East Asian collections in the United States. Copies of the microfilm have been made available by the Library of Congress in film or electrostatic copies. More than one card may be used to report a given title, and each title may be reported by one or more libraries.

R 111 Japan. Mombusho. Daigaku Gakujutsukyoku (Ministry of Education. Higher Education and Science Bureau). *Gakujutsu zasshi sogo mokuroku* (Union list of scientific periodicals). Tokyo, 1966–73. 4 v.
A series of four volumes published from 1966 are not numbered, but in effect cover Japanese holdings of scholarly journals. The volumes are:
Gakujutsu zasshi sogo mokuroku shizen kagaku obun ben, 1966 nempan (Union list of scholarly journals, science, Western languages, 1966). 25,000 different journals, with locations in 253 libraries. 1975 edition seen.
Gakujutsu zasshi sogo mokuroku, jimbun kagaku obun hen, 1967 nempan (Union list of scholarly journals, humanities, Western languages, 1967). 20,000 different journals, with locations in 220 libraries.
Gakujutsu zasshi sogo mokuroku, shizen kagaku, wabun hen, 1968 nem pan (Union list of scholarly journals, sciences, Japanese language, 1968). 25,000 different journals in 316 libraries.
Gakujutsu zasshi sogo mokuroku, jimbun kagaku, wabun hen, 1973 nempan (Union list of scholarly journals, humanities,

Japanese language, 1973). 24,000 different journals, with locations in 295 different libraries.

R 112 Shuppan Nyususha. *Nihon zasshi soran* (Directory of Japanese periodicals). Tokyo, Showa 42– (1967–).
1967 edition lists 9,775 current periodicals, divided into six groups: general periodicals (2,487 titles), scholarly periodicals (1,916 titles), government official bulletins (1,210 titles), organization bulletins (1,571 titles), privately published periodicals (1,289 titles), and public relations periodicals and company bulletins (1,302 titles). Within each group titles are further subdivided by subject. Title index and list of publishers with addresses. 1963 and 1970 editions noted. 1972 edition lists 12,969 titles.

R 113 *Japan English magazine directory.* Tokyo, International Marketing Corporation, 197-.
Fourth edition, published in 1978, lists 788 English-language periodicals published in Japan, including daily newspapers and annuals. The initial alphabetical arrangement is followed by a subject arrangement.

R 114 Carnell, Peter W. *Checklist of Japanese periodicals held in British university and research libraries.* Sheffield, Sheffield University Library, 1976–7. 2 v.
A revision of the 1971 edition, listing some 6,000 titles with Japanese-language contents in 46 British libraries. The second volume includes a list of English-language titles and a subject index.

Periodical Indexes

R 115 Kokuritsu Kokkai Toshokan, Tokyo (National Diet Library). *Zasshi kiji sakuin*, Showa 23– (Japanese periodical index, 1948–). Tokyo, Kinokuniya Shoten, Showa 23– (1948–).
Although a *Zasshi sakuin* (Periodical index) was compiled by Shimotomae Shigamatsu from 1922 to 1941, this was the first serious attempt to develop a comprehensive index, and reliance for much of the control of earlier periodical publications has to be placed on indexes issued by the periodicals themselves. The best guide to these is Amano Keitaro *Zasshi somokuji sakuin shuran* (Collection of indexes to periodicals) (Tokyo, Nihon kosho Tsushinsha, Showa 41 (1966)), which contains 1,334 indexes to periodicals and newspapers published in 1964, arranged by subject. In 1950 the index was divided into two parts, *Jimbun kagakuhen* (Humanities section) and *Shizen kagakuhen* (Natural sciences section). The latter commenced with a new number series, and from 1960 to 1964 was translated into English as *Japanese periodicals index, natural science.* Originally organized by subject headings, but since 1963 by a classified arrangement. This survey of some 1,000 current Japanese periodicals is a major contribution to bibliographical control. 1978 issues seen. Now

being cumulated; Showa 40–4 (1965–9) cumulation, 11 v., published 1976–7, and Showa 45–9 (1970–4) cumulation, 11 v., published 1976 seen. General subject and author indexes for 1965–74, in two volumes and published in 1977, seen.

R 116 Japan. Mombusho. Jimbun Kagaku Obun Mokuroku Henshu Iinkai (Ministry of Education. Committee for the Compilation of a Catalogue in Western Languages of the Humanistic Sciences). *Bibliography of the humanistic studies and social relations,* no. 1–, 1952–. Tokyo, 1955–.

Lists books and articles in some 600 Japanese scholarly periodicals, arranged by broad subject groups. Authors and titles are given in romanized and character forms, and titles are also translated.

R 117 Nihon Gakujutsu Kaigi, Tokyo (Science Council of Japan). *Bunkakei bunken mokuroku* (Catalogue of materials related to culture), 1946–. Tokyo, Showa 27– (1952–).

Volumes 1–10 published from 1952 to 1960 were issued with the title *Bungaku, tetsugaku, shigaku bunken mokuroku.* Includes books, periodical and newspaper articles published since 1945, and each issue is arranged around a central subject, and organized by topics, with an author index. Coverage is extensive, with several thousand entries in each issue. Volume 18 for 1965, published 1966, noted.

R 118 *Current contents of academic journals in Japan.* Tokyo, Kokusai Koryu Kikin, 1975–.

The 1973 issue, published in 1975, indexes 147 journals in the humanities and social sciences, arranging by subject 2,018 articles. The language of the article is noted. The 1976 issue was published in 1978.

COLLECTANEA OR JAPANESE SERIES

R 119 Hamano, Tomosaburo. *Nihon sosho mokuroku* (Catalogue of Japanese series). Tokyo, Rikugokan, Showa 2 (1927). 256 p.

Some 700 series are entered, with the contents of some 18,000 titles arranged in order of their publication in the series. Index to series titles in Japanese syllabic order.

R 120 Hirose, Toshi. *Nihon sosho sakuin,* zotei (Index to Japanese series, revised edition). Tokyo, Kazama Shobo, Showa 32 (1957). 761 p.

Divided into two parts, the first consisting of an annotated list of some 700 series arranged by title in the Japanese syllabic order, and the second a listing of pre-1868 books in series, arranged by title also in the Japanese syllabic order, and stating author and collection in which the title may be located. Reprint of 1957 edition, but including lists of manuscripts found in 1939 edition, Meicho Kankokai, 1969.

R 121 Harvard University. Chinese-Japanese Library. *Japanese*

collected works and series in the Chinese-Japanese Library at Harvard University. Cambridge, 1954. 96 p.
1,027 collectanea, with over 50,000 individual works, arranged by title in stroke order. Both *sosho* or collections of miscellaneous works, and *taikei,* or collections of monographs on specific subjects are included. Represents one of the strongest American collections of this type of material. Romanized title index.

R 122 Kokuritsu Kokkai Toshokan, Tokyo (National Diet Library). *Zenshu sosho saimoku soran* Comprehensive index to collected works and series. Tokyo, Kinokuniya Shoten, 1973–.
The first volume lists some 1,400 collections of materials originally published before 1868, and is based on a number of major Japanese library catalogues. Entries are arranged by title, and under each title individual titles are listed. The second volume will cover modern works, and the third translations. No index to individual titles in collections provided.

ESSAY BIBLIOGRAPHY

R 123 Ota, Tamesaburo. *Nihon zuihitsu sakuin* (Index to Japanese miscellanies). Tokyo, Iwanami Shoten, Taisho 14 – Showa 7 (1925–32). 2 v.
392 collections of essays have been analyzed by subject, with the subjects arranged in Japanese syllabic order. The second volume supplements the first, including works omitted.

Western Languages

R 124 Cordier, Henri. *Bibliotheca japonica, dictionnaire bibliographique des ouvrages relatifs a l'Empire japonais ranges par ordre chronologique jusqu'a 1870, suivi d'un appendice renfermant la liste alphabetique des principaux ouvrages parus de 1870 a 1912.* Paris, Leroux, 1912. 762 col. (Publications de l'Ecole des Langues Orientales Vivantes, 5 serie, tome 8).
Includes some 7,000 books and periodical articles in a wide range of Western languages and Russian, but stressing English and French materials. Detailed bibliographical information, but no annotation. Chronological arrangement is not always the most meaningful. Especially useful for French influence and Catholic missions. Author index. Reprinted by Georg Olms Verlagsbuchhandlung, Hildesheim, 1969.

R 125 Japaninstitut and Deutsches Forschungsinstitut. *Bibliographischer alt-Japan-Katalog, 1542–1853.* Kyoto, Deutsches Forschungsinstitut, 1940. 415 p.
1,624 books in Western languages are arranged by author, with full bibliographical citations. Indexed by year of publication. Valuable to supplement Henri Cordier *Bibliotheca japonica* (R 124).

R 126 Wenckstern, Friedrich von. *A bibliography of the Japanese Empire.* Volume 1: Leiden, E. J. Brill, 1895. Volume 2: Tokyo, Maruzen, 1907.

Volume 1 covers the period 1477–1893, and for the period to 1859 incorporates Leon Pages *Bibliographie japonaise depuis le XV siecle jusqu'a 1859.* Volume 2 continues the bibliography to 1906. Contains 13,200 entries for books and periodical articles. Author index. Continued by:

Oskar Nachod. *Bibliography of the Japanese Empire, 1906–1926.* London, Goldston, 1928. 2 v. Entries for books and periodical articles are arranged by subject, and numbered 1 to 9,575. Korea and Taiwan are included. Author index. Continued by:

Oskar Nachod. *Bibliographie von Japan,* 1927–1929. Leipzig, Hiersemann, 1931. 410 p. Entries are numbered 9,576 to 13,595, and include Korea and Taiwan. Author index. Continued by:

Oskar Nachod. *Bibliographie von Japan,* 1930–1932. Leipzig, Hiersemann, 1935. 351 p. Entries are numbered 13,596 to 18,398, and include Korea and Taiwan. Author index. Continued by:

Hans Praesent and Wolf Haenisch. *Bibliographie von Japan,* 1933–1935. Leipzig, Hiersemann, 1937. 452 p. Entries are numbered 18,399 to 25,376, and include Korea, Taiwan and Manchuria. Author index. Continued by:

Hans Praesant and Wolf Haenisch. *Bibliographie von Japan,* 1936–1937. Leipzig, Hiersemann, 1940. 559 p. Entries are numbered 25,377 to 33,621, and include Korea, Taiwan and Manchuria. Author index.

These volumes constitute a comprehensive bibliographical foundation for the study of Japan through material in Western languages. A further *Bibliographie von Japan,* 1938–1943 was compiled by Hans Praesant and Wolf Haenisch, but not published. A copy of the 3,500 cards, in German only, in bound form and in 3 volumes is held by the Library of Congress.

R 127 Yabuki, Katsuji. *Japan bibliographic annual,* 1956–1957. Tokyo, Hokuseido Press, 1956–7. 2 v.

The first volume arranges 3,600 books and periodical articles by author. No annotation. Some official publications are included. Not restricted to materials published in Japan. Indexes *Contemporary Japan* 1946–55, and *Japan Quarterly* 1954–55. Subject and title indexes. The second volume has entries arranged by subject, and an author, title and subject index to both volumes. It contains 420 entries published in 1956 or before and not in the first volume, and 750 important articles from 11 major English-language periodicals published since 1945.

R 128 Silberman, Bernard S. *Japan and Korea, a critical bibliography.* Tucson, University of Arizona Press, 1962. 120 p.

Similar to companion volumes for India and China, with 1,933 books and periodical articles mostly in English, and arranged under major subject headings. Each subject has a short introduction. A select and annotated work. Author, title and subject index.

R 129 Kokuritsu Kokkai Toshokan, Tokyo (National Diet Library). *Catalog of materials on Japan in Western languages in the National Diet Library, April 1948 – December 1962 (Preliminary edition).* Tokyo, 1963. 306 p.
2,300 books arranged in classified order and published for the most part 1948–62. Useful for locating Supreme Commander for the Allied Powers and official publications. Subject and author index.

R 130 Kokusai Bunka Shinkokai, Tokyo (Society for International Cultural Relations). *A classified list of books in Western languages relating to Japan.* Tokyo, University of Tokyo Press, 1965. 316 p.
5,294 books published from the 17th century onwards and in the Kokusai Bunka Shinkokai Library in 1962 are arranged under 15 major headings, which are further subdivided. Subject approach through the table of contents. Index to authors and persons.

R 131 Kokuritsu Kokkai Toshokan, Tokyo (National Diet Library). *Catalog of materials on Japanese in Western languages in the National Diet Library, formerly in the collections of the Ueno Library, 1872–1960.* Tokyo, National Diet Library, 1966. 166 p.
Some 5,000 books and periodicals are arranged in a detailed subject arrangement, with author and short subject indexes. Important since it represents a period much earlier than similar materials in the main Diet Library collections. 1977 edition reported.

R 132 Fukuda, Naomi. *Union catalog of books on Japan in Western languages.* Tokyo, International House Library, 1967. 543 p.
Approximately 9,800 entries arranged by author. Compilation is based on the printed catalogues, but owing to variations in cataloguing practice at the International House of Japan, Kokusai Bunka Shinkokai, National Diet Library and Toyo Bunko, entries may not correspond to those in the participating library, and there has been much subsequent checking. The most comprehensive catalogue of its kind.

R 133 Kokusai Bunka Kaikan, Tokyo. Toshokan (International House of Japan. Library). *Japan, International House of Japan Library, Acquisition list, 1955–1975.* Tokyo, International House of Japan, 1975. 242 p.
Nearly 4,000 books in English relating to Japan and arranged by subject. No annotation. Author index.

DISSERTATIONS

R 134 Shulman, Frank J. *Japan and Korea, an annotated bibliography of doctoral dissertations in Western languages, 1877–1969.* Chicago, American Library Association, 1970. 340 p.

2,616 dissertations are arranged in a detailed subject order. Each entry is annotated, and has a note on related publications. An extremely thorough and comprehensive study. Institutional, biographical and author indexes. Continued by *Doctoral dissertations on Japan and Korea, 1969–1974, a classified biographical listing of international research* (Ann Arbor, University Microfilms International, 1976. 78 p.). The continuation has unannotated entries, includes dissertations omitted in the parent volume, and is the first in a series of periodic supplements.

TRANSLATIONS

R 135 Inada, Hide Ikehara. *Bibliography of translations from the Japanese into Western languages, from the seventeenth century to 1912.* Tokyo, Sophia University, 1971. 112 p.
A finely worked bibliography of 439 works translated into Western languages, with a note of the original, and annotations. Contains also a bibliography and author, translator, original title and subject indexes.

FILMS

R 136 University of Michigan. Audio-Visual Center. *Film resources on Japan* Washington, U.S. Government Printing Office, 1975. 55 p.
Includes a subject index to 16 mm films, and lists of 16 mm films (annotated), films produced before 1960, sponsored films, 35 mm filmstrips and distributors.

Russian Language

R 137 Akademiia nauk SSSR. Institut narodov Azii. *Bibliografiia IAponii, literatura, izdannaia v Rossii s 1734 po 1917 g.,* Sost. V.S. Grivnin and others. Moskva, Nauka, Glav. red. vostochnoi lit-ry, 1965. 378 p.
7,897 entries for books, periodical and newspaper articles, translations from Japanese, and reviews, arranged under 15 major subject sections, with considerable subdivision and covering the period 1734–1971. Some annotations. Name index.

R 138 Akademiia nauk SSSR. Institut narodov Azii. *Bibliografiia IAponii, literatura, izdannaia v Sovetskom Soiuze na russkom iazyke s 1917 po 1958 g.,* Sost. V.A. Vlasov and others. Moskva, Izd-vo vostochnoi lit-ry, 1960. 327 p.
6,249 entries for books, periodical articles and translations from Japanese, arranged under 18 major sections and covering the period 1917–58. Name index.

Subject Bibliography

RELIGION AND THOUGHT

R 139 Holzman, Donald. *Japanese religion and philosophy, a guide to*

Japanese reference and research materials. Ann Arbor, University of Michigan Press, for Center for Japanese Studies, Bibliographical series no. 7).
992 books arranged in a classified order, emphasizing materials published since 1912 as well as the Japanese aspects of religion and philosophy from the East Asian mainland. Brief annotations. Author and editor index.

R 140 Okura Seishin Bunka Kenkyujo (Okura Institute for Spiritual Culture). *Nihon shisoshi bunken kaidai* (Annotated bibliography on the history of Japanese thought). Tokyo, Kadokawa Shoten, Showa 40 (1965). 432 p.
Some 2,000 printed books and manuscripts are arranged into three major periods from 1868, and then by title. Full bibliographical information is given, followed by an annotation. Ownership noted for manuscripts. Title index arranged by the Japanese syllabic system.

R 141 Earhart, H. Byron. *The new religions of Japan, a bibliography of Western-language materials*. Tokyo, Sophia University, 1970. 96 p.
810 entries for books and articles on the new religions of Japan, divided into general, Shinto-derived, Buddhist-derived, Christian-derived, others and Utopian. Some annotation. Author and subject indexes.

Shinto

R 142 Kato, Genchi. *Shinto shoseki mokuroku* A bibliography of Shinto, a collection of Shinto literature from the oldest times till Keio 4 (1868). Tokyo, Dobunkan, Showa 13 (1938). 646 p.
Some 14,000 books and manuscripts are arranged in three broad periods, with the third period being given subject subdivision. Locations are noted. Alphabetical index of personal names and an index of titles in the Japanese syllabic order. The most comprehensive listing of Shinto materials for the period to 1868.

R 143 Kato, Genchi. *Meiji, Taisho, Showa Shinto shoseki mokuroku, Meiji gannen yori Showa 15-nen ni itaru* A bibliography of Shinto literature from Meiji 1 (1868) till Showa 15 (1940). Tokyo, Meiji Jingu Shamusho, Showa 28 (1953). 737 p.
Some 15,000 books are arranged in a detailed subject order, including Shinto classics, shrines, ceremonies, religious problems and sect Shinto. Alphabetical index to titles and an index to compilers and authors.

R 144 Kato, Genchi, Wilhelm Schiffer and Karl Reitz. *Bibliography of Shinto in Western languages from the oldest times till 1952*. Tokyo, Meiji Jingu Shamusho, 1953. 58 p.
1,138 books and periodical articles arranged by author, with a subject index. Appendix lists another 79 books and articles published from 1941 to 1952. No annotations.

R 145 Kokugakuin Daigaku, Tokyo. Nihon Bunka Kenkyujo

(Kokugakuin University. Research Institute on Japanese Culture). *Shinto rombun somokuroku* (Bibliography of articles on Shinto). Tokyo, Meiji Jingu Shamusho, Showa 39 (1963). 755 p.
35,000 articles selected from some 300 periodicals arranged in a detailed classified order. There is a subject key to the classification. Library locations of articles noted.

R 146 Herbert, Jean. *Bibliographie du Shinto et des sectes Shintoistes.* Leiden, Brill, 1968. 70 p.
1,182 entries for books and periodical articles in English, French and German are arranged in alphabetical order by author. Each entry is numbered and keyed to a subject index. Important since it updates *Bibliography of Shinto in Western languages from the oldest times till 1952* (R 144).

Buddhism

R 147 Ryukoku Daigaku, Kyoto. Toshokan (Ryukoku University Library). *Bukkyogaku kankei zasshi rombun bunrui mokuroku* (Classified catalogue of periodical articles on Buddhism). Kyoto, Showa 6 (1931). 495 p.
15,000 articles selected from 135 periodicals arranged in a detailed classified order with 280 headings. Author and subject indexes arranged in the Japanese syllabic order. A supplementary volume (Kyoto, 1961. 738 p.) covers the period January 1931 to December 1955, and contains some 9,000 articles from 100 periodicals and collections of essays, with a subject index.

R 148 Ono, Gemmyo. *Bussho kaisetsu daijiten* (Annotated bibliography of Buddhist books). Tokyo, Daito Shuppansha, Showa 8–11 (1933–6). 12 v.
Approximately 50,000 entries for Buddhist works, with titles in characters, in Sanskrit and in romanized Japanese and Chinese, full bibliographical information, location of extant copies, if published in printed form, history of translation and size. The last volume is a history of the transmission of the Chinese translation of Buddhist materials and of the Tripitaka.

R 149 Butten Kenkyukai (Society for the study of Buddhist texts). *Bukkyo rombun somokuroku,* kaitei zoho (Catalogue of articles on Buddhism, revised and enlarged edition). Tokyo, Taigando Shobo, Showa 10 (1935). 729 p.
14,223 periodical articles, 1,559 more than in the 1931 edition, arranged in a detailed classified order, with a subject index. The articles selected from 113 periodicals.

R 150 Bando, Shojun. *A bibliography on Japanese Buddhism.* Tokyo, C.I.I.B., 1958. 180 p.
1,660 books and periodical articles in Western languages, and arranged in a general section and under sections for each sect. No annotations. Locations in libraries in Japan stated. Index.

R 151 Ryukoku Daigaku, Kyoto. Bukkyogaku Kenkyushitsu (Ryukoku

University, Kyoto. Buddhist Institute). *Bukkyogaku kankei zasshi rombun bunrui mokuroku* Classified catalogue of theses and papers related to Buddhist studies. Kyoto, Negata Bunshodo, Showa 47 (1972). 680 p.

Lists 9,103 articles published from 1956 to 1970, and supplements the 1931 *Bukkyogaku kankei zasshi rombun bunrui mokuroku* and its 1961 supplement (see R147). Articles are arranged under headings for methodology, texts, history, philosophy, organization, Indian Buddhism, Buddhism in Southeast Asia, Chinese Buddhism, Lamaism, Korean and Japanese Buddhism, Indology, literature, art and religion. Subject and author indexes.

R 152 Beautrix, Pierre. *Bibliographie du bouddhisme Zen.* Bruxelles, Institut Belge des Hautes Etudes Bouddhiques, 19--. 114 p.

Arranges 746 books and articles, mostly in Western languages, in a broad subject arrangement, covering general works, texts and commentaries, history and biography, art and literature, and doctrine and philosophy. Author index. Its importance lies in its provision of Western-language citations.

R 153 Vessie, Patricia Armstrong. *Zen Buddhism, a bibliography of books and articles in English, 1892–1975.* Ann Arbor, University Microfilms International, 1976. 81 l.

762 books, periodicals and periodical articles are arranged under 16 major subjects. No index or list of contents. Useful short historical introduction relating Zen to the United States.

Christianity

R 154 Laures, Johannes. *Kirishitan Bunko, a manual of books and documents on the early Christian Mission in Japan, with special reference to the principal libraries in Japan, and more particularly to the collection at Sophia University.* Tokyo, Sophia University, 1957. 536 p. (Monumenta Nipponica monographs no. 5).

1,428 books and periodical articles arranged by year of publication, in Western languages, and located in 28 libraries in Japan. This is the third edition.

R 155 Ebisawa, Arimichi. *Christianity in Japan, a bibliography of Japanese and Chinese sources, Part I, 1543–1858.* Tokyo, International Christian University, 1960. 171 p.

3,648 books, manuscripts and other materials compiled from bibliographies and other sources and arranged by date of publication. Separate romanized author and title indexes.

R 156 Kokusai Kirisutokyo Daigaku, Tokyo. Ajia Bunka Kenkyu Iinkai (International Christian University. Committee on Asian Cultural Studies). *Nihon Kirisutokyo bunken mokuroku, Meiji ki, part II (1859–1912)* (A bibliography of Christianity in Japan, Meiji era, part II (1859–1912). Tokyo, 1965. 429 p.

Some 8,000 books in Japanese on Christianity and its influence. Arranged into four sections: Christian doctrine, Christian activities, Christianity and forthcoming books. Further sub-divided by class. Information given includes locations. Title and author index.

R 157 Ikada, Fujio and J. McGovern. *A bibliography of Christianity in Japan, Protestantism in English sources, 1859–1959.* Tokyo, International Christian University, 1966. 125 p.
Some 900 books and pamphlets and 286 periodical articles are arranged by author in two sections, with separate title, author and subject indexes. Most entries are in English, but a few are in other Western languages. The periodical article section is not regarded as complete.

SOCIAL SCIENCES

R 158 U.S. Bureau of the Census. *Bibliography of social science periodicals and monograph series, Japan, 1950–1963.* Washington, U.S. Government Printing Office, 1965. 346 p. (Foreign social science bibliographies, series P-92, no. 20).
1,030 periodicals and 1,082 serial monographs, all in the Library of Congress, have been arranged into 14 social science fields and bibliography. Entries are annotated. Separate indexes of titles, authors and subjects.

Statistics

R 159 Japan. Sorifu. Tokeikyoku (Prime Minister's Office. Statistical Bureau). *Sorifu tokeikyoku toshokan zosho mokuroku, washo no bu* (Catalogue of Japanese books in the Library of the Statistical Bureau of the Prime Minister's Office). Tokyo, Showa 30 (1955). 568 p.
Some 9,000 periodicals are arranged in a detailed classification, with an alphabetical title index. Nearly all entries are concerned with Japan. Constitutes the most comprehensive listing of statistical materials for that country.

Anthropology and Social Anthropology

R 160 Nihon Minzokugaku Kyokai, Tokyo (Japan anthropological society). *Minzokugaku kankei zasshi rombun somokuroku, 1925–1959* (Bibliography of periodical articles on anthropology, 1925–1959). Tokyo, Seibundo Shinkosha, Showa 36 (1961). 199 p.
6,000 articles from Japanese periodicals. One-half is concerned with Japan, and materials on Japan are found under 34 general and area subject headings. No index.

R 161 Beardsley, Richard King and Takashi Nakano. *Japanese sociology and social anthropology, a guide to Japanese reference and research materials.* Ann Arbor, University of Michigan Press, 1970. 276 p. (University of Michigan, Center for Japanese Studies, Bibliographical series no. 10).
Some 1,700 entries for periodicals and books published 1946–66,

emphasizing empirical rather than historical or theoretical aspects. There has been a deliberate effort to select the best works available. Author and locality indexes.

R 162 Toshi Shakaigaku Kenkyukai, Tokyo. *Tokyo shakaigaku ni kansuru bunken sogo mokuroku* Comprehensive bibliography of urban sociology in Japan, 1970. Tokyo, Gakujutsusho Shuppankai, Showa 45 (1970). 190 p.
Some 24,000 books and articles are arranged by subject. Author index.

Economics and Economic History

R 163 Honjo, Eijiro. *Nihon keizaishi daiichi bunken* (First collection of materials on Japanese economic history). Tokyo, Nihon hyoron shinsha, Showa 30 (1955). 898 p.
A new edition of *Nihon keizaishi bunken* (1933. 703 p.), with coverage from the beginning of the Meiji period to 1931. Contains 2,800 entries for books and periodical articles. Continued by:
Nihon keizaishi daini bunken (Second collection of materials on Japanese economic history). Tokyo, Nihon hyoron shinsha, Showa 30 (1955). 709 p. 3,000 books and periodical articles compiled from the annual *Keizaishi nenkan* (Economic history yearbook) and covering publications 1932–40. First published in 1942 with title *Nihon keizaishi shinbunken* (New materials on Japanese economic history). Continued by:
Nihon keizaishi daisan bunken (Third collection of materials on Japanese economic history). Tokyo, Nihon Hyoron Shinsha, Showa 28 (1953). 612 p. 2,700 books and periodical articles covering publications 1941–50. Continued by:
Nihon keizaishi daiyon bunken (Fourth collection of materials on Japanese economic history). Tokyo, Nihon Hyoron Shinsha, Showa 34 (1959). 879 p. 5,600 books and periodical articles selected from publications issued 1951–7. Continued by:
Nihon keizaishi daigo bunken (Fifth collection of materials on Japanese economic history). (Tokyo, Mineruba Shobo, Showa 40 (1965). 853 p. Some 5,400 books and articles selected from publications issued 1958–62. Continued by:
Nihon keizaishi dairoku bunken (Sixth collection of materials on Japanese economic history). Tokyo, Nihon Hyoronsha Shinsha, Showa 43 (1968). 819. Covers materials published 1963–7. Continued by:
Nihon keizaishi daishichi bunken (Seventh collection of materials on Japanese economic history). Osaka, Osaka Keizai Daigaku, Nihon Keizaishi Kenkyujo, Showa 52 (1977). 910 p. Covers materials issued 1968–72.
An outstanding series compiled by one of Japan's leading economic historians, and including books and periodical articles by Japanese and Western authors, and not restricted to economic history alone, but including political and social materials also.

Annotations are not only descriptive but also explanatory. Entries are arranged in a classified order, with a title index.

R 164 Remer, Charles Frederick. *Japanese economics, a guide to Japanese reference and research materials.* Ann Arbor, University of Michigan Press, 1956. 91 p. (University of Michigan, Center for Japanese Studies, Bibliographical series no. 5).
1,191 books arranged in classified order, with headings for dictionaries, statistical information, periodicals, economic theory, economic history, finance, agriculture, industry, trade, labour and the corporation. Most entries briefly annotated. No index.

R 165 Sumida, Shoji. *Kaiji kankei bunken somokuroku* (Bibliography of materials on maritime affairs). Tokyo, Nohon Kaiji Shinkokai, Showa 32 (1957). 443 p.
Some 22,000 Japanese books and periodical articles on maritime transportation, shipping, maritime law, ships, routes and harbours, published from 1868 and arranged in classified order. Table of contents serves as a subject approach. No index or annotations.

R 166 Taeuber, Irene Barnes. *The population of Japan.* Princeton, Princeton University Press, 1958.
Bibliography of some 1,500 books, series and periodical articles on pp. 395–455. Materials are largely in Japanese or English, and include the principal population and census series. Some items briefly annotated. No index.

R 167 Nihon Keizaishi Kenkyujo (Japanese Economic History Institute). *Keizaishi bunken kaidai,* Showa 34 nemban– (Economic history bibliography, 1959–). Tokyo, Nihon Hyoron Shinsha, Showa 35– (1960–).
Books and periodical articles on economic history, but not restricted to Japan. Continues *Keizaishi bunken* (Materials on economic history), which covered 1957 and 1958. 1973 issue seen.

R 168 Rosovsky, Henry. *Quantitative Japanese economic history, an annotated bibliography and a survey of U.S. holdings.* Berkeley, Center for Japanese Studies of the Institute for International Relations and the Institute of Business and Economic Research, University of California, 1961. 173 p.
476 monographs, annuals, series and serials, of which 79 are not available in the United States. Arranged in a classified order, with library locations, holdings and annotations given for most items. Separate author and title indexes.

R 169 Ota, Shigehiro. *Shashi, jitsugyoka denki mokuroku* Bibliography of company histories and materials on industrialists. Tokyo, Tokyo Daigaku Keizaigakubu Kenkyushitsu, 1964. 321 p.
In two sections, for companies and individual biographies, both divided by industry. Publications are held in the Economics Department of Tokyo University. Indexes to companies and to individuals.

R 170 Komiya, Ryutaro. *A bibliography of studies in English on the*

Japanese economy. Tokyo, University of Tokyo Press, 1966. 52 p.

554 books and articles, arranged by author, emphasize the period after 1958. Supplements 'Bibliography on economics published in Japan in Western languages, 1956–1958,' *Annals of the Hitotsubashi Academy,* v. 10, no. 1, August 1958, pp. 108–39, and 'Bibliography on economic sciences published in Japan in Western languages, 1945–1955,' compiled by Japan Union of Associations of Economic Sciences, *Japan science review, economic sciences,* no. 3, 1956, pp. 17–32.

R 171 Japanese Economic Research Center, Tokyo. *List of Japanese economic and business periodicals in English, 1969.* Tokyo, 1969. 56 p.

179 periodicals, including official publications, arranged by subject. Title index.

R 172 Nihon Tokei Sakuin Henshu Iinkai. Kawashima Kenkyu Jimusho (Japanese Statistics Index Compilation Committee. Kawashima Research Office). *Nihon tokei sakuin* (Comprehensive Index to Japanese statistics). Tokyo, Nichigai Associates, Showa 50–1 (1975–6). 2 v.

An index of statistics in Japan, updating *Nihon tokei sosakuin* (General index of Japanese statistics) (1959). Contents are arranged by subject in order of the Japanese syllabary, with full indexes in the second volume.

Political Science

R 173 Kokuritsu Kokkai Toshokan, Tokyo (National Diet Library). *Gikai seiji bunken mokuroku, gikai kaisetsu shichijunen kinen* (Bibliography on parliamentary government, in commemoration of the 70th anniversary of its establishment). Tokyo, Showa 36 (1961). 444 p.

In three sections. The first, which contains some 3,600 Japanese books and periodical articles on parliamentary government, is divided into four parts, and has no annotations. The second contains 2,200 books and periodical articles in Western languages, and has a similar arrangement to the first section, except that some entries have brief annotations. The third contains papers and reports, all published before 1894, on the history of the opening of the Japanese Diet. Author index for Western-language materials, and an author and title index for Japanese-language materials.

R 174 Hanabusa, Nagamichi. *Nihon gaikoshi kankei bunken mokuroku* (Catalogue of materials on Japanese diplomatic history). Tokyo, Keio Gijuku Daigaku Hogaku Kenkyukai, Showa 36 (1961). 485 p. (Keio Gijuku Daigaku Hogaku Kenkyukai Sosho 9).

Some 14,000 books and periodical articles on the history of Japanese foreign relations and related fields of politics and economics are divided into four sections by language. The first contains some 5,000 entries for books in Japanese, is arranged by title, and has an author and translator index. The second has some 6,000 periodical articles arranged by year of publication. The third has some 700 books in Chinese, arranged by the Japanese readings of their titles. The fourth has some 2,500 books in English, French and German arranged by author. No annotations.

R 175 Ward, Robert E. and Watanabe Hajime. *Japanese political science, a guide to Japanese reference and research materials,* revised edition. Ann Arbor, University of Michigan Press, 1961. 210 p. (University of Michigan, Center for Japanese Studies, Bibliographical series no. 1).

1,759 Japanese books, series, newspapers and periodicals are arranged in a classified order, with an author index. Concentration is less on the Meiji period and more on recent developments, but with its emphasis on events after 1868, complements the companion bibliography by John Whitney Hall *Japanese history, a guide to Japanese reference and research materials* (R 224). Annotations are descriptive and evaluatory, and in common with other bibliographies in this series, there are introductions to each division of the subject field. Over two-thirds of the titles are not in the 1950 edition.

R 176 *Nihon seijigaku bunken mokuroku,* 1965– Publications of political science in Japan, 1965–. Tokyo, Fukumura Shuppan Kabushiki Kaisha, 1967.

The first part of issue no. 7 is a selected list of 435 articles and 268 books arranged by subject, with an emphasis on Japanese affairs. The items are arranged in two parallel columns, the first with the author in romanized form, the title translated and source, and the second in Japanese. The second part consists of 19 abstracts in English of books in Japanese. No index. No. 10 for 1974 published 1975 seen.

Socialism, Communism and the Labour Movement

R 177 Ohara Shakai Mondai Kenkyujo (Ohara Social Problems Institute). *Nihon shakaishugi bunken* (Bibliography of Japanese socialism). Tokyo, Dojinsha, Showa 4 (1929). 255 p.

396 Japanese books, periodicals, newspapers, pamphlets, and handbills, published from 1882 to 1914 on socialism and related fields, are divided into two sections. The first contains 321 books and handbills arranged chronologically, and the second 75 newspapers and periodicals which have had at least one article on socialism. Index of authors and translators, and of newspapers and periodicals. No annotations.

R 178 Oyama, Hiro. *Nihon rodo undo shakai undo kenkyushi, senzen, sengo no bunken kaisetsu* (Research history of the Japanese labour and social movement, prewar and postwar materials). Kyoto, Mitsuki Shobo, Showa 32 (1957). 296 p.

Over 2,000 Japanese books and periodical articles are arranged in three sections. The first contains 249 books and articles of a general nature, the second 1,220 books and articles of a more detailed nature, and the third 551 biographies, incidents and associated reference materials. Each section is arranged in chronological order and the entries are annotated. Coverage is from the Meiji period to 1956.

R 179 Watanabe, Yoshimichi. *Nihon shakaishugi bunken kaisetsu, Meiji ishin kara Taiheiyo senso made* (Materials on Japanese socialism, from the Meiji Restoration to the Pacific War). Tokyo, Otsuki Shoten, Showa 33 (1958). 337 p.
538 books, newspaper and periodical articles are divided into five periods: 1868–1911, 1912–21, 1922–6, 1927–31 and 1932–45. Entries are annotated. Chronological listing of publications on Japanese socialism appended. Author and title index.

R 180 Uyehara, Cecil H. *Leftwing social movements in Japan, an annotated bibliography*. Rutland, Tuttle, 1959. 444 p.
Some 1,800 books, periodicals and newspapers on the Japanese left wing from 1868 to 1956, with an emphasis on the period from World War I, arranged in a classified order, with some 200 divisions. Each section has a major explanatory introduction. Locations in American libraries given. Author and title index. Reprinted by Greenwood Press, Westport, 1972.

R 181 Japan. Rodosho (Labour Ministry). *Sengo rodo kankei bunken mokuroku* (Bibliography of materials on postwar labour). Tokyo, Showa 39 (1964). 228 p.
6,050 books and series on labour, published 1946–62, divided into nine parts for general works, employment, labour conditions, management and labour, labour movement, living conditions, labour law, social security and culture. No annotations or index.

R 182 Matsu, Sachiko. *An annotated select list of labor statistical materials, post-war to the present*. Ann Arbor, Asia Library and Center for Japanese Studies, University of Michigan, 1975. 78 p.
Annotates in Japanese 374 selected items from the Asia Library's collection.

Law

R 183 Ikebe, Gisho. *Nihon hoseishi shomoku kaidai* (Bibliography of the history of the Japanese legal system). Tokyo, Daitokaku, Taisho 7 (1918). 2 v.
Divided into three sections. The first contains 16 principal legal documents with commentaries; the second has 71 reference works for research on legal history, and an appendix with 18 Chinese legal documents known in Japan; and the third is an annotated list of 153 books arranged by subject. Entries in each section are arranged chronologically, and there is no index. Valuable for the study of Japanese law to 1868.

R184 *The Japan science review, law and politics*, no. 1–. Tokyo, Nihon Gakujutsu Kaigi, 1950–. Annual.
Selected books and periodical articles arranged in classified order, and compiled to introduce current Japanese work on law to the outside world. Last issue noted for 1962, with some 1,000 entries.

R185 Japan. Homufu (Attorney-General's Office). *Horitsu kankei zasshi kiji sakuin* (Index to legal periodicals). Tokyo, Showa 27– (1952–).
Some 470 periodicals are surveyed to compile this major index arranged by a detailed subject classification. Substantial proportion concerned with Japanese law.

R186 Horitsu Jiho Henshubu. *Sengo hogaku bunken mokuroku* (Catalogue of materials on postwar law). Tokyo, Nihon Hyoron Shinsha, Showa 29–41 (1954–66). 3 v.
Over 50,000 books and articles from over 500 periodicals and collections arranged by a detailed classification. The first two volumes cover the whole field of law to 1954, and the third private law only from 1954 to 1962.

R187 Japan. Saiko Saibansho. Toshokan (Supreme Court Library). *Horitsu tosho mokuroku, washo no bu* (Catalogue of law books, Japanese books). Tokyo, Showa 39–41 (1964–6). 3 v.
Some 25,000 books on law, including a substantial number on Japanese law, arranged in a detailed classification. The most comprehensive bibliography of Japanese law books. Separate indexes for author and organization.

R188 Coleman, Rex and John Owen Healey. *An index to Japanese law, a bibliography of Western-language materials, 1867–1973.* Tokyo, University of Tokyo Press, 1975. 167 p.
Some 4,000 books and articles in a detailed subject arrangement cover all aspects of Japanese law, and updates Rex Coleman. *An index to Japanese law 1867–1961* . . . (Cambridge, 1961). No annotations. The 1975 annual special issue of *Law in Japan*.

Education

R189 Kokuritsu Kyoiku Kenkyujo (National Research Institute of Education). *Kyoiku bunken sogo mokuroku* Union list of educational books located in Japan. Tokyo, Showa 25–9 (1950–4). 2 v. (in 3).
Volume 1, published in 1950, contains 14,417 Japanese books, periodicals and periodical articles on the problems of education in general, written 1868–1949, and arranged under eight main headings and a number of subdivisions. No annotation. The general index in this volume has two indexes, by author and subject in the Japanese syllabic order, and a short foreign author. Volume 2 is a catalogue of local Japanese educational materials, with an author index.

R 190 Ishikawa, Matsutaro. *Kyoikushi ni kansuru bunken mokuroku narabi ni kaidai* (Bibliography of materials on education history). Tokyo, Kodansha, Showa 28 (1953). 242 p.
Some 2,000 titles are arranged in six parts, and cover the period 1868–1950, but only the second part is directly concerned with Japanese education. Author and title index.

R 191 Eells, Walter C. *The literature of Japanese education, 1945–1954.* Hamden, Shoestring Press, 1955. 210 p.
Some 1,800 English books, reviews of books and periodical articles relating to Japanese education, arranged in dictionary style, with an index covering all major subjects, individuals, places and organizations named. Over half of the bibliography consists of periodical articles. Annotation is both critical and evaluative. Mr. Eells was an adviser on higher education to the Civil Information and Education Section of the Supreme Commander of the Allied Powers.

R 192 Passin, Herbert. *Japanese education, a bibliography of materials in the English language.* New York, Institute of International Studies, Teacher's College, 1970. 135 p.
Some 1,500 books and periodical articles are arranged under eight subjects, including historical materials before 1920, the American occupation, morals, education, students, teachers, women and specialized problems. Alphabetical index.

R 193 Kano, Masami. *Kyoikugaku kankei sanko bunken soran* (A survey of the reference literature on education). Tokyo, Teikoku chicho gyosei gakkai, Showa 46 (1971). 167 p.
647 reference books, almost entirely in Japanese and related to Japanese education, are arranged in a subject order. Full annotations. Title index.

R 194 Kokusai Bunka Shinkokai (Japan Cultural Society). *Higher education and the student problem.* Tokyo, 1972. 309 p. (K.B.S. bibliography of standard reference books for Japanese studies, Current social problems 1).
A historical introduction is followed by an annotated bibliography listing 722 books and periodical articles in Japanese published 1966–70. Supplement contains material published in 1971. The appendix lists some 160 books and periodical articles in English on education in Japan from 1945 to 1971, and a chronology of events for the same period. Index.

R 195 Teichler, Ulrich and Friedrich Voss. *Bibliography in Japanese education* (Bibliographie zum japanischen Erziehungswesen). Munchen, Verlag Dokumentation, 1974. 294 p.
Includes 2,658 books, articles and reports, published through 1973, and arranged in a detailed subject order, with 23 main divisions. Unpublished dissertations are not included. Lists materials in Western languages only. Author and institution index. More comprehensive and up to date than Walter C. Eells *The literature of Japanese education, 1945–1954* (R 191) and Herbert Passin

Japanese education, a bibliography of materials in the English language (R 192).

R 196 Watanabe, Shinichi. *A select list of books on the history of education in Japan and a select list of periodicals on education.* Ann Arbor, Asia Library and Center for Japanese Studies, University of Michigan, 1976. 153 p.

Lists some 2,400 publications in the Asia Library dealing with general history of education in Japan, higher education and biographies of educational leaders. Text in Japanese.

NATURAL AND APPLIED SCIENCES

R 197 Nihon Gakujutsu Kaigi, Tokyo (Science Council of Japan). *Japan science review, biological section,* 1–. Tokyo, Gihodo, Showa 24– (1949–). Annual.

The 1964 issue, published in 1966, contained 2,284 entries for articles arranged by subject and selected from Japanese periodicals. Those entries with an asterisk have abstracts.

R 198 Nihon Gakujutsu Kaigi, Tokyo (Science Council of Japan). *Japan science review, medical section,* 1–. Tokyo, Gihodo, Showa 28– (1953–). Annual.

Divided into two parts, bibliography and abstracts. Selected articles are arranged by the Universal Decimal Classification, and a number of the articles have abstracts also in the same issue. Pharmaceutical and dental periodicals are represented.

R 199 Fujimoto, Haruyoshi. *Nihon chishitsu bunken mokuroku, 1873–1955* (Bibliography of materials on Japanese geology, 1873–1955). Tokyo, Chijin Shokan, Showa 31 (1956). 711 p.

Some 12,000 articles in two parts. The first, with coverage to February 1941, reproduces the entries of the 1941 edition. The second includes materials published largely between 1941 and 1955. Entries are arranged by regions, then by subject. No author or title index.

R 200 Bonn, George Schlegel. *Japanese journals in science and technology, an annotated checklist.* New York, New York Public Library, 1960. 119 p.

660 Japanese scientific periodicals are arranged under subject headings, which are further subdivided by six kinds of issuing bodies. Well annotated, with a grading of the outstanding periodicals. Indexes cover subjects, titles, issuing bodies and evaluations.

R 201 U.S. Library of Congress. Reference Department. Science and Technology Division. *Japanese scientific and technical serial publications in the collections of the Library of Congress.* Washington, 1962. 247 p.

The first part lists 354 serials in Western languages, and the second 1,136 in Japanese. Both parts are divided into major subject sections. Library of Congress holdings stated. Separate title indexes for Western-language and Japanese serials.

R 202 Schroeder, Peter Brett. *Japanese serial publications in the National Agricultural Library*. Washington, U.S. National Agricultural Library, 1962. 172 p. (Library list no. 72).
1,112 serials are divided into two sections, The first, with multiple agricultural subjects, is divided by issuing agency; the second, with specific subjects, by the subject. Includes Japanese periodicals published in Taiwan. Holdings of the National Agricultural Library stated. Alphabetical title index.

R 203 Kokuritsu Kokkai Toshokan, Tokyo (National Diet Library). *Nihon kagaku gijutsu kankei chikuji kankobutsu mokuroku* Directory of Japanese scientific periodicals. Tokyo, Showa 50 (1975). 1,000 p.
7,087 periodicals being currently published are arranged according to the Universal Decimal Classification. Under each subject division, periodical titles are arranged alphabetically, with information on issuing body and translation of title. Index to titles. 1967 edition replaced the second volume of *Bibliographical list of Japanese learned journals, natural sciences, humanities, and social sciences* (1962).

JAPANESE LANGUAGE

R 204 Tokyo Daigaku (Tokyo University). *Kokugogaku shomoku kaidai* (Annotated bibliography on the Japanese language). Tokyo, Yoshikawa Kobunkan, Meiji 35 (1902). 606 p.
Some 650 books in printed and manuscript form written before 1868 are arranged in Japanese syllabic order. Author and subject index.

R 205 Brower, Robert H. *A bibliography of Japanese dialects*. Ann Arbor, University of Michigan Press, 1950. 75 p. (University of Michigan, Center for Japanese Studies, Bibliographical series no. 2).
995 books and periodicals in Japanese arranged by prefectures, nearly all being briefly annotated. Most entries cited were not inspected by the compiler.

R 206 Kokuritsu Kokugo Kenkyujo, Tokyo (National Language Research Institute). *Meiji iko kokugogaku kankei kanko shomoku* (Bibliography on the Japanese language after 1868). Tokyo, Shuei Shuppan, Showa 30 (1955). 301 p. (Kokuritsu Kokugo Kenkyujo shiryoshu 4).
3,027 books arranged under 17 subject headings covering aspects of the Japanese language, its history, dialects, education, dictionaries, mass communication and linguistics. Nearly all entries were written after 1926. Author index.

R 207 Yamagiwa, Joseph Koshimi. *Japanese language studies in the Showa period, a guide to Japanese reference and research materials*. Ann Arbor, University of Michigan Press for Center for Japanese Studies, 1961. 153 p. (University of Michigan, Center for Japanese Studies, Bibliographical series no. 9).

1,473 books, periodicals and periodical articles arranged under subject headings. Since modern linguistics in Japan may be said to have started in the early Showa period, the time division is appropriate; however some important pre-Showa works are noted.

R208 Yamagiwa, Joseph Koshimi. *Bibliography of Japanese encyclopedias and dictionaries.* Ann Arbor, Panel on Far Eastern Linguistics of Committee on Institutional Cooperation, 1968. 139 p.
1,092 encyclopedias and dictionaries, mostly dictionaries, are arranged in a classified order with annotations. No index. The most comprehensive listing of Japanese-language dictionaries.

JAPANESE LITERATURE AND DRAMA

R209 Ishiyama, Tetsuro. *Nihon bungaku shoshi* (Bibliography of Japanese literature). Tokyo, Okura Kobundo, Showa 9 (1934). 932 p.
Some 750 major classics are arranged by period and then by genre. Full annotation is followed by notes on editions and lists of commentaries and research works. Coverage to the mid-16th century.

R210 Sakanishi, Shio. *A list of translations of Japanese drama into English, French and German.* Washington, American Council of Learned Societies, 1935. 89 p.
Lists some 350 translations of Japanese drama. Author and title index.

R211 Aso, Isoji. *Kokubungaku kenkyu shomoku kaidai* (Annotated bibliography of studies in Japanese literature). Tokyo, Shibundo, Showa 32 (1957). 506 p.
Some 2,500 books are divided first by major period, then by genre or principal works. Principal works are followed by lists of commentaries and research studies. Title index in the Japanese syllabic order.

R212 Nihon Pen Kurabu (Japan P.E.N. Club). *Japanese literature in European languages, a bibliography,* second edition. Tokyo, 1961. 98 p.
Some 1,500 translations in book and article form are arranged under literature in general, classical literature, classical theatre, modern literature, juvenile and folk literature sections and then by author. Author and title indexes. A *Supplement* (1964. 8 p.) lists an additional 250 items. The most comprehensive list of translations from Japanese.

Meiji and Taisho Periods 1868–1926

R213 Murakami, Hamakichi. *Meiji bungaku shomoku* (Bibliography of Meiji literature). Tokyo, Murakami Shobo, Showa 12 (1937). 523 p.
A combined desiderata list and library catalogue. The Murakami

collection is now at the East Asiatic Library of the University of California, Berkeley. The main text lists some 6,000 titles. Other parts include catalogues of poetry and a catalogue of collections. Title index.

R214 Okano, Takeo. *Meiji bungaku kenkyu bunken soran* (Bibliography of studies on Meiji literature). Tokyo, Fuzambo, Showa 19 (1944). 810 p.
Some 2,000 original works and 3,000 critical works are arranged under broad headings for history, criticism, the original works and periodicals. Chronology of important works. Title index.

R215 Bonneau, Georges. *Bibliographie de la litterature japonaise contemporaine.* Tokyo, Kokusai Insatsu Shuppansha, 1938. 102, 280 p. (Bulletin de la maison franco-japonaise, tome 9, no. 1–4, 1937).
3,507 literary works published from the early Meiji period are arranged under 451 authors. Titles are given in romanization, characters and translation. Preceded by a study outline which introduces the works cited in the bibliography.

R216 Fujino, Yukio. *Modern Japanese literature in Western translations, a bibliography.* Tokyo, International House of Japan Library, 1972. 190 p.
Approximately 3,000 entries are arranged by author, noting translations of literary works published after 1868, and books and essays written in a Western language by Japanese authors. Translator, author and title indexes arranged by language.

R217 Pronko, Leonard C. *Guide to Japanese drama.* Boston, G. K. Hall, 1973. 125 p.
An extensively annotated select bibliography, noting 75 books in English. Index. Valuable as an introduction.

Showa Period 1926–

R218 Yamagiwa, Joseph Koshimi. *Japanese literature of the Showa period, a guide to Japanese reference and research materials.* Ann Arbor, University of Michigan Press for Center for Japanese Studies, 1959. 212 p. (University of Michigan, Center for Japanese Studies, Bibliographical series no. 8).
1,248 books, periodicals and periodical articles arranged in a detailed classification for the period 1926–59. The principal part of the bibliography is an annotated listing of Showa authors with their works. Author and editor index.

GEOGRAPHY

R219 Jimbun Chiri Gakkai (Association of Human Geographers). *Chirigaku bunken mokuroku* (Bibliography of materials on geography). Kyoto, Yanagihara Shoten, Showa 28–38 (1953–63). 3 v.
A bibliography of books, periodicals and periodical articles. The first volume has some 3,500 entries published from 1945 through

1951, the second some 10,500 from 1952 through 1956, and the third some 12,000 from 1957 through 1961. The volumes are divided into subject sections. The first has an author and a regional index; the second and third have more detailed subject breakdown, but lack indexes. On geography in general, but has a significant amount of Japanese geography.

R 220 Hall, Robert Burnett and Toshio Noh. *Japanese geography, a guide to Japanese reference and research materials.* Ann Arbor, University of Michigan Press, 1970. 128 p. (University of Michigan, Center for Japanese Studies, Bibliographical series no. 6).
1,486 books and periodical articles are arranged by reference works, periodicals, and by topic groups as physical geography, historical and cultural geography, economic geography and regional descriptive geography. Excludes 19th-century publications. Updates the 1956 edition.

ARCHAEOLOGY

R 221 Okamoto, Isamu and Aso Hitoshi. *Nihon sekki jidai sogo bunken mokuroku* (Bibliography of materials on the Japanese Stone Age). Tokyo, Yamaoka Shoten, Showa 33 (1958). 194 p.
3,870 books and periodical articles published 1868–1965 are arranged chronologically. Author index, and index by districts in Japan. No annotation.

HISTORY

R 222 Kurita,Motoji. *Sogo kokushi kenkyu* (General guide to the study of Japanese history). Tokyo, Chubunkan, Showa 10–11 (1935–6). 3 v.
Some 3,000 books, series, periodicals and historical materials published from 1868 to 1934 are arranged in three volumes. The first contains some 1,100 books and series for the earlier period of Japanese history; the second some 920 books and series for the modern period; and the third some 1,000 historical documents and a title and an author index, both arranged in Japanese syllabic order.

R 223 Otsuka Shigakkai (Otsuka Historical Society). *Sogo kokushi rombun yomoku* Important periodical literature on the history of Japan. Tokyo, Toko Shoin, Showa 14 (1939). 627 p.
22,000 articles, published in 169 periodicals and symposia from 1868 to 1932, are arranged under 29 subject headings, and then by author by the Japanese syllabic system. No annotations or index.

R 224 Hall, John Whitney. *Japanese history, a guide to Japanese reference and research materials.* Ann Arbor, University of Michigan Press, 1954. 165 p. (University of Michigan Center for Japanese Studies, Bibliographical series number 4).
1,551 Japanese books, periodicals and periodical articles are arranged in classified order, organized into five main sections:

bibliographies, reference works, historical sources, periodicals and survey histories. Annotations are descriptive and frequently critical. No index to authors and titles, and this deficiency has been made up by *Index for Japanese history, a guide to Japanese reference and research materials, by John W. Hall* (Canberra. 33 p.).

R 225 Endo, Motoo and Shimomura Fujio. *Kokushi bunken kaisetsu* (Bibliography on Japanese history materials). Tokyo, Asakura Shoten, Showa 32–40 (1957–65). 2 v.
The first volume has three sections: books, series and collected works, and materials in Chinese, Korean and Western languages. Each entry is fully annotated for contents, importance and for critical works. The second volume has a similar arrangement and supplements the first.

R 226 Kokuritsu Kokkai Toshokan, Tokyo. Sanko shoshibu. (National Diet Library. Reference and Bibliography Division). *Jimbutsu bunken sakuin* Biographical literature. Tokyo, Showa 42-47 (1967–72). 3v.
In three volumes, the first on humanities, the second on economics and society, and the third on law and society. Consists of biographical material in book and periodical article form found in the National Diet Library, and published 1912–48.

R 227 Sakamoto, Yoshikazu. *Nihon senryo bunken mokuroku* (Bibliography on the Occupation of Japan). Tokyo, Nihon Gakujutsu Shinkokai, 1972. 349 p.
The first part consists of 6,083 books arranged in a subject order, with titles and authors in Japanese, followed by the same information in a romanized form. Entries are annotated. The second part is a list of periodicals published during the occupation period.

R 228 U.S. Department of the Army. Army Library. *Japan, analytical bibliography, 1972.* Washington, U.S. Government Printing Office, 1972. 371 p. (DA PAM 550.13).
A collection of current books and articles in English arranged by subject, and concentrating on the contemporary situation. Each entry is fully annotated. Nearly one-half of the book consists of documents and data related to the East Asian political scene.

R 229 Hosei Daigaku, Tokyo. Bungakubu (Hosei University, Tokyo. Department of Literature). *Nihon jimbutsu bunken mokuroku.* Tokyo, Heibonsha, Showa 49 (1974). 1,199 p.
Approximately 35,000 Japanese are listed in the Japanese syllabic order, and citations on them in books and articles are noted.

R 230 Ward, Robert E. and Frank Joseph Shulman. *The Allied Occupation of Japan, 1945–1952, an annotated bibliography of Western-language materials.* Chicago, American Library Association, 1974. 867 p.
A major definitive bibliography on the Occupation, including pre-Occupation planning. 3,167 books, periodical articles, most

of which are annotated, are listed in a subject arrangement. Author index, index to periodicals cited, lists of Occupation personnel and personnel index included.

R231 Endo, Motoo. *Nihon shi kenkyusho soran* (Bibliography of studies in Japanese history). Tokyo, Meicho Shuppan, 1975. 402 p.
Some 5,000 works published between 1868 and 1972 are arranged under ten categories. Some 40% of the entries are annotated. Source materials and works in the post-war period are excluded. Title and author indexes.

Local History

R232 Sakamaki, Shunzo. *Ryukyu, a bibliographical guide to Okinawan studies*. Honolulu, University of Hawaii Press, 1963. 353 p.
Some 1,000 primary sources, manuscripts, articles and books, almost entirely in Japanese, but with some works in Chinese and Korean, are arranged in a classified order. Annotated. Separate author and title indexes.

R233 Sakamaki, Shunzo. *Ryukyuan research resources at the University of Hawaii*. Honolulu, Social Science Research Institute, University of Hawaii, 1965. 454 p. (Ryukyu Research Center, Research series no. 1).
3,594 books and periodical articles, approximately one-half being books, arranged by author. Including 400 entries for materials in Western languages, nearly all in English, and 603 microfilms of periodicals and documents mostly in Japanese. Title index to entries in Japanese other than periodical articles. A key to the most comprehensive collection of Ryukyu materials outside Japan.

R234 King, Norman D. *Ryukyu islands, a bibliography*. Washington, Department of the Army, 1967. 105 p. (Pamphlet 550.4).
2,108 entries, a number of which are cross-references, for books, reports and periodical articles, nearly all in English, arranged under broad subject headings, and with an author index. Some entries are annotated.

S. KOREA

The first kind of Korea is reputed to have ascended the throne in 2333 B.C. and the Republic of Korea used this year as a base for its calendar until 1961, when standard Western dating was adopted. Korea was annexed by Japan in 1910, and Japanese rule lasted until 1945. The Republic of Korea was established in South Korea in 1948, and in the same year the Democratic People's Republic of Korea was established in North Korea.

REFERENCE WORKS

S 1 California. University. Institute of East Asiatic Studies. *Korean studies guide*, compiled for Institute of East Asiatic Studies, University of California by B. H. Hazard, Jr. and others, edited by Richard Marcus. Berkeley, University of California Press, 1954. 220 p.

Annotated guide to 491 selected reference works and sources in Japanese, Korean and Western languages on Korea, arranged by major topics. Each section has an introduction. The emphasis is on history. Eight maps show the historical development of Korea, and appendices contain chronological tables. The guide is now seriously dated by the large amount of new Korean reference works and sources which have appeared since 1954. *A Russian supplement to the Korean studies guide* (Berkeley, University of California, Institute of International Studies, 1958. 211 p.) includes valuable Russian-language material.

S 2 Henthorn, William. *A guide to reference and research materials on Korean history, an annotated bibliography*. Honolulu, East-West Center, Research Translations, 1968. 152 p. (Annotated bibliography series no. 4).

612 entries for books and periodical articles, arranged in three major sections for bibliography, modern reference works, and selected source materials for traditional Korean history. Written in a style designed to be helpful to the student, with entries arranged to meet problems which will arise. Will help update the *Korean studies guide* (S 1).

S 3 Han'guk Soji Saophoe (Korean Bibliographical Centre). *Han'guk chamgo toso haeje* Annotated bibliography of Korean reference books. Soul, Han'guk Tosogwan Hyophoe (Korean Library Association), 1971. 272 p.

Contains some 1,100 titles, almost entirely in Korean, and arranged by a detailed subject order. The entries have a very full annotation. Some earlier work is included. Author and title index.

ENCYCLOPEDIAS AND HANDBOOKS

S 4 *Facts about Korea*. Pyongyang, Foreign Languages Publishing House, 1961. 240 p.
Description and history of Korea, with an emphasis on the post-Korean War situation and on conditions in North Korea, stressing its economy and culture. Section on conditions in South Korea. Some statistical information. Not indexed. Not to be confused with a South Korean publication with the same title.

S 5 Yi, Hong-Jik. *Kuksa tae sajon* Encyclopedia of Korean history. Soul, Chinumgak, 1965. 2,085 p.
Historical dictionary of Korean history arranged according to the Korean alphabet, and the most comprehensive of its kind. Has an extensive Korean history chronology from 2333 B.C. No character index. A revision of the two-volume 1963 dition.

S 6 *Pukhan ch'onggam, 1945–68* The yearbooks on North Korea, 1945–68. Soul, Konsandang Munje Ton'guso, 1968. 1,095 p.
Based on the *Chosen chungang yon'gam* (S 16), and surveys political, economic, social, military, education, literature and art fields in North Korea. Appendixes contain documents, a detailed chronology for 1945 to 1968, and biographies of 1,000 prominent North Koreans.

S 7 American University, Washington, D.C. Foreign Area Studies. *Area handbook for North Korea*. Washington, U.S. Government Printing Office, 1976. 394 p.
A country summary is followed by an account of social, political and economic affairs, and of national security. Bibliography and glossary. Research completed May 1975. Revision of first edition published 1969.

S 8 American University, Washington, D.C. Foreign Area Studies. *Area handbook for South Korea*. Washington, U.S. Government Printing Office, 1975. 416 p.
A country summary is followed by an account of social, political and economic affairs, and of national security. Bibliography and glossary. Research completed December 1974. Supersedes 1969 edition.

S 9 *Korea, its people and culture*. Seoul, Hakwon-sa, 1974. 464 p.
A revised edition of *Korea, its land, people and culture of all ages* (1963). Encyclopedic survey of Korea's geography, people, history, thought, education, customs, arts and literature. No index.

S 10 Choson Minjujuui Inmin Konghwaguk. Sahoe Kwahagwon (Democratic People's Republic of Korea. Academy of Sciences). *Yoksa sajon* (Historical dictionary). P'yongyang, 1971. 2 v.
A dictionary of world history, covering all periods down to the contemporary, but with a substantial portion of Korean history, and provides the first extensive interpretation of Korean history from the North Korean point of view.

S 11 *Han'gukhak tae baekkwa sajon* Encyclopedia of Korean studies. Soul, Uryu Munhwasa, 1972. 3 v.
Broad classified arrangement under headings as historical geography, archaeology, government, society, economy, religion, thought, education, customs, language, art, science and technology, and biography, with some 4,000 biographies. Appendices include genealogical and chronological tables.

S 12 *Kugo kungmunhak sajon* (The dictionary of Korean language and literature). Soul, Sungu Munhwasa, 1973. 1,005 p.
In two parts, the first for Korean language and the second for Korean literature. The period until August 1945 is emphasized, and there are 4,500 articles arranged by subject divisions. Appendices contain lists of catalogues of Korean classics and other literary works.

S 13 *Han'guk munhak taesajon* (The encyclopedia of Korean literature). Soul, Munwongak, 1973. 1,390 p.
3,500 articles on important literary figures, works, organizations and periodicals published under 1973 in two main divisions, the first for classics, and the second for modern works. Appendices include a dictionary of literary terms, a catalogue of literary periodicals reference works on literature, and a chronology of Korean literature. Index arranged by the Korean syllabary.

S 14 *Paekkwa sajon* (Encyclopedia). P'yongyang, P'yongyang Chohan Insoe Kongsa, 1974–, v. 1–
The first volume of a projected extensive work in 30 volumes, and intended to be a general encyclopedia, with illustrations related almost entirely to North Korea.

S 15 *Segye paekka taesajon* Encyclopedia of Korea. Soul, Hagwonsa, 1973–4. 20 v.
A substantial and authoritative encyclopedia in Korean, with excellent illustrations. Approximately one-quarter concerned with Korea. Materials arranged according to the Korean alphabet.

YEARBOOKS

S 16 *Choson chungang yon'gam*, 1949– (Korean central yearbook, 1949–. P'yongyang, Choson Chungang T'ongshisa, 1949–
Surveys internal and international affairs relating to the People's Democratic Republic of Korea. Government and politics, culture, social affairs and South Korea are covered. There is a chronology of events. No index but a detailed table of contents. Some issues translated by the Joint Publications Research Service. 1976 issue seen.

S 17 *Han'guk yon'gam*, 1954– Korea handbook, 1954–. Soul, Han'guk Yon'gamsa, Tan'gi 4286– (1953–)
Divided into four sections, the fourth and largest being concerned

with Korea, and discussing foreign relations, government, political parties, statistics, cultural activities, and the major provinces. Appendix lists important government officials. Indexed. A continuation of the *Kyongbuk yon'gam* (Soul, Yongnam ilbosa). 1977 issue noted.

S 18 *Korea annual*, 1964–. Seoul, Hapdong News agency, 1964–.
Arranged by major subjects as chronology, government, foreign relations, and the national economy. 1,500 persons noted in the who's who. English edition of *Haptong yon'gam* (United yearbook). 1978 issue last seen.

DICTIONARIES

S 19 Kauh, Hwang-man. *A new English-Korean dictionary*. Seoul, Omungak Publishing Co., 1964. 2,276 p.
Some 70,000 English words are given Korean equivalents. Usage with Korean translation also stated. The most comprehensive English-Korean dictionary.

S 20 *Taejung chongchi yongo sajon* (Dictionary of popular political usage). P'yongyang, Choson Nodongdang Ch'ulp'ansa, 1964. 536 p.
Contains some 2,500 entries and is valuable for understanding contemporary usage in North Korea.

S 21 Yang, Chu-dong. *Han-Han taejajon* (Chinese-Korean dictionary). Soul, Tong-A Ch'ulp'ansa, 1964. 1,544 p.
Some 4,000 characters are arranged in radical order, followed by their pronunciation in *hangul* (Korean alphabet) and by compounds. A standard *hanmun* (Chinese characters) dictionary. *Hangul* index.

S 22 Martin, Samuel E., Yang Ha Lee and Sung-un Chang. *A Korean-English dictionary*. New Haven, Yale University Press, 1967. 1,902 p.
With some 80,000 words in the Yale romanization of Korean, this new dictionary is reasonably comprehensive, but does not attempt to be exhaustive for *hanmun* compounds. Tables to assist with conversion of the Yale system to the standard McCune-Reischauer and to North Korean systems, but conversion is difficult for the non-specialist. The large format is easier to read than the many smaller print dictionaries previously in use.

BIOGRAPHICAL DICTIONARIES

S 23 Korea (Government-General of Chosen, 1910–45). *Chosen jimmei jisho* (Korean biographical dictionary). Keijo, Chosen Sotokufu, Showa 12 (1937). 2,012 p.
13,000 persons born in the 19th century and before are arranged

by stroke order, with detailed information and sources stated. In addition, there are two lists. The first notes formal names of government offices, with their popular names, their date of establishment and jurisdiction. The second is a list of 15,000 successful candidates to the civil service examinations. Stroke order index to persons by their pseudonyms. A Japanese index arranged in Japanese syllabic order is appended as a separate volume (148 p.)

S 24 Yi, Ka-won. *Yijo myongin yolchon* (Yi dynasty biographical dictionary). Soul, Uryu Munhwasa, 1965. 932 p.
1,670 important persons who lived from the 14th century to the end of the dynasty in 1910, are arranged chronologically. Literary and artistic figures are included, and the *Chosen jimmei jisho* (S 23) is supplemented in this respect.

S 25 *Han'guk ui in'gansang* (Korean biographies). Soul, Sin'gu Munhwasa, 1965. 6 v.
A very selective biographical dictionary with accounts of only some 200 persons. Each volume represents a group of similar persons. Valuable since it gives more extensive treatment for a select number of really important figures. Similar in content to *Inmul Han'guksa* (Biographical history of Korea) in five volumes.

S 26 *Han'guk inmyong taesajon* (Korean biographical dictionary). Soul, Sing'u Munhwasa, 1967. 1,390 p.
Containing some 10,000 biographies, it is less extensive than the *Chosen jimmei jisho* (S 23). Includes prominent people of the 20th century, but no living persons. Some non-Koreans related to Korea have been listed, but this group is not complete. Since this dictionary was compiled in South Korea, prominent persons related to North Korea have not been included. Extensive chronological tables.

Contemporary Biography

S 27 Kasumigaseki-kai, Tokyo. *Gendai Chosenjin jimmei jiten*, 1962 nemban (Who's who in modern Korea, 1962). Tokyo, Sekai Janarusha, Showa 37 (1962). 356 p.
Some 1,600 South Korean and 800 North Korean persons are listed in two separate sections. Entries are arranged by the Japanese syllabary in each section. There are character and romanized indexes. For more up-to-date information on North Korea, the September 1966 issue of *Sedae* has material on 192 North Koreans, and has been translated in JPRS no. 40,950 (9 March 1967). For South Koreans a more up-to-date statement may be found in *Hyongdae Han'guk inmyong sajon*, 1967 (S 28).

S 28 *Hyongdae Han'guk inmyong sajon*, 1967– (Who's who of Korea, 1967–). Soul, Haptong Yon'gamsa, 1967–.
The 1967 edition, the first not to be included as a part of the *Haptong yon'gam* (United Yearbook), contains 3,173 biographies

of living Koreans, arranged by the Korean alphabet. The romanized form of the name is also given. The 1973 edition lists some 4,100 names.

S 29 *Ch'oesin Han'guk insa nok* (Latest Korean biographical dictionary). Soul, Kyongje Tongsinsa, 1974. 921 p.
Some 19,000 brief biographies, giving date of birth, address, education and brief facts on life, including present activities. Names are given in a romanized form also. Appendix gives names and addresses of persons in Korean firms, living in Japan.

S 30 *Kankoku Kita Chosen jimmei jiten, 1977 nemban* (Biographical dictionary for North and South Korea, 1977). Tokyo, Sekai Seikei Chosakai, 1977. 2 v.
The sixth edition of a work which originally appeared in 1966, and now lists 1,958 South Koreans in the first volume, and 1,625 in the second. Accounts for each individual are chronologically arranged. No index.

S 31 U.S. Central Intelligence Agency. *Directory of officials of the Democratic People's Republic of Korea.* Washington, 1978. 119 p.
Some 1,500 officials are arranged by bureau, institution or organization. Alphabetical list of officials. Information from North Korean news sources up to 1978. Revision of a similar publication issued in 1972.

DIRECTORIES

S 32 *The Korea directory.* Seoul, Korea Directory Company, 1958?–
The main section is a list of firms and organizations arranged by type of activity, and then alphabetically. In addition there are a number of appendices and a who's who of foreign residents in Korea. Missions, organizations, government bodies and commercial firms included. 1979 issue seen.

S 33 *Korean business directory.* Seoul, Korea Chamber of Commerce and Industry, 1963?–.
The issue for 1972/3, published in 1973, is noted as the tenth annual edition, and reviews Korean economy and trade, and indexes commodities and firms. 1,243 firms are listed, and there is also a list of service facilities, such as organizations and hotels.

S 34 Kukhoe Tosogwan, Seoul (National Assembly Library). *Kungnae haksul mit yon'gu tanch'e p'yonllam* (Research institutes in Korea). Soul, 1966–7. 2 v.
Altogether some 400 institutes are arranged in the Korean alphabet in a separate sequence for each volume. The second volume, which is in a larger format, has an index by place. For nearly all institutes a translated name is given in English, and objectives, staff, publications and library resources are stated. The emphasis is on science and technology.

ATLAS

S 35 *Taehan min'guk chido* Standard atlas of Korea. Soul, Saso ch'ulpansa, Tan'gi 4293 (1960). 1 v.
26 large coloured maps showing physical features, communications, towns, and villages, at the scale of 1 to 350,000. An index includes some 40,000 place and feature names, arranged by the Korean alphabet with Chinese characters also given. North Korea included.

GEOGRAPHICAL DICTIONARIES AND GAZETTEERS

S 36 U.S. Office of Geography. *North Korea* . . . Washington, U.S. Government Printing Office, 1963. 380 p. (Gazetteer no. 75)
27,000 entries for place and feature names in North Korea, with their classification, and longitude and latitude.

S 37 U.S. Office of Geography. *South Korea* . . . Washington, U.S. Government Printing Office, 1965. 370 p. (Gazetteer no. 95)
26,500 entries for place and feature names in South Korea, with their classification, and longitude and latitude.

S 38 *Han'guk haengjong kuyok ch'ongnam* (Outline of Korean administrative districts). Soul, Pomun ch'ulpansa, 1975. 750 p.
Arranged by provinces, districts and sub-districts, giving villages with number of households and population. Reflects the district reorganization plan of 1973.

S 39 *Kankoku chimei soran* (Survey of Korean place-names). Tokyo, Kankoku Shoseki Senta, 1977. 767 p.
Lists some 20,000 place-names in South Korea, arranged by province and district. Names are given in characters, in the Korean syllabary and in romanized form. Short appendix for North Korean names.

CHRONOLOGICAL TABLES AND CHRONOLOGY

S 40 Chindan Hakhoe. *Han'guksa, yonp'yo* (Korean history, chronology). Soul, Uryu Munhwasa, Tan'gi 4292 (1959). 373, 209 p.
The main text is a chronological table 195 B.C. -A.D. 1945. It also gives the Tan'gi date, the sexagenary cycle date, reign titles, and regnal years for Korean kings, with similar information for China and Korea, and noting major events in Korea and outside Korea. The Western year date is given at the foot of the page. There are two appendices, the first giving a genealogy of the Yi dynasty, and the second a table for the period 918 to 1959 for conversion of Korean dates into Western.

S 41 Kukhoe Tosogwan, Seoul (National Assembly Library). *Han'guk*

sinmun chapchi yonp'yo, 1880–1910 (Chronological tables for Korean newspapers and periodicals, 1881–1910). Soul, 1967. 103 p.
A chronological listing of important events in Korea, with a parallel listing for events outside Korea.

CENSUS

S 42 Korea (Republic). Naemubu. T'onggyeguk (Ministry of the Interior. Statistical Office). *Taehan min'guk kani ch'ongin'go chosa pogo . . .* Report of the first general population census, Republic of Korea. Soul, Tan'gi 4292 (1959). 181 p.
There was no decennial 'complete' census for Korea in 1920, owing to internal disorder. Mid-decade simplified censuses were taken in 1925 and 1935, and a complete census in 1930. A summary census report is available for 1940, and a population survey report for 1944. The first post-World War II census was taken in 1949. This report is based on the 12 interim reports of the 'first' census of 1955. Field enumeration covered sex, date of birth, occupation, education and type of household, whether farm or non-farm. Title does not indicate that this is a summary report. In English and Korean.

S 43 Korea (Republic). Kyongje Kihoegwon. Chosa tonggye-guk (Economic Planning Board. Bureau of Research and Statistics). *Ilgu yukkong nyon in'gu chut'aek kukse chosa pogo* 1960 population and housing census of Korea. Soul, 1963–.
The first volume is a complete tabulation for sex, age, marital activity, literacy, economic activity, occupation and industry. The first part is for the whole of South Korea, and the remaining ten parts are for each province and for Seoul. Two volumes in 22 parts projected, of which volume 1 only seen.

S 44 Korea (Republic) Kyongje Kihoegwon. Chosa tonggyeguk (Economic Planning Board. Bureau of Research and Statistics). *In'gu sensosu pogo* 1966 population census report on Korea. Soul, 1968. 12 v.
Volume 1 covers the whole country and volumes 2–12 Seoul, Pusan and the provinces.

S 45 Korea (Republic) Kyongje Kihoegwon. Chosa Tonggyeguk (Economic Planning Board. Bureau of Research and Statistics). *Chong in'gu mit chut'aek chosa pogo* 1970 Population and housing census report. Soul, 1973–
In volume 1, part 1 is a complete enumeration, and parts 2–12 cover Seoul, Pusan and the provinces. Volume 2 is a 10% sample survey for select topics. Only two parts seen. In English and Korean.

STATISTICAL YEARBOOKS

S 46 Korea (Government-General of Chosen, 1910–45). *Chosen sotokufu tokei nempo, Meiji 43 – Showa 17 nen* (Annual statistical report of the Government-General of Korea, 1910–42). Keijo, Choson Sotokufu, Meiji 45 – Showa 19 (1912–44). 36 v.
Each volume covers area, population, agriculture, forestry, industry, trade, communications, monopolies, religion, education, police, health and finance. The 1942 volume contained 414 tables. Continues *Tokanfu tokei nenkan* (Statistical annual for the Resident-General of Korea) for 1906–9, and published 1907–11 in 3 v. Continued by Korea, South Korea Provisional Government *Choson t'onggye yon'gam*, Tan'gi 4276 yon (Sogi 1943 yon).

S 47 Korea (Republic). Kyongje Kihoegwon (Economic Planning Board). *Han'guk t'onggye yon'gam*, 4285 yon–Korea statistical yearbook, 1952–. Soul, Tan'gi 4286– (1953–)
First published with title *Taehan min'guk t'onggye yon'gam.* From 1961 published by the Kyongje Kihoegwon with title and added title noted above. Gives statistical information for population, economy, social affairs and culture. In Korean and English. Economic statistics for the period 1944–5 for all Korea, and for 1946–8 for South Korea only are found in *Choson kyongje yon'be* Annual economic review of Korea, 1948– (Soul, Choson Unhaeng, Chosabu, 1948–), which suspended publication from 1950–5. 1977 edition seen.

S 48 Korea (Democratic People's Republic). Kukka Kyehoek Wiwonhoe. Chungang T'onggyeguk (State Planning Commission. Central Statistical Board). *Statistical returns of national economy of the Democratic People's Republic of Korea, 1946–60.* P'yongyang, Foreign Languages Publishing House, 1961. 189 p.
174 statistical tables and charts illustrate the industrial, agricultural, transportation and communication, capital construction, labour, commodity turnover, foreign trade, educational, cultural and public health development of North Korea.

BIBLIOGRAPHY

Korean Language

BIBLIOGRAPHY OF BIBLIOGRAPHIES

S 49 Koh, Hesung Chun. *Korea, an analytical guide to bibliographies.* New Haven, Human Relations Area Files, 1971. 334 p.
Lists some 500 bibliographies, published 1895–1970 in eight languages. Comprehensive listing is aimed at, but orientation is

towards the social sciences. Supplementing the main detailed listing are character lists, author index, title index, chronological list, and key to subject coding.

BOOKS PUBLISHED TO 1910

S 50 Courant, Maurice. *Bibliographie coreenne*. Paris, Leroux, 1894–6. 3 v. (Publications de l'Ecole des Langues Orientales Vivantes, 3 serie, v. 18–20)
Some 3,000 books in Korean published to 1890 are arranged in subject order with descriptive and analytical annotation. Author and title index. A major Western contribution to traditional Korean bibliography. Supplemented by:
Supplement a la Bibliographie coreenne (jusqu'en 1899). Paris, Imprimerie National, Leroux, 1901. 122 p. (Publications de l'Ecole des Langues Orientales Vivantes, 3 serie, v. 21)
Original work and supplement reprinted by Burt Franklin, New York.

S 51 Toyo Bunko, Tokyo (Oriental Library). *Toyo bunko Chosen-bon bunrui mokuroku, fu Annam-hon mokuroku* (Classified catalogue of Korean books in the Oriental Library, with an appended catalogue of Annamese books). Tokyo, Showa 24 (1939). 100 p.
Some 1,000 Korean books arranged in traditional Chinese bibliographical order. Information on modern editions of early Korean books given.

S 52 Maema, Kyosaku. *Kosen sappu* (Record of early Korean books). Tokyo, Toyo Bunko, Showa 19–32 (1944–57). 3 v. (Toyo bunko sokan 11)
Some 8,000 books arranged by title in the Japanese syllabic order. Nearly all entries are annotated with an indication of location. No index to authors or to titles by stroke.

S 53 Soul Taehakkyo. Tosogwan (Seoul National University Library). *Kyujanggak toso mongnok Han'gukpon ch'ong mongnok* Catalogue of Korean books and manuscripts in the Kyujang-gak collection, Seoul National University Library. Soul, 1965. 691 p.
The Kyujanggak or the Yi dynasty Royal Library was founded in 1776. Under the Japanese occupation of Korea it was transferred to the Keijo Imperial University (the present Seoul National University) in 1931. Over three-quarters of the 8,000 entries were published after 1850. The remainder are fairly well representative of all periods since 1700. The books are arranged in the traditional Chinese bibliographical order, with a title index in the Korean alphabet and a character key. Some selected titles are annotated. An important bibliographical tool, since it is now possible to order books listed on microfilm. An earlier edition commenced publication in 1964, and was issued in a number of volumes.

S 54 Kukhoe Tosogwan. Seoul. Sasoguk (National Assembly Library. Reference Division). *Han'guk goso chonghap mongnok* (Union catalogue of Korean books). Soul, 1968. 1,439 p.
An attempt to develop a comprehensive listing of some 37,000 Korean books. Arranged by title in the Korean syllabary. Both manuscripts and printed books are listed and locations are given. Items published to 1910 are included. Author index.

S 55 Fang Chaoying. *The Asami collection, a descriptive catalog.* Berkeley, University of California Press, 1969. 424 p.
Lists over 900 titles of Korean printed books, and also manuscripts and rubbings, and covering the whole range of Korean traditional culture, with some emphasis on law and government. Entries have detailed bibliographical descriptions and full annotations. The materials are held by the East Asiatic Library of the University of California at Berkeley.

S 56 Koryo Taehakkyo, Seoul. Minjok Munhwa Yonguso (Korea University. Korean Culture Institute). *Han'guk toso haeje* (Annotated bibliography of Korean Books). Soul, 1971. 981 p.
A selected and annotated list of older Korean books, published to 1910, and superseding the shorter *Chosen tosho kaidai.* Some 5,300 titles in 29,000 volumes are listed in Korean syllabic order. Subject index and author index.

BOOKS PUBLISHED 1910–45

S 57 Kungnip Chungang Tosogwan, Seoul (National Central Library). *Changso pullyu mongnok* (Classified catalogue of books in the collections). Soul, 1961–2. 5 v.
The books listed are published almost entirely in Japan, but some publications in Japanese and Korean published in Korea are included. Books on Korea are arranged in a separate sequence in the last volume, with a similar classification to that in the main text. A revised and enlarged edition of Korea (Government-General of Chosen, 1910–45) *Shinshobu bunrui mokuroku* (Classified catalogue of new books) (Keijo, Showa 12–13 (1937–8). 3 v.).

S 58 Kungnip Chungang Tosogwan (National Central Library). *Goso mongnok* (Catalogue of the Oriental Classics in the Central National Library). Soul, 1970–2. 3 v.
The first two volumes list 12,063 titles published to 1945, and arranged under nine subject divisions: philosophy, various schools; religion and education; politics and law; language and literature; history and biography; geography and physics; architecture, engineering and military; agriculture and art; and general and miscellaneous. The third volume lists 4,497 titles published after 1945, and arranges these also under nine divisions not identical with those in the first two volumes. Author and title index arranged by the Korean syllabary.

BOOKS PUBLISHED SINCE 1945

S 59 Yang, Key Paik. *Reference guide to Korean materials, 1945–1959.* Washington, 1960, 131 p.
A master's dissertation at Catholic University of America, and based on materials selected from the Korean collection of the Library of Congress. 800 items are arranged in a classified order, and most items have short annotations. The selection stresses reference works. Separate author and title indexes.

S 60 Koryo Taehakkyo, Seoul. Asae Munje Yonguso (Korea University. Asiatic Research Centre). *Bibliography of Korean studies, a bibliographical guide to Korean publications on Korean studies appearing from 1945 to 1962*. Seoul, 1961–5. 2 v.
Volume 1 lists 863 books and periodical articles, arranged in subject order. Each entry is fully annotated, and the period covered is from 1945 to 1958. The subject index gives greater subdivision than the main text. Index to authors. Volume 2 has a similar arrangement, but covers the years 1959–62, again with 863 entries.

S 61 Harvard University. Harvard-Yenching Institute. Library. *A classified catalogue of Korean books in the Harvard-Yenching Institute Library at Harvard University*. Cambridge. 1962–6. 2 v.
The first volume contains 3,414 books and periodicals, and the second 3,200. Both volumes are arranged in a classified order, and the second volume has an author and title index to both volumes arranged by the Korean alphabet. The Harvard collection is strong on traditional Korea, and individual writings, genealogical records and rosters of examination passes are well represented. The number of modern works is second only in size to the collection of the Library of Congress. Volume 3 will contain 12,000 titles, and will have a separate list for North Korea, noting 1,145 titles.

S 62 Yang, Key Park. *Maiguk kukhoe tosogwan sojang charyo mongnopchip* (North Korean publications in the Library of Congress collection). Soul, 1970. 755 p.
List of 2,468 North Korean publications in the Library of Congress, arranged in classified order.

S 63 Koryo Taehakkyo, Seoul. Minjok Munhwa Yonguso (Korea University. Korean Culture Institute). *Han'guk nonje haeje* (Korea, an annotated bibliography). Soul, 1972–3. 2 v.
The first volume contains 1,284 books and 9,909 articles published since 1910 with full annotations, and is concerned with Korean language and literature. The second volume on Korean history notes 1,777 books and 8,333 articles. Indexes include author index and title index in each volume.

TRADE BIBLIOGRAPHY

S 64 *Ch'ulp'an taegam* (Register of publications). Soul, Choson Ch'ulp'an Munhwa Hyophoe, 1949. 108 p.

Lists 1,400 publications, issued from 1945 through 1948, arranged in major subject groups. Supplement to *Ch'ulp'an munhwa* (Publishing culture), no. 7, April 1949.

S 65 *Han'guk ch'ulp'an yon'gam*, 4290– Korean publications yearbook, 1957–. Soul, Taehan Ch'ulp'an Munhwa Hyophoe, Tangi 4290–(1957–).

More of an in-print catalogue than a record of books published in the previous period. The 1968 issue, the latest noted, lists books published from 1955. Entries are arranged in Korean Decimal Classification order. Issues also noted for 1963, 1964, 1966, 1972, 1974 and 1977. The 1957 issue has title *Ch'ulp'an yon'gam* (Publications yearbook).

S 66 *Choson toso* Korean books. P'yongyang, Kukze Sedom, 195–?–.

Issued on an irregular basis, and listing books for overseas distribution. Entries translated into Russian, Japanese, English and Chinese. In the absence of an available North Korean bibliographical record, this is the best listing available. Only a small proportion of the total number of periodicals and books published in North Korea are listed.

Choson ch'ulp'anmul such'urip sangsa, Pyongyang (Korean Publication Export and Import Corporation) *Choson toso ch'ongmongnok* General catalogue of Korean books, (Pyongyang) was issued aiming at the foreign market for Korean books, with copies reported for 1963–70.

S 67 *Choson toso mongnok* (Catalogue of Korean books). P'yongyang, Choson Ch'ulp'anmul Such'urip Sangsa, 195–?–. Monthly.

Supersedes *Choson toso* (S 66). Copies reported published from 1959–65.

NATIONAL BIBLIOGRAPHY

S 68 Kungnip Chungang Tosogwan, Seoul (National Central Library). *Han'guk somok* Korean national bibliography, 1945–1962. Soul, 1964. 722 p.

The National Central Library was formerly the National Library, and from 1923 to 1945 it was the Library of the Government-General of Korea. The bibliography lists 21,660 books, periodicals, dissertations, music scores, maps and principal official publications published from 1945 through 1962. Entries are arranged by the Korean Decimal Classification. There are two indexes arranged by the Korean alphabet, the first for books and the second for dissertations. No author index. Continued by:

Taehan min'guk ch'ulp'anmul ch'ongmongnok, 1963–64 Korean national bibliography, 1963–1964. Soul, 1965. The first part contains some 4,000 books and yearbooks, including government publications, and is arranged by the Korean Decimal Classification, and the second 580 periodicals and newspapers arranged by frequency of publications. Index to authors and titles. Annual volume for 1975 published in 1976.

S 69 Kukhoe Tosogwan, Seoul (National Assembly Library). *Changso mongnok Han'guk toso p'yon* The classified catalogue of books in Korea. Soul, 1966–72. 2 v.
The first volume contains some 7,500 titles, and the second, for the period 1966–72, some 10,500 titles. Author and title indexes.

OFFICIAL PUBLICATIONS

S 70 Korea (Government-General of Chosen, 1910–45). *Chosen sotokufu oyobi shozoku kansho shuyo kanko tosho mokuroku* (Catalogue of the chief publications of the Government-General of Korea and its agencies and offices). Keijo, Chosen Sotokufu, Showa 5- (1930–).
Publications are arranged under 28 subject divisions with no index. Issues for 1930, 1932–3, 1936 and 1938 have been noted. Korean official publications are also noted in *Kancho kanko tosho mokuroku*, Showa 2–12 (Catalogue of government publications, 1927–37) and its continuation *Kanko kancho tosho geppo*, Showa 13–18 nen (Government publications monthly, 1938–43) (see R 93).

S 71 Kukhoe Tosogwan, Seoul (National Assembly Library). *Chongbu kanhaengmul mongnok* Government publications in Korea. Soul, 1966–.
Books and serials are arranged by issuing agency. First volume covers 1948–65. The fourth covering 1970 was published in 1971.

PERIODICALS AND NEWSPAPERS

S 72 *Choson chongi kanhaengmul mongnok* (Catalogue—newspapers and periodicals from Korea). P'yongyang, Choson Kukche Sojom. Annual.
Issues for 1949, 1951, 1958–62, 1968 and 1972–4 reported. 1974 issue in Korean, English and Russian.

S 73 Korea (Republic). Kongbobu (Ministry of Information). *Chonggi kanhaengmul sil t'ae illam, 4294* (Directory of Korean periodicals and newspapers, 1961). Soul, 1962? 1,503 p.
Divided into five sections. The first contains 38 newspapers arranged by place, the second lists six newspaper agencies, the third 30 weekly periodicals, the fourth 158 monthlies, and the fifth is a miscellaneous section with 61 entries. Information given on date of first issue, numbers of copies published, and lists editorial staff. Lacks comprehensive index.

S 74 Yi, Pyong-mok. *Han'guk ui taehak chonggi kanhaengmul* Bibliography of university periodicals in Korea, 1945–1964. Soul, Yonse Taehakkyo Tosogwan Hakkwa, 1964. 265 p. (Library science series of Yonsei University no. 15).
724 titles, including 147 university newspapers and 85 catalogues and bulletins, are arranged by title in Korean alphabet order. Classified index to titles. Also contains a directory of institutions

of higher education, listing 1,537 departments in 164 institutions, with disciplines index. Intended as aid to library exchange.

S 75 Yang, Key Paik. *Han'guk sinmun chapchi ch'ong mongnok* Catalogue of Korean periodicals, 1883–1945. Soul, Taehan Min'guk Kukhoe Tosogwan, 1966. 230 p.
799 entries for periodicals published in Korea, 234 for periodicals published outside Korea, and 105 for newspapers published in or outside Korea. However some entries are cross-references. The titles are arranged alphabetically in each section. Characters and dates of issue are given. The fourth section is a chronological list arranged by date of first issue from 1892 to 1944. Index of titles arranged by the Korean alphabet.

S 76 U.S. Library of Congress. *Union card file of Oriental vernacular serials, Chinese, Japanese and Korean. Korean file*. Washington, 1966. 2 reels.
Contains 3,037 holdings cards from leading American academic institutions for Korean-language periodicals. Available from the Library of Congress on microfilm or on electrostatic reproduction in card size.

S 77 Kukhoe Tosogwan, Seoul. Sasoguk. Yollamkwa (National Assembly Library. Reference Division). *Kukhoe tosogwan sojang ch'ukch'a kanhaengmul mongnok* Catalogue of periodical publications. Soul, 1968. 152 p.
The first section is concerned with Korean publications and lists some 750 periodicals held in the National Library, giving holdings and frequency. In addition 750 government periodicals arranged by bureau, 450 university periodicals arranged by university and some 120 newspapers are listed.

S 78 Park, Yang Ja. *Korean publications in series, a subject bibliography*, 1945–1965. Washington, 1967. 148 l.
396 series are arranged under 17 major subjects, with each entry listing titles of volumes published in the series, and based on the collections of the Library of Congress. Author, series and titles index. Thesis in partial fulfilment of the requirements for MSLS degree at Catholic University of America, Washington, D.C.

S 79 Yang, Key P. *Union list of North Korean serials and newspapers in five U.S. libraries.* Washington, 1971. 144 p.
In manuscript only and compiled by the head of the Korean section of the Asian Division of the Library of Congress. Contains 342 entries. Titles not holdings updated to 1979 on manuscript copy. Title index. Reprinted by the National Assembly Library as *Pukhan chapchi sinmun mongnok* (Catalogue of North Korean periodicals and newspapers).

INDEXES

S 80 *Chonggi kanhaengmul kisa saegin*, 1960– Korean periodicals index, 1960–. Soul, Taehan Min'guk Kukhoe Tosogwan, 1964–.
An index to 155 scholarly and official periodicals, arranged by

subjects. Newspapers, statistical and recreational periodicals are excluded. Each issue contains some 3,500 entries. Lists of periodicals indexed, and index to authors appear in the last issue for each year. The 1960 issue duplicates the *Haksul chapchi saegin*, 2960 (Index to Korean learned periodicals, 1960). No issue was published for 1961/2, but there is an issue of the *Haksul chapchi saegin*, 1961/2. 1963 and 1964 are annual volumes. Quarterly from 1965. This series now includes coverage from 1945. 1977 issue seen.

S 81 Kukhoe tosogwan, Seoul (National Assembly Library). *Hanmal Han'guk chapchi mokch'a ch'ongnok* Catalogue of contents of Korean periodicals published in the end of Yi dynasty, 1896–1910. Soul, 1967. 138 p.
Contents of 29 periodicals are listed, but some issues are lacking.

S 82 Yonse Taehakkyo, Seoul. Chungang Tosogwan (Yonsei University. Central Library). *Chonggi Kanhaengmul chesaegin*, 1967– Index to Korean periodical literature of, (1967–). Soul, 1969–
1968 issue indexes 321 Korean periodicals held by Yonsei University Library.

S 83 *Dong-A ilbo saegin* Dong A ilbo index. Soul, Dong A ilboso, 1970–7. 5 v.
A detailed subject index covering the years 1920–34 for this major Korean newspaper. Volume 5 for 1932–4, published 1977, seen.

THESES AND DISSERTATIONS

S 84 Kukhoe Tosogwan, Seoul (National Assembly Library). Han'guk *paksa mit soksa hakwi nonmun ch'ongmongnok, 1945–1968* List of theses for the doctor's and master's degree in Korea, 1945–1968. Soul, 1969. 573 p.
Lists 2,178 doctoral dissertations and 10,885 master's theses, each grouped by subject. Separate author indexes. Continued by *Han'guk paksa mit soksa hakwi nonmun ch'ongmongnok, 1969–1970* List of theses for the doctor's and master's degree in Korea, 1969–1970, (Soul, 1971. 271 p.), which lists 850 doctoral dissertations and 3,650 master's theses, with author index. Volume 3, published 1972, noted; volumes 5 and 6, published 1973 and 1974, seen.

Chinese and Japanese Languages

S 85 Sakurai, Yoshiyuki. *Meiji nenkan Chosen kenkyu bunkenshi* (Bibliographic record of Korean studies in the Meiji period). Keijo, Shomotsu Dokokai, Showa 16 (1941). 421 p.
Some 600 books in Japanese on Korea, published 1868–1912, are arranged in eight sections. Full annotations. Author and Title indexes, arranged by the Japanese syllabary.

S 86 Beal, Edwin G. and Robin L. Winkler. *Korea, an annotated*

bibliography of publications in Far Eastern languages. Washington, Library of Congress, 1950. 167 p.
528 books, periodicals and periodical articles arranged in subject order, with a combined author and select subject index. Stresses the modern period and does not include some 1,687 older Korean books in the Library of Congress at the time of publication.

S 87 Kondo, Kenichi. *Chosen kankei bunken shiryo somokuroku* (Catalogue of materials on Korea). Tokyo, Chosen Shiryo Kenkyukai, Showa 36 (1961). 180 p.
4,333 books in Japanese, emphasizing history, social sciences, technology and industry, are arranged by the Nihon Decimal Classification. No index.

Western Languages

S 88 Gompertz, G. St. G. M. *Bibliography of Western literature in Korea from the earliest times until 1950.* Seoul, Dong-A Publishing, 1963. 263 p. (Transactions of the Korea Branch Royal Asiatic Society of Great Britain and Ireland no. 40)
2,276 books and periodical articles arranged in a detailed subject order. No index. A revision of H. H. Underwood 'A partial bibliography of Occidental literature on Korea from early times to 1930', *Transactions of the Korea Branch Royal Asiatic Society*, v. 20, 1931, and first supplement, *Transactions*, v. 24, 1935.

S 89 Kulhoe Tosogwan, Seoul (National Assembly Library). *Soyangbon Han'guk munhon mongnok, 1800–1963 (nosabon p'oham)* Bibliography of Korea, publications in the Western language, 1800–1963 (in the Russian language). Soul, 1967. 227 p.
This publication reprints:
Helen Dudenbostel Jones and Robin L. Winkler *Korea, an annotated bibliography of publications in Western languages* (Washington, Library of Congress, 1950. 155 p.), which has 632 books, periodicals and official documents, mostly in English, published between 1886 and 1951, but emphasizing those issued after 1930. Indexed.
Yi Sun-hi (Soon Hi Lee). *Korea, a selected bibliography in Western languages, 1950–1958.* Washington, 1959. 55 p. A master's dissertation at Catholic University of America, with 500 entries for books arranged in subject order, and almost entirely in English. Indexed.
Yong-Sun Chung. *Publications on Korea in the era of political revolutions.* Kalamazoo, Korean Research and Publication, 1965. 117 p. 967 entries supplement the two preceding bibliographies, Includes Far Eastern-language material also. Indexed.
U.S. Library of Congress. Bibliography Division. *Korea, an annotated bibliography of publications in the Russian language.* Washington, Library of Congress, 1950. 84 p. Notes 436 books and periodical articles.

S 90 U.S. Department of the Army. *Communist North Korea, a bibliographic survey, 1971*. Washington, 1971. 130 p. (DA Pamphlet 550–11)
Major emphasis is on the period 1965–70, but includes background bibliography on Korean history and the Korean War. Some 300 books and periodical articles are arranged in a subject order. Fully annotated. Numerous background appendices on the North Korean army, population, government and politics, and the economy. Pocket of maps, including a road map of North Korea at a scale of 1:250,000, four 1:1,000,000 maps, and maps on railroads, forests and land utilization.

S 91 Ginsburgs, George. *Soviet works on Korea, 1945–1970*. Los Angeles, University of Southern California Press, 1973. 179 p.
Lists 1,126 books, articles and dissertations are arranged by subject. Gives a strong emphasis to North Korea. An extensive valuable introductory survey is also included. Author index.

PERIODICAL AND NEWSPAPER INDEXES

S 92 Elrod, Jefferson Mcree. *An index to English-language periodicals in Korea, 1890–1940*. Seoul, Yonsei University, 1960. 214 p.
A master's dissertation for George Peabody College for Teachers. 2,970 entries from a group of ten periodicals published in Korea and mostly edited by missionaries, but including the important *Transactions of the Korea Branch Royal Asiatic Society*. Also published by the National Assembly Library in 1965.

S 93 Elrod, Jefferson Mcree. *An index to English-language newspapers published in Korea, 1896–1931*. Seoul, National Assembly Library, 1966. 66 p.
1,250 entries are indexed from the *Independent*, 1896–9; *Korea Daily News*, 1904–5 and 1909; *Korea repository*, local edition 1899 (weekly);*Seoul Press*, 1907–10 and 1927–37; and *Seoul Press weekly*, 1905.

S 94 Kang, Sang-un. *Han'guk kwangye oeguk nomun kisa ch'ong mongnok* A list of articles on Korea in the Western languages, 1800–1964. Soul, Tamgu Dang, 1967. 192 p.
Title is misleading since it commences with articles published in 1890. Based on a review of the more general American periodicals indexed in the *Readers' guide to periodical literature*. Arrangement is by chronological periods, and then by subject. Altogether there are some 5,700 entries, of which approximately 900 were published before 1945.

S 95 Chon, Munam, *Index to English-language periodical literature published in Korea during 1941–1968*. Seoul, National Assembly Library, 1969.
Covers 16 English-language periodicals and contains some 3,600 subjects and author entries, arranged in alphabetical order.

Films

S 96 Butler, Lucius A. and Chaesoon T. Youngs. *Films for Korean studies, a guide to English-language films about Korea.* Honolulu, Center for Korean Studies, University of Hawaii, 1977. 167 p.
333 English-language 16 mm films are arranged by title, with running time, summary of contents, and source from which film can be obtained. Subject index and list of producers and distributors.

Subject Bibliography

BUDDHISM

S 97 Tongguk Taehakkyo. Pulgyo Munhwa Yonguso (Eastern University. Buddhist Culture Institute). *Han'guk Pulgyo ch'ansul munhon ch'ongnok* (Selected bibliographical outline of Korean Buddhism). Soul, 1976. 474 p.
Lists some 2,000 titles arranged by period, then by subject, with some annotations. Title index.

SOCIAL SCIENCES

S 98 Chungang Taehakkyo, Seoul. Mullikwa Taehak. Kyoyuk Hakkwa (Chungang University. College of Arts and Sciences. Education Department). *Han'guk kyoyuk mongnok* Korean education index. Soul, Tangi 4293 (1960) – 1966. 2 v. The first volume covers the period 1945–59, and the second 1960–4. Arranged by a detailed subject classification, and containing some 30,000 articles in Korea. Each volume has an appendix for books.

S 99 Yonse Taehakkyo, Seoul. Sanop Kyonguso Yonguso (Yonsei University. Industrial Economics Institute). *Sanop kyongje munhon mongnok* . . .(Catalogue of materials on industrial economics). Soul, Yonse Taehakkyo Ch'ulp'anbu, 1961–5. 2 v.
Lists over 11,000 books and periodical articles published in the fields of business and economics, with over 5,000 from 1945 to 1960 in volume 1, and over 6,000 from 1961 to 1964 in volume 2. Each volume is divided into major subject fields, which are further subdivided. Lists of periodicals, annuals, and dictionaries in economics and business are appended.

S 100 Bureau of the Census. *Bibliography of social science periodicals and monograph series, North Korea, 1945–1961.* Washington, U.S. Government Printing Office, 1962. 12 p. (Foreign social science bibliographies, Series P–92, no. 8)
Lists 38 periodicals and 3 monograph series, giving considerable bibliographical and other information for each entry. Materials cited can be found at the Library of Congress. Separate subject and title indexes.

S 101 Bureau of the Census. *Bibliography of social science periodicals and monograph series, Republic of Korea, 1945–1961.* Washington, U.S. Government Printing Office, 1962. 48 p. (Foreign social science bibliographies, Series P92, no. 9)
127 periodicals and 134 monograph series in the Library of Congress are arranged under 14 social science fields and bibliography. Each entry is annotated. Separate subject, title and author indexes.

S 102 Bark, Dong-suh and Jai-poong Yoon. *Bibliography of Korean public administration, September 1945–April 1966.* Seoul, U.S. Operations Mission to Korea, 1966. 174 p.
A short list of 99 Korean books and government publications, arranged chronologically, is followed by 1,355 articles on Korea divided into 17 main divisions and then chronologically, and by 513 master's theses, also arranged by major subjects. Valuable for the non-Korean speaker to learn what is being published in the public administration field in Korea. No index.

S 103 Knez, Eugene Irving. *Han'guk illyuhak e kwanhan munhon mongnok* A selected and annotated bibliography of Korean anthropology. Soul, 1968. 235 p.
537 periodical articles and books in Japanese and Korean have been selected from the collections of the Library of Congress and arranged by subject. Author and title indexes. Each entry is fully annotated, and the bibliography is intended to be an introduction to Japanese and Korean materials for Western scholars.

S 104 Fraser, Stewart E. *North Korean education and society, a selected and partially annotated bibliography* . . . London, University of London, Institute of Education Library, 149 p. 1972.
Approximately 1,000 periodical articles, books and unpublished materials are divided by language into English, German, Russian, Korean, Japanese and Chinese sections, but mostly in English and Korean. No index.

S 105 Kukhoe Tosogwan, Seoul (National Assembly Library). *Chong ch'i haeng chong pop ryul nonmun ch'ongnok* (An index of Korean periodicals on politics, administration and law, 1945–1972). Soul, 1972. 855 p.
Some 40,000 articles are arranged in a classified subject order. Includes also a list of doctoral dissertations. Author index.

NATURAL AND APPLIED SCIENCES

S 106 Miki, Sakae. *Chosen isho shi* Bibliography of Korean medicine, ancient and medieval. Sakai, Showa 31 (1956). 477 p.
Lists over 400 medical books arranged into six groups: early Korean medical books, Chinese medical books published in Korea, Korean books on materia medica, Korean medical books published in China and in Japan, and catalogues of Korean medical books. Index to titles by stroke.

S 107 Schroeder, Peter Brett. *Korean publications in the National*

Agricultural Library. Washington, National Agricultural Library, U.S. Department of Agriculture, 1963. 25 p. (Library list no. 79)

Includes 79 periodicals and 110 monographs in English or Korean and mostly published in South Korea. The holdings of the National Agricultural Library are noted. Author index, list of titles in English and list of publishers appended.

S 108 Han'guk Kwahak Kisul Chongbo Ssent'o (Korean Scientific and Technological Information Centre) *Bibliography of scientific publications of Korea, volume 1, 1945–1965*. Seoul, Korea Scientific and Technological Information Center, 1966. 484 p.

10,664 periodical articles in English and Korean are arranged in a detailed subject order, covering natural and applied sciences. Only the English-language titles of articles given. Author index.

MUSIC

S 109 Song, Bang-song. *An annotated bibliography of Korean music*. Providence, Asian Music Publications, Brown University, 1971. 250 p. (Asian Music Publications, Series A, Bibliographic and research aid no. 2)

1,319 books and periodical articles in Japanese, Korean and Western languages. Author index and subject index.

HISTORY

S 110 Blanchard, Carroll Henry. *Korean war bibliography and maps of Korea*. New Albany, Korean Conflict Research Foundation, 1964. 181 p.

An extensive unannotated bibliography on the Korean war. In the first part some 900 books are listed by subject; in the second some 200 books from foreign publishers, including materials from Communist countries; in the third some 360 periodicals which have had articles concerning the war; in the fourth some 5,330 articles from these periodicals arranged by subject; and in the fifth 25 black and white maps. Comprehensive, but no table of contents or index.

S 111 Han, U-gun. *Han'guk kyongje kwan-gye munhon* (Annotated bibliography of Korean economic history, 1570–1910). Soul, Soul Taehakkyo, Mullikwa Taehak Tonga Muhhwa Yonguso, 1966. 223 p.

Lists 3,229 entries, nearly half for the period 1877–1910, with an emphasis on taxes and the land system, and based on the collections of the Kyujang-gak archives.

S 112 Kukhoe Tosogwan, Seoul (National Assembly Library). *Han'guksa yon'gu nonmun ch'ongmongnok* Catalogue of articles in Korean studies. Soul, 1967–1970. 2 v.

A bibliography of books and periodical articles almost entirely in Japanese and Korean. The first part, for the period 1900–66, has nearly 7,000 entries arranged in subject order, with an author index. The second part, for the period 1967–9, has 6,000 entries arranged by subject, with an author index.

S 113 Korean National Committee of Historical Sciences. *Historical studies in Korea, recent trends and bibliography (1945–1973).* Seoul, 1975. 627 p.

In three sections, the first and largest listing some 3,000 books and articles in Korea, with translation of titles, and romanization of the Korean. The first section is preceded by short historical essays. Author index.

T. MONGOLIA

Outer Mongolia, or the present Mongolian People's Republic (MPR), proclaimed its independence from China in 1911. However, more Mongols still live in the People's Republic of China than in the MPR, and there they are concentrated in Inner Mongolia, which has been extended to include a large part of the former Western Manchuria. The MPR was formally established in 1924. Extensive references to the Mongols and to Mongolia may also be found in the section on China.

HANDBOOKS

T 1 American University, Washington, D.C. Foreign Area Studies. *Area handbook for Mongolia*. Washington, U.S. Government Printing Office, 1970. 499 p.
A short country summary is followed by four sections, for social, political and economic affairs, and for national security. There is an extensive 24-page bibliography and an index. Coverage of the handbook is to December 1968.

T 2 Sanders, Alan J.K. *The People's Republic of Mongolia, a general reference guide*. New York, Oxford University Press, 1968. 232 p.
An encyclopedic guide to the People's Republic of Mongolia, includes lists of members of the 1966 Parliament, the party, government, press, education, literature, statistics, economy, short biographies, a gazetteer, chronology and map. Information is through 1966.

DICTIONARIES

T 3 Boberg, Folke. *Mongolian-English dictionary*. Copenhagen, Munksgaard, 1954–5. 3 v.
A Mongolian-English dictionary comprises the first two volumes, which contain over 18,000 Mongol words and expressions. The third volume is an English-Mongolian dictionary keyed to the Mongolian words in the preceding volumes.

T 4 Lessing, Ferdinand D. *Mongolian-English dictionary*. Berkeley, University of California Press, 1960. 1,217 p.
The emphasis of this dictionary is on modern Mongolian. The strictly archaic language is avoided, and technical Buddhist phrases and words are in an appendix. Entries are arranged alphabetically, and English meanings, Mongol and Cyrillic transcriptions are given. Cyrillic index.

GAZETTEER

T 5 U.S. Board on Geographic Names. *Mongolia* . . . Washington, U.S. Government Printing Office, 1970. 256 p. (Gazetteer no. 116)
Some 13,000 entries for place and feature names in Mongolia, with their classification, latitude and longitude.

BIBLIOGRAPHY

T 6 Iakovlena, E.N. *Bibliografiia Mongol'skoi Narodnoi Respubliki.* Moskva, Izd. Nauchno izdaltelstvo assotsiatsii po izuchenuiiu natsional'nykh i kolonial'nykh promlem, 1935. 230 p.
A bibliography by one of the leading Soviet Mongolists includes 2,422 entries for books and periodical articles in the Russian language on the Mongolian People's Republic and on the Mongols and Mongolia. Materials published from the beginning of the 18th century to 1934 have been included. The arrangement is first by topic, then by year. Entries for books are annotated. The index lists authors, translators, editors and titles of works by anonymous authors. For a selection of the more recent Russian literature on Mongolia refer to Robert A. Rupen *Mongols of the twentieth century* (T 10).

T 7 Iwamura, Shinobu and Fujieda Akira. *Moko kenkyu bunken mokuroku, 1900–1950* Bibliography of Mongolia, 1900–1950. Kyoto, Kyoto Daigaku Jimbun Kagaku Kenkyujo, Showa 28 (1953). 46 p. (Toyoshi kenkyu bunken bessatsu dai 1)
Contains approximately 1,500 entries of books and periodical articles in Japanese, and is arranged by author, considered by the compilers to be the most useful approach. Articles far outnumber books. No annotations or subject index.

T 8 Washington (State) University. Far Eastern and Russian Institute. *Bibliography of the Mongolian People's Republic.* New Haven, Human Relations Area Files, 1956. 101 p. (Behaviour science bibliographies)
Major sections on general materials, economics, linguistics and materials in Japanese. The first and last sections have further subdivision. There are approximately 1,200 entries, and nearly all are annotated. One-half of the entries are in Japanese, and the remainder are in Western languages, except for the section on economics which is almost entirely in Russian. No index.

T 9 Chang, Hsing-t'ang. *Meng-ku ts'an kao shu mu* (Reference catalogue on Mongolia). T'ai-pei, Chung hua Ts'ung shu Wei yuan hui, Min kuo 47 (1958). 278 p. (Chung hua ts'ung shu)
Divided into broad subject divisions further subdivided by language. There are 1,831 entries, of which 1,123 are in Chinese, 376 in Japanese and 28 in Mongol. 304 entries are in Western

languages, of which nearly two-thirds are in English. Both books and articles are included. Sources of compilation are stated. No annotations or index.

T 10 Rupen, Robert A. *Mongols of the twentieth century*. Bloomington, Indiana University and The Hague, Mouton, 1964. 2 v. (Indiana University publications, Uralic and Altaic series, v. 37)

The first volume is a major suvey of modern Mongol history, and the second is an unannotated bibliography of over 3,000 books, periodicals and periodical aricles, principally in Russian and English, with nearly four-fifths in an alphabetical listing by author. The key to this bibliography is provided by a short subject index. Easily the most extensive bibliography on Mongolia. This is not a publication of Indiana University Press.

INDEXES

AUTHOR AND TITLE INDEX

This index also lists translated titles which are included in the reference works cited. A reference code in italic refers to an author and/or title appearing in an annotation.

CHINESE, JAPANESE AND KOREAN CHARACTERS FOR TITLES

A 15 東洋學文獻目錄

A 47 日本東洋古美術文獻目錄

A 49 日本における東洋史論文目錄

N 20 タイ語文献総合目録

O 17 現代ベトナム民主共和国人名辞典

P 8 太平洋戦史文献解題

Q 3 中文工具書指引

Q 4 古今圖書集成

Q 20 中國年鑑

Q 21 支那年鑑

Q 22 中國年鑑

Q 23 新中國年鑑

Q 24 中國總覽

Q 25 申報年鑑

Q 26 人民手册

Q 27 中華民國年鑑

Q 30 國語字典

Q 31 中文大字典

Q 32 辭海

Q 35 中華成語辭典

Q 37 中日大辭典

Q 39 新英漢詞典

Q 41 中國人名大辭典

Q 42 中外人名字典

Q 43 中國文學家大字典

Q 44 中國歷代書畫篆刻家字號

Q 50 中華民國人實錄

Q 55 現代中國人名事典

Q 56 現職新中國人名辭典

Q 65 中國工業工場總覽

Q 76 中華人民共和國分省地圖集

Q 79 中國地名大辭典

Q 80 中國古今地名大辭典

Q 87 1821－2020年二百年曆表

Q 88 中國年曆總譜

Q 90 中國大事記

Q 91 新華月報國內外大事記

Q 92 中華民國統計摘要

Q 98 四庫全書總目欽定

Q 99 江蘇省立國學圖書館總目

Q 100 國會圖書館藏中國善本書錄

Q 102 近百年来中國文文獻現在書目

Q 103 圖書年鑑

Q 104 生活全國總書目

Q 107 全國新書目

Q 109 全國總書目

Q 113 中華民國出版圖書目錄彙編

Q 114 現代中國關係中國語文總合目錄

Q 118 中華民國圖書總目錄

Q 121 國立中央圖書館藏官書目錄 第一輯

Q 122 近百年來中譯西書目錄

Q 123 清代禁燬書四種

Q 125 四川省各圖書館館藏中文舊期刊聯合目錄（初稿）1884–1949

Q 126 全國中文期刊聯合目錄，1833–1949

Q 127 中國現代文學期刊目錄初稿

Q 129 紅衛兵資料目錄

Q 132 中國雜誌指南

Q 136 中國文新聞雜誌總合目錄，日本主要研究機關圖所館所藏

Q 141 中文雜誌索引

Q 143 人文月刊

Q 144 期刊索引

Q 145 日報索引

Q 146 人民日報索引

Q 147 全國主要報刊資料索引

Q 148 中文期刊論文分類索引

Q 149 中華民國期刊論文索引

Q 151 中文報紙論文分類索引

Q 152 中文期刊人文暨社會科學論文分類索引

Q 153 中國近二十年來文史哲論文一分類索引

Q 154 中華民國期刊論文索引

Q 155 新華月報刊參考資料索引

Q 156 中文報紙文史哲論文索引

Q 157 中國叢書綜錄

Q 158 台灣各圖書館現存叢書子目索引

Q 159 中國隨筆索引

Q 160 中國隨筆雜著索引

Q 161 中華民國博士碩士論文索引

Q 169 中國文献西譯書目

Q 194 中國合作文獻目錄

Q 197 經濟論文分類索引

Q 209 中國法制史書目

Q 211 教育論文索引

Q 212 圖書館學論文索引

Q 215 中國醫學書目

Q 216 中國醫籍考

Q 217 科學技術參考書提要

Q 218 中國礦業期刊論文索引

Q 226 中國農學書錄

Q 228 農業論文索引

Q 230 中國藝術考古論文索引

Q 240 中國通俗小說書目

Q 241 中國現代文學作家作品評論資料索引

Q 249 曲海總目提要

Q 250 元代雜劇全目

Q 251 明代雜劇全目

Q 252 明代傳奇全目

Q 253 北京傳統曲藝總錄

Q 254 中國戲曲總目彙編

Q 256 中國音樂書譜目錄

Q 257 中國古代音樂書目

Q 259 中國地學論文索引

Q 262 中國史學論文索引

Q 263 中國古代中世紀史報刊論文資料索引

Q 266 明代史研究文獻目錄

Q 286 國立北平圖書館方志目錄

Q 287 國會圖書館藏中國方志目錄

Q 289 臺灣公藏方志聯合目錄

Q 290 中國地方志綜錄 增訂本

Q 294 中國地方志聯合目錄

Q 302 新疆研究文獻目錄, 1886–1962. 日本文

Q 304 臺灣文獻資料目錄

Q 305 臺灣文獻分類索引

Q 306 臺灣文獻目錄

R 2 日本の参考図書

R 3 古事類苑

R 4 廣文庫

R 5 佛教大辭典

R 6 日本歴史大辭典

R 7 世界大百科事典

R 10 讀史総覧

R 15 朝日年鑑

R 19 廣辭苑

R 20 日本國語大辭典

R 21 大漢和辭典

R 22 大字典

R 27 日本人名辭典

R 28 大人名事典

R 29 西洋人名辭典

R 34 日本紳士錄

R 35 人事興信錄

R 38 文化人名錄

R 42 全國各種團體名鑑

R 44 職員錄

R 46 日本官海名鑑

R 48 會社年鑑 上場會社版

R 49 日本職員錄

R 51 會社總覽 未上場會社版

R 56 全國學協會要覽

R 58 全國研究機關總覽

R 60 全國大學一覽

R 61 日本經濟地圖

R 62 日本歷史地圖

R 65 日本分県地図地名総覧

R 68 全國市町村要覽

R 69 日本地名事典

R 71 新日本史年表

R 72 國史大年表

R 73 索引政治經濟大年表

R 74 國勢調査報告

R 77 日本帝國統計年鑑

R 78 日本統計年鑑

R 79 本邦書誌の書誌

R 80 國書解題

R 81 國書總目録

R 82 明治期刊行圖書目録

R 83 東京書籍商組合圖書總目録

R 84 出版年鑑

R 85 書籍年鑑

R 86 出版年鑑

R 87 帝國圖書館和漢圖書分類目録

R 88 帝國圖書館和漢圖書書名目録

R 89 帝國圖書館・國立圖書館和漢圖書分類目録

R 90 全日本出版物總目録

R 91 國立國會圖書館藏書目録

R 92 國立國會圖書館藏書目録

R 93 官廳刊行圖書目錄

R 94 官廳刊行物總合目錄

R 96 國が編輯,監修し政府關係團體出版社が發行した刊行物一覽,未定稿

R 99 明治·大正·昭和翻譯文學目錄

R 100 明治·大正·昭和邦訳アメリカ文學書目

R 101 現代筆禍文獻大年表

R 102 連合國軍總司令部から没收を命ぜられた宣傳用刊行物總目錄

R 103 昭和書籍雜誌新聞發禁年表,上

R 104 東天紅 明治新聞雜誌文庫所藏目錄

R 106 帝國圖書館雜誌新聞目錄

R 107 雜誌年鑑

R 109 日本年鑑類總目錄

R 111 學術雜誌總合目錄

R 112 日本雜誌總覽

R 115 雜誌記事索引

R 117 文科系文獻目錄

R 119 日本叢書目錄

R 120 日本叢書索引

R 122 全集叢書細目總覽

R 123 日本隨筆索引

R 140 日本思想史文獻解題

R 142 神道書籍目録

R 143 明治、大正、昭和神道書籍目録

R 145 神道論文總目錄

R 147 佛教學關係雜誌論文分類目錄

R 148 佛書解説大辭典

R 149 佛教論文總目録

R 151 佛教學關係雜誌論文分類目錄

R 156 日本キリスト教文獻目錄、明治期

R 159 總理府統計局圖書館藏書目錄、和書の部

R 160 民族學關係雜誌論文總目錄

R 162 都市社會學に關する文献總合目錄

R 163 日本經濟史第...文獻

R 165 海事關係文獻總目錄

R 167 經濟史文獻解題

R 169 社史實業家傳記目錄

R 172 日本統計索引

R 173 議會政治文獻目錄

R 174 日本外交史關係文獻目錄

R 176 日本政治文献目錄

R 177 日本社會主義文獻

R 178 日本勞働運動社會運動研究史

R 179 日本社會主義文獻解説

R 181 戰後勞働關係文獻目錄

R 183 日本法制史書目解題

R 185 法律關係雜誌記事索引

R 186 戰後法學文獻目錄

R 187 法律圖書目錄，和書の部

R 189 教育文獻總合目錄

R 190 教育史に關する文獻目錄並に解題

R 193 教育學關係參考文獻總覽

R 199 日本地質文獻目錄

R 203 日本科學技術關係逐次刊行物目錄

R 204 國語學書目解題

R 206 明治以降國語學關係刊行書目

R 209 日本文學書誌

R 211 國文學研究書目解題

R 213 明治文學研究文獻總覽

R 214 明治文學書目

R 219 地理學文獻目錄

R 221 日本石器時代總合文獻目錄

R 222 總合國史研究

R 223 總合國史論文要目

R 225 國史文獻解說

R 226 人物文獻索引

R 227 日本占領文献目錄

R 229 日本人物文献目錄

R 231 日本史研究書總覽

S 3 韓國參考圖書解題

S 5 國史大事典

S 6 北韓總鑑

S 10 력사사전

S 11 韓國學大百科事典

S 12 國語國文學事典

S 13 韓國文學大事典

S 14 백과사전

S 15 世界百科大事典

S 16 朝鮮中央年鑑

S 17 한국연감

S 20 대중정치용어사전

S 21 漢韓大事典

S 23 朝鮮人名辭書

S 24 李朝名人列傳

S 25 韓國의 人間像

S 26 韓國人名大事典

S 27 現代朝鮮人名辭典

S 28 現代韓國人名辭典

S 29 最新韓國人士錄

S 30 韓國北朝鮮人名辭典

S 34 國內學術및研究團體便覽

S 35 大韓民國地圖

S 38 韓國行政區域總覽

S 39 韓國地名總覽

S 40 韓國史年表

S 41 韓國新聞雜誌年表

S 42 대한민국 간이총인구조사보고

S 43 1960年人口住宅國勢調査報告

S 44 人口센서스報告

S 45 총인구및주택조사보고

S 46 朝鮮總督府統計年報

S 47 韓國統計年鑑

S 51 東洋文庫朝鮮本分類目錄

S 52 古鮮册譜

S 53 奎章閣圖書目錄 韓國本總目錄

S 54 韓國古書綜合目錄

S 56 韓國圖書解題

S 57 新書部分目錄

S 58 古書目錄

S 62 米國國會圖書館所藏資料目錄集

S 63 韓國論著解題

S 64 出版大鑑

S 65 韓國出版年鑑

S 66 조선도서

S 67 조선도서 목록

S 68 韓國書目

S 69 藏書目錄—韓國語圖書篇

S 70 朝鮮總督府及所屬官署主要刊行圖書目錄

S 71 政府刊行物目錄

S 72 조선 전기 간행물 목록

S 73 定期刊行物實態一覽

S 74 韓國의大學定期刊行物

S 75 韓國新聞雜誌總目錄

S 77 國會圖書館所藏逐次刊行物目錄

S 80 國內刊行物記事索引

S 81 韓末韓國雜誌目次總錄

S 82 定期刊行物諸索引

S 83 東亞日報索引

S 84 韓國博士및碩士學位論文總目錄

S 85 明治年間朝鮮研究文獻誌

S 87 朝鮮關係文獻資料總目錄

S 89 西洋本韓國文獻目錄

S 94 韓國關係外國論文記事總目錄

S 97 韓國佛教撰述文献總錄

S 98 韓國教育目錄

S 99 産業經濟文獻目錄

S 103 한국 人類學에 관한 文獻목록

S 105 政治行政法律論文總錄

S 106 朝鮮醫書誌

S 111 韓國經濟關係文獻

S 112 韓國史研究論文總目錄

T 7 蒙古研究文獻目錄

T 9 蒙古參考圖書